MW00464096

Advance Praise for **And the Rest Is History**

"Although I have known national security journalist Ken Timmerman for over twenty years, he only told me how he barely escaped execution by radical Islamists in a Beirut cellar a few years ago. His professionalism, modesty, and faith are qualities seen far too rarely in today's ego-driven field of journalism."

—**Fred Fleitz, Former National Security Council Chief of Staff under President Trump**

"Ken Timmerman is a superb investigative reporter—and old school—which means he does his research. His behind-the-scenes adventures in Iraq, Syria, Egypt, Israel, and even France are a terrific read for those of us who share his passion for tracking down the facts, not molding the facts to a 'narrative.'"

—**Peter Schweizer, president of the Government Accountability Institute and *NY Times* bestselling author of *Clinton Cash* and *Profiles in Corruption***

"*And the Rest Is History* is a memoir that reads like a rollicking, page-turning novel. From the cold war through the war on terror and beyond, Ken takes us on the wild adventure that has been his life as a global-trotting reporter: we enter war zones and the halls of power, eavesdrop on conversations with world leaders, terrorists, arms dealers, and spies, and become witnesses to extraordinary history. Dripping in vivid detail, his unforgettable story will have you riveted from page one."

—**Monica Crowley, Ph.D., Former Assistant Secretary of the Treasury**

"Real reporters don't follow the pack. Ken Timmerman takes us down roads where few reporters have managed to go before and knows how to evoke people and places with remarkable grace."

—**Walid Phares, FoxNews National Security and Foreign Policy expert**

Also by Kenneth R. Timmerman

FICTION

The Election Heist

ISIS Begins

Honor Killing

The Wren Hunt

NONFICTION

*Deception: The Making of the YouTube Video
Hillary and Obama Blamed for Benghazi*

*Dark Forces: The Truth About What
Happened in Benghazi*

*Shadow Warriors: Traitors, Saboteurs,
and the Party of Surrender*

*Countdown to Crisis: The Coming Nuclear
Showdown with Iran*

The French Betrayal of America

Preachers of Hate: Islam and the War on America

Shakedown: Exposing the Real Jesse Jackson

The Death Lobby: How the West Armed Iraq

*La Grande Fauche: La Fuite des Technologies vers l'Est
(Gorbachev's Technology War)*

*Fanning the Flames: Guns, Greed,
and Geopolitics in the Gulf War*

WWW.KENTIMMERMAN.COM

AND THE
REST IS
HISTORY

AND THE REST IS HISTORY

TALES OF HOSTAGES, ARMS DEALERS, DIRTY TRICKS, AND SPIES

KENNETH R. TIMMERMAN

Foreword by Rabbi Abraham Cooper, Associate Dean, Simon Wiesenthal Center

A POST HILL PRESS BOOK
ISBN: 978-1-63758-476-7
ISBN (eBook): 978-1-63758-477-4

And the Rest Is History:
Tales of Hostages, Arms Dealers, Dirty Tricks, and Spies
© 2022 by Kenneth R. Timmerman
All Rights Reserved

Bottom Cover Photo by Rich Gibson
Interior Design by Yoni Limor

Post Hill Press
New York • Nashville
posthillpress.com

Published in the United States of America
1 2 3 4 5 6 7 8 9 10

For Niclas, Julian, Clio, Diana, and Simon

Table of Contents

Foreword...xv
Preface..xix

Chapter 1: Illusions 1
   1: Illusions 3
   2: There Are Only Good Drivers in Lebanon............................ 5
   3: Crossing the Green Line.. 10
   4: Interrogation 15

Chapter 2: Captivity 19
   5: Cellmates 21
   6: Bang, Bang. You Dead... 27
   7: Bastonnade... 33
   8: Beirut Underground 36
   9: Arafat's Headquarters.. 41
   10: On Angels' Wings 49
   11: The Monastery 53

Chapter 3: Apprenticeship 59
   12: The Village Leagues 61
   13: 'Actually, Major, I Can Confirm That.'............................ 63
   14: The Princess and The Lamp... 64
   15: First Blood 68
   16: Silence in the Hashish Fields..................................... 73
   17: Voila du Boudin... 77
   18: A Message from the Mountains 83
   19: Hungry Guns, Exploding Cats 88

Chapter 4: Tales out of School 99
   20: How I Became an Arms Dealer....................................... 101
   21: The Boys with the Plastic Keys.................................... 105
   22: 'Who's Shipping to Iran?' 109
   23: Blacklisted by Saddam 113

Chapter 5: Need Juice.. 127
   24: Iran-Contra, the Real Beginning................................... 129

25: 'That's the Sound of Freedom' 131

26: By the Rivers of Babylon 136

27: Courtship 144

28: The Damavand Project 146

29: 'We Hate Your Country' 149

30: Fanning the Flames 156

31: Bernard, the Arms Dealer 162

Chapter 6: Treachery **169**

32: Game of Missiles 171

33: The Paris Ayatollah 174

34: Stabbed in the Back 177

35: Izzy Stone, KGB Spy 180

36: Legends 182

37: Saddam's Nephew 188

Chapter 7: Hostage Negotiations **193**

38: How I Became an Israeli Spy 195

39: The London Safe House 198

40: Coffee with Hezbollah 204

41: Back Door Man 214

Chapter 8: Choosing Sides **217**

42: The Baghdad Arms Fair 219

43: Search Warrant, French-Style 223

44: Pierre Salinger's Yogurt 226

45: The Intelligence Underworld 228

46: A Communist, a Capitalist, and a Socialist... .232

47: Affairs of State 235

48: The Best Article I Never Wrote 241

49: My Contribution to the War Effort 243

Chapter 9: And I Thought It Wasn't Political **247**

50: The Uranium Plant That Couldn't Exist 249

51: BNL and the Death Lobby 251

52: 'Our Bible' 256

53: 'Oh My, That's the Defense Minister!' 262

54: 'Saddam's Secrets' 265

Chapter 10: Visitors **269**

    55: 'No Arms Shipments, No Scandal' 271

    56: Return to Lebanon 275

    57: Saddam and the Jews 278

Chapter 11: Open the Windows **281**

    58: Bill Clinton's 'Funny Facts' 283

    59: A Matter of Physics 287

    60: SCUDS on Tel Aviv 292

Chapter 12: Persona Non Grata **297**

    61: 'If You're Not a Journalist, You're a Spy!' 299

    62: 'We Will Keep You a Long Time' 303

    63: Simon Wiesenthal's Sources 305

    64: 500 Million Reasons 306

    65: The Fist of God 310

    66: Putting on the Chain 312

Chapter 13: 'Watch Your Back' **317**

    67: Welcome to the Swamp 319

    68: The China Plan 323

    69: *Time* Magazine 326

    70: An Obituary of the "Mainstream" Media 330

Acknowledgments **339**

"In peace we can make many of them ignore good and evil entirely; in danger, the issue is forced upon them in a guise to which even we cannot blind them."

–C. S. Lewis, *The Screwtape Letters*, p. 148

Foreword

By Rabbi Abraham Cooper, Associate Dean, Simon Wiesenthal Center

I n 2008, I was approached by Kurdish and Iraqi diplomats[1] with a request to create a UN exhibition commemorating the twentieth anniversary of Saddam Hussein's gassing of five thousand of his Kurdish citizens.

To prepare for the exhibition, my colleague, Liebe Geft, the director of our Museum of Tolerance, and I traveled to Kurdistan to hear from survivors of that horrific day in 1988.

This orthodox rabbi had one request: to pray at the site of the mass grave of five thousand innocent Muslims.

As I grappled to find the appropriate words for a prayer, I remembered a conversation I had with the namesake of our institution, Nazi hunter Simon Wiesenthal, one of the few world leaders to denounce Saddam's crimes against humanity. He warned that the silence and apathy greeting the atrocity would be interpreted as a green light by other tyrants for future atrocities. He was to be proven right over and over again.

Standing in that windswept cemetery, the souls of the innocents seemed to be silently screaming, "How could the world let this happen? Why the silence and apathy from the world?"

---

1   Mike O'Sullivan, "Los Angeles Museum of Tolerance Exhibit Recalls Gassing of Kurds," *Voice of America*, March 17, 2010, https://www.voanews.com/a/museum-of-tolerance-exhibit-recalls-gassing-of-kurds-88430247/163375.html.

I knew the answers. They were supplied by a courageous investigative journalist, Kenneth Timmerman, years before. He could detail where the poison gas came from, who sold the helicopters, and so on.

I first learned about Ken Timmerman years before from my colleague Shimon Samuels, who was the Paris-based European director of the Simon Wiesenthal Center and who alerted me to alarming news that Ken had published about the German connections to Saddam Hussein's poison gas programs.

Poison gas is a sensitive subject for the Simon Wiesenthal Center, whose mission is to teach the lessons of the Nazi Holocaust and to help the world avoid repeating the horrors of the past. The idea that Saddam Hussein might be getting poison gas technology from Germany to use against Israel was beyond horrifying.

The founder of the Simon Wiesenthal Center, Rabbi Marvin Hier, and I decided to commission Ken to do additional research. We released his *Poison Gas Report* in late 1990. It identified eighty-six West German companies as major supplies of Saddam Hussein's burgeoning WMD programs. It was the first of several collaborative projects we did together.

As I got to know Ken and his wife, Christina, better, I realized he was no ordinary reporter. His energy was prodigious. One week he was in Paris, the next in Washington, then he flew to Israel and Jordan and onward to tour machine-tool plants in Germany, always meeting sources who were willing to compare notes because he actually had notes to compare.

But his uniqueness went way beyond this extraordinary ability to drill down into complex subjects. It was Ken's *story*.

As you will read in this book, Ken started his career as a young American liberal, went to Beirut, and promptly got taken hostage by terrorists. It's the classic American story of a transformation. He came out of that experience a changed person, born again to his Christian faith and with an unshakeable devotion to the cause of freedom.

That devotion led him to do things many journalists would not consider, including helping his own government and that of Israel.

Ken went on to dedicate his life to exposing terrorists, or as Simon Wiesenthal put it, "the murderers of tomorrow." His many books are full of them.

You will find this book a good place to understand yesteryear's crises and today's challenges. I can only hope that Ken Timmerman's dedication will inspire a new generation of journalists who will pursue their stories the old-fashioned way—seeking out the truth—wherever that journey takes you.

G-d bless you Ken for always taking that journey.

Rabbi Abraham Cooper
Simon Wiesenthal Center
Los Angeles

Preface

I never wanted to be a journalist. In fact, as a young aspiring novelist, I held the profession in contempt. It was for lesser mortals, I argued, drawing on my Gauloises-stained beard in the book-lined parlor above Shakespeare and Company in Paris, where I edited an expatriate literary review. Journalists wrote short sentences and shunned ambiguity, I declaimed. Journalists couldn't write dialogue or create landscape. A journalist would never dream of writing an entire book just to evoke a color, as Flaubert claimed he had done with *Salammbô*, his ode to ancient Carthage and the color ochre. At best, journalism was a pastime that a "real" writer only engaged in to "blunt the instrument" of his talent, as Ernest Hemingway famously wrote. Journalism was—well, just boring.

I certainly had a lot to learn.

If there is one thing my life as a journalist over the past thirty-five years has *not* been, it's boring.

I have covered war, espionage, and intrigue for major news organizations in the United States and around the world, including the *New York Times*, *Newsweek*, *Time* magazine, *Reader's Digest*, CBS News, ABC News, *Le Monde*, *L'Express*, Le Point, and many others. That was when these organizations still tried to be "mainstream" and did not pull punches, obfuscate, self-censor, and lie to protect their political allies.

Only when I was fired from *Time* magazine in 1994 for investigating a story that threatened President Bill Clinton and many senior officials in his administration did I begin to understand that the mainstream media was dead. Like many other countries in Europe and the Western world, we now have a politicized media in the United States. But unlike other countries, in all but a few cases our media refuses to acknowledge its ideological affiliation. So added to bias, you have hypocrisy.

But this book is not a diatribe about the media. Instead, it tells the backstory of a very rich period of recent history from one reporter's perspective as that perspective broadened and deepened with time. As a product of the late 1960s and early 1970s, I questioned authority and was a fierce individualist, making me a natural leftist. By the mid-1990s, I discovered to my surprise that those same values now made me a conservative. History would be nothing without irony.

Some of my friends have urged me to write a memoir of sex, Paris, and the expatriate literary set that gathered around Shakespeare and Company. It was riotous and raucous, sinful and fun. But they will have to wait.

This book will take readers on a traveling circus from Paris to Prague to Beirut, Damascus, Baghdad, and beyond. It will introduce you to spies and terrorists, arms dealers and crooks, and along the way reveal a few surprises about the secret underbelly of public events in ways I guarantee you never would have expected.

All the rest, as they say, is history.

Chapter 1:
Illusions

1: Illusions[2]
On the border between Germany and Czechoslovakia

The border guard marched right out of my dreams and into the harsh, metallic corridor outside our compartment, banging on the glass door.

"Papers!" he said in German, Czech, and then French. "*Papiers!*"

The train had come to a halt during the night in a pine forest at the edge of West Germany. Now the sun was beginning to turn the patches of sky between the trees a sullen grey, and I watched the border guards outside, shuffling between military trucks parked parallel to the train tracks. It was dark, dreary, and cold. In the sodium lights, you could see swamps of mud from melting snow.

Suddenly, the door to our compartment slammed open, and a giant beard in a uniform filled the entire space. I was holding out my American passport, and his eye caught it right away.

"Get up!" he said brusquely. "Who are you hiding behind your seat?"

I got up obediently, turning to look behind me. Then the guard burst into laughter, and several of the other passengers in the compartment joined him.

"Welcome to Czechoslovakia," he said.

I was teaching English in Paris at the time, and had just launched an expatriate literary journal called *Paris Voices*. This was my first foray behind the Iron Curtain, and I had no real-world guidance of what to expect.

My girlfriend's parents had given me the Prague address of a family friend named Olga, who had worked for them as an *au pair* in the early 1960s. Olga was now in her mid-thirties and was married to a signatory of Charter 77, the civic movement led by Václav Havel that called for an end to Communist rule.

Solange, my girlfriend's mother, had given me presents for Olga and Jiri: a washable tablecloth, paper napkins, stockings, chocolate, and an inexpensive French pullover. When I arrived at their large apartment and saw the polished antiques, the telephone, the hand-blown crystal goblets, and the dark bookshelves crammed with books and records, I felt foolish.

---

2   This section was published in the *Paris Metro 40th Anniversary Edition*, September 2016.

"Sshh!" she said when I started to ask her about Charter 77. "Not here."

She pointed to the walls and then to her ears. "The walls have ears, even for silly things like chocolate and stockings," she said.

A thick haze of coal smoke choked the streets. It entered your lungs like a fist that opened and closed against your will. Olga took me down to a local tavern just off the Staroměstské náměstí, the Old Town Square, not far from the Charles Bridge. At 4:00 PM on a Saturday afternoon, it was absolutely packed. People were eating sausages, drinking beer and *slivovic,* and talking at volumes that rivaled those of a Washington, DC, bar at happy hour. I could barely hear Olga, let alone what anyone at the next table was saying. I got it. Even if the walls had ears, all they could hear here would be gobbledygook.

A while later, her husband joined us.

"In 1968, we all believed," Jiri said. "Soviet Communism was like an old coat we had outgrown. It was springtime, we were young, all we saw were possibilities. Just the thought of freedom was a drug that loosened our tongues."

"After the crackdown," Olga continued, "we were just waiting for the police to show up at our door. The Soviet tanks were everywhere. I wondered if I would ever smell the sea again."

An army colonel came in through the door, and the wave of cold air he brought with him seemed to chill the entire room. For a few moments, as he approached the bar and ordered a beer, no one spoke. He exchanged a few pleasantries with the barman, echoing off the walls like broken crystal. Then he downed his beer quickly, dropping a large bill. The barman returned the change. When the colonel tried to leave it as a tip, the barman pushed it back at him, queen's pawn to QP4.

"Things are different now," Jiri said once the colonel left. "It's only a matter of time. They think they are winning, but they have lost."

"But we will get a call later on, asking us what we were speaking to you about," Olga added.

Later, I met a young music teacher, who, unlike Olga and Jiri, had made his peace with the regime. He claimed to have studied the West and found our system wanting.

"Here I have everything I need," he told me. "I have a job, an apartment, even a house in the country. I have economic security but have to watch what I say. In the West, you can say what you wish but you have to struggle to live. Which is better?"

In the magazine article I eventually wrote about this trip for *Paris Metro*, a new expat magazine, I compared the vision of these two, as if they represented a fair choice.

How wrong I was. And how little did I understand the sweetness of freedom or its cost.

But I would learn.

2: There Are Only Good Drivers in Lebanon
On the Mediterranean between Cyprus and Lebanon

"*Siroco, Siroco*, this is Israeli navy ship. Do you read me, over?"

It was nine o'clock at night, beginning week six of another war in Lebanon. The sea was calm, and our Greek captain was used to dealing with the Israeli gunboats.

"Israeli navy ship, this is *Siroco*. I wait your instructions, over."

He cut the engines, and an eerie quiet engulfed us, stretching like a caged tiger into the night. In the distance we could see the running lights of several other ships also waiting for clearance to approach Jounieh. Once the shelling had closed the Beirut airport weeks earlier, this small fishing and pleasure port had become Lebanon's main window onto the world.

I joined a small group of Lebanese men who had crowded up at the bow, talking excitedly, seemingly oblivious to the low-slung gunboat circling us silently in the darkness. One man, bald on the top, his white dress shirt open halfway to his waist, wore a heavy gold cross. He offered me a beer from a cooler at his feet.

"You see that?" he said, pointing to an orange glow on the distant shore. "That is the Palestinians finally getting their due."

The Israeli gunboat hailed us again with a staccato burst of sound, falling like a saucer into the dull emptiness of the sea. Almost simultaneously, a bomb burst over Beirut, illuminating the mountains beyond.

"Oh, *yeah*!" a short, stocky man cheered. "That is just below my village in the Djebel Druse."

The Druse were Muslims, and I must have looked confused because the bald man with the cross started to laugh.

"You probably think we Muslims and Christians hate each other," he said.

I shrugged evasively.

"Ask Ali here what he thinks of the Palestinians," the bald man went on. "Ali, tell the American how much you love the Palestinians," he said, prodding him with his beer.

Ali was a Shiite from a village called Bint Jbeil in South Lebanon, not far from the Israeli border. He turned toward me and spat on the deck.

"They invaded our country," he said.

"Didn't they lose theirs?" I said naively.

"What theirs? Some rocks in Palestine you can't even wipe your rear end with. Let the Arabs take them if they care so much."

I was excited and apprehensive, not knowing what to expect. After seven years of holding forth at Shakespeare and Company and leading a thoroughly frivolous life of poetry and prose, of drinking bouts and easy girls, I knew I had to start listening, following the facts. It was scary, in a way, because it meant entering someone else's reality you couldn't control.

In a matter of weeks, I would come to doubt everything I thought I knew and to believe things I never thought I could.

It was the beginning of a long career.

+ + +

I wrote my first dispatch later that night, a sixty-second piece on war profiteering for the English service of Radio Holland International. I don't think it ever aired, but I remember describing the crowd of refugees in Larnaca, most of them poor Christians, pleading with the deckhands to let them sneak on board the ferry so they could return to their families. The indifferent Greek captain was charging $180 for one-way passage, close to twenty times the normal fare. Only a handful of the wealthy—or the reporters—could afford to pay.

I shared a taxi with Associated Press feature writer Mort Rosenblum to the Alexander Hotel, which towered above the twisting streets of Ashrafieh like a tacky monument of aluminum and glass. The run-down lobby was the swollen heart of Christian East Beirut. People were crammed into overstuffed chairs, hanging on sofas, slumped against the walls by the teletype machine. Shrapnel had pockmarked the dingy marble floor tiles, and the walls had turned yellowish brown from cigarette smoke. The AP had superstar status because of the size of its weekly bill, and Mort offered to use his pull to get me a room. But when the manager told me it would cost $150 per night, cash up front, I politely demurred. At that rate, I could only afford to stay in Beirut for a week—without eating.

An M113 armored personnel carrier struck with a blue Star of David was parked out front—not exactly the BMWs you might expect. The Israel Defense Force (IDF) had converted the chintzy coffee shop overlooking the empty parking lot into a press office. I could see the officers through the glass in their relaxed military fatigues and felt like I was about to enter the belly of the beast, the heart of enemy territory. At least, that is what I had been taught from the screaming anti-Israel headlines in the French press.

I bumped into a cameraman I had met during the crossing from Larnaca. We shared a beer at the bar.

"How do you get across to the West?" I asked him.

"Wait for a ceasefire. And avoid the Israeli checkpoints. They know they can't stop us, but they always try."

+ + +

I found a room with a Christian family for twenty dollars a night not far from the Alexander. After walking around for a day, getting the feel of the city, I decided to phone the father of one my students from Paris. He was a surgeon at St. George's hospital in East Beirut. They were Christians—Greek Catholic, I learned later, although the distinction meant nothing to me at the time. Dr. Riachi invited me to visit his home that evening to meet some friends. I figured it was a good way to bide the time until I could cross into West Beirut, which, of course, was the real story.

The houses in their neighborhood along the southern rim of East Beirut looked like enormous blockhouses, a far cry from the dilapidated structures crumbling on top of each other where I was now staying. As I got closer, I noticed huge circles of fresh cement in virtually every house along the street. Most of the windows were crisscrossed with tape to prevent them from shattering.

A Bangladeshi servant in a white coat ushered me inside to a living room where dense clusters of bodies were talking and sipping on drinks.

"Nadia told me to be expecting you," Dr. Riachi said. "Excuse us for the cramped conditions."

He explained that three other families were temporarily staying at his house because they had been bombed out of their homes in West Beirut.

"The Israelis have made them refugees?"

"Oh no," he said. "The Palestinians."

One of his houseguests was a member of parliament from Nabatieh, a heavily Shiite district in South Lebanon. He was a distinguished older gentleman accustomed to power with a large, expressive forehead who had no reason in the world to spend a minute on an insignificant visitor like me. And yet he did, eager and I think amused to watch the scales drop from my eyes.

"First, the Israelis forced us out of our home in Nabatieh," the deputy said. "We were the last ones to leave when they invaded; we had to be. And so we moved up to our apartment in Ras Beirut, and then the Palestinians put an RPG-7 through the living room window, setting everything on fire. They said we had been collaborating with the Israelis."

Somewhere an angel was fluttering its wings, driving away the stereotypes I had learned in Paris.

Dr. Riachi invited me to join them up in the mountains for dinner. Once our small convoy got out of the city, we drove up twisting roads, hugging the steep ravines, then emerged onto a ridge with a spectacular view of the sea. The lights of the city stretched below us like a river of diamonds toward the distant port and abruptly ended in a jagged line just to the west, cutting the city in two. Half the city was bathed in light and activity, the other half plunged in the outer darkness.

We were shown to a large table at the edge of the stone terrace perched over the cliff. The entire back wall of the restaurant was covered with bright red Bougainvillea. Bunches of bright flowers spilled onto a long table that was crowded with hors d'oeuvres and fruits. Many Americans today are familiar with Lebanese food and would find nothing extraordinary in the lavish plates of hummus, *baba ghanoush* and fresh yoghurt decorated with swirls of red pepper, the giant platters of spring onions and hearts of lettuce, the bowls of dark green *tabouleh* sprinkled with grains of barley, the grilled liver brochettes, the skewers of frog legs, and the mountain of fresh strawberries, cherries, plums, and grapes that dominated the far end. But this was my first encounter with the extravagance of Lebanon. I felt I had been magically transported to a Roman saturnalia, where the revelers ate until they burst, then emptied their stomachs in some hidden vomitorium so they could return to the feast. We ate and drank *arak*, the anisette beverage that was so similar to French *pastis*, and the war seemed far away. Strings of clear Christmas lights peeped out of the forest of grapevines that formed a natural pergola over our heads, and people were laughing and talking loudly in a babel of languages. As I learned from the Riachis, our fellow revelers were Christians and Muslims and Drusis, about equally apportioned, and normally lived in both the Christian east and the Muslim western sectors of Beirut. This mountain restaurant, and many others like it, was neutral territory, a secret haven where ordinary people—or at least the noncombatants—could make their separate peace and pretend to live the dream of Lebanon as the Switzerland of the Middle East, which otherwise had been extinguished by seven years of feudal bloodletting.

Suddenly, we heard a loud whooshing and saw the bright orange tailpipes of two Israeli fighter jets plunging into the darkness below, streaking down toward the city. It was too dark to identify them, but there could be no doubt where they had come from or what their mission was. In that instant, the restaurant fell quiet. People eating at distant tables jumped up and joined us at the parapet, staring into the dark half of the city below as if to divine the target of these beasts of prey. We saw tracer bullets arc up into the sky from a dozen points on the ground, and then we saw the Israeli jets pull sharply upwards, afterburners lit, and stand out against the clear night sky, like rockets rising almost vertically into the heavens. In the next instant we saw the red-orange blooms where their bombs hit the darkened city, eerily silent, and the entire restaurant erupted into raucous applause and catcalls before the distant rumbling of the explosions and the jet noise poured over us.

"Isn't it your city, too?" I asked Dr. Riachi.

"You mean, why is everybody so happy to see the Palestinians get bombed?"

He nodded toward his friend, the Shiite deputy from South Lebanon. "Why don't you ask him?"

The deputy had risen with the others, not applauding but smiling wistfully, gently shaking his head as if in approval. When he rejoined us at the table, he gestured to the crowd at the parapet.

"People have memories," he said. "For seven years, most of the people you see here were getting bombed day and night by the Palestinians. Many of them, like our host, lost their homes and had to rebuild them, sometimes two or three times. Where was your international media when Christians or Drusis or even Shia in the South were the victims? The Hotel Alexander was empty for seven long years. No one dared walk the streets of Ashrafieh. Many didn't even dare go to work."

"You asked me why I drove an American car," Dr. Riachi added. "Well, it's very simple: it's the biggest and heaviest vehicle I could find. I had to drive an open stretch of road on my way to and from work every day, about three hundred meters each way. When I left the last Kataeb checkpoint at the Qarantina I had to step on the gas and get down below the steering wheel and pray that I could hold it straight and go fast enough not to get hit by the Palestinian snipers along the river. Every day I had to do that. I wound up spending quite a bit on body work—but just on the car, not on me." He laughed. "We have a saying that in Lebanon, there are only good drivers. All the bad ones are dead."

3: Crossing the Green Line
Beirut

The next morning, they announced a ceasefire over the radio, and I resolved to make my way into West Beirut. While I was beginning to doubt the sympathies I had brought with me from Paris, I just couldn't see a story that any Western media would publish based on what I had heard and seen over the past few days.

The narrow streets winding down to the avenue by the museum crossing were choked with traffic and exhaust fumes, which I took as a good sign. An Israeli M113 was parked alongside the road in front of a tank, its cannon muzzle covered with a cloth bag. I presented my passport to the Israeli soldier at the oil drums barring the road. He looked like he had stepped out of a Hollywood audition with an M-16 slung casually below his waist, shirt untucked, and Foster Grant shades.

"Why do you want to go in there? Everybody else is trying to get out."

"I'm a reporter."

"It's closed," he said with a shrug.

"What do you mean? They just announced on the radio that it was open."

He ignored me and waved his arm lazily at a taxi driver who had left his car in the line and was approaching him on foot, apparently trying to pick up fares from the people crossing over from West Beirut. The man threw up his arms in exasperation and turned around.

I decided to hang around. A few Lebanese families were anxiously peering across the Green Line, waiting for relatives to emerge from the besieged West. I took the lens cap off my Leicaflex, snapped a few pictures, and mentally noted the place and the caption. A plainclothes Lebanese security officer came over to me and shouted in English, "No photographs. Move along." I hurriedly stowed the camera in my shoulder bag and fell back into the crowd.

After a bit of wandering, I stumbled on a smaller roadblock in the midst of a dense network of streets farther up. There was a wall of sandbags and no Israelis, just a guy in a Bob Marley T-shirt and sunglasses, sitting on an oil drum in front of a bombed-out doorway, an M-16 propped lazily against his jeans. I asked if I could pass.

He held up his hand. "Wait a few minutes."

Soon, an old man carrying a leather pouch with his identity papers came up to the guard and whispered a few words. The militiaman nodded and pointed the two of us down an alley. On the crumbling wall of an abandoned building someone had painted an arrow in white, so we entered and made our way down a long hallway, stumbling over the rubble in the darkness until we turned a corner, and the hallway ended in bright sunlight, where a man-sized hole had been blown out of the wall.

Suddenly we were on a wide, abandoned avenue, and the little man I had followed headed off at a martial pace, just like the rabbit in *Alice in Wonderland*. The buildings on either side looked like once-elegant sandcastles eaten away by the tide. Seven years of almost constant shooting and artillery fire had blown out all the windows and turned the street to chunky dust, except for masses of green vines sprouting up everywhere—hence the name of this no-man's land, the Green Line. Up ahead, a huge mound of red earth blocked the road. As we approached, I saw several guerilla fighters—I assumed they were Palestinians, though they wore no insignia—milling about, smoking cigarettes and drinking tea. One of them tipped his fingers to an imaginary cap as we approached their position. He waved us through.

I turned onto the main boulevard along the hippodrome and the resi-dential neighborhood of Mazra'a. Despite the ceasefire, not a single car was visible. Bags of rotting garbage were everywhere. They sat in platoon-like ranks in companies, a whole regiment of grey garbage bags lining the shut-tered shops along this once-elegant street, many of them gnawed open by rats and others looking for food. The stench was overpowering, a mix of rotting olives, rancid meat, and sun-baked diapers. A few children ran in and out of a building down the street. As I was about to get my camera, a bald-headed man in a neat safari suit came out of nowhere and gently grabbed my arm. I was sweating in the heat, but his touch was dry.

"Your papers, please," he said. "Where are you going?"

I told him the name of the humanitarian organization I intended to visit and write about.

"Okay, but first you have to go to the Foreign Press Office for a pass. Just ask anyone for the *Jamia Arabiya*."

A pair of Israeli fighters descended out of the clear blue sky and roared past us. I turned to look for cover but noticed that the man was not paying them any attention. He was staring at me.

"What about them?" I said, indicating the retreating planes.

"They're just practicing. Maybe like you."

He handed me back my passport and sent me on my way before I could say a word.

+ + +

When I finally reached the *Jamia Arabiya*, I was directed to the PLO's chief flak, Mahmoud Labadi, who was giving a tour of bombed-out areas to a pair of British reporters. Labadi had become a familiar face to Western television viewers that summer. With his large designer glasses, fashionable haircut, and casual jacket, he could have stepped off a college campus, not a refugee camp. I found him a few blocks away, explaining the ordnance the Israelis had been dropping on the civilians of West Beirut. At the end of a sidewalk display of what purported to be cluster bomblets, exploding dolls, and other evil wizardry was a brass shell casing filled with a yellowish powder. He dipped a piece of cardboard into it, lit it, and set it on the ground, where it gave off a huge amount of smoke.

"White phosphorus," Labadi explained. "You can identify it by the smell. Also by the burns, because it penetrates beneath the skin.

This is what the Israelis are dropping on our homes. You call them incendiary bombs."

I had read stories about these PLO allegations but never imagined I would be looking at the actual chemical used in illegal incendiary bombs. Somehow it seemed not very threatening, like a high school chemistry experiment. And maybe it was. Labadi had obviously performed this demonstration many times and had no fear of getting burned.

"Now let me show you where the Israelis are dropping these," he said, setting a course for the Arab University. The two Brits hung back for an instant, watching the sky for Israeli planes. The street was deserted, except for us.

"This is a city of death," Labadi said. "You should say that in your columns. People are afraid to come out into the streets, thanks to the Israelis and their American helpers."

The tall reporter with the paunch wrote down the phrase in his notebook, but the shorter reporter was looking at me instead.

"Say," he said. "Who are you with, anyway?"

I told him I was working as a stringer for the English-language service of Radio Netherlands.

"Well, we arranged for a private briefing and don't appreciate you barging in on us," he said.

"Seriously," I said. "It's not like this is a scoop."

That was obvious even to me, after what I had learned over the past few days. Then it occurred to me that the two Brits were slothfully taking dictation from Labadi and that I had just rubbed their noses in it. Dumb!

"Mr. Labadi," the British reporter called out. "This man isn't with us. I consider his presence an intrusion."

Labadi apologetically asked me to wait for him back at his office. So I left the three of them at the university and headed back.

One of his aides gave me a form to fill out for my press pass while I waited for the chief flak to return. I filled it out and handed it to him, along with my letter of accreditation.

"You need two identity photos," he said.

"Identity photos?"

"One goes on the pass, the other is for file."

I hadn't thought to bring photos. Nobody had told me I needed them until now.

"Don't you have a photo machine around here? Somewhere at the university? We've got them in Paris in the metro."

The aide laughed. "This isn't Paris. The only machines that still work are in East Beirut."

"But I just walked here from East Beirut."

"Then you can walk back."

I was furious with myself. *How stupid!* I had studied hard to learn about Lebanon, the seven years of the civil war. I had followed the events since the June 6 invasion very closely, memorizing names and dates and places. I had identified several aid organizations in West Beirut I was hoping to use as a base to report on the lives of ordinary people trapped in war and had made contact with the PLO in Paris and in Athens en route. They enthusiastically approved my request to visit the city as a novelist-cum-writer-cum-radio stringer, and each time they said I would be greeted with "open arms." No one had ever mentioned the need for ID photos. I felt like a dunce.

I started walking back toward the museum, wondering if the cease-fire would last long enough for me to get photos made and return across the Green Line before nightfall, when a mud-smeared Mercedes came out of nowhere and pulled up alongside me. The bald-headed man who had checked my papers earlier was at the wheel. Thinking he was offering me a ride, I told him I had to go back to the museum to get ID photos.

"Get in," he said.

We were the only car on the street, and the bald-headed man drove quickly. He turned a corner and we headed away from the museum, and I began to get nervous. I said something about Labadi being busy and asking me to meet him back at his office as soon as I got the photos, but he just raced through the back streets, ignoring me. A few minutes later, we pulled up at a roadblock in front of a heavily guarded villa. The guards recognized him and let us pass. The last thing I noticed was long sections of garden hose spliced together in the middle of the street. This, I would learn, was the PLO's alternative water system hooked up to West Beirut's numerous private wells. It was the only water I would drink for several weeks.

4: Interrogation

A pair of guerilla fighters in dusty green fatigues escorted me into the villa, where a civilian interrogator was waiting. He had sallow skin and several days of dirty beard. His stomach hung over the trousers of his light green safari suit, and his fingernails were long. He sat at a large glass desk flanked by ornate glass-enclosed bookcases packed with ancient pottery and artifacts. I was guessing that the PLO had seized the villa from a wealthy Lebanese family.

He was holding my passport, which the soldiers had taken from me once we got out of the car.

"You are American," he said.

"Yes."

"Born in New York."

"Yes."

"You have a Jewish name."

"Actually, it's not," I said. "My family is—"

"Shut up!" he slammed my passport onto the desk. "You have a Jewish name. You look Jewish. You were born in New York, the city of the Jews. You have a camera. You are an Israeli spy. *Sharmouta!*"[3]

He jumped up and cocked his fist but then thought better of it and said something in Arabic to the two soldiers and waved me out of his presence.

I was in a state of shock. I had come to Beirut thinking that the Palestinians were the powerless victims of a massively well-armed nation state, the Arab David fighting a Jewish Goliath. After all, that was the story the Western media was putting out. And I was sure that would be the story the two British reporters I had met earlier would write. But suddenly, I had slammed into reality in the form of a PLO political cadre who had real power over me, and he was convinced I was a spy.

The two guerilla fighters took me outside and herded me back into the dilapidated Mercedes. We drove for a few minutes in the shadows of bomb-nibbled apartment blocks, then arrived at what looked like a military complex. We left the car by a roadblock and went through a large gate into a courtyard, then up a flight of steps and through a series of

---

3   Literally, "whore." More generally, filth, dirt, excrement.

corridors. Guerilla fighters were sleeping in rooms on both sides; others were drinking tea or playing cards. At the end was an office, where an older man in crisp military fatigues was seated at a desk looking at a file.

"You speak to the Colonel," one of the guards said.

"Sit down," the Colonel said in perfect English. He went over the same questions as the political cadre, carefully writing down my answers without comment. His businesslike manner was reassuring, and I began to hope that this was all just a huge mistake. He asked who I had spoken to at the PLO, wrote down their names, and then asked how I had crossed over to West Beirut. When I told him that I had followed an old man through an abandoned building, he stopped writing and stared at me.

"You mean you just walked in here?"

"Yes."

"My soldiers are jittery. They could have shot you, and there's nothing I could have done about it. Don't you realize this is a war zone?"

Israeli warplanes passed overhead, and he pointed to the darkened window behind him. "Do you think I have these shutters closed because I like to sit in the dark? It's to conceal our position. You think you can just walk the streets and nothing will happen?"

I felt dumb but a bit relieved. I was thinking that it must be harder to shoot somebody you think is just plain dumb, rather than a brilliant spy.

He began thumbing through my address book, and my worry returned. I had the names and phone numbers of political contacts in East Beirut, people whose names he undoubtedly would recognize.

"Who is Adib Yitshack?" he asked. I drew a blank. It sounded ominously Jewish the way he pronounced it.

"Can I see?"

He slid the address book over to me, and I understood.

"That's the name of the street of the Hotel Alexander, where I thought I would stay."

A large map of Beirut occupied an entire wall of his office. He stared at it for a moment, seemingly lost in thought, then shook his head again, exasperated.

"I spent ten years in the United States. You have a saying: the best defense is a good offense. Do you know who said that?"

"We use it in football."

"Yeah, it was Notre Dame, I think. Look, if you want to get out of this, you'd better stick to that story."

"What story?"

He slapped the folder with my information onto the desk angrily. "You just walk in here with no papers and say you want to write about the war. I might be inclined to believe you. But other people are going to think you're a spy. We've had people come in here with airtight credentials who turned out to be spies."

"What are you saying?"

"I'm just saying, stick to your story. Having no credentials, nothing in writing besides a letter from some radio no one has heard of, might be what finally saves you."

He made a final annotation in Arabic at the bottom of the paper he had been writing on, then waved me off, shaking his head. "Goddamn stupid Americans!"

✦ ✦ ✦

The guards ushered me down another long hallway overlooking a courtyard, then up a flight of stairs to a bare office, where a man was waiting. He was closer to my age, wore a pistol in his belt, and spoke broken English. He offered me tea from a pot on his desk, then indicated that I should empty my shoulder bag: Leicaflex, a few notebooks, rolls of film, address book, wallet, and identity papers all wound up on his desk, where he inventoried them in Arabic on a plain sheet of paper. Then he opened my wallet.

"Money," he said. "How much money?"

I didn't know whether this was a joke, since he could see for himself, or whether he was asking for a bribe.

"Around five hundred pounds," I said.[4]

I was curious whether he would pocket the cash, but instead, he wrote down the sum and put the money and my passport into a plain white envelope on the desk.

"Belt," he said next.

I tried to make him understand that my belt had a practical function, but when he offered to assist me in taking it off, I rolled it up and placed it with the rest of the things he had stuffed in my bag, hoping he wouldn't see the zipper. Inside, I had stashed enough cash to last me several weeks.

---

4   Around $170.

"Write name," he said. I looked at the lines of Arabic writing, wrote "for contents of bag," and signed. My mind raced over the events of the past few hours, but I could find no order, no logic, no reason why this was happening. The man ushered me politely into the next room, where a few fighters in uniform sat around, cleaning their rifles, smoking, drinking tea. One of them had a fresh bandage wrapped around his left foot. He smiled, extended a pack of cigarettes. Another soldier stood on the balcony. I pointed to the sky.

"More planes?"

"*W'allah*," the man with the bandaged foot shrugged. "They come, they not come. What we do?"

After a few minutes, we heard footsteps in the corridor, and a guard came in and motioned with his AK-47 for me to get up.

"Where are you taking me?"

"Someplace safe," he said with a grin.

We went down two flights and headed across the courtyard to a much taller building, perhaps seven or eight floors, on the far side of the compound. It looked like so many seaside apartment buildings in Beirut, with small balconies at each floor and a pale yellow façade. The only access from the courtyard that I could see was a basement door, its metal covers folded back. We went down a half-dozen steps and through another metal door, entering a darkened room, where half a dozen fighters lounged about a cheap metal desk and chairs. They laughed as I came in, then one of them got up and went to a metal door at the far side of the room and inserted a key, pushing it open.

For an instant, my mind froze, unable to comprehend what was happening. It was pitch black inside, but the smell of human sweat and excrement and cigarette smoke was overwhelming. As they pushed me into that pit, I could feel densely packed bodies shift slightly so I could pass, like a carpet of squid. All I could see were a pair of orange coals floating in the darkness, too faint to illuminate what had to be faces bathed in smoke. And then the door snapped shut behind me, forever closing me off from the world I had known for twenty-eight years.

I wanted to shut my mind and block it all out, but the darkness was thick and palpable, and it sucked me inside like Jonah into the whale.

Chapter 2:
Captivity

5: Cellmates

"You have cigarette?" a voice in English whispered. For some reason, they hadn't emptied my shirt pocket upstairs, so I had a pack of Gauloises, a disposable lighter, and a piece of candy a six-year-old Lebanese boy had given me for good luck before I crossed the Green Line into West Beirut. I grabbed the cigarettes and felt around in the darkness until I found the man's arm.

"Somali!" someone jeered.

He sang at them in Arabic, and the room broke into muffled laughter.

Someone lit the stub of a candle behind me and placed it on the metal frame of a cot. My body threw weird shadows onto the mass of flesh before me, warping the distinctions between human and darkness like a Rembrandt painted on water. In the heat, most of the men had stripped to their underwear. Some lay on filthy foam mattresses on the floor, clothes bunched into pillows beneath their heads. Others sat or lay on cots at either end of the cell. You couldn't move without bumping into something you couldn't see. Bare backs and chests glistened with clammy sweat that exuded an indescribable odor I soon identified as hopelessness, resignation, and fear.

"Sit," Somali told me.

I saw the newcomer space near the corner and wrapped my bare arm across my nose, hoping to filter the stench from the plastic bucket that served as the latrine. Now it was time for the cell leader to conduct his interrogation of me.

Ali was Palestinian. He was fit and clean, compared to the rest of them, with an almost military bearing. His eyes sparkled with humor as Somali transmitted the outline of my story. I gestured to show the size of my two small children.

"You, six months," Ali started to laugh. "Six months talk *Arabi* very good!"

I tried to laugh with him, but the thought of staying in this place one day, let alone six months, was a shock. *Six months!* It couldn't be. I had come here as their friend. And now I was their prisoner.

"The Colonel said he'd be coming for me later," I ventured.

"Oh, the Colonel," Somali said. "*Boukra. Boukra, inch'allah!*" Tomorrow, God willing. My heart sank.

Those first hours underground were the longest in my life. There were fifteen of us in the cell, which couldn't have measured more than sixteen by ten feet. They all smoked to hide the kerosene-fringed stench of the latrine bucket and their own clothes, and I smoked with them, but it just made the air thicker and more fetid. Relying on Somali's English, I tried to learn something about them.

Fouad announced that he was a Palestinian Liberation Army soldier, thumping his chest, perhaps thinking to impress or scare me, since I was, after all, an Israeli spy. He was the only one in the cell who had a cot to himself, and he seemed to have special privileges—extra cigarettes, candle stubs, a lighter. His dark hair fell in a greasy lock over a low forehead. Beneath his dirty white shirt, you could see ripples of fat. He was not just a bully, but, I soon learned, he was also our dedicated snitch, a greasy informer. The others feared him and held him in contempt. "He once murdered someone—with a knife!" Somali whispered, rolling his eyes in terror so that even in the dim light they showed white in his deep black face.

Ramadan and Anwar were Egyptian laborers who were arrested at a checkpoint trying to leave West Beirut during a lull in the fighting. They looked like they were born dumb, carrying loads of sticks on their backs, peasants in dirty *dish-dash* dresses. But they constantly smiled and made the best of things. Whenever Ramadan said something, Anwar repeated it as if it were the smartest thing he had ever heard. "No bombing today," Ramadan remarked. "No bombing today!" Anwar shouted out to the rest of us, and they both laughed. Ramadan liked to crack his knuckles. Anwar did the same.

"The Fatah people, they keep them for a week or two, slap them around, then let them go," Somali said as we discussed our cellmates. "That's how they tell Beirut, you not leave."

"So everybody is a hostage," I whispered. "The entire city!"

He nodded.

Two of the men were Drusis, soldiers in Walid Jumblatt's People's Socialist Party, PSP. Both had been here more than a week; one of them had scoops of flesh missing from both thighs. They, too, had been taken at a checkpoint trying to leave.

Perhaps the strangest was a skeletal-looking Palestinian whose name nobody knew, who was lying face-down on a thin foam mattress. Two years ago, someone had thrown him through a window, and according to Somali, he hadn't uttered a word since. On his back was a large crimson patch, raised from the skin like hot wax, cross-hatched with a web of thick lines. It was as if he had been branded with a waffle iron.

Suddenly, there was noise out in the guard room: scuffling feet. My heart leapt—perhaps it was the Colonel, coming down to tell me it was all a mistake.

"*Hot, khobès,*" Ali the cell leader said.

A guard banged on the door and slid open the judas, and Somali went over and took a bag of flat Lebanese bread. The cell erupted into frenzied activity. Someone opened the door and handed in a pan of stewed tomatoes and two bottles of water, our dinner. Even the man with the crimson brand managed to sit up and move to the floor, where the rest of us were crouching like animals in the light of a candle stub. We scarfed up the tomatoes with stale bread and passed the water bottles hand to hand. Someone burped. Fouad hawked up phlegm, then lit a cigarette. My first meal as a captive was over in less than three minutes. I returned to the sour-smelling blanket I had found on the floor.

That night, as I lay awake listening to the other men trying to sleep, with Fouad coughing richly, Somali nervously smoking, Ramadan and Anwar cracking their knuckles, and someone else moaning, I learned not to let my mind wander. Because when I did, I wanted to moan just like my invisible cellmate across the room. I thought of Julian and Clio, my infant children, and how I would get down on all fours and they would crawl all over me, like the statue of Zeus and his infants in the Tuileries Gardens. They probably wouldn't even remember me in ten years, and all of it, for what? What had I possibly hoped to achieve by coming here? To report on what? How stupid had I been! What could possibly be more important than running with them in the park, reading them stories at night? It soon became obvious that such thoughts led directly down to the pit, so I learned to train my mind. I focused on visualizing the courtyard outside. How many sandbags had there been? How many soldiers? Where was the gate that led to the street and to freedom? I tried to remember everyone's name. I focused on remembering the Arabic words I was learning, and I kept hearing a voice: *Your story doesn't end here*, over and over, like the snippet of a song you repeat when you walk. *Your story doesn't end here.*

Eventually, I fell asleep.

+ + +

Finally it was morning, and the short bald Syrian who headed the guard detail shone his flashlight through the judas, blinding us purposefully one by one. Everyone crowded to the door. This was roll call, PLO style. Each of us spoke his name and the date he was taken. The Syrian wrote carefully in his dirty notebook: Ali, Fouad, Somali, Salih, Omar, Ramadan, Anwar, Nasser, Mahmoud, Hassan, Fa'ad, Saleem, Nayef, Rahsan. As the new arrival, I was last. He couldn't pronounce my name and was writing something with a scowl.

"Herrr-mani?" he said. He was so short he had to stretch up to reach the judas.

"No, Timm-merrr-man," I said again, insisting on each syllable.

"OK, OK, Herr-man-man," he said, waving me away.

I returned to my place by the latrine jug, sunk in a gloom as foul and insidious as the vapors of the piss pot next to me. I was locked in an underground cell somewhere in West Beirut. My captors alone were aware of who and where I was, and they didn't even know my name. I felt like the tree in Wittgenstein's forest that fell with no one to hear. What difference did a life make without witnesses? The voice inside me screamed the answer: *every difference!*

Over the next three and a half weeks, I would lose most of my illusions and learn hard lessons that have stayed with me ever since. I would learn that I could bear physical pain and hopelessness beyond anything I had ever imagined and that I could forgive those who inflicted it. I would learn that I was ready to take another man's life in order to gain my freedom or lose my life in the attempt. I would learn again to pray, and most important of all, that I was not alone: I had a Savior who had endured far worse than anything I could imagine, and he was very real and would stay by my side when I most needed him.

+ + +

"*Quickly! Yallah! Quickly!*" the guard shouted as he herded me back to the cell. Before he could get the door open, another explosion made the floor tilt, throwing us against the wall.

I had been at the *hammam* down the hall, where they let us out one by one to wash and use the toilet. This was a ritual accomplished in the morning after Karaki, the resident cook, banged on the judas and brought glasses of sweet tea to accompany the dry bread and olives he gave us for breakfast. For *hammam*, one of the guards dipped a plastic urn into an oil drum and scooped up a half-liter of water, our daily ration for washing. The urn had a handle and a long spout and was normally kept in toilets to perform the ablutions that replaced toilet paper in much of the Muslim world.

"*Yallah!*" the guard shouted again as the hollow sucking roar of the Israeli aircraft died away. He was the small older one called the Syrian, and his small dark eyes darted frantically from pillar to duct, trying to figure which posed the greatest danger. He was scared.

Out in the guard room, everything was in confusion. The air smelled of cordite, people were coughing, and the fighters were shouting at each other as the Palestinian anti-aircraft guns rattled away, chasing the departing aircraft. In the dim light from a Sterno lamp on the desk I could see white smoke billowing down the steps from outside. Then somebody shouted "*Tehran!*" again and the Syrian wrestled the door open and nearly threw me into the cell. He slammed the door shut just as the plane dove toward us, sucking all the air out of the building like a giant pair of lungs, and then the bomb hit and popped me like a cork me into a mass of bodies, sweating, tense, and afraid.

Most of my cellmates were crouching on the floor, hiding their heads between their knees. Some muttered prayers, begging Allah to keep the roof from collapsing and burying us alive. Even Fouad started cracking his knuckles, huge cartilage snappers my grandmother always warned would make your bones ache when you got old, filling the silence between bombs. Two or three were smoking nervously. By the glow of their cigarettes, I waded through Jell-O to the far corner of the cell, where I pressed my back into what I hoped was a supporting column. I figured if we took a direct hit, I had a better chance of surviving there.

Each time the bombs hit, I could feel the walls shake. All of a sudden, I really wanted to grow old. When I was a spoiled teenager reading Dostoyevsky, I thought it was romantic to pretend I wouldn't live past thirty. Now I desperately wanted to see my grandchildren grow up.

Rahsan the Syrian was sitting across from me. "We're all going to die," he said, looking up to his god. Like the others, he was a fatalist who believed everything was in Allah's hands and that he was powerless to assert any control over what happened to him. But because in real life he was a Shakespearean actor, he added some theatrics to the mix. He was small and fine-featured, and when the sucking began again, he tucked his head between his legs and waved like a scarecrow at the emptiness. Then the bomb hit and toppled him over, and in the aftermath, we could hear the sharp crack of automatic rifles nearby and the crazed popping of mortars and rockets and the rapid bursts from the anti-aircraft guns out in the street, and Rahsan looked up from the ground, rolled his eyes, and smiled. We had survived, *al-hamdulillah.*

I was queasy and weak from lack of food. My stomach was empty of everything but fear, and the fear seemed to be devouring everything. "*Ken!*" Rahsan shrieked, just before another bomb hit. I crossed myself and began to pray out loud, something I hadn't done for years. I started by asking God to forgive me for shouting out his name in vain when the bombs hit, for not praying in ordinary times, for turning to him only in weakness and danger. Then I started to make him promises. I promised to baptize my children if I survived, I promised to light candles in churches, I promised to go to Mass, finding in the mysteries of the Catholic Church with its miracles and martyrs greater power than the purely rational Presbyterianism I had been brought up with. I prayed with confidence that only he was powerful enough to get me out of this darkness, out of Death's strong grip. And then I begged him to accept my prayers and to forgive me again for not praying before and to hold me to my promises, and then the bombing stopped, and I knew he was listening and he was real.

I began praying every day, not just during the bombardments, but at ordinary moments, trying to trick my mind into making time disappear. One morning, I skied an entire mountain I knew as a teenager in Vermont, and that was a form of prayer, too. With infinite slowness, I left the Antelope and entered the woods, stopping to feel His presence in the silence between the trees. How good it was to feel the deep, soft snow beneath my skis, to shift my weight for a quick turn, to float on top of it and sit backwards and sink down to a stop. I tugged on a pine branch and felt the snow fall on my face, cool and refreshing like angel dust.

A bang on the door interrupted my descent, calling us to the judas to take a bag of dried *khobès*, a plate of olives, and a pan of a sludge that might once have been brown beans. Thanks to him, I spent a whole morning on that mountain, not in this pit.

6: Bang, Bang. You Dead.

The bombardments continued intermittently for more than a week. They came without warning and followed no discernable pattern, day or night. Sometimes they lasted for hours, sometimes just a few quick passes of the jets, like a matador performing a series of veronicas on a bleeding bull. One morning that felt like a lull, I had a shock while visiting the *hammam*.

"*Vous parlez français?*" a voice hissed from somewhere in the darkness behind me. Karaki, the chief cook, part-time guard, and *hammam* attendant, had just handed me the urn with my half-liter of water and was pretending not to notice. I hissed back, "*Oui.*"

"*Si jamais vous sortez d'ici, contactez l'ambassade française. Dites leurs qu'il y a deux français ici.*"

"*Comment tu t'appelles?*" I asked. Karaki still pretended not to notice, consumed as he was by withdrawing the two tomatoes and bits of onion from a giant pot of boiling water. That was how he did it. First, bring twenty liters of water to a boil, then add salt, an onion, and two tomatoes. Let simmer for thirty minutes, remove the onions and tomato, and serve. We called it Palestinian soup. We lived on it for weeks.

"Pellay, *comme le footballeur*," the voice said.

"Pellay!" Karaki shouted at the sound of his name, banging his metal spoon noisily against the pot. "No talk! No talk!"

He ran to a door behind me and slammed shut a judas located at knee height. Pellay must have been crouching on all fours to call out to me. Then Karaki grabbed the water urn from my hands and pulled me away from the toilet area. "Finished *hammam*," he said. "No *hammam* today."

For several days, I contemplated the momentous information I had just learned: there was another Westerner, probably two, in this hellhole with me, and he seemed to have hope in the French embassy. Since I had never set foot in the US embassy in Beirut and had no illusion they might be looking for me, let alone care whether I lived or died, the thought that the French embassy might care about hostages was incomparably sweet.

One night, after a period of intense bombardments, an officer came down to the guard room. I knew he was an officer because Fouad, the informer, and Ali, the cell boss, crowded each other cheek to jowl at the judas to hear what he was saying.

I had become friends with a Shiite from South Lebanon who had been thrown in with us. He had thin blonde hair and blue eyes—showing his Circassian descent. He was as stocky as a football player and pale as a ghost. Ali Hakim spoke reasonably good English and regularly translated for me the snippets of news we overheard from the guards' radio.

"What are they saying, Ali?"

He just shook his head. This was unusual for him. Usually he was eager to show his knowledge of English and would translate avidly.

"*Amreeki,*" I heard the officer say.

"They are talking about me, aren't they?" I whispered.

"I can't!"

"*Yahoud!*" I heard. "*Jassoos!*" I looked Ali squarely in the face because he knew I had learned those words.

"They say you are a Jew, a spy," Ali said finally. "The Israelis are getting closer. The guards are complaining that you are eating their food. They asking officer why they don't kill you."

Obviously, if Ali Hakim had heard this, so had everyone else in the cell. I went back to my corner and began praying, crossing myself and calling loudly on the name of Jesus.

The next morning after an Israeli artillery barrage, the old Syrian guard opened our door and pushed someone inside.

"Quickly, *yallah!* Quickly!" he shouted in between the shell bursts.

The man must have been folded in two when he came through the door, for as soon as the Syrian slammed it shut, he stood up and towered above us. He wore a dirty white T-shirt and blue jeans, and in the glow of a candle stub, I could see he had a gold tooth. "*L'Amérloque, tu es là?*" he said, blinded by the sudden dark.

"*Oui*," I said. I moved through the pressed bodies toward the door and grabbed him by the arm and half-guided, half-dragged him over to my spot.

That was how I first met Jean-Yves Pellay.

+ + +

Over time, he became my guide, a guardian angel sent to instruct and lead me out of the darkness into the light. But it wasn't obvious at first. I guess it never is.

As we whispered back and forth to each other for what seemed like days, I gravitated between horror and fascination. At first blush, he was everything I had been taught to despise in Left Bank Paris. A busted officer in the French Foreign Legion, he had joined a shadowy right-wing group and claimed to know men who were still on the run for having tried to assassinate General de Gaulle two decades earlier. He had been wounded in the French incursion in Chad, lay in a coma for days, and claimed to carry shrapnel in his chest beneath a large metal plate that showed through his filthy T-shirt. He came to Israel through family contacts and went to South Lebanon to offer his services to the puppet army commanded by former Lebanese Army colonel Saad Haddad, whom everybody accused of being an Israeli stooge. The Palestinians picked him up after he had laid mines, his combat specialty, at several intersections near the Beirut airport. The idea was to booby-trap the Palestinian retreat into the Borj al Barajneh refugee camp as the Israelis advanced into Beirut proper. A fellow légionnaire working for the Palestinians had tortured him with electricity to discover his crimes, but he never confessed.

"I said I would beat the crap out of him once we were back in France," Jean-Yves said. "He thought that was funny and turned up the *gégène*."[5]

As we got to know each other over several days, my horror turned to fascination and then trust. After all, everything I was seeing and hearing was so totally beyond my experience that it seemed foolish to judge a man just because his politics appalled me, especially since we both appeared to be marked for death by our captors. I began to think that his experience and easy relationship with weapons could mean the difference between dying like a rat in the dark and surviving to tell the story another day.

---

5   This was an old term for a hand-cranked electrical torture device the Foreign Legion used during the Algerian war, with electrodes connected to the genitals.

"The Israelis are advancing," he said during a tank barrage. "You can hear them marching down the street toward us."

It was true. When I pressed my ears to the walls, I heard what seemed to be the distant rumbling of tank treads pounding the ground.

"If they break through the walls, we have to grab their guns," he said with a nod to the guards outside. "Have you ever fired a kalash?"

I had not, so he held out his two hands as if gripping an imaginary weapon, cocked the recoil spring, and released it. "You flick down the safety with your right thumb. When you fire, the barrel pulls up and to the right. So when you squeeze the trigger, you have to hold it down and in, like this…."

"Down and to the left," I said.

"When the time comes, you must not think." He looked me square in the eye. "No regrets. Not a second! It's them or us."

To hear him say it, the idea of us fighting our way out made sense. After all, there were rarely more than a handful of soldiers out in the guardroom, and of those, even fewer were armed. Already, the Palestinians were taking Lebanese prisoners outside and shooting them in the alleyway—at least, that's what Ali Hakim had been telling me. If we stayed here much longer, we would be dead anyway.

The bombardment that afternoon clinched it.

Now there were two of us pressed into the corner to feel the walls dance. The bombardment began with several volleys from the Israeli gunboats. Jean-Yves educated me to distinguish between the softer explosions from the naval shells, the sharp *cra-aaack…whoosh!* from the tanks, and the sheer brute force of the aerial bombs that shattered the concrete above our heads, making it fall back to earth with a sifting sound like tiny pebbles against glass. He also helped me to understand the variety of Palestinian weapons fired in response, from the dull *thmp—thmp* of the mortars to the multi-barreled *Katyushas* that created a haunting hum like a pipe organ, to the single explosive tear of the GRAD rockets. It sounded as if the Israeli tanks were walking up the street toward us, and it wasn't just Jean-Yves and I who heard it.

"Come on, Israel!" Ali Hakim hissed in English, thinking no one else would understand.

Just two weeks earlier, I had thought of the Israelis as oppressors, as the US and European media reliably portrayed them. Now I prayed they would blow through the walls of our prison to set us free.

Outside in the guard room, it was sheer chaos. Fighters from nearby positions collapsed at the bottom of the stairs in an out-of-breath heap, coughing from the smoke and dust of the explosions. They were nearly as many of them as there were us, but in the violence of the bombardment, we were all going to die. Only God himself could distinguish between terrorist and victim in the junk-heap wreckage the bulldozers would rummage through later on. It wasn't a pleasant thought.

Another bomb and another group of soldiers came crashing down the staircase bringing a man and a woman. The woman had long brown hair and high cheekbones and was prattling away with a Midwestern twang that reminded me of my sister-in-law from Chicago. She could have had the perky good looks of a college cheerleader if she hadn't been dressed for a Beirut barricade. The man was older and taller, his hair going to grey. Both of them wore safari jackets with lots of pockets. The man was saying something about how the Israelis were bombing indiscriminately with no regard for civilian casualties, and she was translating into Arabic with lots of hand gestures. I scoffed as I thought of the two British journalists I had met with Mahmoud Labadi just before I was abducted who had been saying the same thing.

Jean-Yves elbowed me in the ribs. "Journalists. You know them?"

"They're Americans," I said.

Without hesitation, he elbowed his way to the judas, where Fouad the informer was hissing to one of the guards, pleading with him to open the door.

"Get out of the way, dog," Jean-Yves said in English. Fouad just glared at us, so Jean-Yves yanked him aside, pulling him by the collar like a slobbering mutt.

Then he leveled his eyes to the opening of the judas and began to whistle "The Star-Spangled Banner." I rushed to his side and whistled with him. I could see now that each of them was carrying a shoulder bag, and they had laminated passes around their necks. Neither had a camera or pretended to take notes. It was almost comic because to look at them as we whistled, it was obvious they were just as terrified to learn that the Palestinians were holding hostages—*right there in the same room!*—as they were of the shelling outside. The woman started to look our way, but the man grabbed her wrist and shook his head. "Look at me!" he said forcefully. "Do what I do. And don't say a *word* about *that*."

He turned his back to us and pretended to peer inquisitively at the stairs leading back up to the street, the direction of freedom and the Israeli bombs. He was worldly-wise, that one, oh yes.

Jean-Yves then began to whistle "La Marseillaise," and I joined in.

I heard the man turn to the soldier escorting them. "I think the worst of it is over," he said, trying to sound matter-of-fact, hiding his nervousness. "Shouldn't we be getting back to see Mister Labadi?"

The woman translated, her hands waving toward freedom, but the soldier cut her off. "Not safe! Not safe!" he shouted. And then the short, mean-tempered Palestinian guard who everyone called Abu Sa'ar thrust his Mephistopholean goatee into the judas and barked something at us, slamming the steel shutter closed.

A few hours later, long after our cowardly visitors had left, a generator sputtered to life in the distance, and the bare bulb out in the guard room slowly came to light. I was rubbing my eyes from the glow when Abu Sa'ar burst in, revolver drawn, his eyes red and crazy, shouting at Jean-Yves.

"Up! Up!" he shouted, waving the pistol wildly.

Jean-Yves hauled himself up, tall and ghostly-thin, and picked his way through the bodies until he reached the far wall. Like the others, he had taken off his trousers because of the heat; and in his underwear, with the greasy T-shirt hanging emptily from the plate in his chest, he looked so frail and spindly-legged that a single push could knock him over.

I watched helplessly as tiny Abu Sa'ar waved the pistol with both hands, shouting for Jean-Yves to stand this way, no, over there, hopping from side to side like a bantam coq clearing the barnyard, glaring at us and waving the gun to make sure no one got close.

And then time seemed to stand still. I realized that the door to the cell was still open, and Karaki, the old Syrian, and a crowd of others were looking on with curiosity. Crazy Abu Sa'ar was hopping from foot to foot, too far back for Jean-Yves to lunge at him, and then he racked the slide. Everyone froze, and I understood in that instant that the sound of the gun going off in the small confines of the cell would probably blow out my eardrums, and there was absolutely nothing I could do to stop him. Beads of sweat glistened on the hairs of Abu Sa'ar's jet-black goatee as he danced from foot to foot, shaking the pistol, screaming orders, but Jean-Yves stood his ground, towering over him like a scarecrow, a sarcastic leer on his face. And then I watched in horror as Abu Sa'ar went still and squeezed the trigger, and I couldn't believe he was actually doing this. I heard in my mind the deafening roar, and then there was just a tiny click and Abu Sa'ar burst into laughter, dropped his arms, and staggered toward the door. He was laughing so hard he could hardly speak. "You dead!" he choked, doubling over. "*Francowi!*" he made a pop, puckering his lips. "Bang, bang. You dead."

7: Bastonnade

The next morning, he came for me.

"*Amreeki! Yallah!*" he shrieked, banging on the door. I jumped into my jeans and polo shirt, stiff enough to crack by this point, and was tying my jogging shoes when Abu Sa'ar grabbed my arm and yanked me to my feet. "*Tetla!*" he said. "Out!"

Jean-Yves clenched his hands on an imaginary rifle stock. "Down and to the left," he whispered.

Two more guards joined us and marched me toward the staircase. Pressed to the judas of the next cell I saw a pair of terrified eyes, trying not to make contact with mine. Could that be the other Frenchman Jean-Yves had mentioned?

"Where are you taking me?" I shouted bravely for his benefit. It occurred to me as they half pushed, half pulled me up the stairs, cradling their Kalashnikovs with calm professionalism, that they could be taking me out to shoot me like the others. I resolved to make that as difficult for them as possible. But how? I couldn't see how I was going to grab a rifle and make any use of it before they knocked me to the ground or just shot me. There were too many of them.

It was so bright outside that it hurt. The hot summer air was rank with the smell of rotting garbage and excrement, but at least it dried the damp from my clothes. I was desperate to find some way out. Squinting to keep my eyes from hurting, I saw that the wall of sandbags separating the courtyard from the street was still intact, but now a half-dozen soldiers lounged behind it. They were dragging me toward what must have been the main building, where they had interrogated me when I first arrived, but it was unrecognizable. The courtyard was full of rubble and rebar, wires dangled in front of us; the walls beyond were shot through with holes the size of windows. The upper floors of the building had collapsed, sitting on top of each other. At the very top of the rubble, a pair of overstuffed chairs sat between pieces of wall, looking out into empty space. Even if I managed to get free, there was nowhere to run.

Upstairs, a young officer in a pressed uniform was waiting by a metal desk, along with Nasser and Salih from my cell. He had a long rod in his hand, and he was tapping it against his leg with a sinister smile. It looked like several strands of metal-shielded electrical cable twisted together with white tape. He saw me take it in. Then he handed it to Abu Sa'ar, who sneered with anticipation.

"Sit!" Abu Sa'ar shouted, slapping the rod against the desk.

I looked around. There were no chairs.

"Sit!" he screamed, waving the metal rod at me. "Now!"

I got down on the floor, and Nasser and Salih kneeled on either side of me.

"Why talk-y Frenchman?"

"He's in my cell."

"No talk-y!" Abu Sa'ar shouted. "Shoe! Shoe!"

The young officer gave orders to Nasser and Salih, who removed my shoes, then slipped my bare feet between the stock and the strap of a Kalashnikov. Nasser hesitated, glancing at me furtively, asking forgiveness.

Abu Sa'ar screamed at them again until they turned the rifle so the strap wound my feet tightly against the stock. Then they lifted the rifle, rolling me onto my back.

The next thing I knew, my feet exploded with pain as I had never experienced before. Abu Sa'ar was grinning. He tapped the rod against the palm of his hand, watching my feet twitch. I tried to prop myself up on my elbows to look him in the eyes, but he just swung at me anyway, grunting with the effort. "*Yahoud*!" he shouted.

"No!" I shouted back.

He hit me again. "*Yahoud*! Jew! *Yahoud*!"

He whacked away at the soles of my feet, and the pain was so complete that it blotted out everything else in the room. It was thick, dull, and heavy, like a sledgehammer slamming into concrete.

"*Yahoud*!" Abu Sa'ar screamed each time he hit me.

After a while, I stopped shouting back and just focused on the pain. In between blows, I could feel the molecules of my feet rearranging themselves, furiously rubbing against each other, creating heat, and then exploding when he hit again.

After a dozen or so strokes, I stopped looking at Abu Sa'ar. Each blow from the metal rod drove the mass of red-hot pain further up into my body. I started thinking it was a carnival hammer game, and with each blow, Abu Sa'ar was coming closer to ringing the bell. My head fell to the side, and I must have let out a convincing groan, because the officer waved his hand for Abu Sa'ar to stop. He was puffing and red-faced with exhilaration, sweating like a pig. He waved the truncheon over me as if gauging which part of my body to hit next.

"Up!" the officer said. He gave orders in Arabic, and Nasser and Salih pulled me up onto my feet. "Run!" the officer said.

I looked at him incredulously. I could barely keep my balance. The ground was so far away it felt like I was standing on stilts.

"Run!" he shouted.

So I raised a foot, teetering, gingerly testing it against the floor. It felt huge and numb, somehow unattached to my body. "More fast!" the idiot shouted. Holding onto Nasser and Salih, I pulled up the other foot, then again, and again, slightly faster each time. It was like wading across a bed of coals in cement shoes. My feet were thick and heavy, while from the waist up I became lighter and lighter and began to float, like a white sheet borne up in the wind. Abu Sa'ar beat time against the desk with his truncheon.

Nasser and Salih brought me back downstairs, and I collapsed onto the filthy blanket on the floor. As I lay there, drifting into unconsciousness, I felt in the numbness another presence at my side, and I saw the face of my Savior on his cross, looking at me with a gentle smile. He didn't say a word. But his eyes were full of compassion as he felt my pain and took it onto himself, even as the blood dripped from the wounds in his hands. And then I realized that the pain I was enduring was but a fraction of what he had suffered for me. And I sobbed quietly, just beginning to comprehend the enormity of his sacrifice and his love.

8: Beirut Underground

We had several days of almost nonstop bombardments after that, from air and sea and land. Even though they had put Jean-Yves back into a punishment cell, the days we had spent together made me less afraid of the bombs because now I could tell them apart and make an educated guess at how far away they were from our position.

From what I learned from Ali Hakim, who translated the *Radio Falastin* broadcasts the guards listened to religiously, the Israelis had taken the airport, just 1500 meters away, and were pushing deep into the city. Ali and I fantasized how we would make our escape, spring Jean-Yves, and then fly through deserted streets toward the museum and freedom. "We're going to take him, man. We're taking him with us," Ali said. "We're not going to leave him behind."

That evening, a dozen soldiers crowded around the metal desk outside, flicking from one radio station to another. Abu Sa'ar and a guard we called "Moustache" were convinced they had pushed the Israelis back, but an older man who had joined them disagreed. He was tired and dirty and apparently had been much closer to the fighting than the others. When the younger men wouldn't shut up, he threw his rifle onto the desk and unstrapped his cartridge belt and slammed it down as well. "Maybe the Israelis will go easier on you without those useless pistols you like to wear," he scoffed at them.

"He's calling them many names," Ali Hakim said.

Indeed. The older man was working himself up into quite a lather, pounding the desk, slapping Moustache and Abu Sa'ar, who instead of fighting back just cowered like beaten dogs. It was great fun to watch, with Ali Hakim calling the blows like a referee. The end was near, and if the older man hung around, it looked like sanity would prevail and we would make it.

+ + +

It was that night when I realized they had all fled. "Abu Sa'ar," a voice whispered in the darkness. "Abu Sa'ar!" It stretched out into a groan and then a wail. "Abu Sa'ar!" the voice shouted, growing frantic, as mortar bombs and tanks shells exploded in the distance. He started banging a teacup against the metal door. Fouad lit a candle stub, and I saw it was Nasser and that he was in pain.

"*Na'im!*" Fouad growled. "Sleep!"

"I'm dying," Nasser wailed, clutching his stomach, his black curly hair gone damp with sweat. He went on banging the cell door with the cup, trying to get someone's attention. "Abu Sa'ar!" he shouted. He had gone pale, and his eyes were wide with fear. He must have been really sick to call for that sadist, I thought.

Finally, the Syrian warder shuffled down the stairs from outside, swearing and shouting, jangling the keys. It had taken nearly fifteen minutes for someone to hear Nasser's screaming over the sound of the bombs and fetch the Syrian, the only man with the keys to our cell.

The next morning, Salih confirmed my impression. He was brought down earlier than usual from work upstairs and whispered to Fouad and Ali Hakim that the officers were leaving. They were packing up archives and files and what little furniture was still intact and piling it into trucks. They didn't know what to do with us, so they were leaving us behind. A few more direct hits and what remained of the building would collapse on top of us anyway, burying us alive. And you could be sure no one would be coming to dig us out of the rubble.

+ + +

That night, Fouad served dinner, since Karaki had been called back into the ranks to fight. He opened the door and handed us a huge tin of sardines and a bag of bread. To my amazement, no one wanted to eat, not even Ali Hakim.

"Sardines? Nah. I don't eat that stuff," he said.

We were weak from malnourishment; this was the first protein we had been offered in weeks. I devoured the sardines with relish, soaking up the oil. I intended to survive, no matter what. I was going to fight— whether it meant clawing my way through blocks of concrete and steel or foolishly grabbing somebody's gun. And so I ate.

"*Tehran!*" someone called from outside.

When the bomb hit, it nearly shook the metal door off the hinges. I dove for the corner, pushing into my jeans and gingerly wrapping my shoes around my swollen feet. The fighters began streaming down the stairs almost immediately, coughing and shouting, hurrying each other.

None of the officers we had grown used to over the past three weeks were among them. Just frightened kids with guns.

"What are they saying, Ali?" I asked.

"You don't want to know, man."

I could hear the familiar words *ashnabi*, foreigner, and *Yahoud*, Jew.

"They want to kill you, man."

He just shook his head, resigned. Adip, an Armenian sandwich seller who had joined us a few days earlier, looked at me briefly, crossed himself, and then guiltily went back to his corner. I couldn't blame him, though. He probably had teenage kids and a wife and lived in some god-awful shack in the shantytown by the airport. Why should he put himself out for some idiot American he'd never met?

Down and to the left. Even if they were just kids, there were so many of them. *Lord Jesus, guide my hands*, I prayed. *I am yours.*

✛ ✛ ✛

The bombardments continued all night and into the next morning, hitting so close that the ventilation duct by the *hammam* burst its supports and rattled against the ceiling. We could feel the shells slam into the concrete above us and then hear it drift back to the ground like sand. In the end, an officer we had never seen before rushed down into the guard room to evacuate the child soldiers because of the danger. "*Yallah yallah yallah!*" he shouted, herding them up the stairs. By morning, we were alone.

"That's it!" Ali shouted, panicking. "We're trapped, man! They've all gone away."

He started banging on the door, and soon, the entire hallway erupted with people banging on cell doors, hostages I had never seen or heard before. It was an amazing sound, the revolt of the condemned, the Beirut underground. Men who apparently had been resigned enough to their fate just hours before, all of a sudden realized they were about to die.

We tried to pry the door off the hinges, but the bolts were too solid, even when three of us went at it together.

The thought that we were trapped underground in a building about to collapse didn't frighten me as it had the night before. With the lull in the bombardments and the echoing emptiness that greeted our banging, I felt as if a protective angel had come down among us, gathering us under his wings.

+ + +

And that's when the officer came. He had one star on his shoulder boards beneath the Palestinian Liberation Army eagle. He called out in French, "*'Y a des français ici?*"[6]

I looked at Ali, and he looked at me. Was this real? Or a trap? In the next instant, I knew it didn't matter. Either the Palestinians had finally woken up to the fact that they had Western hostages and could trade them for something with the French, or they had figured out what Jean-Yves and Pierre had really done and were going to kill them. Either way, it was better than dying like a rat underground, I thought.

"*'Suis là!*" I shouted through the judas. "There are three of us."

By the time someone found the key and opened the door, they had retrieved Jean-Yves from the punishment cell. "Don't forget Pierre. He's over there," he told the French-speaking officer, pointing down the hall.

In the nearly three and a half weeks I had been held captive, I hadn't once seen or heard Pierre. He was younger than I was and, like me, had no military background. But he spoke Arabic, and a sense of adventure had prompted him to go to Lebanon earlier that year and join the Christian militia of Major Saad Haddad. When Haddad ordered Jean-Yves north to mine the outskirts of the Beirut airport in Borj al Barajneh, he sent Pierre along as interpreter. All of this I had learned from Jean-Yves, who told me that during the first interrogation after their capture, Pierre simply lost it. I didn't understand what that meant until now, when they dragged him out of his punishment cell. He held his hands before his face, as if to shield it from a beating, and was sobbing. "I am a good man," he said in English. "I am a good man, I am a good man. Don't kill me."

"Nobody's going to kill you," the officer said, switching to English. "You go home now."

Jean-Yves and I traded a glance full of suspicion. We said nothing, but both of us knew what the other was thinking: if this was a trap, we would go out fighting. Given our weakened state, we wouldn't last long against the officer and the two well-fed guards who accompanied him. But we would fight to get free or die trying.

They led us upstairs, and the Mediterranean sun blinded me so much it hurt. I wanted to cover my eyes but couldn't because of the rubble. We

---

6 Any Frenchmen here?

had to negotiate our way over huge slabs of concrete, twisted rebar, and chunks of furniture where the barracks had once been. Although I had seen the impact of the bombardments a few days earlier when they took me upstairs for the *bastonnade*, the extent of the destruction hadn't hit me until now. Of the eight-story building where we had been held, only one floor was left standing above our cellar. All the walls had been blown into dust, collapsing the cement-slab floors on top of each other like a stack of pancakes. It's a wonder we were able to get out at all.

The street was covered in several inches of concrete chunks and sand from the barricades, and electric lines waved and hung down to the ground like toilet paper on Halloween. Two cars were waiting for us: a white Mercedes, its windows blown out, and a battered red Toyota sedan with sagging bumpers.

"Where are you taking us?" Jean-Yves demanded.

The officer nodded, all business. "You go home now."

For an instant, looking at the officer, the two cars, and the hot, rubble-clogged street empty of soldiers and traffic, I could almost believe that the war was over and that the officer was telling us the truth.

So we got into the cars. As we turned around, I tried to read the name on the blue street sign, but it was in Arabic. (I tasked myself to learn to read Arabic and Farsi later on.) But a bit further down, we crossed another street and the sign was in French, "*Rue el Khartoum*." Later, I would find it on the map as well as the street with the Arabic name where we had been held hostage, Shara Abu Sahl. It bordered the Sabra and Shatila refugee camps on the southern edge of Fakhani by the sports stadium.

We passed the mosque I had seen on the way in. The destruction was far greater than what I had seen when I first walked through West Beirut three and a half weeks earlier. Whole streets were impracticable, choked with rubble, wrecked cars and triple-A guns, pools of water from the broken water mains. No one was about except clutches of soldiers and a street vendor selling cigarettes.

Soon we reached Mazra'a and the boulevard Saeb Salaam, which seemed to have survived intact. Instead of turning right toward the museum, we went the other way. The drivers began to race ahead at breakneck speed, perhaps anticipating that we might be getting uncomfortable.

We came to a complex intersection, a jumble of roads and red earthen-work barricades, topped by a flyover from the airport road.

"Israel?" I asked the driver, pointing down the road toward the airport.

"*Ah*," he said, meaning "yes." He looked nervously at the soldier sitting next to him, who had never taken his finger from the trigger of his Kalashnikov. "*Fi Isr-ra-el wa hamatash mia'a metre*," he said with a nod. The Israelis were just 1500 meters away! He stepped on the gas, taking us in the other direction.

Three and a half weeks ago, I was avoiding Israeli positions because I saw them as an obstacle to my plan of entering West Beirut to report on the siege. Now I was eager to stumble upon those same Israeli positions, knowing they meant freedom, not just for me but for all the Lebanese who were being held hostage by the Palestinians, just as we were. I knew now that I was going to survive and that I was not the same person I was just weeks ago.

For a brief instant before we turned up into smaller residential streets, I saw the sea, sparkling in the hard Levantine sun. I drank in the salty air and closed my eyes and imagined myself, like this battered giant of a city, stumbling down the cliffs into the Mediterranean. It would be great to rip off my clothes and run out into the water like any normal person. But I shook it off. I had to focus on staying alive.

9: Arafat's Headquarters

A few minutes later, we pulled up in front of a modern apartment building, with wraparound balconies still clinging to the upper floors. Just across the street was an elegant Ottoman structure with broad loggias and arched windows flying a French flag. No bombs had fallen here. Jean-Yves and I exchanged a glance. Was it true? Was it here we were going to be released?

And then, sitting on a folding chair in front of the apartment building with a dozen uniformed soldiers, we saw Karaki, our prison cook. Now he wore a black cowboy hat and sunglasses, a Kalashnikov slung smartly across his shoulder. The sunglasses were a necessity, not a fashion statement, since he had been held prisoner underground for two years, and his eyes, like ours, were having a hard time adjusting to the sun. But he looked fit and trim in his clean Syrian army fatigues. He tipped the cowboy hat ever so slightly to me, finger to his lips, slipping a few cigarettes into my shirt pocket.

"You're not in Fakhani," he warned.

"Where are we?"

"Sanayeh."

That meant nothing to me, but Pierre's eyes filled with panic.

"That's where Arafat's supposed to be," he hissed to us in French.

As soon as he heard Arafat's name, Karaki growled at us, "No talking!" and walked away.

To Pierre's horror, Jean-Yves called one of the guards over and demanded cigarettes.

"*Hot, cigara!*" Jean-Yves demanded, tapping the man's breast pocket where he could see a pack of cigarettes.

The young soldier grinned and shook out a cigarette for Jean-Yves. "And for my friends as well," Jean-Yves said.

When he had lit our cigarettes and walked away, Pierre lost it. "You can't do that!" he hissed. "You don't understand the way they think."

"Shut up, Pierre. You want a smoke or not?"

For what seemed like hours, we hung around the front of the building with the guards, free but not free to go. They even fed us lunch: more bread, more olives, and triangles of Vache Qui Rit.

"What do you think they're going to do with us?" Pierre said.

The answer came later that afternoon, when one of the guards who had accompanied us during the drive to Sanayeh came to fetch us, carrying a ring of keys. He marched us into the building and down the stairs into an underground passageway. It was so narrow we had to squeeze sideways to pass because the walls were stacked floor to ceiling with wooden ammunition boxes. Down the corridor was a steel door beneath the stairs. He opened it and invited us into the blackness: another cell!

"You said you were taking us home," Jean-Yves said.

"Not long here. Just wait for big man, okay?"

Our new prison was somewhat cooler than Fakhani and the air a bit better, but it still took some time to find a spot to sit down. Invisible bodies shouted as we stepped on them.

When our eyes adjusted, we could see that the cell was actually the boiler room of the apartment building, which appeared to have been commandeered as a military headquarters for Arafat and the leadership, as well as an ammo dump. There was a broken cot occupied by an obese, fifty-something Lebanese ambulance driver, one chair, and a wooden door propped up by ammo boxes that was the bed for two Palestinian boys who had been caught stealing. On the floor was another door spread with a filthy blanket on which the three of us sat. Elias, the ambulance driver, told us in French he had been held here for six days already. Beneath the stairs were a couple of plastic water bottles.

"Not for drinking," he warned us. He pointed below the belt. "It's all there is," he explained.

"No *hammam*?"

"No *hammam*."

Pierre buried his head in his hands and began to moan, while Jean-Yves and I felt our way around the boiler room. After a few minutes, we discovered three possible means of escape: the grill above the door, which we found could be easily removed; through the brick chimney of the boiler; and by the door itself. Jean-Yves had pocketed a metal bedspring in Fakhani, and in the light of a candle stub, we bent it to make a tool for picking the lock.

"What are you doing?" Pierre said, alarmed.

"Go to sleep!" Jean-Yves said.

"They're going to kill us."

"That's possible. And so what are you doing about it?"

We moved away from Pierre and decided to wait out the night and assess our new guards' habits until we could find a suitable moment to try picking the lock. "Then we head across the street to that building with the French flag," Jean-Yves whispered to me.

While that was a lot closer to freedom than we had been in weeks, it still seemed many bullets away.

+ + +

They didn't feed us that night, and we spoke in whispers about what to do if they tried to transfer us again. Jean-Yves had given up on Pierre, so it was just the two of us. One would take the driver from behind, while the other would knock the guard's weapon away. Jean-Yves showed me the point of the windpipe to go for.

"Squeeze with all you've got. And don't let go!" he said.

This was murder on intimate terms, and it turned my stomach into mush. But if it came to that or being shot, he was right. The next time they transferred us would be the last; of that, we were certain. But could I actually do it? I didn't know.

We drifted into sleep only to be woken up by a woman's voice outside, deep, hoarse, and guttural. She was speaking Russian. Jean-Yves and I jumped up on the chair and caught a glimpse of her through the ventilator grill as she and her group walked by. She was blonde and towered over her Palestinian escorts and wore the visored cap of the Red Army. Another woman in a Red Army uniform walked with her, translating her words into Arabic for the Palestinians. They stayed for a half hour or so just outside our door. Were they Soviet advisors to the PLO? That would be one hell of a story, I was thinking.

In the morning, the young guard who had given Jean-Yves cigarettes opened the door and told us politely he would escort us to *hammam* one by one. He had a wispy little moustache and pimples.

"They were wrong," Jean-Yves said when he came back, motioning to our cellmates. "It's just outside. Keep your eyes open and we'll compare notes."

"Take a bottle with you," the guard said in English. He indicated the plastic water bottles filled with urine.

I followed him upstairs and across the street, toward the building with the French flag. High-rises climbed the hill behind us. Between them I caught glimpses of the sea shimmering in the heat, frustratingly close and yet unattainable. Someone had strung a clothesline between two scraggly eucalyptus trees in the courtyard with underwear and T-shirts. Windows in the surrounding buildings were filled with colorful laundry. It almost seemed normal, worlds away from Fakhani, like Bastia or Toulon on an ordinary summer day.

The guard gave me a plastic jerrican of fresh water and showed me where to empty the urine bottle in the stall of a waterless toilet.

"Take your time," he said in perfect American English. "Here it's not prison."

Was he joking, I wondered? I had spent the night locked in a dark boiler room with five other people, sleeping on empty ammo boxes, and had just been escorted at gunpoint to the toilet. As if reading my thoughts, he started talking.

"I came back here at the beginning of the summer," he said. "I'm going to be a junior at DePaul University. Do you know it?"

I was so taken aback I couldn't say anything.

"I was born here, but my uncle lives in America," he added. "I've been in school in the US since I was twelve."

"Any idea what they plan to do with us?" I asked.

"Oh, yes," he smiled. "They're going to release you just as soon as the big boss comes."

"The Colonel?"

"Oh, no, the big *big* boss," he said, raising a hand above his head with a laugh.

"What do you think?" I asked Jean-Yves when I returned, blinded from my brief exposure to the sun.

"If it's Arafat, we'll probably get out. He wants to keep on good terms with *our* government. Don't forget, you're a Frenchman now, *mon pôte.*"

+ + +

An hour later, there was a tremendous commotion out in the hallway. I climbed up onto the chair to look through the vent and saw a serious bodyguard detail, with crisp fatigues and shiny machine pistols. They were crowding around a short man whose face I couldn't see because of the Soviet-style military cap he was wearing. He looked like he was on some kind of inspection tour, and he turned the corner down the hallway to another area we had not been allowed to enter.

A half hour or so after they went through, the guard came back and called the "three Frenchmen" outside. Karaki was on post, sporting his black cowboy hat, and gave us an informal salute. A swarthy soldier with a thick black moustache indicated we should get in the back seat of the Land Rover parked outside. Jean-Yves nudged Pierre into the middle. I went around to the other side. Up front were the driver and an armed guard. It was just as we had rehearsed. Jean-Yves and I took the windows, with Pierre in between.

"Where are you taking us?" Jean-Yves asked in French.

The driver threw up his hands. "*Arabi?*"

"*Mafi Arabi. Francowi, engleesi?*"

The guard spoke a few words of English.

"We take you Mahmoud Labadi."

"You mean, you take us home?"

"Yes, home!" he seemed pleased with the word.

Jean-Yves pretended to stare out the window, but I knew exactly what he was thinking "*Tu te souviens de la route du musée?*" he said beneath his breath.

Yes, I nodded. I knew the way to the museum.

"*On y est?*"

"*Plus ou moins,*" I said, pretending to smooth out my sweat-caked jeans. So far, so good. We were headed back down the Boulevard Saeb Salaam toward the museum and would have to turn right to reach the *Jamia Arabia* where Labadi had his office.

"*Si jamais ils prennent le mauvais sens....*"

Oh yes, I knew exactly what we would do if they took a wrong turn. We would try to grab their guns and open the doors to escape. And we would surely die.

Pierre looked terrified but kept quiet this time.

"*Jamia Arabiya?*" I said to the driver when we passed the airport road and seemed headed for the mosque.

"Yes, yes. We see Mahmoud Labadi."

Our nervousness must have affected him because he kept pointing the way to reassure us. I nodded to Jean-Yves—so far, he seemed to be telling the truth. The "OK" cigarettes the guard had given us were wretched and wonderful at the same time. Would they be the first of our liberty or the last of our lives?

When we passed through the bombed-out souk, with panels of corrugated tin hanging in every direction, I reached across Pierre to slap Jean-Yves on the knee. That was it! Labadi's office was just a street away.... But the road was blocked with the remains of a fallen building and the wheels of the Land Rover started to spin. Immediately, we snapped back on our guard. They could still turn around and go a different way. I saw Jean-Yves bite his lip.

"We find new road," the driver said, throwing up his hands in excuse. "Bombing here, maybe two, three days? This, Beirut. Road always new."

I felt light-headed when I saw Labadi's sidewalk display almost exactly as I had left it three and a half weeks ago. A small Peugeot with diplomatic plates was parked outside.

Labadi was waiting with a young Frenchman who could have been a student, thin and jaunty and fair-haired, except for a military set to his jaw. I got him aside in the movement and whispered that I wasn't French. "*Mes enfants sont nés en* France. *Nous habitons* à Paris. *Je vous saurai infiniment gré de me permettre de devenir français pour au moins un jour,*" I babbled.[7]

He nodded quickly, and we separated. Then it was Labadi's turn.

"What is your profession?" he asked me in excellent French. He obviously didn't remember me from twenty-four days ago, and I didn't think it was a good idea to remind him.

"Freelance journalist."

"What about you?" he asked Jean-Yves.

That's all, I thought?

"Photo journalist. And you have two cameras of ours we'd like to get back. A Leica M-4 with a telephoto lens and a Leicaflex that belongs to my colleague."

"Okay, I'll see about that. And you?"

He turned to Pierre, and I held my breath. Pierre was just capable of blurting out the truth and telling him that he had volunteered for the South Lebanon army as an interpreter and had taken part in a massacre by the airport.

"I'm-ma-a- a journalist, too," he stammered.

I couldn't believe it. Labadi was not questioning us. He didn't care about our answers. This was just a kabuki dance. A deal had been done, and we were part of it.

"Okay, you get back in the Land Rover and follow the other car."

"Where to?"

"They have orders to drop you off at your embassy on the rue Clemenceau. You are free to go. Goodbye."

He shook hands with the young consular officer, and they exchanged a few words. Then the Frenchman got into his car and waited while we turned around. We drove slowly up through Fakhani, bumper to bumper.

Jean-Yves and I were just shaking our heads in wonder at how easy it had been when the windowless white Mercedes that had taken us to Sanayeh the day before honked its horn wildly, swerved around us, and forced the Land Rover to the side of the road.

---

7 My children were born in France. We live in Paris. I would be infinitely grateful if you would allow me to be French for at least this one day.

Pierre started to freak out. "*Fais rien, fais rien, fais rien, fais rien!*" he shouted. Don't do anything!

The Frenchman guiding us saw what was happening and quickly jammed the Peugeot into reverse and screeched his tires in the rubble as he joined us. A PLO cadre in a safari suit leaned through the window, smiled, and said something to the driver, who got out and opened the trunk.

"Five seconds, that's it," Jean-Yves hissed.

Then we saw that the cadre was heading for the Mercedes. He came back with a large manilla envelope, which he handed through the window to Jean-Yves, while two other men loaded something into our trunk. Then he waved his arm at the French Consul, "*Yallah, yallah,*" and we set off. Jean-Yves emptied the contents of the envelope onto his lap and gave a huge grin. Inside were his and Pierre's passports, cash, watches, and even the pink cards from Saad Haddad and the Hebrew passes permitting them to circulate in areas controlled by the Israel Defense Force.

"Either they can't read Hebrew, which I doubt, or else they wanted pretty bad to trade us for something," he said.

My papers and my money weren't in the envelope. But hey, I thought. This close to freedom, I'm not going to push my luck.

We drove across Hamra and a residential district, which had not been heavily bombed, and then the French embassy gates came into view. We kept silent until the PLO Land Rover pulled up before the palatial Ottoman building, with its climbing Bougainvillea and deeply shaded yard below the street. Jean-Yves and I shook hands wordlessly with the Palestinian driver. Then Pierre joined us in a sudden burst of animation. He took the driver's hand and pumped it vigorously, swearing away in a gutter Arabic even I could understand.

"Israel, no! Long live Palestine!" he said.

He flashed the victory sign at the driver, who gave him a puzzled look and then began to laugh, circling a finger around his temple. "*Inte majnoon,*" he said. You're crazy.

"What'd you say that for?" Jean-Yves asked once the man had left.

"We're still in West Beirut."

"You'd better worry what you're going to say to the SDEC rather than yucking it up with the Pals." The SDEC was the French equivalent of the CIA, except that it was run by the military. They would surely be asking all three of us why we had been kidnapped and what we had seen.

The French consul general, a professorial-looking man in a sports jacket and open collar, greeted us in the majestic entry hall of the embassy.

"Had anything to eat?" he asked right off.

Our eyes must have bugged out of our heads because he gave a laugh and then called a steward, asking him to bring lunch for three up to the balcony, along with beer and wine.

Jean-Yves and I exchanged a look of disbelief, then broke out laughing. A half-hour ago we had been hostages, desperately planning some hair-brained escape that undoubtedly would have gotten us killed, and now we were back in France, where order, reason, and impeccable manners were the norm. And we were about to be fed!

Up on the terrace, they served us hot lamb stew on real plates with silverware, French bread, and a liter of wine! The knife and fork felt awkward in my hands. It was as if I had forgotten how to eat in any position except for squatting on the floor. Jean-Yves and I clinked glasses and saluted the consul.

"Don't rush," he said. "But don't take too much time, either. We have a convoy leaving in fifteen minutes for Baabda and we'd like you to be in it. You never know how long the ceasefire will hold."

10: On Angels' Wings

We finished the meal, lit cigarettes, and then the consul ushered us out front, where five embassy cars were jockeying into a long curving line in the driveway. All were equipped with what looked like dashboard-mounted short-wave radios, and though there were just the three of us as passengers, we had to bounce from car to car to find seats. The cars were so heavily loaded that the trunks sagged, and the drivers were nervous. Were they packed with weapons? Cash?

Jean-Yves and I got in with a lieutenant colonel whose freshly pressed uniforms were hanging in the side window. Jean-Yves asked him what regiment he was with but got cut off straight.

"Look, Mister. We don't have to take you out of here if you don't want. You see nothing, you say nothing. Got it?"

We exchanged a long glance. The lieutenant colonel was a short balding man with large horn-rimmed glasses whose developing paunch made him look like a desk bureaucrat rather than someone on active duty.

It was exactly 11:45 on the morning of Friday, August 6, when our convoy passed through the French embassy gates on its way out of West Beirut. I had been held hostage for twenty-four days, Jean-Yves and Pierre for over six weeks.

+ + +

We stopped behind the Residence des Pins, the French ambassador's official residence in the heart of elegant West Beirut, which the French had evacuated early on during the siege. It had become a favorite target of the Israeli gunners, since the PLO had set up artillery positions just outside the walls. The Ottoman palace had taken a pounding, and the majestic umbrella pines that surrounded it had been snapped in pieces as if a tornado had gone through. We could see Israeli tanks on the other side of the broken forest and the hippodrome, which fronted the Residence. Our lieutenant colonel got out of his car, sweating.

"What the—what are they doing?" he said.

A Lebanese couple was running towards us from the main building, looking for a ride out of West Beirut. Behind them came several men carrying large metal trunks and shipping cases, which they loaded into the cars.

"The Israelis really gave you a pounding, didn't they?" Jean-Yves remarked. "I guess they don't like us as much as the Pals do."

"You're starting to piss me off," the lieutenant colonel said. "You can both get out here and walk if you'd like."

We embarked a Lebanese guide who squeezed into the front seat with Jean-Yves. Just minutes after we left the residence, he waved the colonel to stop at a dust-choked crossroads, where a woman was carrying a baby and a bundle of clothing on her head. She turned her head and gave us a long, pitiful look, holding out her baby, pointing to herself and then to the sky. We would see many more of them on our way out, all of them pleading for a ride before the screaming airplanes returned.

After a brief palaver with the guide, the French colonel flicked on the radio. "We're changing routes!" he said crisply.

The Lebanese guide hadn't stopped our convoy because of the woman but because he was worried about land mines up ahead. We turned into back streets, slowed through a couple of Palestinian road-blocks, and emptied out into a broad avenue sweeping uphill to the Galerie Semaan crossing point in South Beirut. The avenue was choked with people fleeing the city on foot, so we advanced at a crawl, with the colonel honking and swearing as he pushed through the crowd. Through the open windows, you could hear people calling to each other and talking excitedly until they reached the last roadblock where they went silent and filed sullenly past the wired Palestinian soldiers, many of them not old enough to shave. I couldn't help wondering which person in line would punch the ticket and get taken off the street and thrown into the hole, like so many others we had met.

We zigzagged through the sandbags and oil drums into the no-man's land and reached the Israeli checkpoint just minutes before the crossing point closed and the war began again in earnest. The two-day ceasefire was over.

+ + +

From the twisting mountain road above Baabda, we entered the gates of the compound housing the temporary residence of the French ambassador. A crowd of embassy employees swarmed over us as we pulled up, unloading the trunks and carrying what appeared to be switchboards, transmitters, and other electronic gear. Some of the crates were so heavy that two men had to carry them, one on either end.

"Communications gear, pretty sensitive stuff," Jean-Yves told me as we went upstairs. "They also got the PLO archives. The PLO has all kinds of trinkets they got from us that neither of us want to fall into the wrong hands."

"What are you saying?"

"That's what they traded us for. They couldn't have gotten that stuff out of West Beirut without diplomatic cover. We were just the pigeons they used to make the stew."

The French ambassador, Paul-Marc Henri, came down the elegant staircase from lunch to greet us. He drilled down almost immediately on Jean-Yves, who gave him a quick rundown of his involvement with Major Saad Haddad.

"Let's get one thing straight," Ambassador Henri said. His face had gone slightly red from lunch, and with his healthy corpulence and shock of thick wavy silver hair, he looked like an Irishman, not French. "We're glad to have been able to get the three of you out, but it's not the type of thing we could do a second time. Besides, you know there's a law against serving in a foreign army, right?"

Jean-Yves laughed. "I wouldn't be the first."

"That's not my business, Mister. I just wanted to warn you before my colleagues have a go at you."

+ + +

It was a little after two in the afternoon, and I was sitting out on the upper terrace of the ambassador's residence overlooking the city, jotting down some notes, when I heard the distant roar of Israeli jets. I turned to one of the French military officers who had so helpfully offered us cold beer and cigarettes just a few minutes earlier and asked if I couldn't borrow his binoculars. He refused. So I scanned the horizon, eyes aching from the sun, until I spotted the planes, which were already over the city. How different it was from just a few days ago, when we were on the receiving end! There was no intense sucking sound, no pulling the guts out of the building, no fearful whispers, "*Tehran!*" The fighter jets seemed so far away, lost in the heat spume of the horizon as they dove down silently into the city by the sea. Then we saw a thick column of grey smoke rise up from the ground and a giant fireball down below and tracers arcing up, and then the soundtrack caught up to us with the great roar of the afterburners and the explosion and the crackling triple-A fire. It was like being in a movie theater.

The next morning, *L'Orient-Le Jour* carried a front-page photo of a giant crater in a residential area the Israeli jets had hit during that raid. One of the surrounding buildings looked familiar. I thought for sure I saw a French flag flying outside. As I read through the article, my head began to spin. The air strike had hit a building in Sanayeh, just across the street from a French school. The Israelis had allegedly used a new weapon the Palestinians were calling an "implosion bomb" that caused the entire building to collapse into itself, creating a crater twenty meters deep. Mahmoud Labadi and his propaganda machine claimed the bombing had killed more than two hundred civilians. But as I knew, because I had been in that building just three hours before it was hit, there was not a civilian in sight, unless you counted the Russian Natashas, and they were long gone anyhow. Whatever special weaponry the Israelis may have used—and some speculated later it was a fuel-air explosive—the massive amounts of ammo stockpiled in the corridors intensified the explosion and no doubt added to the depth of the crater.

And then it all made sense: the Palestinian officer, Karaki, the young Palestinian educated in America, even Mahmoud Labadi—their eyes had been clouded by angels who were hovering by me the whole time, obscuring me with their wings, making me invisible to the evil one, guiding me to freedom.

11: The Monastery

The lieutenant colonel with the short temper who had escorted us in the convoy turned out to be the French military attaché. Once he realized that we knew that he knew we had been in the building in Sanayeh the Israelis had leveled just hours after we had left, he was anxious to get us as far away from official French territory as possible. Witnesses to Palestinian double-talk, so to speak. Who knows, maybe he had fed the "implosion bomb" nonsense to the media in the first place.

He made a few calls and then drove us down the hill and up the coast to Antelias, an Armenian Christian suburb between Beirut and Jounieh, then back up into the mountains to the Greek Catholic monastery in Raboué. This is where we were to "cool off" (*au congelateur*, as he put it) until the French authorities could decide what to do with us. They would be contacting the US embassy over the weekend to arrange my repatriation, which in fact they never did.

The monastery was housed in a modern building that looked like a cliffside hotel, all windows and concrete and pillars, with a magnificent view of the sea and the Beirut coastline. Walking out across the dry, rugged landscape pungent with thyme and rosemary was like entering a haven of peace, a strange new world of gentleness and timelessness that was healing in itself. If the intention of the French military attaché had been to get us off his hands and far from the news media in East Beirut, his choice of refuge could not have been more fortuitous, and I thanked him inwardly for it. The isolation, the calm ordered life of the Patriarch and his acolytes, and the kindness of the seminary students and staff helped me readjust to normality from life as a hostage in an underground cell.

When I arrived, I had nothing but the clothes on my back, which had gone stiff with filth. I scrubbed them and myself for a good hour. When I came out of the shower, I found clean clothes and sandals on the floor left there by Andrew, a Greek-Australian seminary student who had befriended us. I felt like a pilgrim after a long arduous journey, fragile and unsure of step and speech. The first time I walked up into the hills, my muscles ached. But this was good pain, I reckoned. And I was surprised that my feet seemed to have healed with hardly a trace of the bludgeoning they had received. They were still black and blue and sore as hell, but the sharp pain had been replaced by a dull ache, and even that faded as I walked.

In the evening, after a meal taken in the company of a half-dozen French embassy employees who had been evacuated with us from the Residence des Pins, we went out onto the balcony with Andrew and sipped a chilled white wine from the Bekaa Valley. We watched as East Beirut burst into flames where Palestinian rockets hit an oil depot at the port near Qarantina, an event I now realized wouldn't find its way into any Western newspaper because it didn't fit the media narrative: Palestinians good, Lebanese Christians and Israelis bad.

"For eight years it has been like this," Andrew said. "Last week, the rockets hit within a hundred meters of the monastery. Look at this land! It's beautiful, isn't it? And yet, it's hard to imagine there ever being peace, although there are few places in the world more in need of it."

We went down to the cool sanctuary, where we knelt side by side and prayed together before the cross. I watched Andrew kiss the icons of Jesus and the Virgin Mother and felt a tugging in my soul for the certainties I reckoned he must feel from his faith.

"I was ready to kill a man to win my freedom," I said. "If I had heard somebody saying that just six weeks ago, I wouldn't have believed them."

"It is not a sin, Ken. When you must kill or be killed, it is not a sin. What is sinful is taking pleasure in killing. But to kill in order to survive…. You have taken part in the agony of Christ. That's why you are here. He has already forgiven you."

We looked up at the face of our Savior and contemplated him for a while in silence.

"Did you feel his presence?"

"He was always by my side," I said. "Always."

Andrew mumbled a prayer and made the sign of the cross.

"You must learn to testify to his truth. He pulled you out of the darkness, out of the jaws of death. You have been reborn through your faith in him," he said. "He saved you for a reason."

"Amen," I said. "I just don't know what it is."

"You will."

I am still trying to answer that question today, although in a sense the answer is obvious. I was blessed to return to my two infant children and to watch them grow up. I was blessed to find Christina and smart enough to chase her and convince her to marry me. Together we brought up five children, and that has been the greatest accomplishment and greatest joy of my life, bar none. And I have shared my faith with them and many others as best I could.

+ + +

A few days later, during an extended ceasefire, Jean-Yves and I hitchhiked down to Antelias and along the coast road to Beirut, hoping to tell our story to French or US reporters at the Hotel Alexander.

I remembered the suite of rooms used by the Associated Press and found a chain-smoking, overweight reporter named Terry Anderson sitting at a desk covered with newspapers, empty food wrappers, an over-flowing ashtray, and a teletype machine. As I told him the outline of our story, he kept leafing through a stack of copy, not taking notes.

"Tortured?" he asked.

I described the beating on the soles of the feet, the *bastonnade*.

"Any marks?"

I shook my head, no.

"Were they shooting people?"

I said that's what we were told, but we didn't know for sure.

"Look," he said, almost angrily, waving the stack of copy and pulling at his moustache. "There's a lot going on. There's a war on, right? I don't have time to assign a reporter to check your story with the Palestinians. And I'm certainly not going to waste my time by calling the French. I wish you well. But I've got other things to do."

When we next saw each other, a year later in Damascus, Terry apologized for his abruptness. We drank most of a bottle of whiskey together and parted friends.

In March 1985, he was snatched from the streets of Beirut and held hostage by Iranian-backed terrorists for more than six years. I thought about him constantly, and the knowledge that Terry and others I knew were suffering the same fate I had known—but prolonged for years and years—ultimately compelled me to do things that most journalists would never contemplate. I will tell that story in a later chapter of this book.

+ + +

I learned later why the Israelis waited until 2:00 PM to bomb the Palestinian headquarters in Sanayeh, well after Arafat had come and gone.

It had nothing to do with us.

Arafat's driver, it turned out, was an Israeli spy—a real one. Throughout the entire summer of the war, the IDF was able to track Arafat's whereabouts using the first battlefield reconnaissance drones, and never once did they lose patience and drop a bomb on him, no matter how great the temptation. Defense Minister Ariel Sharon seemed to enjoy toying with him, bombing places he had been just a few hours earlier. Eventually, it worked. Not long after we were released, Arafat threw in the towel and with help from the French, negotiated his departure from Beirut. And the rest is history.

When people ask me today how I got out, I answer without hesitation: by the grace of God. Because nothing else can explain what actually happened. By rights, the Palestinians should have taken me out into the street and shot me like the others. After all, they suspected me of being an Israeli spy, and at the end, only kids with guns were left guarding our prison. How else explain the apparition who asked if there were Frenchmen present and instantly accepted me when I called out? Or the fact he had come to free us, not execute us, as Jean-Yves and Pierre surely deserved had the Palestinians figured out what they had done? Or the reaction of the French consul at the handover, who masked his surprise at finding three of us, not two? It would have been so easy for him to cast me aside, and yet, he didn't. Or the fact we were released just before the total annihilation of the building in Sanayeh, when the Palestinians could have delayed our departure for any reason at all? There is no logical explanation for any of it except for pure dumb luck, a string of happy coincidences, each more unlikely than the last.

Or this: God had sent his angels to guide me out of the darkness into the light. Instead of almost certain death, he raised me up, a sinner, to live and to bear witness to his faithfulness, to the unbelievable, unearned mercy of his love.

+ + +

When we were still with the French, I asked the consul general how they had known we were being held hostage.

"We received a call a month ago from the British embassy. We didn't know your names and had no idea how many you were. It seems Fatah had kidnapped an Irishman, a teacher at the American University, who spoke to Jean-Yves in the same prison and notified his embassy when he got out that Fatah was holding two Frenchmen. When we called our contacts in Fatah, they said they had no French prisoners. Until yesterday, that's where things remained.

"Then we got a call last night from our contact telling us to pick up three French citizens in front of the PLO press office at 11:00 AM this morning. We thought there were only two of you. You are a lucky man, Monsieur Timmerman. It looks like somebody screwed up and they released you by mistake. You owe your freedom to the fact they took you for French. The Americans never could have gotten you out."

The angels were swirling around us in battalions and regiments as the full import of what he was saying hit me.

Now came the question that was gnawing at me. "Did the Americans even know I was there?"

"If they did, they never contacted us, and we are just about the only ones still on good terms with the PLO."

I vowed then that if I ever crossed paths with the despicable couple whose attention we desperately tried to attract by whistling our national anthems through the judas, I would spit in their faces.[8]

---

8   Some time after I finished drafting this section, I happened upon Kai Bird's *The Good Spy: The Life and Death of Robert Ames* (New York: Broadway Books, 2014). Bird's account of Beirut before the 1983 embassy bombing included fascinating details about a young American woman named Janet Lee Stevens, a freelance journalist in Beirut, a city with very few female journalists, even fewer of them freelance. Ms. Stephens had fallen in love with the Palestinians and had excellent contacts, and squired outsiders to meet with them. According to Kai Bird, she became known as the "little drummer girl" because of her devotion to the Palestinian cause. During the siege of Beirut, she led British spy novelist John LeCarré around the Fakhani district, where we were held captive. While I was convinced that the couple visiting our bomb shelter-cum-prison were both Americans, the woman very well could have been Janet Stevens, who was born in Saginaw, Michigan. She died on April 18, 1983, while visiting the US Embassy in Beirut, reportedly trying to convince a US diplomat who died with her in the cafeteria to funnel US aid money to Palestinian families. The man with her was in all likelihood an anti-Israeli activist named Franklin Lamb, who wrote years later that Janet Stevens was carrying his child when she was killed. He was outed by *New York* magazine in a November 1, 1982, article for having fed fake information to the *Washington Post* about Israeli cluster bombs he claimed to have gathered when he "led an August mission" to Beirut.

Chapter 3:
Apprenticeship

12: The Village Leagues
Nablus

It seemed like it had been raining for weeks, and every place I stayed had no heat. The fall after my captivity, I spent the better part of a month roaming Israel and the West Bank, visiting Palestinian refugee camps and universities, interviewing deposed Palestinian mayors, visiting with Jewish "settlers," and attending lectures and conferences. I soaked up every bit of knowledge I could, trying to find some connection between the Palestinians and Israelis I was seeing here and those I had met in Beirut, but they seemed to come from different planets. The swagger and brashness of the guerilla fighters in Beirut was nowhere to be found.

Then I happened upon a young man I'll call Mohammad, who invited me to spend the night at his parents' cinderblock-and-cement house in the Askar refugee camp in Nablus. This was completely against the rules of the Israeli military occupation at the time, which enforced a strict curfew on the camps. As he told me the story of his family, I began to understand.

Mohammad's cousin had been sentenced to four years in jail at the age of fourteen for throwing stones at IDF jeeps. He had been released a month before my visit but was arrested again for being a member of the PLO. Mohammad's older brother ran a small marble factory inside the camp, but the Israeli civilian authority had closed it down for taxes. The mother sewed for a living, his father drove a bus, and Mohammad worked as a mechanic. The house was so cold the hands of his sister's two-year-old son felt like ice. Her husband was in jail.

At five o'clock the next morning, I was awakened in the sofa by the call to prayer from a nearby mosque. Mohammad's parents got up quietly to attend the *Fajr* (dawn) prayers, and when they returned, they informed me that many of the men had left the camp two hours earlier for jobs in Israel. They were the lucky ones.

I went outside shortly before six to watch the sun rise above the surrounding hills. A flock of birds crossed the sky. Beneath it lay squalor and misery and hopelessness. Suddenly it hit me: the PLO fighters in Beirut had been free, and that is what made them so different from their families in the West Bank. They were the masters, they were in control, and no one could impose their will on them. What they did with their freedom was another matter. But Mohammad, his family, the university students, and so many others I met that fall yearned for the same freedom the fighters enjoyed, and that yearning was far more powerful than anything else.

After breakfast of sweet tea, *khobès*, olives, white cheese, and marmalade, we walked through the camp to meet some of his friends. When people think "refugee camp," they think of the tent cities set up by international relief organizations to temporarily house victims of war or natural disaster. But there hadn't been tents in Askar for decades. It was a real city, with its souk, its shops, its narrow dirt alleyways clogged with children kicking soccer balls. Most of the houses were built of cinderblocks; many had a second floor. They had electricity and running water, even if the sewage ran in open canals through the streets.

"Why don't you move out of the camps?" I asked Mohammad. "What about the Village Leagues[9] the Israelis have been setting up so people can get a fresh start?"

He looked frightened for the first time since we had met. Not even when we went through the Israeli checkpoint to enter the camp had I seen fear like this on his face.

"Sshh!" he whispered. "Not here."

We came to a soccer field, and after making sure there was no one in sight, he explained.

"In Jenin, the Israelis went to the big families and offered them money if they would leave the camps and move to Jericho. In Ramla, they offered one man six million shekels. They told people in Gaza they had built free houses for them in Silwad, near Jerusalem. We have all heard these stories about the Village Leagues. But the houses the Israelis built are empty. No one will leave the camps," he said.

"Why not?"

"These camps show that we exist," he said. "Without these camps, there is no Palestinian people."

"Is that what the PLO says?"

He looked around furtively, then quickly passed his hand across his throat and changed the subject.

---

9   The Village Leagues were a brief, failed attempt by the Israeli occupation authorities to reward Palestinians who agreed to move out of the refugee camps into brand new villages built for them by Israel.

13: 'Actually, Major, I Can Confirm That.'
Jerusalem

In those days, I was writing human interest stories for a new national newspaper called *USA Today*, so I had no need to run with the journalist pack. But one day, I joined them for a briefing by the IDF spokesman, Major Raanan Gissin, at the Beit Agron press building in Jerusalem, not far from the US consulate-which-was-not-an-embassy, because the subject was close to my heart.

Major Gissin was combative by nature and liked to challenge and prod and goad Western reporters, knotting his bushy black eyebrows expressively. On this day, he was handing out booklets with astonishing photos of heavy weaponry, including Soviet tanks and 122mm D-30 field guns, which the IDF had captured in South Lebanon from underground PLO stockpiles during the 1982 war. It was enough to equip two full armored divisions, Major Gissin said. One of the largest storehouses, near Sidon, was secured behind a vault door with a digital locking device it took Israeli technicians several days to crack. Both the weaponry and the security equipment had been supplied by the Soviets, he claimed.

I tuned out as Gissin sparred with some wiseacre from the *New York Times*, I think it was, who asked him if he was trying to set up Israel as a US ally fighting a proxy war against the Soviet Union and started fantasizing what all that weaponry was about. Eventually, I wrote a novel combining that astonishing piece of information, which got almost zero media coverage, and my own experiences as a hostage in Beirut.[10]

Later in his briefing, Major Gissin showed us gun-camera footage of the Israeli air strikes on West Beirut. He had a large photograph of the Cité Sportive mounted on posterboard to illustrate his point.

"Many of your colleagues wrote about 'indiscriminate' IDF air strikes," he said scornfully. "Well, look at the evidence for yourselves: ninety-five percent of our bombs fell within one hundred meters of the sports stadium. Why? Because that is where the PLO concentrated its triple-A guns. This was a military target."

---

10 The novel, *Soldiers Without a Country*, was intended as the first of a three-volume series that I called *The Lebanon Chronicles*. Volume II was called *The Time of the Assassins* and chronicled the mid-1980s when the country was rife with hostage-takers and intelligence-agency murderers. Volume III, *The Return of the General*, was my fantasy about the return of General Michel Aoun, who I got to know well during his exile many years later. Of the three volumes, I have only written the first—and not yet published it. General Aoun did finally return to become president of Lebanon in 2016, not as a national hero but as a stooge of Iran and its Hezbollah militia.

I raised my hand, and Gissin called on me. "Actually, Major, I can confirm that. I was held hostage in a military building that was within that hundred-meter radius, and your guys pounded us day and night."

Several of the reporters scowled at me, so I shut up.

Later, Gissin came up to me after the other reporters had left. I was looking through the exhibit of captured weapons he had put together.

"So you are the American who was kidnapped by Fatah."

I shrugged. "No one much wrote about it."

"You weren't the first, you know. *You* should write about *that*."

"None of these guys want to hear it," I said.

"Well, if you change your mind, we might be able to help you."

Gissin suggested I do a little research into other reporters who had been taken hostage by the PLO and whose publications had suppressed the story. "You might be surprised by what you find," he said.[11]

14: The Princess and The Lamp
Cairo

I had been bitten by the Middle East. Far from deterring me from ever setting foot in the region again, my twenty-four days as a hostage during the siege of Beirut made me thirsty to learn more. I endeavored to learn Arabic and sought every opportunity to return to the region to learn about the lives of ordinary people, not just the headline stories of power and money.

A friend in Paris offered me a job in Cairo, where his small company had a contract to install interior signs in the massive Ain Shams hospital in Heliopolis the French were constructing. He rented a small villa to house me and a coworker, and in the mornings, I would go to the lineup where the day-laborers came seeking work. Since none of them spoke more than a few words of English, it gave me a great opportunity to learn Arabic.

The Egyptians are known for being a happy-go-lucky people. Unlike some of their Arab neighbors, they never seemed to cast blame on others but accepted the bad things that happened to them with fatalistic and usually

---

11   Eventually I took him up on his suggestion, although I never contacted anyone in the Israeli government for help. See: "How the PLO Terrorized Journalists in Beirut," *Commentary*, Jan. 1, 1983. https://www.commentarymagazine.com/articles/how-the-plo-terrorized-journalists-in-beirut/

good-humored equanimity. One evening when I was out with Jérome, my co-worker, we watched a baker's delivery man walk down a crowded street, balancing a baking pan piled high with flatbread on his head. His dish-dash, the long robe the peasants wore, was filthy, and his hands and face were black with dirt. But he kept smiling a gap-toothed grin, all the while holding an animated dialogue with the people he was passing.

All of a sudden, he disappeared. It was like a trick shot in a movie, where you photograph someone walking in the woods, stop the camera, move the person off screen, and start filming again, so it looks like they have vanished in thin air. People started laughing, pointing, and covering their mouths. And then we saw him, nearly five feet below, submerged in a sinkhole created by a burst sewer pipe, the tray full of bread still balanced perfectly on his head. He was laughing, too, as if falling into a deep hole of raw sewage was the funniest thing in the world.

Much of those two months were marked by a thin, raven-haired young woman I met in a collective taxi on the way home from work. I was leaning backwards from the front seat, speaking to Jérome in French, when she caught my eyes and smiled. She began talking a mile a minute in excellent English, twirling her dark hair behind an ear, posing first one way, then another, her dark eyes locked on me. She said she was studying sociology. Then it was film. Then her father was a professor, who had taken her to the United States for several years. Like so many things about Amayni I would learn over the next two months, the truth was always approximate. She cultivated a Durrellian sense of mystery, of dark secrets and forbidden practices that never quite squared with the real world. I gave her my card with the address of our hotel (we had not yet moved into the villa) and invited her to join me for dinner that night at eight.

"I'll be your guide," she said. "I'm gonna take you someplace that is truly Egyptian."

When I met her down in the lobby that evening, she grabbed my hand and we set off at a breakneck pace, leaving the broad avenues near the Nile and weaving through narrow residential neighborhoods choked with shoppers. Cairo had so many smells! From the kebab joints to the juice stalls to the spice merchants with bags of cumin and cardamom and turmeric and pepper, it was powerful and exotic, and it all belonged to her. After a while, we reached a side entrance to the ancient al-Azhar mosque compound, and then she took off at full speed, plowing into a Daedalus of narrow streets. Old men were smoking water pipes in tiny ill-lit cafes, and as we reached deeper into the neighborhood the asphalt gave way to packed dirt and dried mud. A group of street urchins started to follow us, begging for *baksheesh*. We reached an area where the buildings seemed to collapse into rubble. Whole families were living in cardboard shacks as untethered goats nosed through their belongings. Amayni seemed lost. A young man approached us, offering to sell hashish, and she panicked, tugging me forward at a near-hysterical pace. The street got narrower, and the crowd of urchins disappeared. The young man kept following us, shouting something at her now, and Amayni was clearly frightened. Suddenly the street ended, blocked off by a hatchwork of fresh wooden beams sealing the area between two buildings. Amayni squeezed in between, waving urgently for me to follow. She broke out into a run until we reached a main street. Up ahead was a large, well-lit café and beyond it was a restaurant, surrounded by streetlights. Way in the distance, I could see al-Azhar behind its mud-colored walls.

"Did you see those walls?" she said, once we were seated at a table inside.

"What was that?" I wondered.

"It's called *Batnia*—hashish," she said with a huge grin. The tea lights on the table made the amber streaks in her brown eyes seem to dance. "I've never gone there before on foot. It's the most dangerous place in Cairo. They say people just disappear there and never come out."

"So you just wanted to see it?"

"Well, I couldn't go there alone, could I?"

We ordered kebabs and salad, and she fished out a cigarette and asked me for a light.

"What time is it?" she said, suddenly anxious.

"Ten o'clock."

"My mother made me promise I would be back at eight thirty. She always beats me when I'm late."

She snuffed out the cigarette, half-smoked, then fished out another and began going through her purse.

"He stole my lighter."

"Who stole your lighter?"

"That man who wanted to sell us hashish."

"He didn't take your money."

"That lighter is better than money," she said.

"Check your pockets. It's probably there."

She found it but stuffed it in her purse before I could see it.

When our food came, she told the waiter to put wrap the kebabs in bread and pack them into a paper bag. "We have to go," she said.

We found a cab, and she gave the driver an address and then fished out another cigarette and lit it with a disposable butane lighter. She saw me looking at her and grinned. "You see? I lied," she said.

We stopped in front of a dingy church with a crumbling low dome and soot-filled windows protected by heavy iron bars. I offered to see her to her door, somewhere in the tenements down the dust-filled street, but Amayni jumped out of the cab and leaned into me before slamming the door. "Just go!" she said forcefully, ashamed. I still had the bag with our dinner on my lap and tried to hand it to her, but she was gone.

+ + +

Toward the end of my stay, we went to Khan al-Khalili for dinner. This is the trinket market catering to tourists on the other side of the al-Azhar mosque from Batnia. Amayni was wearing beige jeans and a cheap T-shirt from Banana Republic. When the waiter seated us, he addressed her in English and pulled out the chair for her to sit down.

"You see?" she said triumphantly, once he had taken our order. "When I wear rubbish like this, people take me for a foreigner. But when I dress up like a princess, I just look like a maid. This city is so small, so small."

At 9:00 PM on the dot, the lights went out. We were sitting in a loggia, one floor above the street, and I marveled at how people reacted to the power cut: they just continued walking silently in the dark, as if it had never happened. Waiters glided from table to table, bringing candles and kerosene lamps.

When we finished our coffee, Amayni grabbed my wrist.

"Turn over your cup."

"What do you mean?

"Like this," she showed me, putting her saucer on top of her cup and turning both of them over and setting them back on the table. I followed her instructions, curious where this was going. After a minute or two, she lifted the cup and peered intently into the pattern the Arabic coffee grounds had made in the saucer. The kerosene lamp gave her tiger eyes.

"You will live a very long time," she said finally.

"You think so?" I laughed.

"No!" She shook her head and gave me an angry pout. "I *know* so." Pause. "It is written," she added.

"Is that all?"

She plunged into the coffee grounds again, her head moving back and forth slightly, as if she were holding a silent dialogue. Suddenly, she jerked backwards and stirred her spoon abruptly through the grounds, scattering whatever she had seen.

I was taken aback. "What is it?" I asked.

"No. I can't tell you," she said.

She took me outside to one of the trinket shops and insisted on buying something for me as a gift.

"I know what you need," she said.

She mumbled something to the shopkeeper, who directed her to a dark corner stacked with blackened kerosene lamps. She picked one out, settled her purchase, and made sure the shopkeeper wrapped the fragile glass sconce in newspaper so it wouldn't break.

"Once you leave Cairo, you can rub your Aladdin's lamp and make me pop out. I'm going to be your genie," she said. "And you're going to take me with you, far away."

15: First Blood
Beirut

My work in Cairo completed, I flew to Beirut in early April 1983 with Amayni's lamp carefully tucked into my shoulder bag. By husbanding my resources and avoiding hotels, I had enough money to spend another month on the road. I found a room in a hostel in West Beirut that I wound up sharing with a young French photographer named Annick, who was dating a Lebanese Air Force pilot, a rare breed. She had dirty blonde hair and bit her fingernails, with the rough manners of a no-nonsense working-class girl. Square-jawed but cute, she dressed like a guy, in jeans and T-shirts, and once she made clear there would be no sex between us, we got along just great. She had been wounded in an ambush while driving with the Lebanese pilot two months earlier in the Shouf, the Druse-dominated mountains above Beirut. "You don't realize until later that they can be firing in the air or firing at you and it makes the same sound," she said.

Together, we hopped jeeps with French officers in the Multinational Force to tour bombed-out areas of Beirut, and choppered offshore to the *USS Guadalcanal* with the Americans. It was a curious time, in between wars. Everyone could feel the tension just beneath the surface, but no one could quite put their finger on what it was.

When I asked a Lebanese taxi driver to take me to Fakhani, where I had been held hostage, he nearly refused. "You mean where the PLO had their headquarters?" he said. "We call it Tarik Jdideh." There were no detailed street maps of the area, so I asked him to let me off alongside the sports stadium, which looked like a modern version of the Colosseum in Rome. Through its broken walls and gaping holes, I could see the wreckage of a Soviet T-54 tank and a dozen dushkas, the truck-mounted AAA artillery that the Palestinians had trained on the Israeli jets.

The buildings facing the stadium had been heavily bombed. Many of them were nothing more than piles of rubble, cinderblocks, rebar, and splintered wood. Nothing of any value had been left by the looters. When I came to the north end of the stadium, I saw the sign for Shara al Khartoum. I felt curiously detached and unemotional as I walked through the broken streets, with the balconies and the upper floors collapsed on top of one another and giant holes blown out of the front rooms. I found the pile of rubble where the sandbagged roadblock in front of our prison had been, then I found the hole punched through the wall where we had been taken outside to Baghdadi Street, now patched up. I went inside the courtyard and found a large stain of dried blood at the head of the stairs leading up to the heaped rubble where the barracks had once been. The actual street address of the wrecked building was 167 Shara al Ghana (rue 69), parallel to Shara al Khartoum.

A bakery and a greengrocer's were open down the street. "They had two prisons there," Adip the baker said. "One was for soldiers and was run by a Jordanian Colonel named Abrami. The other one was mostly for Lebanese people who were trying to leave Beirut." The key to the cellars, which were still locked, had been taken by a French officer who had come to inspect them about a month ago, he added. "The whole street was full of Katyushas and dushkas during the siege."

A woman named Soubra told me more. "We left early on for the mountains," she said. "The PLO demanded we pay them fifteen thousand Lebanese pounds so we could leave, or else they said they would blow up our building." That was around $5,000 at the time. "We came back three days before the Palestinians left Beirut and everything was broken, everything was down."

Another woman, Mrs. Fadel, remembered the name of the Palestinian commander, Captain Toufik Jebel Abutarik. "He told us he wanted to go to Switzerland and maybe come back to Beirut in a few months. He said if he found us back here, he would kill us. They treated this whole city like a supermarket with no checkout. Anybody could just come in and take what they wanted, if they were Palestinian."

I walked farther south through the Shatila camp, where Lebanese Forces militiamen had slaughtered three thousand Palestinian civilians in the infamous massacre shortly after the PLO evacuation from Beirut in September 1982. I kept looking for familiar faces. Had Karaki shed his uniform and blended back into a life of petty crime? What about the other prison guards or the fighters? Rumors abounded that the PLO still had hundreds of fighters in the Beirut camps.

One young man who called himself Abu Sa'ar—not the guard who had beaten me the summer before—admitted that he had been a PLO fighter during the siege. "I used to think we had to distinguish between the Zionists and the Jews," he said. "Now, after the war, I say we must take revenge against all Jews everywhere. We don't need an Arafat, but a Hitler." Needless to say, that remark did not make it past the censors at *USA Today*—not because of what it said about Jews, but because of what it said about Palestinians.

A week later, I returned to the sports stadium with a French officer who offered to show me the tunnels. I hadn't seen them during my first visit because the entrances were hidden behind house-high mounds of rubble, but now it was hard to miss them. They were large enough for a tank to go down, with cement walls that were a good twenty inches thick. The Israelis had emptied them of weapons months ago and padlocked the blast doors, but the officer told me they had huge underground galleries, barracks, infirmaries, and weapons stores, with escape holes every fifty meters or so. "The PLO could fire their Katyushas from the streets and then drive them down into the tunnels before the Israeli fighter jets arrived," he said. "The galleries and shelters go on for miles."

It was another untold story from the siege of Beirut.

+ + +

I had arranged to interview former Lebanese president Camille Chamoun on Monday, April 18. He had continued to play an influential role in Lebanese politics long after leaving the presidency and was considered an architect of the temporary alliance between the Maronite Christians and Israel that drove the Palestinians from Beirut. His thick, almost opaque glasses put him at a distance from the world, which a shortening attention span helped to accentuate. We met in the "throne room" of his vast apartment in the high streets of Ashrafieh. He was the ageing don of a major Lebanese clan, whose soft skin and smooth hands bespoke a life of command, not service.

He was spouting what I recognized as the party line: there had never been a civil war in Lebanon between Christians and Muslims but a war between patriotic Lebanese and traitors who supported the Palestinian occupiers. Added to that was a new hostility toward Israel, which I guessed he was using to distinguish himself from his arch-rivals, the Gemayels, who were wedded to getting Lebanon to sign a US-brokered peace agreement with Israel, something Arabists like Chamoun abhorred. "The origin of all that is happening in the Middle East has two causes: British aid to the Zionists during the League of Nations mandate, and the subsequent division of Palestine," he said. I was a bit disappointed. An original thinker, he was not.

Suddenly, the windows of his apartment rattled violently, shaking against the frames, and I felt the explosion beneath my feet. It was around one in the afternoon.

"What's that?" I asked.

"Probably just the Multinational Force blowing up another batch of Palestinian landmines," he said. Then he continued his lecture on the violations of Lebanon's sovereignty.

He droned on for another minute or so, but I had stopped listening. Outside, I heard the first emergency siren go off, then it became a syncopated brass band of sirens from emergency vehicles from all different directions.

"I'm sorry, but I've got to go," I said. "Something's afoot."

"Young man, this is Beirut. Something is always afoot."

But he didn't take it badly, and we left on cordial terms.

I flagged down the first taxi I saw and asked what was happening.

"It's the US embassy," the driver said. "On the Corniche."

"Let's go!" I said.

When something bad happened in Beirut, people had a tendency to get off the streets, wary of getting caught in the crossfire. With the Green Line between East and West Beirut dismantled, we could drive from Ashrafieh to the Corniche in West Beirut without stopping for a single checkpoint. With the thin traffic, we made it in less than ten minutes.

The elegant seaside neighborhood had largely been spared over the past summer. But when I turned the corner and saw the embassy, I was shocked: the whole facade of the massive seven-story building had been peeled back like a sardine can, so you could see the offices inside. Desks and sofas and file cabinets were leaning at precarious angles, about to slide into the abyss; several floors up, a body dangled in the air, held in a maze of cabling. Smoke from the still-burning fires filled the air, along with dust from the explosion. Ambulances and fire trucks were screaming, and a handful of US Marines had formed a security perimeter, keeping bystanders at a distance. For the first ten minutes or so, I was the only reporter on scene.

Sometime later, once the wire agencies had arrived, a young political officer covered with dust emerged from the wreckage to give us an update. He was about my age and gave his name as Ryan Crocker. He didn't have a body count yet, but there had been American casualties, in addition to several dozen Lebanese. However, he assured us, Ambassador Robert Dillon had survived. "He was standing at the back of his office, about to go out for a jog, when the bomb went off," Crocker said. "He managed to climb down to safety out the back window on electric cables."

USA Today ran my story the next morning under a joint byline. It was my first front-page story, and I was proud. But I realized that afternoon as I watched other American reporters go to work, asking survivors "how they felt" after the bombing, that I wanted to know more. I wanted to know what had actually happened, who had commanded it, and why. How did you expect survivors to feel, anyway? Like it was Christmas?

It would take years of research and many unusual sources to find answers to those questions. Although I didn't know it then, the April

1983 Beirut embassy bombing was my first encounter with a mysterious Lebanese terrorist named Imad Mughniyeh. His masters in Tehran had just declared war on America. With the embassy bombing, they drew first blood.

16: Silence in the Hashish Fields
Damascus

It was my second summer in the Middle East, but the first time that I really experienced the overwhelming hypocrisy of Ramadan. While it was supposed to be a "holy" month in which believers focused their minds on Allah through daytime fasting and abstinence, including from cigarettes, in reality, people just shifted their schedules so they slept most of the day then gorged themselves at banquets throughout the night. Government offices opened at 10:00 AM and closed for the day at 2:00 PM, and what bureaucrats you could find were even more ill-tempered than usual, since they were unable to drink tea and coffee or even to smoke. The Kurdish manager at the cheap hotel where I was staying near the old market in the center of town patted his belly and laughed. "Everybody get fat during Ramadan," he said. "Pray to God when sleep, ho-ho!"

One big advantage to not staying at the Sheraton, where I drank whiskey and made peace with AP reporter Terry Anderson, was that for the most part, I slipped under the radar of the Syrian intelligence goons keeping an eye on the international press corps, who obligingly crowded together in one place. I learned to avoid the blue Volvo taxis lined up in front of the Sheraton, since the drivers were goons or reported to them. I walked a lot and took taxis off the street, habits that would stay with me and keep me safe for many years.

Yasser Arafat and the PLO bosses had moved from Beirut to Tripoli but maintained a number of bases and training camps in Lebanon's Bekaa Valley. Fighting erupted that June for control of these camps between Arafat loyalists and fighters who threw their lot in with a dissident Palestine Liberation Army colonel named Abu Musa, who vowed to reform Fatah, put an end to corruption, and get back to killing Jews. In reality, as I would learn that summer, the Fatah rebellion was fueled by Syrian president Hafez al-Assad in a bid to take over the PLO.

All the Palestinian groups had set up shop in Damascus, which had international phone service and great restaurants, something the Bekaa Valley did not. As I went from office to office, picking up snippets of information and lies, I kept looking for familiar faces. Luckily, I saw none. I was incognito.

One day, I hitched a ride with a group of Abu Musa fighters into the Bekaa Valley town of Hammara, in hopes of meeting the rebel leader. We left the international highway well before the border, cutting south along a rough dirt track that snaked down the mountain through a series of Syrian army outposts with spectacular views of the lush, hashish-filled valley below. Near the bottom, we zigzagged through anti-tank trenches that formed the actual border. "Smile for the cameras," our driver said. "This is the most heavily photographed area in the world."

In the dusty little village, our Land Rover stopped at a Shell station, and the three fighters in the back lowered their windows, casually pointing their AKs in the air. The attendant feigned a smile as he filled the tank and waved us off without paying. I doubted they were on account.

I forget the name of Abu Musa's sidekick who greeted me and gave me a tour, but his bluntness was a refreshing change from the stale rhetoric of Damascus. The main reason they had rebelled was because Arafat had gone soft, he said. "Arafat can climb onto my little finger with all the other Arab leaders," he said in English. It was his crude but effective way of contrasting their youthfulness and vigor to the "Old Man."

His soldiers watched every car that approached the farmhouse with suspicion, including ours. It was pretty clear things were going to blow up, so rather than take up their offer to stay the night, I decided to head back with a group of fighters through the mountains into Syria. A dozen of us piled into a dilapidated Kama truck that was missing its hood. As we rumbled past the Syrian position in nearby Aita el Foukhor, dripping foul-looking liquids as we rounded the curves, the crush of somber-faced fighters lurched and bounced without a word. I couldn't help thinking that we must look like something out of the *Grapes of Wrath* fleeing the dust bowl down below.

"At least in Beirut, we had the beach," one of the fighters said to me in English. "Here?" He spat derisively, then repeated it in Arabic, and the other men grunted their agreement. Life in the dust bowl of the Bekaa was not for them.

+ + +

One late June afternoon, I joined a dozen' or so correspondents at Fatah headquarters in Damascus to wait for Arafat, whose exact whereabouts were unknown. Terry Anderson thought he was stuck in Tripoli, surrounded by Fatah dissidents. Others said his convoy had been attacked at Chtaura, a key crossroads in the Bekaa that Arafat loyalists had taken back a few days earlier. When he finally pulled up in his royal blue Chevrolet Caprice, it was clear he had been through the wringer. Several bullets had lodged in the armored glass of his car, and the side panels and roof were scraped as if they had taken a roll. Usually a show-off for the cameras, he rushed past us without a word. A few minutes later, a convoy of Syrian army vehicles screeched to a halt and a handful of soldiers jumped out. They hauled Arafat from the building, along with a couple of aides, and tossed them unceremoniously into Soviet jeeps. Word spread they were taking him to the Damascus airport. Since the Syrians hadn't been able to kill him on the road, they were expelling him.

A few days later, I ventured back to the Bekaa. This time, I took a collective taxi to the Syrian border outpost up on the ridgeline and walked down through Lebanese Customs to where the road spilled into the dusty towns of Majdel Anjar and Deir Zenoun on the edges of the valley and then the long straight road toward Chtaura, where Arafat's men were supposed to be. Syrian soldiers were encamped all over the hills. A lookout with binoculars and a radio was scouring the valley from a broken electric tower, not quite hidden by trees. A handful of tanks had pushed into the ripe wheat and hashish fields after Majdel Anjar, their crews smoking and drinking tea in the shade of their silent mounts. I was hoping to find a taxi to take me to a village outside Baalbek, where I had arranged to spend the night with a PFLP unit, but there wasn't a car in sight. In the distance, I could see a plume of smoke rising from the plain.

Suddenly, from up ahead came bursts of automatic weapons fire and then a couple of larger explosions in the distance. Then everything went deathly silent.

I waved to a pair of Syrian soldiers manning the roadblock before Deir Zenoun. "*Saba khair*," I called. They returned the greeting, and we chatted for a few minutes in a mixture of pidgin Arabic, English, and French. I said I was a journalist and pantomimed the fighting between Arafat and Abu Musa.

"Arafat, very crazy," said the younger of the two soldiers, whose name was Marwan.

"Arafat finished," I said. "Gone."

The two of them thought that was a good joke. "You go Abu Musa?" Marwan asked.

"Sure. Why don't you come with me?"

I offered him a cigarette, and we walked about fifty yards as the road plunged into ripening wheat. Then he stopped dead in his tracks, waving a hand in front of him as if to ward off the evil eye.

"Big danger! Big, big danger!" he said. "We go back!"

"You're a soldier," I said. "You are brave! We go together."

I went ahead a few paces and waved for him to join me, but he just shook his head. "Big danger!" he called after me. "Arafat, not finished. Arafat, very bad!"

No matter how much I cajoled him, Marwan stood his ground. So in the end, we smiled and waved to each other, and I headed up the road through the wheat and hashish fields toward Deir Zenoun, where it sounded like the fighting had just finished.

At first, I listened for Marwan, just in case he had changed his mind and was coming to join me. In the sudden stillness, I missed him. Perhaps I should have tried harder to convince him to walk with me into town. After a few hundred meters, I ventured a look back, but he was gone. I stopped for a moment and watched the empty blacktop quiver in the sun. It was so hot and so quiet I fancied I could hear the wheat ripening, but it was just my heart pounding. I suddenly realized it was so quiet because the cicadas had stopped singing. I was about to turn back to the checkpoint, but it occurred to me that if anyone *was* hiding in the wheat or in the hashish fields beyond, as Marwan seemed to fear, they would undoubtedly shoot me if I gave them a second chance. The utter silence was unnatural. It was like somebody had just turned off the sound. I was beginning to think this was a very bad idea.

I could see the outlines of buildings up ahead, and as I got closer, I could see smoke and smell the thick stench of burning rubber. But still, there wasn't a sound anywhere: not an engine, not a bird, not even a lone cicada, creaking. Things must be really bad if the cicadas fell silent, I thought. I was starting to feel very exposed.

The road bent around a building into town, and then the intense heat just whacked me, blowing me back. Now I saw what had caused all the smoke, because it was billowing up, great coiled rolls of it, from two burning pickups. Further down, flames poured out of a wrecked truck that had been blown onto its side, its twin ZU-23 anti-aircraft tubes pointing recklessly at a nearby building. In the distance came bursts of automatic weapons fire and then the scream of an ambulance, but there didn't seem to be a person anywhere, not even in the windows. The fighting in this part of town must have ended just minutes ago, and people were still too scared to venture out.

A pair of angels swept past, brushing me with their wings. Or else it was just pure dumb luck. At any rate, the Palestinians were preoccupied with shooting each other, not looking for Westerners—this time, at least.

17: Voila du Boudin
Souk el Gharb, Lebanon

In those early days, I shunned the high-priced hotels and the watering holes frequented by international correspondents. Part of it, of course, was a lack of funds. But even when I had the money, I never liked running with the pack. I preferred stories with ground truth soaked up from ordinary fighters and their victims, not the tall tales of the politicians.

I spent the night in a farmhouse in the middle of nowhere with a group of PFLP fighters, a left-wing faction founded by Palestinian "doctor" George Habash. Their reps in Damascus were eager to have a reporter visit, to show what "real" Palestinian fighters were doing in Lebanon (i.e. not fighting each other, but killing Jews). So over a dinner of Palestinian soup, garnished with olives, dried cheese, and old bread, they boasted of nighttime guerilla raids and slaughtering civilians, and I took notes, realizing there was probably no way I could verify a thing they said. After many glasses of sweet, hot tea, I visited the hammam, washing my hands with water from an oil drum, and we all retired to old blankets on the floor, just as we had done in my Fakhani basement when I had been a hostage. The more I thought of it, there wasn't much that set them off from my jailers the previous year, except that they weren't getting bombed day in and day out—and I was a guest, not a hostage. In the morning, they drove me in the back of a Toyota pickup through the hashish fields to Chtaura, where I took a collective taxi to Beirut so I could file. They were a friendly-enough lot, but they gave me the creeps, and I was happy to get shut of them. They could just as easily have kept me as let me go. That was Lebanese logic.

A few days later, a contact with the Lebanese Forces, the Christian militia founded by the martyred boy-president, Bashir Gemayel, offered to squire me around the Shouf mountains above Beirut so I could report on the battle between the Phalangists and the Progressive Socialist Party (PSP), the pro-Syrian, pro-Palestinian Druse militia commanded by Walid Jumblatt. Two off-duty militiamen joined us for the ride, tight blue jeans and designer tees and cropped black moustaches and hair. As we careened around the ravines, they snapped back the bolts of their M-16s and stuck the barrels out the windows. And laughed. After all, this was their weekend *off!*

We approached an unmanned checkpoint. I got out my passport and press pass, but Gaby pointed for the driver to go around the oil barrels without stopping.

"That's an Israeli checkpoint," he said. "Sometimes they stop us, sometimes they don't. Sometimes they let the PSP guys get through, just to give us something to do."

He pointed to a pair of Israeli soldiers sitting on the roof of an M113 in the rocks beyond the road, smoking, pretending not to see us.

The entry to Souk el Gharb was deserted. Small stone houses lined both sides of the road, many of them bombed out years before. You could tell the older damage because thick vines and brush covered the ruins in luscious green mounds; occasionally, you could see a patch of sky break through, a jagged reminder of cannons gone silent. Like so many other towns up in the mountains, Souk el Gharb was built right to the edge of a ravine with spectacular views of Beirut and the sea.

Major Oskar was in his late thirties but was already losing his hair. He looked like he had stepped out of an insurance brokerage, sucked in his stomach, and put on a militia uniform for the weekend. But he was in charge of the four hundred or so Phalangist fighters in the area and, as I soon learned, commanded utter devotion from his men. We met him behind a wall of sandbags on the flat roof of his command post, peering at the PSP positions just below us through binoculars. Two soldiers lying prone next to him practiced sighting their Browning .50 caliber machine gun.

"This is our last stand," he told me, waving at the panorama. "These mountains used to be half Christian. For over a century, we lived side by side with the Druse. Then we invited the Palestinians into our house, and they took our mothers and our sisters and kicked us out. Now the PSP has taken over from the Palestinians—and the Israelis, instead of helping us, just stand aside."

He showed me the Israeli positions hidden in the trees down below, just behind the last checkpoint. I counted four or five halftracks and two large field guns. Below the Israelis, he pointed out the PSP positions. Through his binoculars, I saw a bunch of military trucks and nearly a dozen T-54 tanks, barrels pointed our way but covered with canvas bags.

"I'll take you to our forward position at the top of the town so you can see what the PSP has above us," he said.

"It looks pretty quiet."

He grunted. "Just wait until it gets dark."

It was close to sunset, so after a quick tour of the forward positions, where he greeted his fighters with a gentle slap on the back, we repaired to Major Oskar's quarters. He, his wife, and their seventeen-month-old baby had set up house in the upper floor of a sumptuous villa owned by a Christian family that had fled to Beirut when the fighting here intensified last fall. Despite the Louis XV chairs and the elegant veneer table, we dined on camp rations, bottled water, and sweet tea as a constant procession of junior officers filed in to bring him updates from the field.

The shelling started at midnight. Oskar gave me an Israeli flak jacket and a US Army Kevlar helmet and took me up to the roof. I counted twenty rounds and saw the flashes where the last ones hit just beyond the village, maybe a hundred meters higher up the rocky hillside.

Major Oskar clicked on the microphone of his walkie-talkie and gave a quiet order. I was waiting for the sky to erupt with return fire from the 155mm howitzers hidden behind the houses across the street, but nothing happened.

"You're not shooting back?" I asked.

"Not unless they hit our people. Most of the time, they're just training the new guys."

A half hour later, I heard the dull thud of another distant departing round, followed by another, and then a steady stream of thuds for several minutes. At the bottom of the village, someone fired several bursts from a machine gun, and then the guns fell silent.

Major Oskar grinned when I asked him what that was about. "We can't let them think we are sleeping," he said. "Then they might do something *really* stupid."

Walid and Samir, the two militiamen who had driven up with us from Lebanese Forces headquarters near the port of Beirut, stayed up most of the night, keeping watch. When I got up the next morning just after dawn, they joined me for coffee at the Louis XV dining table, now dressed in militia uniforms.

"How often do you come up here?" I asked them.

"Two nights a week," Walid said. "Samir works at the port during the day. I'm at the Université de St. Joseph, studying business."

"So this is how you spend your weekends?"

"Something like that."

Walid joined the fighting when he was a teenager, near the start of the civil war. "I told my mother I was going out to play cards with some friends, so I needed to take a gun. Instead, I went to join the *Ketaeb*"—as the Christian militia was known in Arabic.

Major Oskar came down from upstairs along with a handful of soldiers, two of them wearing nothing but shorts and t-shirts and carrying refurbished AK-47s, the cottage industry of the village. Another one came in wearing swimming trunks and sandals, an automatic pistol strapped in a holster around his bare chest.

"This is like World War I, a war of positions," Oskar said. "My strategy is to lure the PSP soldiers out of the villages at night so we can shoot them."

I was taking notes, and I must have paused and given him a quizzical look. "Why would I want to shoot at them *in* the villages?" he said. "The Druse are Lebanese. We don't want to destroy Lebanon. We want to save it."

Later that morning, as I was getting ready to drive back to Beirut, an Israeli captain named Yitzhak came to pay his respects. He and Major Oskar embraced each other on both cheeks and exchanged small talk in Hebrew and drank tea.

"I've got a present for you," Captain Yitzhak said.

He nodded to his driver, who opened a wooden crate in the back of the jeep and brought out four M-16s, minus their magazines.

"We confiscated these from some of your guys at the checkpoint two days ago," Yitzhak said. "I thought you might like to have them back."

Major Oskar watched him depart, the open jeep bumping and whin-ing in low gear, and gave a short laugh. "Tonight, he'll probably tell his guys to lob a few shells in our direction—just to show the Druse that they are being even-handed. If they don't leave Lebanon, even I will join the Resistance. It's time for all the foreign fighters to go. All of them."

Gaby was loading his battered BMW with a bushel of plums and two bags of snap beans, ready to head back to Beirut.

"If you see the French," Major Oskar said, "ask them when they're coming up here to help us."

It was another example of what Jean-Yves liked to call "Lebanese logic," the stark, in-your-face contradictions and absurdities that no one seemed to find absurd. Major Oskar wanted the foreign fighters to go, but first he wanted *them* to help *him* against his enemies. Even the Israelis got caught up in it.

I told Major Oskar I would pass on the message.

+ + +

Two nights later, I had the opportunity to do just that, when Major General Jean-Claude Coullon, commander of the French contingent of the Multinational Force in Beirut, invited me to his officer's mess.

General Coullon was no ordinary French army officer: he was a légionnaire. His men had taken up quarters in the Residence des Pins, the Ottoman palace that until recently had served as the official residence of the French ambassador. When I was escorted to the dining hall to join the general, I was stunned to encounter over a hundred officers, most of them wearing the white kepis of the French Foreign Legion and dress uniforms, all standing at attention. Once we took our places at the center of the long table, shaped like half an *H*, the immense hall fell so silent you could hear the birds in the inner courtyard beyond. Then a sergeant major shouted out, "*Tiens!*" and the room erupted in thunder and song, each line punctuated by 120 large men rapping their boots against the stone floor:

Voilà du boudin, voilà du boudin, voilà du boudin

Pour les Alsaciens, les Suisses et les Lorrains,

Pour les Belges, 'y en a plus, Pour les Belges, 'y en a plus,

Ce sont des tireurs au cul.

Pour les Belges, 'y en a plus, Pour les Belges, 'y en a plus,

Ce sont des tireurs au cul.

And with that, General Coullon lifted his glass of wine, nodded to his men, and they all drank to the Legion and noisily sat down to eat.

"I know your story," the general said after making sure a steward filled my plate with a generous assortment of tabbouleh, kibbeh nayyeh, spicy zucchini, and other appetizers. "You were held with one of our men from the 2e REP."[12]

"That's true, *mon générale*," I said. "He was a good ambassador. But he hadn't prepared me for the food."

Coullon laughed and had a steward bring us more wine, a 1971 Pomerol from Château Clinet. "Unlike your compatriots, we think wine improves good food and makes our soldiers more courageous."

"I see the Palestinians didn't raid the cellar."

General Coullon looked almost out of place at this mess. He was half the size of most of the men, and he wore steel-rim spectacles that made him look more like an engineer than a war-fighter. But he was steeped in the history of the Legion. When I told him I had just come down from the Shouf, his eyes narrowed.

"My men all remember the battle of the Djebel Druse," he said. "All légionnaires do."

"Remind me," I said.

"It was 1926. We still sing about it today."

And so General Coullon told me about the forays of the Legion into the mountains above Beirut two generations ago, and I recounted the close succession of Israeli, Druse, and Christian Ketaeb checkpoints on the twisting mountain roads today. I told him about Major Oskar and his men and how they were eager for French support. I told him about the ambivalence of the Israelis to the Christians who traditionally had inhabited the Shouf mountains and their apparent connivance with the Druse.

---

12   2nd Régiment Étranger de Parachutistes, a famed Foreign Legion unit that had jumped into Kolweizi, and fought in Morocco, Algeria, and Indochina. This was Jean-Yves's regiment.

"Yes, but it's not just any Druse," he said. "They are working with Jumblatt's men, the PSP. There *are* other Druse, people we know."

I caught a not-so-distant gleam in his eye, a glimmer of desire.

"So. Are you thinking of going into the Shouf?"

We were eating quail his men had shot in the mountains north of Beirut on exercises with the Lebanese army. "Do you know the French phrase, '*J'ai des boules?*'" he said, putting a hand to his throat like he was holding back something that was expanding very rapidly. It meant, politely put, that he'd really like to do that more than anything else in the world.

"So you would like to go," I said.

"I have no orders from my political command to deploy beyond Beirut," he said carefully, making sure that I noted his words. "But tell me more about the Shouf."

I remain convinced that if the United States and our partners had intervened more forcefully during the summer of 1983 in Lebanon, in keeping with the desires of the overwhelming majority of the Lebanese people and our military leaders on the ground, we could have avoided countless disasters, hostage-takings, and tens of thousands of deaths caused by a runaway, emboldened Iran.

But history had it another way. Instead of striking back after Iran launched its war against us that April when they blew up our embassy and drew first blood, we just sat back and pretended nothing was happening—with deadly results.

18: A Message from the Mountains
Beirut

We couldn't land the first time because of the fighting.

The approach to the Beirut airport was impressive. Our Middle East Airlines 737 from Paris was flying low over Hamra, the nightclub district of West Beirut, heading into the setting sun. The flight path came so close over the rooftops that you could see men smoking waterpipes and the cleavage of spectacular women as they stepped out of low-slung BMWs. Barely two weeks had passed since the Iranians had massacred 241 US Marines and 63 of their French counterparts in near-simultaneous truck bomb attacks near the airport, and the city was tense. As we dropped closer to the runway, we hit a wave of turbulence, and then out the window I saw red tracers shooting past our wings. That's when the pilot punched it, driving us back into our seats. The luggage compartments shuddered, something metallic smashed in the rear galley, and a few people shrieked as the engines whined, and we suddenly saw stars out the windows, not city streets. We couldn't have been more than a few hundred feet in the air when the pilot pulled up. I had never felt anything quite like it.

We spent the night in Larnaca, Cyprus and made another attempt to fly into Beirut the next morning, this time successful. I had become friends with a young Lebanese Druse named Khaled, and he invited me to stay with his parents at their apartment on the Christian side of the Galerie Sema'an. As I was still freelancing—writing for the *Atlanta Journal-Constitution* and doing radio work for RKO and a French cable news network—I was excited not just to save money but to benefit from the experience and contacts of Khaled and his family, who turned out to be prominent members of the Yazbek community. These were the "other Druse" General Coullon had mentioned, and they were staunch enemies of the Jumblatt clan and the PSP.

When the plane touched down, Khaled took the gold cross he had been wearing in Europe and flipped it around so it fell down his back. A driver was waiting to pick him up on the other side of passport control. As he hefted our bags into the trunk, he handed Khaled a 1911 Colt .45 semi-automatic pistol. "Welcome home, Sheikh Khaled," he said.

Khaled's mother, Jamal, adopted me. Every evening when I returned from interviews, she made sure I ate a gigantic meal with the family and the innumerable relatives and guests who crowded their large apartment with its blown-out bay windows to confer with her husband, Sheikh Farid. When I told them I would be staying for dinner one evening in West Beirut, they insisted on sending a driver to pick me up, since the once-open crossings between the Muslim and Christian sector were now tightly controlled.

I was late. When I finally got through the last checkpoint at the museum and found Khaled and his driver, Ali, it had been dark for an hour. Ali had placed his .45 between the two front seats and was caressing its smooth black steel as I got in back. During the daytime, the pistol stayed underneath his seat. But at night it became a stark reminder of how bad things had gotten since the glory days just after the 1982 war when the city briefly reunited.

Ali maneuvered skillfully around the gaping holes opened by last night's artillery duel and used speed, skill, and prayer to avoid tonight's. I saw a flash somewhere up in the mountains, and then a sudden explosion rocked the car, and the sky turned red. Ali swerved the car to avoid the spray of dirt and asphalt and shrapnel. Gunners responded from invisible rooftops. Each time a shell landed nearby, Ali moaned, "Al-llaaah…." But instead of slowing down, he stepped on the gas as if he could outrun the bellowing hellhounds pursuing us. And he did.

Pulling into the open garage beneath the building at the Galerie Sema'an, he shut off the engine, lit a cigarette, and let his breath out in a heap. Suddenly, in the rearview mirror, headlights appeared then blinked off. The other car nearly touched our bumper as it pulled silently to a halt.

"Who's that?" I said.

Khaled paused getting out.

"That's Amin."

"He was behind us the whole way? I saw nothing."

"Some people are paid for that, Ken."

Amin got out and gave me a wave and a gap-toothed grin. He was built like a chunk of rubble, full of rebar and concrete. Even his forehead was knotted with muscle.

No one lived in the building these days besides Sheikh Farid and his family. Squatters had made off with everything, right down to the window frames, floor-tiles, and bidets. At the peak of the Civil War, the Syrians had poured five feet of concrete along the outside walls, with slanted loopholes no larger than silver dollars so that a pair of snipers could control the entire crossroads below. It was desolate and downright bizarre, like living in a Hollywood movie set or a cemetery.

Jamal was in the couch knitting blankets for orphans, while in half-sobs and hiccups women recounted to her the same events their husbands undoubtedly were telling Sheikh Farid in the men's reception room, where they sat along the walls in stiff-backed upholstered chairs. Jamal patted the shoulders of the girl next to her, drew her close, and then held her for a long time, burying the girl's swollen face in her hair. I doubted the girl was more than sixteen.

Jamal was aunt, mother, and Greek chorus all at once. "Where is the poor child to go?" she moaned when I came in. "First it was her mother and brother killed in the shelling. Now her father is butchered by those animals. It's been nine years since we've been able to go home. When will it stop? Can you tell me, *Monsieur Ken*? When is your president going to do something?"

I said nothing. A servant brought me coffee. I had heard this lament so many times, from so many different Lebanese, that I knew it by heart. All their problems were caused by foreigners; if only the Americans or the French or the Israelis would kick the bad ones out, everything would be fine. It wasn't rocket science to figure out there was no magic wand for Lebanon, no foreign savior who could jump into their lives and rip out the hatreds they had nurtured in their hearts for generations. The horror was reinvented every day by one and all, and no one did a thing to make it stop. How do you say that to people who have become friends?

Sheikh Farid opened the sliding doors. By the taut, detached look on his boxer's face, I knew he had made a decision. He motioned Khaled and me inside.

The men of the tribe were all standing around a cedar-wood coffin clicking their amber prayer beads, except for two grey-bearded clerics come down from Baaqline who sat in armchairs in their white turbans and black robes, presiding over the gathering. The old solemn faces nodded as we came in. Sheikh Farid took my arm.

"See for yourself," he said quietly.

But there was no body to see. What once had been Sheikh Farid's cousin had been arranged in the coffin in four plastic bags, the members grouped together as if by convenience or some queer respect for anatomical order. Thankfully, the eyes were facing downwards into the pillow. The skull had been split in two by an axe. It was a gruesome display of a gruesome murder, with no attempt at making it appear more palatable.

"He was taking care of my house in the mountains. He knew everyone in the village. I had given him the keys. When we realized the village was about to fall, I begged him to bring his family down to Beirut, but he refused. That was when his wife and son were killed, during the last shelling before the village fell. He remained behind to bury his dead.

"During the forty days mourning, not one of the Jumblattis disturbed him. Not one. We share the same beliefs, the same traditions.

They left his daughter unmolested when she went out to find food. You would think they had drunk their fill of blood.

"There were no weapons in the house!" He raised his voice, speechifying now. "I even arranged to send him money to pay the new taxes the Jumblattis imposed. Let them take my money, let them ransack my house. But why this? What has happened to us that we kill our own?"

We had both been looking at the coffin while Sheikh Farid, dressed in a worn tweed jacket that was too small for his barrel chest, tried to reassemble his dead cousin with his words. Soon the bare light bulb dangling overhead faded to a filament, then went out. Almost immediately Ali appeared in the doorway, handing Sheikh Farid a gas lamp. Since I was the taller, I reached the handle upwards to hang it over a crook in the electric wire, and the ghostly aura of the spiting butane spread like blue fire to the white turbans and the grey beards in the corner.

"This is how it always starts, my friend. I am the only one to speak out against that monster. And he is afraid of me. Because he knows I speak for the heart of our people. A day will come when the mountains will turn against him, to cleanse themselves of the blood he has spilt."

"How many men do you have?" I asked him.

A glimmer of an old fire lit up his eyes; the hint of a smile, then a shrug.

"It's not the numbers but where and how you strike. This is a message. And like any message, it calls for just the right response."

Silence descended on the room, a silence nourished by the now-steady draw of the butane lamp, the vacant bluish-white stare of the men around me, the determined set of Sheikh Farid's jaw. Though his tweed jacket seemed out of harmony with the traditionally clad elders, like them, he was born and bred of the mountains, his viscera unchanged for generations.

"*Ya, Lubnan,*" he murmured, almost to himself. "Poor Lebanon."

Although I stayed with them for several more weeks, I never asked how he responded to the murder, and he never volunteered an answer. And he stayed alive.

19: Hungry Guns, Exploding Cats[13]
Tripoli, Lebanon

The PLO civil war moved up to Tripoli that autumn, along Lebanon's northern coast, where the Syrians were shelling Arafat and his supporters in the refugee camps, pretending the dirty work was being done by Palestinian dissidents. The Syrians were on Mount Turbol, overlooking the camps Nahr el Bared and Baddawi. Even though the Lebanese media pretended the Syrians didn't exist, their tanks were parked in plain sight in an olive grove above the city, and the tank crews made no bones about the fact they were Syrian, not Palestinian. We drank tea with them one day, and they'd shoot at us the next when we went to report on Arafat and his men down below.

It was a crazy little war, even by Lebanese standards. A handful of us would drive up in the morning in a collective cab, roam around looking for news, then drive three hours back to Beirut before nightfall so we could file our dispatches to Paris, London, New York, and, in my case, Atlanta. If we left Tripoli early enough, we'd stop for drinks in a mountain tavern overlooking the sea, just thirty minutes and a world away from the war.

One day, I drove up with a Czech correspondent I had met at the UPI bureau where we filed our dispatches. Václav Bervida was not particularly adventurous when it came to covering the fighting (nobody much cared about it in Prague). But he was happy to get out of Beirut, and he turned out to be great company. On our first foray together, we were joined by a French photojournalist named Roger Auque. He turned out to be a total nutcase. Certifiably insane.

In a patch of dusty sunshine at the top of the Baddawi camp, Roger spied an old man sitting on a fruit crate, keffiyeh wrapped around his head, his huge gnarled hands swatting flies. Roger thought he would make a great picture. Václav spent the next fifteen minutes looking for a safe place to leave his car, so it wouldn't get hit by shrapnel. By the time we caught up to Roger, he and the old man had been joined by a pair of twelve-year-olds who had set up a 60mm light mortar. Roger was egging them on, trying to get them to fire off a round toward the Syrian tanks. The old man was shooing them to get lost.

---

13   This section was published in *War, Literature & the Arts*, Autumn 2018.

"Why don't you send a birthday card to Hafez al-Assad?" Roger cajoled the kids.

"You've got to be out of your mind," I said.

"Come on, it'll be a great picture," Roger said. He looked like a cartoon caricature, safari jacket stuffed with film, chin-length hair, twirly moustache, red scarf. He crouched and moved with his camera crab-like around them, pretending to find the best place to shoot.

"They're actually going to do it," Václav said. He started down the hill.

"Roger, you are truly messed up," I said.

"Come on, come on, you're going to be famous," Roger egged on the kids.

And then the kid with the mortar bomb did it. He popped the mortar into the tube, and the two of them giggled and put their fingers in their ears, and Roger started snapping pictures. I gave it thirty seconds before we had incoming.

"See you back at the car at four," I said. Then I jogged down the hill to where Václav had taken cover a couple of streets down. I had reached the count of forty when a tank round slammed into the upper floor of the building across the street from where Roger and the kids and the old man had been. Once the shrapnel and the dust had scattered, I stuck my head around the corner but didn't see anyone. They must have run for cover just in time.[14]

Václav was short, stocky, and sported a gnarly dark beard. He had a constant twinkle in the eye that for some reason made me think of the Russian anarchist, Mikhail Bakunin. Even the Palestinian kids could tell he was a Slav, not American or French. As we worked our way lower down into the camp, a teenager in fatigues came up to Václav, holding out an assault rifle for him to examine.

"Mister, mister," he said. "Nobody knows where this comes. Mister, you know?"

"I don't have a clue," Václav whispered to me. He took the rifle and pretended to examine it authoritatively, then he announced that it came from Hungary.

"Hungry?" the kid repeated.

---

14 Roger Auque was taken hostage by Hezbollah in January 1987 and held for nearly a year. Later in life, he went into politics and was appointed French ambassador to Eritrea by President Sarkozy before dying of brain cancer in 2014. In a tell-all memoir published after his death, *Au Service Secret de la République* (Paris: Fayard, 2015) he revealed that during much of the time he spent overseas as a reporter, he was engaged in secret missions on behalf of French intelligence and Israel's Mossad.

"That's right. It's a hungry rifle. It needs to be fed."

The fight for the camp erupted into extreme violence for ten- or twenty-minute spurts, a gushing wind like a sudden storm; then it fell quiet, and the bullets stopped, with only an occasional mortar or tank round bursting nearby. The Syrians and the Fatah rebels occupied the high ground, allowing them to pour enfilade fire down the main street of the camp, where two thousand people still lived. Arafat's men hunkered down and made occasional sorties, still succeeding those first days in keeping their enemy at bay. Václav and I stopped off at an UNWRA school flying the blue UN flag near the bottom of the hill, where several dozen families had taken refuge. To while away the time, kids took cafeteria trays and slid down the corrugated tin roof of the bomb shelter entrance, even as bombs exploded nearby.

After several day trips back and forth, our PLO contact told us that Arafat would speak to us that evening at 10:00 PM. I had hooked up with a photographer from UPI and decided to stick around to meet Arafat, then see if I could get a hotel or a late-night ride back to Beirut.

That afternoon, the rebels made their final push. They came down from Mount Turbol and took up positions in an olive grove just beyond the crumbling apartment buildings at the top of the camp, where Arafat had his offices until a few days earlier. As they advanced, camp residents began rising up out of the shelters, as if carried by a flood, and flowed downhill seeking safer ground inside the city of Tripoli itself. Late in the afternoon, even the fighters began clearing out. The UPI photographer and I were the last reporters left in the camp. We had holed up on the ground floor of a house along the main street, and every ten minutes or so, groups of three or four exhausted fighters, many of them bleeding, would crash into our shelter to escape the automatic weapons fire tearing down the street. When they sensed a lull, or perhaps that the enemy had stopped for tea, they would crawl across the junk-strewn concrete and then roll into the drainage ditch beyond. It was the only way to actually leave the camp. To reach the relative shelter of the city, you had to cross the main street and the drainage ditch, and then it was a two-hundred-meter sprint across open ground to the next group of buildings at the edge of the camp.

We were trapped. And the UPI photographer and I and the fighter who was serving as our guide knew it. But the longer we waited, the closer the rebels advanced toward our position, and none of us had any confidence they would respect our protests that we were press.

Finally, it started to get dark, and we decided to make a run for it, first the soldier, then me, and finally, the photographer. I was carrying a Sony professional cassette recorder in a leather case around my neck that I used for my radio work. It had full stereo capabilities that let you dub from one channel to the next and weighed a good ten pounds. I decided to carry the microphone and my notebook in one hand and hold the recorder against my chest with the other and record whatever happened. I whispered a brief, out-of-breath commentary to set the scene in both French and English, then ran in a crouch across the street and dove into the drainage ditch, rolling to keep the cassette deck from hitting the ground. It was still recording, so I waved to the photographer and he made his move, pointing his camera toward the shooters, taking pictures as he ran. This time, I could see the bullets as they kicked up sand and dirt all around him. But he made it, and together we ran across the broken field and collapsed into the shelter at the bottom, completely out of breath from the run, the fear, and the adrenaline.

"You were lucky," he said when we could breathe again. He poked at my Sony.

I looked down and saw that it was still recording but that the decibel meter on one channel had gone dead.

"Not there. There," he said, pulling at a tear in the thick leather casing where the tape recorder had been covering my chest. Whether it was from a rock when I crashed into the drainage ditch or from a passing bullet, I never knew. But an angel got up and, unfolding his wings, flew off into the night. The Lord had much more for me to do, much more to teach me, many more trials for me to endure.

✝ ✝ ✝

We made our way to Arafat's new headquarters in Latfi, a residential district on the outskirts of town, where a crowd of reporters was waiting for the Old Man to appear. Our arrival, fresh from the battle they had been hearing about on the radio, was the most exciting thing that had happened to them all day. A French reporter named Jean-Paul Kauffmann took me by the arm and led me into a corner. At first, I was flattered—I had been reading his eyewitness dispatches from Beirut and Tripoli in *Le Matin de Paris* and admired his literary skill.

"So what was it like in Baddawi?" he asked. "What happened?"

"*Ouf*," I said, using a French expression that could mean anything from "not much" to "whatever."

"No, really. What was it like? We've been hearing all day that the camp was about to fall."

"Why do you think there are so many loyalist troops in here?" I said.

He latched onto that. "You mean, they have fled?"

I gave in and started to talk. "One of the last guys we saw leaving was this idiot on the back of a pickup, hanging onto the grips of an anti-aircraft gun as they bounced in the potholes. He was wearing Palestinian flags like a sandwich board, back and front, shooting up the mountain like a maniac. And through all of it, you could smell the honeysuckle and roses people were growing just beyond the walls, mixed in with the cordite. It was surreal."

Suddenly, it occurred to me that I would be reading about sandwich man in his dispatch the next day, and I kicked myself.[15] "How about you, what did you see?" I asked.

He pulled out a notebook and flipped through the pages. "We went to the morgue. They had fourteen dead and forty-five wounded, both civilian and military."

I knew the hospital and the morgue well. Everyone did. But I had a special reason to go back there as soon as I could, and it wasn't to number the dead. "Pretty quiet? No shelling?"

"Calm."

Suddenly, three GRAD rockets slammed into the neighborhood in quick succession and made the lights go out. Like mortars, the GRADs could land at street level because of their ballistic trajectory, but they were several times more powerful than the mortars.

"Someone is making us a target," a British voice said in English.

About ten minutes later, an officer came in and gave us the all-clear, and most of the reporters left. They'd had enough of waiting for Arafat that night. Besides, they knew he was going to dish out more lies.

History was full of them.

---

15   *Le Matin de Paris* did indeed publish an eyewitness account of the fall of Baddawi the next morning under Kauffmann's byline that described sandwich man. Like Roger Auque, Kauffmann was taken hostage by Hezbollah a few years later and released after intense French government negotiations with Iran.

+ + +

Arafat's number two, Abu Jihad, arrived first, pulling up in a dark blue Alfa Romeo. I thought it was an odd car for a guerilla commander to be driving around Lebanon, but then I thought, why not? If you had all the money he'd stolen and could choose any car you wanted, why not pick an Italian sports car with leather seats and then equip it with bulletproof glass and armor-plated doors?

Arafat himself arrived, wheels squealing, in a white Jeep Wagoneer with two carloads of bodyguards and almost ran over people lounging outside in the courtyard. A couple of local TV cameramen had stayed behind, and they turned on their lights. The Fatah chief was wearing pressed olive fatigues over a crisp green dress shirt and a pistol with silver inlay in the handle. If you listened to his calm, good-humored presentation, you would think it was just an ordinary day in the life, not a day when his men had made their last stand—and lost. It was a great lesson in image over substance.

At 1:15 AM, there were no cars on the street, no taxis, no hotels, and nowhere to go. I was beginning to wonder why I had hung around to listen to Arafat, when I knew full well my editors wouldn't want anything from him in my dispatches, since they could get it off the wires. The deathly quiet was unnerving and made me feel exposed, as if a thousand eyes were tracking me from behind curtains. Plus, it was getting cold, and all I had on was a polo shirt and a thin leather jacket. Sleeping outside was not an option, nor was walking around. I had to find shelter.

All the windows on the street were dark, either from the power cut earlier or because everyone was in bed, so I went into the first open apartment building I found, walked up to the top floor, and started knocking on doors. After the third try, I thought I heard movement inside and began to wonder if this was a bad idea. What if someone came out firing an AK-47, thinking I was a burglar? I figured that by now, enough people must know that I was inside the building, so if someone wanted to offer me hospitality, they would. So I brushed the broken glass and debris off the cement faux-marble tiles in the stairwell and sat down, back to the wall, trying to find a comfortable position. I resolved to try to get some sleep.

For the longest time, I couldn't stop shivering. But in the end, I must have drifted off because the next thing I knew, it was three in the morning and I no longer felt the cold. I had been woken up by the deep thump of a departing artillery round from somewhere nearby. It's astonishing how quickly you can go from deep sleep to total alertness at the sound of danger. Less than two minutes later, the broken window across the street blossomed bright red as the first incoming round ripped the covers off the night.

For the next hour or so, the gunners on both sides traded fire. You could almost hear them thinking in between rounds: was that enough to shut him up? Can't we just get back to sleep? And then one of them broke the lull, and they traded another volley.

But at four o'clock, either the annoyance factor had kicked up a notch or someone important had woken up because suddenly both sides went at it without letup. I could see the reflection of a not-so-distant fire in the windows across the street, and then a shell must have landed just below because half the windows shattered, driving slivers of flame through the air until they hit the pavement like rain. In one of the apartments just above me, a woman started to wail. Another round hit close by, and the walls jumped. It went on like that for fifteen minutes or more until the guns were no longer hungry.

+ + +

The next time I opened my eyes, it was light outside. It wasn't the light that woke me but the sound of a door opening just above me. A middle-aged woman in a long nightdress peered down at me from the landing, then called her husband to join her. The man saw me, shook his head, and shut the door. In the distance, I could hear ambulances screaming. I was glad the night was over and I could get back to work.

The emergency room at the Islamic Hospital that morning was standing room only as family members sought their loved ones. There were so many wounded that the ambulance medics left them on stretchers on the floor. A forty-year-old Lebanese man slipped in a pool of blood as he rushed in, sobbing, carrying his infant daughter. A medic caught his arm, and together, they placed the shivering girl on a vinyl-topped counter because the two operating tables were taken. A young nurse smoothed the wet hair from the girl's face and stared down at her with a tenderness I suddenly found heartbreaking. I swatted a fly off my forearm and saw that it had left red tracks.

Down one corridor, they had stacked the dead, too busy to haul them off to the morgue. A volunteer medic arrived with a bunch of body bags and struggled to slip one over a pair of gnarled bare feet. I wondered if the young nurse would come help him. Maybe, like me, the medic had come to the hospital just to be in her presence. Windows rattled against their hinges up above us as another artillery round slammed into a nearby building.

I waited an hour or more, taking notes, trying to find someone of authority who could give me an actual body count but really just waiting until things had calmed down enough so I could take the young nurse aside and interview her. She had a Brancusi face, with a broad forehead and an intentness that seemed to focus all the emotion of this place on whoever she looked at with those brilliant green eyes. She seemed fragile and yet strong all at once.

"You were wonderful," I said once the stretchers had cleared. "How can you deal with all those children and those horrible wounds?"

"I was born here," she said. "In Baddawi, the camp. Perhaps you have been to Baddawi?"

"I was there when it fell to Abu Musa yesterday afternoon."

"Don't talk to me about Abu Musa!" she said, with a sudden burst of anger. "You know who led the assault? It was Ahmed Jibril, the Syrian. He boasted about it on the radio this morning."

For an instant, I thought she might be angry with me. "I'd like to write about you," I said. "What's your name?"

"My mother named me Thara'a. It means 'wealth.'"

"Wow," I said. "How could she have known?"

"Known what?" she smiled.

"How beautiful you would become."

She blushed and looked around quickly to make sure the medics were still busy with patients. Then she brushed her hand gently against mine, pointing to my notebook.

"My mother is Lebanese, but I am Palestinian. You can write that I need to see the wounded, to hear the bombs, to see the blood," she said, without flinching as another artillery shell slammed into cinderblocks nearby. "These are my people. I want to die here in Tripoli!"

"Please don't be in a hurry," I said.

+ + +

I ran into Václav at Arafat's headquarters later on. It was now official that Baddawi had fallen to the rebels last night. My UPI colleague's photographs were the last taken by any Western photographer from inside the camp. After we had escaped, it turned into a rout.

"Have you noticed anything about the shelling?" Václav said.

"Yes, it's coming to a neighborhood near you. My guess is, the Syrians want to put pressure on the local muckety-mucks to kick Arafat out of Tripoli."

Václav was nervous about his car. He was keenly aware of the immense privilege his Communist editors had granted him by shelling out for the old Peugeot and wanted to make sure nothing happened to it.

"How about I give you the low-down from last night and we grab lunch up in the mountains?"

"It's deal," he said with a fake Russian accent. Václav loved to make fun of the Russians. It's one of the many reasons we hit it off.

My hunch about the shelling turned out to be right. Václav drove toward the port, thinking that was about as far away from Fatahland as you could be on this particular day. But the Syrian gunners seemed to follow us wherever we went. Václav was a nervous driver. He actually stopped at stop signs and red lights, unlike the Lebanese. He braked for cats—and there were lots of them. With every shell that landed, they seemed to leap out of basements, their fur electric. It would have been hilarious if they didn't look like they were just about to explode.

We reached the coast road, and this gave us a clear view across the ruins of the artillery marching in our direction, digging up the dirt.

"I don't think you need to worry about the police," I said. "Go faster!"

Václav started sweating, and the last thing I saw as we cleared the edge of the city at 70 mph, with tank shells exploding just behind us, was a kid on a skateboard, calmly weaving back and forth to avoid the shell holes and the debris.

+ + +

We feasted that afternoon at a restaurant in a small village up in the mountains, with a spectacular view of the sea way below. We shared two bottles of Ksara wine from the Bekaa and talked about our families.

Among the many things we had in common was an aversion to returning to our home countries. In my case, it was the dread of working for a small-town newspaper in America. For Václav, it was the dull stupidity of Communist rule in Prague. He never said it in so many words, but I suspected he was not a Party member and had gotten the Beirut post because no one else at *Rudé právo* wanted it.

"Your countrymen are hard at work," he said, pointing to the sky. "Why don't you call them to join us and we'll order another bottle of wine."

We couldn't yet hear the fighter jets, but this was the second group that had flown by. We were still on the road when the first group had roared overhead, but we hadn't been able to see them through the trees. Now, in the distance, I could see a faint outline of four aircraft approaching the Lebanese coast from the sea. As they came closer, it seemed to me that the sound of the engines was distinctly different from the Israeli F-16s from last summer.

"Those aren't ours," I said. "Look at the wings. Do you see how small they are? And how they kind of sweep back from the fuselage? They're Super Étendards. It's like the entire French naval aviation is on exercises."

"Is bad joke," Václav said. "So what are they up to?"

We left the table and followed the aircraft up the stairs from the terrace and out into the parking lot, until they disappeared without giving any sign of turning back.

"They're headed for the Bekaa," I said.

Twenty minutes later, the planes returned and disappeared out to sea. I figured it was time to settle the bill and head back to Beirut.

On the radio, maybe a half hour later, they announced that the French had just bombed the headquarters of Islamic Amal in Baalbek, the Iranian-backed group believed to have been responsible for the twin truck bomb attacks on the French and American Marines three weeks earlier. The radio said the initial death toll was more than fifty, but within days, the truth came out that a mole within the French foreign ministry had tipped off the Iranians so they could evacuate their people. The only casualties were a local shepherd and a bunch of sheep.

But it took more than two decades for the full story of the Nov. 17, 1983, fiasco to come out. President Ronald Reagan had ordered US Marine Corps fighter jets to lead the airstrike, but at the last minute, Defense Secretary Caspar Weinberger pulled the plug, leaving the French to go it alone. Weinberger argued that the US would lose its allies in the Arab world if it took part in such a raid—a ridiculous statement given the fact that the Arabs were then mired in an epochal bloodletting with Iran that would leave more than one million dead on both sides. They hated the Iranians and would have applauded the raid.[16]

A few days later, I was leaving the UPI office in Hamra when someone ran up behind me and grabbed my arm. I recognized the sparrow-thin fingers before I saw her, and a thrill shot through my veins.

"You're not dead!" Thara'a said. "Look, I'm not dead, too!"

As the Syrian bombardments reached progressively into the heart of Tripoli proper, including the Islamic Hospital, Thara'a's mother had ordered her to leave the city and visit relatives in Beirut.

"I am so sad to leave," she said. But despite all her efforts to make a sad face, the joy leapt out of her heart, and we embraced on the street.

---

16   In the second chapter of *Countdown to Crisis: The Coming Nuclear Showdown with Iran* (New York: Crown Forum, 2005), I recount the federal court testimony of Rear Admiral James (Ace) Lyons in a lawsuit against Iran brought by families of the 241 US Marines murdered in Beirut in which he described an intercept proving Iran's responsibility for the October 1983 terrorist attack. Lyons told me the US jets were "gassed and loaded" on deck, awaiting takeoff to join the French, when the stand-down order came from Weinberger. See www.kentimmerman.com/countdown.htm, pp. 23–26.

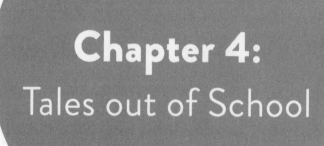

Chapter 4:
Tales out of School

20: How I Became an Arms Dealer

Colonel Mark Broman was right out of central casting: tall, trim, with short black hair tinged with grey, who seemed to be in uniform even when wearing a suit. He stood ramrod straight and spoke with a watered-down Texas accent that sounded like he was chewing food. Covering the walls of his spacious office suite on the rue la Boétie were pictures of him flying US Army helicopters in Vietnam, citations, awards—even a picture of him in full dress uniform shaking hands with President Reagan. I met him while doing a story on NATO and the Euromissiles. We hit it off from the start, and I spent long hours with him in the US Embassy Annex, which also housed the CIA station. He was planning to retire in two months and join a defense publishing and consulting group. And he wanted to hire me.

"I'll tell you the secret about the US and Germany," he said. "The politicians complain we still have two hundred fifty thousand troops in West Germany forty years after the war. But when I ask friends in the German military about it, none of them want us to leave. 'You Americans make us better Germans.'" He said it with a disarming smile and a gentle rap on his gigantic wooden desk, as if that summed it all up.

Broman introduced me to his future business partner, Professor Paul S. Cutter, from Santa Clara, California. Cutter was as extravagant as Broman was reserved. A chain-smoker with a thick black moustache and unruly hair, he loved to drink and tell stories about the six years he spent in Moscow with the United States Information Agency (*wink wink, nod nod*). Later, he returned to the Soviet Union undercover as a geologist, an importer-exporter, and sometimes, as he put it, as a "delegation appendage." His real job was with the CIA's "exhibits" division. "I made my contribution to the cause," he said. It was a self-satisfied understatement meant to imply big things he couldn't talk about.

Cutter's plan was to build European Defense Associates into a giant defense publishing and consulting group that would have its hand "in a lot of pies." He had lined up partners in Israel, France, the UK, and the

United States, many of them US Army officers, like Colonel Broman, about to retire. "This is your opportunity to get in at the ground floor" was his pitch.

He had just published a lengthy account of Israel's 1982 air war against Syria that blew me away. He described in detail how Israeli F-4 "Wild Weasels" jammed Syrian air defenses in the Bekaa Valley, so that follow-on waves of F-15s and F-16s were able to knock fifty Syrian MiGs out of the sky without a loss. Cutter had interviewed top Israeli generals and defense industry executives who described the technology. While it didn't exactly read like a Tom Clancy thriller, remember: this was the beginning of the Tom Clancy era, and Americans were fascinated by exotic technologies that until recently had been closely guarded secrets. This was the real deal. I was hooked.

So when the two of them asked me to travel to Cairo on a special mission, I wouldn't have dreamed of saying no.

They were grooming me to become an arms dealer, with the blessing of the "highest levels" of the US government.

+ + +

Cairo

Broman set me up with his counterpart at the Office of Military Coop-eration at the US Embassy in Cairo. If Major Rasmussen found anything unusual about a journalist inquiring about buying F-4 fighter-bombers, he didn't let on.

"The Ministry of Defense is eager to sell the older planes, but the Air Force is against it. You're going to have to navigate between the two," Rasmussen told me. He walked me through the regulatory steps needed to get the planes released to a foreign purchaser, but since Broman was involved, he didn't expect it would be overly complicated. "Mark knows all the traps," he said. I was now one of the club.

Cutter had been insistent that I stay at the Nile Hilton, the most prominent hotel in Cairo, and that I send him a telex shortly after arriving. That evening, when I got back from dinner with Amayni, the front desk clerk handed me a thick envelope. When I opened it upstairs, I was stunned. Cutter had sent a ten-page pro forma contract for 32

F-4 fighter-bombers, 350 M48A5 Patton main battle tanks, and a dozen C-130-A Hercules military transport aircraft, along with full specifications, prices, and documentary requirements for each. Any illusion that I was working as a journalist ended at that moment.

It took a day to set up an appointment with the head of the MoD Department in charge of surplus military equipment. Major General Ussery Katib offered me Turkish coffee and asked if it was my first time in Cairo. I told him that I had lived in Heliopolis the year before while working on the hospital at Ain Shams. "So you speak Arabic," he said, delighted.

"Just a bit," I said.

I laid out the proposal as it had been explained to me. EDA represented the Government of Paraguay, which was interested in purchasing between twelve and thirty-two used F-4s from Egypt. We understood that the planes had been declared surplus, since Egypt was scheduled to receive F-16s from the United States in the coming months. Would Egypt consider selling them?

"Absolutely," the General said. "But you realize this has to be done through Washington."

"Of course," I said. "That's why I came through OMC."

He agreed to meet again the next day after discussing the proposal with his colleagues. Before I left, he took another look at the end-user certificate from General Alejandro Fretes Davalos of the Paraguayan Air Force I had handed him earlier.

"Are you sure Paraguay *has* an air force?" he said, pulling on his white moustache. I think he actually gave me a wink.

"That's what I was told," I said.

"You might want to check it out."

As I left the MoD compound, I mulled over what he said. I took a taxi back to the Nile Hilton, changed out of my suit, and walked over to the American University library. What I learned was disturbing: Paraguay did indeed have an air force, but no jet fighters, only a handful of trainers and helicopters. The purchase of these F-4s would not just double the size of the Air Force, it would be like upgrading the family car from a Model T to a stable full of Formula-1 racers. And then there were financial issues. I learned that the gross national product of the entire country of Paraguay was $1.3 billion, while government military expenditures for the most recent year were just $46 million. If Paraguay purchased all thirty-two of Egypt's F-4s at $3.2 million each, the $102.4 million expenditure would be more than double its entire defense budget! Something was not right.

Thus began my crash course in fake end-user certificates and the world of black-market arms deals. I waffled through the next day's meeting and headed back to Paris to confront Colonel Broman.

"You lied to me," I started out, brimming with self-righteousness.

He looked truly surprised. Then he smirked, giving his desk a slap.

"You mean, you didn't get it?" When I continued glaring at him, he went on. "There are some things you don't talk about openly. But everybody understands all the same."

"Spell it out for me."

"Not here," he said.

We ducked into a noisy café a few blocks from his office.

"It's Iran, isn't it?" I said.

"It's all part of the Initiative."

"What makes you think the Egyptians, who are Saddam Hussein's best buddies, would be caught dead selling their F-4s to Iran?"

"Easy," Broman said. He rubbed his thumb against his first two fingers. "Money."

I shook my head. "I don't believe it. They would be furious if they ever found out."

"What makes you think they don't know?" he said. An image flashed in my mind of General Ussery winking at me as he suggested I find a better story than Paraguay. Maybe Broman was right. "Don't be such a prig. This has all been wired in Washington," he added.

That was a line I would hear often over the next year. At times, it seemed tantalizingly close to the truth. When I got "Professor" Cutter to talk about it during one of his fly-bys through Paris, he described a colossal struggle between the United States and the Soviets to gain influence in post-Khomeini Iran. "This thing has to be supported with a lot of deals," he said. "The US is going to get in there very quickly with a lot of free stuff. So it will be damn good to get some things done before that happens. Because once they start delivering the goodies for free, who the hell is going to get paid?"

Broman retired a few weeks later, and together we opened an office for EDA in Paris with money transferred by Cutter's team in Santa Clara, California. I focused on learning about the French defense industry, leaning on Broman's contacts. But I also monitored the telex traffic and cautiously made copies when Broman was not around. Just in case.

21: The Boys with the Plastic Keys
Basra, Iraq

The massive bloodletting between Iran and Iraq was mired in its fourth year. The French defense contractors I was starting to meet were making out like gangbusters on the war and loved to talk about it. Now that Lebanon had gone south, Iraq became the story.

I had been planning to head back to Beirut that February, but when Shiite gunmen shot up the Commodore Hotel bar, not far from the UPI office in Hamra where I worked, I called it off. I reckoned that wasting good booze was a bad omen, since it meant that Iran's proxies felt confident they were powerful enough to write new rules. Shortly after that, the kidnappings began in earnest. I felt an angel leap off my shoulders, opening up a vision of endless torment, chained to a bedpost in a Bekaa Valley farmhouse in the dark. That was not where I wanted to be, for sure.

I finagled my way to Baghdad in the dead heat of summer to attend a "peace" conference hosted by Saddam Hussein. Needless to say, only his friends attended, but to my surprise, the circle of friends of this secular tyrant was rapidly expanding. Two State Department officers at the bustling US Interests Section in Baghdad, Ted Kattouf and David Newsom, openly spoke to me about a new US "tilt" toward Iraq.

Our government minders organized a trip down to Basra, Iraq's second-largest city and the scene of a recent Iraqi "victory" in the war. We traveled in a convoy of two luxury motor coaches and a few jeeps down the main highway, hugging the border with Iran, the same highway the Iranians had successfully cut twice already in the war.

"You can see that the Iraqis are confident," said Pascal Boniface, a young Socialist Party defense analyst. He was trying to impress an attractive female Swiss journalist across the aisle.

"Do you think the Iranians can see us?" she asked.

"They wouldn't dare shell a convoy of foreign journalists," he said.

Patrick Denaud, a CBS News cameraman assigned to work with me on this trip, had to clap both hands over his mouth to keep from laughing.

Our luck held, and once we rolled into the Basra Sheraton, we learned why. The four-story atrium, draped with flowering Bougainvillea that cascaded down the tiered balconies in a replica of the Hanging Gardens of Babylon, was completely deserted. We were the only guests. From the sandbagged bar on the roof, opened for our benefit, we could see a half-dozen coastal tankers and bunkering ships in the Shatt al-Arab waterway, some of them at anchor, others shot full of holes and beached at crazy angles in the muck. On the other side of the hotel, away from Iran, a few black-robed women carrying shopping bags hugged buildings and hurriedly pushed through head-high walls of sandbags to the market. The Iraqi army had conducted a massive artillery campaign against the child soldiers dragooned into Khomeini's Islamic horde, stomping at them like hobnailed boots squashing bugs. They drove them back from the border through sheer brute force, so Basra was now out of range. Three weeks after the battle was over, Basra's residents were still shell-shocked.

It was one hundred degrees Fahrenheit by ten o'clock the next morning when we departed for the front.

The first sign that things were getting serious was the pontoon bridge over the Shatt al-Arab, with a misspelled sign that read, "Far well." Our luxury motor coach rumbled slowly across the murky waters, heading toward a marshy lowland where the skeletons of uprooted palm trees littered the bare ground.

"That used to be the border," Patrick said. "We are now in Iran."

Our Ministry of Information guide was smoking quietly up front with a half-dozen soldiers who had joined us in the hotel parking lot. Only about a dozen of us had signed up for the trip. Neither the French socialist Lothario nor the Swiss girl was among them.

About a mile in, we saw sand-colored pickups and Range Rovers speeding across dusty side roads, their windshields and windows smeared with mud. "That keeps down the reflections," Patrick said. "The Iranians will shoot at anything that catches the sun."

"Like us," I said.

"For example."

We both laughed nervously.

A few minutes later, we arrived at a checkpoint and were ordered off the bus into a group of waiting Range Rovers, their windows smeared with mud like the others. Their engines gave off enormous amounts of heat in an effort to keep the air conditioners working. Even so, we started to sweat almost as soon as we got in.

Our first stop was a command bunker, about a ten-minute drive due east into Iran. Our four-car convoy spread out at twenty-meter intervals along a giant earthwork berm that sheltered us from the two hundred thousand Iranians who faced us somewhere in the shimmering distance. An open tent had been set up, and a ten-ton truck arrived and began distributing huge blocks of ice for the troops. Inside the bunker, an officer welcomed us with ice-cold refreshments and snacks. Window air conditioners, set at ceiling level into the corrugated tin walls, wheezed like old hunting dogs dreaming of the chase.

The forty-year-old Iraqi division commander described the recent battle for us.

"I felt sorry for my men," he said, and the group of staff officers around him tut-tutted and shook their heads knowingly. "It broke their hearts to kill so many boys. They just kept coming, wave after wave of them, clutching their plastic keys. We had to chain our men to the machine-guns to keep them from giving into pity and running away."

He gave a quick, barking laugh, and his officers joined in. It was my introduction to Baathist humor. I gave an involuntary shudder as the meaning of what he said sunk in. The boys were sent out to breach the minefields. They walked shoulder to shoulder, clutching the plastic keys Khomeini had told them would unlock the gates of heaven when they died. To the Iraqis, they were like Halloween ghouls. They were terrified of them.

"We'd like to shoot at the front," Patrick said, indicating his video rig.

The general conferred with his officers. After some back and forth, with two of them vigorously shaking their heads to veto the proposal, he turned back to Patrick and smiled. "I think we can arrange that."

An aide gave each of us a bottle of chilled water and we headed topside, where by now it was 120 degrees. It was so hot that you didn't actually feel your sweat because it dried as soon as it reached your skin.

We packed into two Land Rovers, one for us and the second as armed escort, and headed through a cut in the berm that was rutted from tank traffic. The driver picked up speed and began an active discussion with the officer up front about which road they should take as we entered the valley of the turrets.

"What's on your side?" I asked Patrick.

"Just dust," he said, peering through the gaps in the smeared mud. "And tanks."

Every twenty meters or so, a tank turret emerged from the hard-scrabble dirt, and as we got close, we could see that the tanks had been buried in pits, with just enough room around them for a man to walk. This was right out of Soviet armor training manuals, I learned later. A soldier emerged from a trench, carrying a block of ice for the tank crew.

We drove at breakneck speed for another five minutes due east into Iran, then the officer up front pointed, the driver cut the wheel hard, and we skidded in the desert gravel and dust and swerved into a vacant tank pit. "Let's go," the officer said.

Outside, the wind was howling, and it reached into our clothing, sucking the liquid out of our bodies and reducing our visibility to perhaps one hundred meters until the distance became a vague, shimmering mass of dust and sand and diffused light. We climbed down into the trench and advanced another two hundred meters until we reached a mud-crusted wooden ladder at the end.

"Up," Patrick pointed. "Do your stand-up and let's get out of here."

So I stood out in the Iranian desert with my back facing the hordes of invisible Iranian soldiers and practiced the couple of sentences I had composed while we were driving. I vaguely remember the concept—that here in the desert between enemy lines, Iraqi troops were battling the elements as much as their enemy, Iran. Patrick shot two or three takes, and then we heard the muffled booms of departing artillery, and Patrick turned me around just in time so I could see the white puffs of smoke.

"Incoming!" he said and dove down into the trench.

Our escort's radio exploded in static just as the shells landed, whistling just beyond us. "We can't go back," he said, indicating the trench we had taken to the front. "Follow me!"

The Iraqi officer scrambled up to the desert floor and fell flat to the ground, where I joined him. Patrick was having problems with the weight of his camera in the heat, so he handed it up to me, then crawled up the rocky dirt to the top. "This way!" our guide said. And then he was off.

Patrick had turned red and could hardly breathe. We had both run out of water, and he was dehydrating quickly. I grabbed him under the shoulder and ran in a crouch after our guide. Patrick stumbled out of my grip and lurched forward, pulled by the weight of the camera. Now we could hear a change in the Iranian artillery. Instead of whistling overhead, it went silent after the thud of the outgoing rounds, and in the next instant, I saw the flash and then heard the sound of the incoming shell, ramming into the trench we had just left. They were bracketing us. Our guide ran toward us and grabbed Patrick under the arms and half-carried, half-dragged him across the open ground as I lugged the camera. All of a sudden the two of them disappeared, and with the heat and the shimmering light and the exploding shells, I thought for an instant they had been vaporized. But my legs kept moving until I crashed down on top of them in a hidden trench.

Despite the unexpected drama for us, the brief shelling was nothing to write home about, as it hit no Iraqi targets. It was a hard, brutal, bloody slog of a war. I would go back to Baghdad and different parts of the front repeatedly, and rarely did it get any better.

22: 'Who's Shipping to Iran?'
Paris

A broad range of characters came streaming through the EDA office on the rue Léon Vaudoyer in the fifteenth arrondissement to meet with Broman and with Cutter when he was around. There was the foulmouthed lawyer from San Francisco hawking used C-130s from Australia, the silver-haired French military pilot who flew DC-3s full of weapons into Chad for French intelligence, a former French Resistance fighter who claimed to have a "nuncle" at the NSA, a portly Greek shipping baron from London, an Israeli arms dealer who claimed he could acquire "anything" from Israeli stockpiles, and the scions of several French noble families who made their livings from their address books. All of them were trying to sell arms to Iran, and all were convinced that the Americans held the keys to the kingdom. Watching them interact with Broman and Cutter was like watching a carefully orchestrated mating ritual among thieves.

Cutter grew progressively suspicious of me and warned his partners to avoid me. But he kept talking. They all did. In fact, they seemed to revel in boasting of their exploits over open phone lines, as if this was further proof that their actions had been approved by the "highest authorities" of the US government.

By the time Broman closed the EDA office for lack of funding in late October, I realized I was sitting on a wealth of material. So I took it to Joel Bernstein, the Paris bureau chief of CBS News where I had been working as a stringer. After a few phone calls, they put me on a TWA flight to New York to discuss the story in person. By the end of November, I had a signed contract with CBS News with a significant advance and was assigned to work with *60 Minutes* producer Bill Wilson and correspondent Bob Simon on a segment devoted to clandestine US arms sales to Iran. We started work on it nearly two full years before the Iran-Contra Initiative became public.

✦ ✦ ✦

Charles Miseroy St. Claire had the tough chin and clear eyes of his Dutch ancestors, and a *crème brulée* complexion he inherited from his Indonesian side. He had just spent several weeks with Iranian arms buyers, first in Vienna, then in Geneva. Now he was driving to Paris to finalize shipping and financial arrangements on his latest deal with Cutter. He agreed to meet me at 5:00 PM in the lobby of the Paris Hilton for drinks two weeks before Christmas. A *60 Minutes* cameraman was hiding behind a forest of potted palms, and I was wired for sound.

I had rehearsed repeatedly with producer Bill Wilson how I was to get St. Claire talking about the deal he was negotiating to sell the Iranians a dozen Bell AH-1G Huey Cobra helicopter gunships. According to St. Claire, the choppers were sitting in a hangar on the military side of the Frankfurt airport and were controlled by the CIA. That was why he was coming to Paris: he believed Cutter's CIA connections could get them released. They also were closing a deal for eighty M48A5 tanks, the same tanks Cutter mentioned in the pro forma invoice he had sent me in Egypt an eternity ago. Cutter claimed the tanks were in Israel, but St. Claire believed they were sitting in a NATO depot in the Netherlands.

St. Claire had telephoned when he was with the Iranians a few weeks earlier. "I have seen the money with my own eyes," he told me. "They have between five hundred million and a billion dollars in blocked accounts at the Crédit Suisse, and it's all there just to buy guns!" That was the type of quote Bill wanted me to get now—on camera.

Our plan was simple: as soon as I saw St. Claire coming through the front door, I was to whisper into the microphone taped inside my suit and indicate to the cameraman where he was. I would then stand up, careful not to expose the wires, so St. Claire would see me and come over. We would shake hands, I'd order drinks, then we would sink into the gigantic leather armchairs in our isolated area of the lobby near the elevators. And I would gradually lead him to the water and see if he would drink.

By 5:15 PM, I was a wreck. St. Claire had not arrived. I whispered into the mike if I could get up and walk over to the front desk to see if he had left a message. The cameraman shook his head, so I stayed put for another fifteen minutes. Even though it was winter, I was sticky with sweat beneath my suit and tie.

Finally, at six o'clock, I got up and went to the front desk. St. Claire had in fact called just a few minutes earlier and left a message for me with the concierge, saying he wouldn't arrive until late that night. So we moved to Plan B, which was for me to record my telephone conversations with him and Cutter until we saw another opportunity to get them on camera. With no equivalent of Radio Shack in France, I jury-rigged a French telephone cable to an RCA jack and plugged it into my mini-cassette recorder.

That night, Cutter called me to find out where St. Claire was. I asked him how the tank deal was going. It was as if he knew that I was taping the conversation.

"I just sent my man out there to get that first eighty out, and I don't think they'll get out before the first of the year. Once that's shipped out of Israel, we'll look to the balance. The total is about seven hundred units. How many will pass inspection, God only knows. The figure of three hundred is probably realistic—probably another eighty could come out of Israel. The rest are in Korea."

"What about the embargo?" I asked.

"Who's shipping to Iran?" Cutter said. "Do you know anyone who is shipping to Iran? I don't."

"Where are they shipping to, then?"

"A lot of places. There's Turkey, Pakistan. There's Saudi, the Emirates. There's Latin America. Nobody's doing business with Iran. Where did you get that from?"

Uh-oh, I thought; he's on to me. But if we were going to get a *60 Minutes* piece out of this, I had to get him saying the word, Iran. I tried another tact.

"So it's being processed in other ways?"

Cutter seemed not to hear me, but he came back to Iran like a dog that smells rotting meat in the forest.

"There really is a change taking place over there. It's a concerted effort. You can expect something to happen within three months. I expect, sooner."

I knew he was referring to the rumors swirling around Ayatollah Khomeini's health. Just ten days ago, former president Bani Sadr had told me that two French cardiologists had flown to Tehran after Khomeini had a heart attack, and a number of newspapers had run with the story.

"Is that related to this deal?" I asked.

"I don't know. What deal? There are lots of deals. This thing has to be supported with a lot of deals. There are more channels than one. I'm only concerned with what we have on the books because I think the stuff that's coming in is going to be free, where we just don't make any money on it. I don't even have any glory or anything. I would say we have less than thirty or forty days to deliver stuff—after that, it's all going to be free."

Better, I thought. But still not conclusive.

Almost as soon as Cutter hung up, St. Claire called to tell me he had finally made it to the Paris Hilton. We talked about the recent hijacking of a Kuwaiti airliner to Tehran, during which the hijackers had killed two Americans. That same day, the *Atlanta Journal-Constitution* ran a story of mine revealing that two of the hijackers had been part of the team that had hijacked an Air France flight to Tehran four months earlier that Iran claimed they had arrested.

"Our friends in the US are running scared because of the hijacking," St. Claire said. "Today is the wrong time for this kind of deal. Believe me, I know."

"I was just speaking with Paul, and he didn't seem particularly worried," I said.

"Look, I have a very grave concern about this whole thing," St. Claire said. "And I'll tell you what my grave concern is. That somebody is ripping somebody off. If the government of Iran is being ripped off by the middleman, then you've got a helluva problem on your hands. And there's this guy, Paul Cutter, sitting all alone by himself out in California."

The last time I had seen St. Claire, just before I went to New York to meet with the CBS News execs, he had shown me a pro forma invoice for eighty M48A5 tanks that Cutter had sent him, where he had upped the price from $750,000 to $1.7 million each.

"You told me it was the Ayatollah's son who'd asked that the higher price appear in the documents. For kickbacks."

"Look, I can BS with the best of them. You're a journalist. Just watch out how you use that information," St. Claire said.

I realized then that he was putting me on notice: if there was a leak in their operation, they knew it would be coming from me.

23: Blacklisted by Saddam
Baghdad

I was becoming a regular at the Palestine Méridien Hotel in Baghdad, with its fresh French pastries, exquisite filet mignons, and well-stocked (but often over-cooked) wine cellar. By now, I had learned the dos and don'ts of working as a foreign reporter in Saddam Hussein's Iraq, a very different place from free-wheeling Lebanon or even despotic Syria.

For one thing, I never wrote down the name of my sources. That lesson I learned on my first trip to the Iraqi capital, when two of my notebooks "disappeared" from my hotel bureau drawer while I was at dinner. I complained to the hotel manager, and a few hours later he called me down to his office to reiterate my complaint to a plainclothes security officer, who promised he would interrogate the entire hotel staff to find my missing property. It wasn't hard to imagine what that would look like, and a rush of guilt came over me as I thought of the Filipino chambermaids and Pakistani bagboys. I wasn't supposed to have called their bluff, so now they were calling mine.

"I'm sure it's just an honest mistake," I said. "Maybe I left them down at the bar. I'm sure they will turn up."

And turn up they did, three days later—in exactly the same drawer between the same two shirts where I had left them. Of course, by now, every page had been copied. I don't think the Iraqi goons were able to extract much of use, since during that trip I had stayed with my "minder" pretty much the whole time. The only unscripted comments, written hastily in a stall in the toilet outside the hotel bar, were nearly indecipherable even for me. And they concerned what was becoming my favorite Baghdad story: French arms sales.

Truth be told, the Iraqis were actually eager for the world to know more about their growing arms relationship to the French. I was getting extensive briefings from the Iraqi ambassador and his military attaché in Paris, and the glossy embassy newsletter regularly carried stories about how the Iraqi Air Force had launched a "tanker war" against Iran's oil exports in the Gulf using French-supplied Exocet missiles. From the French defense industry types, however, I heard a substantially different story, and that was one of the reasons I was back in Baghdad in late January and early February, as the Iranians geared up for their annual human-wave offensive.

By now, I had spent a full year learning the French arms industry. I knew the companies and was on a first-name basis with their flaks and key marketing officials. In many cases, I had toured production plants normally off-limits to foreigners. I met their overseas reps at international arms exhibits, such as the first Cairo International Defense Exhibition that I had covered the summer before. These were the guys who were their eyes and ears on the ground in sensitive places. Here in Baghdad, we all knew there was no such thing as an "innocent" meeting, so except for the military attachés and the embassy officials, I never met any sources in their offices. Instead, we spoke in whispers on hotel balconies, sometimes for hours. Or even better, in the noisy bar at the Méridien.

In addition to my regular gig with the *Atlanta Journal-Constitution* and shooting video footage of the front for CBS News (I had written the CBS instructions for booking satellites and the names of our official contacts in Baghdad in large clear letters for all to see on the inside cover of a notebook), I now had a letter of introduction from a glossy French defense magazine. They had offered to pay a small fortune—close to $10,000—for a feature story on French arms sales to Iraq, and they specifically wanted me to interview French technicians and military trainers in Baghdad. The magazine was well known, and all the French companies were regular advertisers. So that letter really loosened tongues. Part of it was occasioned by a commercial rivalry between the French and the Americans. Except for the Exocet missile, which became infamous during the Falklands war when the Argentinean Air Force used it to sink the British destroyer *HMS Sheffield*, French weaponry had not been tested in war. To the arms salesmen, I was free advertising. And Iraq was not just their biggest client; for many of them, it was their *only* client.

I took pages and pages of notes during these long, whispered conversations. Often, the defense techs would notice I had written something down incorrectly, so they would jot in my notebook the previously unknown configuration of the new Mirage F1s that the French had just begun to deliver two months earlier.[17] They made sure I got the correct spelling of the Cyrano twelve-mode fire control radar made by Thomson-CSF. And they began talking of Iraqi plans to purchase the latest French fighter jet, the Mirage 2000, and perhaps even assemble it locally.

"General Amir has big plans," one of the corporate reps involved in these talks told me. "He's been put in charge of the Scientific Research Council, a new group that is handling all future military projects. You should see him while you are here."

Now that I had a name, I began asking all of them who he was. A guy from Thomson was telling me about Saad 13, the top-secret military electronics factory they had built near ad Dour, a rural area just south of Tikrit known for its ironclad support for Saddam. When I mentioned the general's name, he paused. He must have counted until thirty before he said anything, visibly trying to figure out how much I knew. "You can't put anything past General Amir," he said finally. "If you walk into his office holding a set of electronic schematics and pretend it's something that it's not, he'll call you out. He can read the damn things upside down!"

And this general who stayed out of the limelight—no one even whispered his last name at this point—was in charge of the whole she-bang. He was their bread and butter, their lunch and dinner. He was smoked salmon and caviar and retirement in St. Tropez. The French were close to finalizing a monumental arms package with General Amir worth 50 billion francs—around $6 billion with a vastly overvalued dollar. It was

---

17   They were known as "EQ5," for the Exocet version, and "EQ6" for an even more sophisticated fire control radar capable of launching a laser-guided missile, the AS-30L, that later would get me—and the French—in so much trouble.

the biggest single arms sales agreement the French had ever negotiated. He was champagne every day for the rest of their lives.

So *you bet* I wanted to meet General Amir.

The man from Thomson told me how. "You must go through Section Six. That's a military intelligence unit that monitors our access to General Amir. In Arabic, they call it *sirballa*."

He was kind enough to draw me a map and to make sure I understood exactly how to get there. He even gave me the name of the major in charge of liaison and his phone number!

Even though we were in the middle of a war, in many ways, it didn't feel like the middle of a war. I had recently stopped smoking and had taken up jogging and so went for long jogs before dinner along the Tigris just as the fish restaurants were stoking charcoal braziers to cook the giant greasy river carp known as *masgouf*. Every so often, an enterprising waiter would trot after me to get me to patronize his restaurant. All the while, I was shadowed by a green and white Mercedes full of plainclothes minders from the *moukhabarat*, who kept shaking their heads at my bizarre behavior. Why would anybody choose to run if they weren't being chased by someone with a gun? They glided after me on a separate paved track that ran parallel to the riverside promenade. All the strollers knew to stay away from them.

But I saw things during these jogs. I drank in the ubiquitous posters of Saddam Hussein, plastered over the lintel of every shop and eating establishment like a swash of blood to keep the Angel of Death at bay. I noticed the young men with their equally ubiquitous Saddam moustaches lingering on the sidewalks, smoking, always dressed in clean shirts, mysteriously idle, watching. One evening, I saw a Roland missile launcher being moved in a small convoy across the river from the presidential palace. The Roland was the upscale French version of the Hawk, which the US shipped to Iran via Israel during Iran-Contra. This one was mounted on an eight-wheeled truck. When I mentioned it to the Thomson guy, he nearly freaked out. "That's part of CORAD," he said.

"What's that?"

"*Centre d'Opérations Roland Air Defense*. When it's finished, it will mesh Iraq's Soviet, Italian, and French radar into an integrated system for the control and defense of the entire national air space. This is a NATO-grade program, with hardened fiber-optic links, buried command-and-control bunkers, and multiple redundancies. It's designed to withstand a full-scale air assault by a modern air force. Think, Israel."

Or, as it turned out, the United States.[18]

+ + +

The chief minder assigned to me was named Fuad. His official job was to set up my "program": trips to the front and interviews with Iraqi officials who pretended to have authority they didn't have. I spent much of the daytime hours with him, going from one office to the next, learning little. We would say good-bye to each other at around 6:00 PM. And then the real work began, and I would meet the arms salesmen.

If I was going to visit Section 6, it would have to be during office hours. That meant ditching Fuad. So I mulled over several ideas until I came up with what I thought was a workable plan.

That morning, I mixed it up a bit. Instead of meeting Fuad at 9:00 AM in the hotel dining room after breakfast, I sauntered in through the front door a half hour late and joined him in the lobby.

"Where have you been?" he asked, clearly angry.

"I was out for a walk."

"We must be at the foreign ministry by 10:00 AM. We must hurry."

Both he and I knew there was no need to hurry for anything. It wasn't as if the place was crawling with foreign journalists or that the Iraqi PR machine was suddenly stretched to the limits because of a public scandal. After the deputy foreign ministry droned on for ninety minutes about Israel seeking to keep the Arab world in a perpetual state of underdevelopment, and that was why Israel was backing Iran in the war, we returned to the car and headed back to the hotel.

It was just after 11:30 AM. Our next appointment was at 12:45 PM with the president of the People's Assembly, an appointed body of Saddam Hussein lackeys that resembled an elected parliament like

---

18 CORAD was the successor to a 1981 contract the French codenamed KARI (Iraq spelled backwards in French). It integrated thousands of Soviet-supplied AAA fire units with sophisticated French radar and the Roland-2 missiles using buried fiber-optic communications links. When I told the air attaché at the U.S. Embassy in Paris about CORAD a few years later during the build-up to Operation Desert Storm, he was visibly shocked. The French had never whispered a word about it in all the conversations he'd had with them about their arms deliveries to Saddam. He made sure that changed, and the initial waves of US attack aircraft rolled into Iraq like limos on the New York Thruway once our Apache attack helicopters flying nap-of-the-earth in the dead of night knocked out the CORAD radar and the buried command, control, communications (C3) bunkers. I will return to my contribution to the war effort in a later chapter.

masgouf resembled *sole meunière*. On the ride back to the hotel, I asked our driver, Adel, to stop the car so I could walk.

"What are you doing?" Fuad said.

"Just getting some exercise. I'll see you back at the hotel in an hour. I know the way."

Fuad grudgingly let me get out, and I watched the two of them drive off. Once they entered the traffic, I walked out to the median of the divided expressway and ran to the other side and hailed an orange and white cab. I gave the driver the name of the intersection where Section 6 was located and pumped my legs as he took off.

When we turned onto the side street the man from Thomson had given me, I paid the driver and got out. There was no mistaking where we were.

Section 6 was headquartered in a low-slung box of a villa secluded behind an eight-foot wall with a guard shack outside. Even though it was mid-February, the temperature was already in the low eighties, the sun was hot, and the corrugated tin made the air shimmer. The guard had the door open to get some air. He came out as I approached the gate.

"I'm here to see Major Zuhair," I said. "For General Amir."

"Fadlak, habibi," he said, gesturing for me to go inside. The magic names had done the trick.

Inside, the villa resembled a doctor's waiting room, with cheap plastic chairs ringing the walls and a few end tables covered in magazines. A uniformed lieutenant sat behind a metal desk, and a European I didn't recognize was patiently waiting, expensive leather briefcase at his side.

"I'm here for Major Zuhair," I repeated. "To see General Amir."

"Ah," he said, nodding. "General Amir, not here."

"That's okay. I need to see Major Zuhair to set up a meeting."

"Wait, mister," he said. He went to the door leading to an office inside, knocked twice, then, bowing his head, he pulled the door shut behind him. It's remarkable how in a military dictatorship no one asks you for identification or even your name. If I was able to find my way to this unmarked office and knew the name of the man inside, clearly I must have business there. No one else would be crazy enough to show up.

Just as I was thinking I had aced it, I glanced through the window and saw Fuad and Adel talking to the guard outside. The guard pointed in my direction, and Fuad must have seen me at that point because he ducked back behind the tin shack out of sight.

Damn, I thought. He's better than I thought. Or maybe crossing the street and hailing a cab in the opposite direction had been a bit too obvious, and when he didn't see me behind him, he simply ordered Adel to make a U-turn.

The lieutenant ushered me in to see Major Zuhair, leaving the European with his attaché case wondering who I must be. He pointedly refused to look at me while we waited. Not even a covert glance.

"Do you have an appointment?" the major asked me in perfect English.

"No. But I am here to do a story on the State Organization of Technical Industries for a French defense magazine, and everybody tells me that General Amir is the man I've got to see."

He scrutinized the letter I handed to him, wrote down my name, and then handed it back to me. "This is something you need to set up from Paris."

"I understand. But I didn't realize before I left that General Amir was the man in charge. It would be great if he would talk to me. I can guarantee you we'll give him a good spread!"

The major didn't laugh, but as he got up to see me to the door, he nodded with grudging admiration. "Well, you found us. I will call you if anything comes up. Where is your car?"

We had walked right past the European with his attaché case and were now facing the guard shack. Fuad and Adel were nowhere in sight.

"I took a taxi," I said.

"No, I meant the Information Ministry car."

"I don't know. They're probably out on the street somewhere."

We shook hands, and I went out on the street. I could see Fuad and Adel inside the closed guardhouse, sweating buckets. Since I had played the game of ditching them, they apparently intended to return the favor. I waited a good ten minutes for them to come out and drive me back to the hotel, but they stayed put, sweltering in their pride.

I met them back at the hotel lobby. Fuad was dark with rage.

"Your program is over," he said.

"We can still go see the president of the People's Assembly if you like," I said.

"No. Your program is finished for today."

"You know, Fuad, reporters can only write what they can see."

"Sure."

"So if we can see nothing…."

The prospect of foreign reporters seeing nothing made his face light up. "Then you will write nothing?"

"Wrong. We will write about the things that we were not allowed to see."

"Never mind. As far as the army is concerned, everything is secret. We cannot let you see anything."

+ + +

My informants had given me an additional critical piece of intelligence: the man now responsible for negotiating the details of the 50-billion-franc arms package, General Bernard Carlier, had just arrived in Baghdad and was staying in room 1010 of the Rashid Hotel.

The Rashid became famous during the two Iraq wars as the government-owned caravansary where foreign journalists were required to stay. In the mid-1980s, though, the few reporters who visited Baghdad preferred the Méridien, and not just because of the food, the bar, or the fauna that gathered on the pool deck. The expats all believed that the Rashid was equipped with a giant, well-staffed basement, off-limits to ordinary mortals, where interpreters fluent in a variety of European languages manned banks of reel-to-reel tape decks wearing giant headsets, taking notes. Listening devices were embedded in the air conditioning vents, the lights, and the consoles around the bedsteads, all designed by the East German Stasi or the Romanian Securitate, or so the expat mythology had it. Even in the Méridien, people with information would only talk in the bar or on balconies.

If I could get General Carlier to confirm the story—or even just to respond to his name—it would be front-page news back in Paris.

I knew I had to tread lightly. Carlier's predecessor, General René Audran, had been gunned down outside his Paris home just two weeks earlier, apparently an Iranian-government hit subcontracted to Action Directe, a hard-left anti-NATO terrorist group. The Iranians didn't reproach Audran for selling arms to the Iraqis but for promising to sell weapons to Iran and backing out of the deal (the same sin committed by Swedish premier Olof Palme, who was gunned down in Stockholm one year later). Audran had been scheduled to travel to Baghdad while

I was there to sign the 50-billion-franc contract. Carlier was his last-minute replacement.

Both Audran and Carlier worked for the Direction Générale de l'Armement (DGA), a miracle of the French bureaucratic mind that was totally foreign to the Pentagon. The DGA was run by a small cadre of technocrats, most of them civilians, who combined engineering expertise with management skills. They oversaw the French state-run arsenals, as well as overall defense R&D and procurement. Audran and Carlier were in charge of foreign arms sales and worked under a civilian armaments engineer, Henri Conze. I had interviewed the convivial, wily, Gauloises-chain-smoking, pro-American Conze several times, thanks to an introduction from Colonel Broman.

I caught up with him just as he was leaving his room in the Rashid Hotel.

"*Ah, mon Général Carlier,*" I addressed him in French.

He did an abrupt about-face, a look of astonishment on his face. I introduced myself and said I was doing a feature article on French arms sales to Iraq and understood he had come to Baghdad to sign the 50-billion-franc arms deal.

"How did you find me?" he said.

"I have many friends. Including Henri Conze."

He nervously looked in both directions, then fixed me with steely eyes. "*Monsieur,* I don't know you," he said. "But keep your mouth shut until I get back to Paris the day after tomorrow."

He ran off down the hall before I could shake his hand. But I had all the confirmation I needed.

✦ ✦ ✦

When I returned to Paris, I ran my final traps. I bounced information I had learned in Baghdad from Thomson, the radar-manufacturer, off the guys from Dassault, who produced the aircraft. I took the information from Dassault's Baghdad rep and bounced it off the folks at Aérospatiale and Matra, who made the missiles that equipped the Iraqi Mirages. In Baghdad, the reps generally talked amongst themselves, so even if they wouldn't discuss what they themselves were doing, they knew everything about their colleagues and were happy to share it. As I polished off the rough edges, the story took shape.

"There's no way I can run this," the editor who had offered me the ten grand told me. "Our advertisers will go nuts. The Defense Ministry will kill me."

So he offered me a substantial "kill" fee, and I took it to his competitor, who published it as a cover package six weeks later.[19]

Meanwhile, I went to Jacques Isnard, the defense correspondent at *Le Monde*, and gave him a rundown of what I had learned. At first, he scribbled a few notes. Then he seemed to zone out and sketched tiny circles in the air above his notebook with his pen as he worked through something in his mind.

"Don't tell me any more," he said finally, tossing down his pen. "Get me a draft, *quatre feuillets*, and I'll run it by my editors." These were the days before word processors, so length was still measured in the number of double-spaced pages—four, in this case.

I returned the next day with my copy and met him in the same cramped office. His desk was stacked with newspapers, and the bookshelves held an entire library of SIPRI yearbooks and Janes defense reference volumes on armored vehicles, ships, and aircraft, each of them weighing about fifty pounds. The smoke from his Gauloises had gone blue from the sodium lights outside, vainly trying to shed light on the miserable late winter afternoon. He read my copy without a word, then stabbed out his cigarette and got up before he had even finished the first page.

"Wait here," he said.

It was a Thursday. *Le Monde*'s inventive publication schedule required its readers to engage in a mental calculus to determine when the events it reported transpired. The issue published today at noon bore Friday's date. We always joked that *Le Monde* was the only newspaper in the world where you could get yesterday's news dated tomorrow.

Ten minutes later, Isnard returned and told me his editors wanted to run my story on the front page above the fold that weekend. Over the next hour or so, we went over the text, with Isnard making a few minor corrections. By the time we were done, the French remained pretty much as I had written it. (As a former lit major, I found *Le Monde*'s literary style, with its subordinate clauses and gerundives, easy to imitate).

The story was a bombshell and gave me my first Andy Warhol fifteen seconds of fame. Titled innocuously, "Iran-Iraq, the war of the cities," the

---

19   "Do Arms Hold the Key to Success in Iraq?" *Défense & Armement*, April 1985.

subtitle carried the real message: "Baghdad's army can't exploit the power of the weapons delivered by France."

I began, French-style, with an anecdote.

"Commenting on Iraq's technological superiority, a foreign military attaché in Baghdad recently said: 'The officers of Iran's regular army are better trained and more motivated than the Iraqis. Think of something very smart that is technically feasible, and you can be sure the Iranians are figuring out how to do it. The Iraqis have never had this type of initiative. If they had been able—for example, to launch a real offensive—the war would have been over years ago.'"

Ouch. And that came from one of Saddam's *friends.*

The problem, I noted, always quoting those unnamed foreign military attaches, was "the heavy-handed control of the Baath Party over the Iraqi armed forces." The Air Force was arguably the worst, with political "commissars" assigned to each squadron who would choose the targets before every mission. "They will use four MiG-23s to destroy a machine-gun nest, while flying alongside an Iranian troop convoy without firing a shot, because the convoy wasn't in their op order," an unnamed "expert" told me.

Isnard and his editors had no problem with my unnamed "experts" and the foreign military attachés. They knew exactly who I had been talking to, if not by name at least by function. And they could smell the truth when it was dished up like three-day old fish on their plate.

I went on to explain that Iraqi pilots would drop their bombs from ten thousand feet rather than take the risk of losing aircraft by conducting close air support. Even worse, they were missing their targets with the fabled Exocet missile—by a long shot. "In 1984, Iraq claimed to have hit 67 merchant ships in the Gulf, but only 24 of those strikes were confirmed by maritime sources," I wrote. In January, the ratio was even worse: six confirmed hits out of out of twenty-six Exocet launches.

The Iraqis stockpiled ultra-sensitive infrared seekers in crude hangars in the desert, exposed to the sand-filled *khamsin* winds; because Saddam and the conspiracy-minded Baathists who surrounded him feared the technicians might get too close to their foreign mentors, as soon as they were trained how to maintain one piece of equipment, they were moved to another unit and ordered to service something different.

To cover their failings, the Iraqis blamed the French: bad equipment, insufficient maintenance, and defective spare parts, self-serving accusations that made the French furious. I got an earful of that while I was in Baghdad. This article—and the more detailed feature piece than ran the following month—was my hat-tip to my sources: I heard you.

I ended the *Le Monde* piece in classic French style, with hard intel disguised as analysis. "The French government has never been entirely at ease with its arms sales to Iraq," I wrote, "to the point that French defense contractors had to insist with the government to extend generous credit to Iraq to open the way to new contracts, such as the Mirage 2000."[20]

+ + +

I broke the story about the negotiations over the new $6 billion arms contract in *Jane's Defence Weekly* two weeks later, then fleshed out the themes from *Le Monde* in a feature story in *Défense & Armement*. My sources in the French defense industry—many of them now friends— loved it. For one thing, it helped them push back against the Iraqis, who had been demanding billions of French francs in damages for allegedly "defective" weaponry the French had delivered. But it also assuaged their pride. When I covered the Paris Air Show that summer for the French-language *Show Daily*, all the champagne bars along the chalet line at Le Bourget opened to me. Each morning as I made my rounds, I plotted out exactly where I would be at midday to get the best access to the most secretive officials, with a fabulous lunch thrown in. I even arranged with friends at Dassault for a special Saturday lunch with my two children, Julian and Clio, so they could watch the air show from the balcony of the chalet. It was an experience they never forgot and that we repeated many times. And a jolly time was had by all.

But the Iraqis hated me for it. When my new editor at *Défense & Armement*, Stéphane Ferrard, asked the Iraqi Defense Minister for an interview to respond to my article, the Embassy didn't merely reject his request: they told Ferrard that his magazine, and me in particular, were banned from Iraq until further notice.

Blacklisted by Saddam Hussein. That was a distinction worth wearing on my sleeve, it seemed to me.

---

20 "Iran-Irak: Guerre des Villes. L'Armée de Baghdad ne sait pas exploiter la puissance des armements livrés par la France," *Le Monde*, March 17–18, 1985.

At the time, I was dating the Iraqi military attaché's secretary, an Assyrian woman named Marie. After a lovely dinner she prepared for me in her small flat in a non-descript building just beyond the Périphérique, we wound up where one usually ends up at such moments. We never "talked shop" beyond the purely logistical questions of visas and flights and hotels for my trips to Baghdad, which she helped to clear. She never once asked me a question about who I had interviewed in Baghdad, and I never quizzed her on her attitude toward Saddam's regime. I thought we genuinely enjoyed each other's company, as well as a certain physical compatibility. I loved her throaty accent in French. I loved her dancing eyes. I loved the sharp aquiline features of her face, and the rest of her, as well. So there she was, hands firmly on my shoulders, rising up at the waist, and suddenly she stopped moving and bore into my eyes with a penetrating, earnest, and thoroughly unerotic question:

"*Pour qui tu roules, Ken?*"

"*Pour qui je roule?*"

"*Ouai. Pour qui? C'est louche ce que tu fais.*"

I was floored. She turned her face back and forth as she stared down at me, as if driving in a knife. *Who was I working for?* As in, what intelligence agency had me in their employ?

"Nobody," I said. "Me."

"I don't believe you."

"You don't have to," I said. And with that, I got up, got dressed, and left her apartment.

I saw her a couple of times after that at Iraqi embassy cocktail parties or receptions but never again engaged her in conversation. The idea that she had been used by her government to extract information from me and that her sexual favors had been purchased, not given freely, was the biggest turnoff I had ever experienced.

Many years later, I would learn much about Iraq's captive Christian population and the compromises many of them committed in order to survive, first under Saddam, later under the Kurds. But this was my first encounter with *une hirondelle*[21]—or, as we say less poetically in English, a honey trap. It stung me to think I was such an easy play.

---

21 Literally, "a swallow."

Chapter 5:
Need Juice

24: Iran-Contra, the Real Beginning
Paris

After several weeks island-hopping in Greece, I returned to Paris in August to investigate a story I had heard whispered on balconies in Baghdad: Saddam was building the bomb. The evidence was fragmentary. One source provided me with a detailed briefing on a series of underground air bases the Iraqi Air Force had built to shelter their aircraft from a nuclear blast. He gave me the name of the builder, a Belgian company called Sixco, the location of each base, and a vivid description of how the aircraft started takeoff underground, brakes on, with seven meters of concrete to protect the facility from the blast of their white-hot afterburners. "The planes are airborne by the time they emerge from the underground runway," he said.

The Saudis had spent $12.5 billion to build similar anti-nuclear aircraft shelters and a deeply buried command bunker beneath King Khaled Military College to rival Cheyenne Mountain in the US. My source provided a schematic drawing of the underground Saudi command bunker, which *Défense & Armement* reproduced when it ran my piece that fall. Sparking this wave of nuclear blast-proof construction were secret nuclear weapons programs in both Iran and Iraq, I wrote, with details that later were confirmed by UN arms inspectors in Iraq. The Iranian part of the nuclear equation remained a secret for another twelve years.[22]

At the end of September 1985, I received a call from CBS News in New York, hiring me to investigate a story their State Department producer, Charlie Wolfson, had been working out of Tel Aviv. It seems Wolfson had stumbled on a joint US-French plan to spring the hostages in Lebanon. They knew by this point that the hostage-takers were all controlled by Tehran, so the plan was to purchase their release by delivering weapons to Iran. Since I had already been working on a similar story for the past year with *60 Minutes*, New York thought it natural to bring me in.

---

22   "The Race to Armageddon," *Défense & Armement*, November 1985.

129

The spark for Wolfson came when a DC-8 registered to an apparent CIA proprietary in Miami took off from Tabriz, Iran, disappeared over Turkey, and resurfaced in Tel Aviv. Sources in Israel told him that several Americans got off the plane, including an official from the National Security Council, who disappeared into the US Embassy before the plane flew off to the Ivory Coast. The *Times* of London was reporting that a second CIA plane, a Boeing 707, had made two trips from Israel to Iran via Malaga, Spain, carrying 1,250 TOW missiles on each rotation. In the month preceding the "mystery" flights, the *Times* reported, a high ranking NSC official was seen on several occasions in London, meeting the Secretary General of Israel's Foreign Ministry, David Kimche, a former Mossad officer.

CBS News identified the NSC official who met with Kimche as Jock Covey and told me they believed the planes had been flown by Israeli military pilots. They wanted to know what more I could find out about this alleged US-Iran arms pipeline through Israel.

My first call was to Claude Lang, one of the French arms brokers I had met while working for European Defense Associates the year before. Lang was the former French resistance fighter who claimed to have a "nuncle" at the National Security Agency. He spoke with a deep nasal twang that reminded me of a meat grinder.

"Did you hear about Paul?" he said.

"Hear what?"

"He's been arrested. In Orlando."

"Orlando? What in the world was he doing there?"

I had never heard Cutter mention Orlando—or even Florida, for that matter—as a market stall in the global arms bazaar. I was genuinely surprised.

"It was a Customs sting. He went there to buy TOW missiles."

When I remained silent for too long, Lang added, "Natela warned me when I got back from vacation in August."

Natela was Paul's twenty-something daughter who was attending the American University of Paris. Paul had introduced me to her briefly, if reluctantly, and made sure that I kept my distance from her, which I did. She hadn't called me, that's for sure.

"That wasn't your deal, was it?" I asked.

"I don't know anything about TOWs," Lang growled.

Neither Lang nor his French partners had been indicted or approached by any US official, suggesting that Cutter had a new channel to the Iranians. "I was shocked to hear the news. I had always thought he was officially supported by the US government," Lang added.

That was what Cutter had always claimed, of course. So had Broman. So had all of them.

Next I called Nour Bizri, a Lebanese businessman who claimed he had become personal friends with Ahmad Khomeini, the Ayatollah's son. I knew he had been negotiating with Cutter for tanks and aircraft for Iran. He had always been suspicious of me because I was a reporter, but he took my call.

"I put up the performance bond for those TOWs," Bizri said. "Paul never paid us. He sold those TOWs and I never saw a dime."

I wasn't sure how much of that was true, but soon I discovered that Bizri's partner, Charles St. Claire, had been arrested in Southern California as part of the same sting operation—the same St. Claire I had been hoping to surprise in a hidden camera interview at the Paris Hilton the year before.

The plot thickened.

25: 'That's the Sound of Freedom'
Johannesburg

It was always great to get out of Paris in the autumn, when the cold rains came and a cinderblock sky descended on the city until it crushed the Seine and the damp reached through windows and doors into your bones. This year I was headed due south to the other side of the Equator, where it was late spring. *Défense & Armement* had commissioned me to do a spread on Armscor, the national arms manufacturing establishment of the Republic of South Africa, the original embargo-buster.

I had reservations about the trip, worried that somehow just by showing up in South Africa I would be lending support to the apartheid regime. But that soon gave way to pure fascination. There was so much to see and to learn and to absorb; and Jo'burg was no Baghdad. When I jogged through the streets in the early evening, no regime goons trailed behind me in a green Mercedes.

Farny, my Armscor guide and companion for much of the three weeks I was there, could have leapt out of the pages of Rudyard Kipling, right down to the singsong accent of the high veld. With his pencil-thin reddish beard and green eyes cross-hatched from decades of squinting into the austral sun, he embodied the frontier mentality that drove the Afrikaners to protect the claim they had staked to the Cape even at the cost of international shunning. We had a nonstop discussion over three weeks about apartheid and what would come afterwards, a future he and most of his compatriots knew was inevitable.

"We are not a country of racial groups but of minorities," he said. "Even if Mandela became president, there'd be no change in the economic situation of blacks. Minorities practice apartheid among themselves." Prophetic? No, just insightful.

Later I would meet Kwazulu Chief Mangosuthu Buthelezi, where I heard much more on this score. While Mandela and the African National Congress dismissed him as a collaborator of the white apartheid regime, Buthelezi dismissed *them* as communist stooges who were collaborating with the Soviets and Cubans in Namibia and Angola to transform South Africa into a Soviet base.

Farny and I flew and drove all over the country. We went up to Durban on the east coast to visit the naval shipyard. We went down to Cape Town to visit a missile plant. We flew in a six-seat crop duster far into the northwest, landing at a tiny airstrip in the middle of the vast savannah that stretched inland from the South African coast up into Namibia, which Farny referred to as "South-West."[23]

The South African Defense Force had beaten back a massive Soviet-backed offensive in Namibia earlier that year. As chief of staff General J. J. Geldenhuys explained to me in Pretoria, they even captured Soviet officers when they overran the guerilla bases of the South West Africa People's Organization, SWAPO. The embarrassment made the Soviets a bit gun shy after that, which is why they pushed their Cuban brothers to the front lines. Farny played coy when I asked him where exactly we had landed. I knew we had flown deep into the bush of Namibia, but how far north exactly was a mystery. He had arranged for me to take part in a live training exercise of the 4th South African Infantry Brigade on their 155mm G-5 guns. Armscor was very proud of these towed howitzers, which they had developed using the base-bleed patents of renegade

---

23   As in South West Africa, the name it was known by while still a German colony.

ballistics engineer Gerald Bull. With its unusually long 45 caliber barrel, the G-5 could hit targets forty-two kilometers away, nearly ten kilometers farther than any gun in U.S. inventory—or in Iran's, for that matter.

"I hear the Austrians have a similar gun they developed with Mister Bull," Farny said. "But when the Iraqis started using them on the battlefield, the barrels melted after a hundred rounds. Something tells me they have been looking for a replacement."

Iraq and Iran always lurked at the back of our discussions. The war between the two had sparked a boom market for defense contractors around the world. The rumor in Baghdad was that the Iraqis had sent a buying team to South Africa the year before to try out the G-5 guns and were so impressed that they had purchased them on the spot.

"In fact," Farny said with a wink, "I am told that General Janoob himself flew up here last year. You might want to ask Major Jacobs about that when we get back to base."

We had driven out into the bush to meet field artillery commander, Major Swanepoel ("Swaney"). He had propped himself in the passenger seat of an armored car, one leg on the ground, a cup of tea on the dashboard, giving quiet commands in Afrikaans into the radio when we arrived. A moment later, eight trucks towing the giant 155mm howitzers roared over the horizon, kicking up dust. When the first one started maneuvering into firing position just behind us in the bush, Swaney pointed to my watch. "Mobility is the key to good gunnery, as our Iraqi friends know. They're supposed to be able to do this in seven minutes or less. Why don't you keep track?"

One after the other, the gun crews jumped out of the cabs and went to work. I counted the seconds it took the troopies to dig the stabilizing spades into the dry red earth and lower the firing plates. I counted minutes more as they brought up the white bag propellant and placed the plastic-cased high-explosive round into the semiautomatic loader, which rammed it home. The whole idea, Swaney explained, was for the gun crew to get in, fire a barrage, and get the hell out before the enemy located them and fired back.

Seven minutes to the second after the last gun arrived, they were all in position. The eight team commanders stood at attention along the gun line, waiting for Swaney's command.

"Want to do the honors, Mister Timmerman?" he said.

I glanced at Farny to see if he really meant it. For an instant, the thought crossed my mind that we might actually be in range of the SWAPO or Cuban forces and that this might not be just an exercise. After all, why go to all this trouble of deploying an entire artillery battery just for a visiting journalist?

But Farny reassured me that they were serious, and he steered me over to the first howitzer and instructed the gun commander to hand me the cord. "You will want these," he said, handing me a pair of foam earplugs.

The commander had a loudspeaker mounted on top of his vehicle, and his disembodied voice crackled in the gentle wind. "Three...two... one...*fire!*" he said. I pulled the cord and felt the ground shake all around me and the cord snap out of my hand but realized that my gun hadn't gone off.

"You've got to *pull* it, manny," Farny laughed. "*Pull!*"

So I fished the cord out of the dirt and gave it a yank with both hands, and the ground shook as the gun went off.

"That's the sound of freedom!" Farny boomed.

+ + +

A second piece of the Iraq story fell into place when we visited a brand new, state-of-the-art munitions plant. Boskop, southwest of Johannesburg near the town of Potchefstroom, had been built to replace an older gunpowder plant close to Soweto. Boskop used automated machine tools purchased from West Germany and was run by a skeleton crew of sixteen men, including the plant supervisor. Separate production units made different kinds of explosives. The newest was devoted to filling 155mm artillery shells with a slurry of TNT and RDX.

"We can push out five hundred shells per eight-hour shift, eight hundred if we have to," Mr. Kootzee, the plant manager, told me. "And it's all for export. Eight hundred thousand rounds worth, all said and done."

Farny and the plant manager exchanged a wink, and their eyes strayed out to an open loading door, framed in sunlight.

"We're going to have tea," Farny said. "Join us in Kootzee's office when you feel like it."

We had just spent half the morning talking about industrial accidents, the main reason they were closing the Lenz plant in Soweto and moving their munitions-filling operations here to Boskop. I could hear the automated filling lines whomping and sucking in the semi-darkness behind me, so the light and the fresh air beckoned. I had a good camera with me that I had used to snap photos of the ultra-modern production line. "Just don't show the nameplates on the machines," Farny had said. Keeping up the pretense of the worldwide trade embargo on South Africa meant that the German-built machine tools had sprung from Zeus's thigh.

I jumped down from the loading dock. The backside of the plant was a vast open-air warehouse set behind a twelve-foot-high barbed wire fence with giant sodium perimeter lights. Pallets of wooden crates were stacked three high the entire length of the building, covered loosely with blue tarps. As I walked alongside them, it was easy to read the black block letters stamped on the sides: Ministry of Defense, Baghdad, Iraq.

Not only all for export, I thought—but for just one client. That's what Farny and Kootzee had wanted me to see.

+ + +

Commandant Piet Marais was a giant of a man who had a tendency to stoop when speaking with shorter people like me. As chairman of Armscor, he welcomed me into his office for well over two hours and spoke with astonishing frankness. On his desk, I saw a model of the giant G-6 wheeled howitzer that I had climbed over at the factory. A self-propelled version of the G-5, it was gangly, tall, and huge—so huge, I felt like I was about to fall out of a third-story window when I had climbed the ladder and peered out of the gunner's hatch. "Farny!" I hissed, jerking my thumb toward the miniature G-6. My guide obligingly took a picture of me with the Armscor chairman and his "Rhino" in between.

We talked extensively about the UN arms and trade embargo, which in fact had driven Armscor into self-sufficiency. "If we can't buy it, we make it," Marais said. "And if we can't make it, we steal it—from our enemies or from our friends."

That got us to discussing other countries subjected to arms embargoes, such as Iran and Iraq, both of which had approached Armscor for badly needed supplies. "We made our choice," Marais said. "We chose Iraq."

While making sure I understood that this part of our conversation was "off the record," a stipulation I respected until the history of South Africa's arms sales to Iraq became well known, he proceeded to confirm everything I had heard and then added a great deal more.

Yes, General Janoob had come to South Africa the year before and fired the G-5 gun. Not only was he impressed by how quickly it could "shoot and scoot," but he was especially impressed at how little training the crews needed to be able to use it effectively. "We couldn't make those guns fast enough for the Iraqis," Marais recalled with a chuckle. "They fire off rounds like you or I crack nuts. They are shooting like *hell*."

Then he told me the inside story of Gerald Bull, who at the time was an esoteric figure, unknown to the general public but a legend within the artillery world. His subsequent exploits to build a "super-gun" for Saddam Hussein and his assassination—possibly by Iraqi agents, who suspected him of two-timing them with Israel—became front page news. Bull originally wanted to make a much smaller field gun with a 39 caliber barrel. "We are the ones who opted for the longer barrel," Marais said. At the peak of their cooperation, Marais and his team actually managed Bull's Space Research Corporation for eighteen months. "And nobody knew," he said.

South Africa was new to the arms export business, that much was clear. So when General Janoob insisted as a condition to the G-5 contract that South Africa cut off all arms sales to Iran, Piet Marais agreed on the spot. Unlike other arms salesmen, he scrupulously kept his word.[24]

26: By the Rivers of Babylon
Baghdad

A lot had changed since the Iraqis had blacklisted me for revealing their incompetence in using high-tech French weaponry. For one, the Iraqis actually got better (somewhat). More to the point, they had a new story they wanted to tell; and who better to tell it than the man who seemed to know their Order of Battle inside and out and who had dumped on them

---

24   Swedish arms dealer Karl-Erik Schmitz discovered the South African pledge to his dismay in June 1984. As Iran's principal buyer of military explosives, Schmitz had signed contracts with Armscor to load 3,700 tons of gunpowder, part of a larger shipment destined for Iranian munitions plants. But in June 1984, as a cargo vessel was heading for the Cape, Pretoria informed him the deal was off. To make up the shortfall, Schmitz appealed to a little-known association of European munitions producers, the European Association for the Study of Safety Problems in the Production of Propellant Powder (EASSP), which soon became a convenient cover for a cartel whose sole purpose was supplying both belligerents with heavy munitions. Without Piet Marais's revelations, I would have missed this huge story.

in public? I was invited to Baghdad in late January 1986 by the Defense Minister himself. He offered me the carte blanche access my editors had been demanding.

My host, General Adnan Khairallah, was Saddam's cousin. In February 1986, the few of us in the West who actually followed what was going on in Iraq (and myself excluded, they were mostly arms dealers, geeks, and spooks) saw him as Saddam's ally and alter ego. And we were wrong. He turned out to be a Saddam rival. We would learn that later with a vengeance, when Saddam eliminated him like a Mafia don, ordering his agents to sabotage Khairallah's helicopter.

The other thing none of us saw, because it was taking place in the background, was that Saddam's other rival, Iran, was poised to make a devastating breakthrough on the battlefront, thanks primarily to several thousand TOW anti-tank missiles shipped to Tehran as part of Iran-Contra.

My reporting over the previous year had attracted the attention of a wealthy publisher in Germany, who recruited me away from the French defense magazine that had published my earlier Iraq stories by offering me $10,000 per feature, an enormous sum that was twice what I had been earning. Even though the dollar had plunged from the astronomical heights of the previous year, when it pushed beyond ten francs, it was still well above seven francs. Having lived through the Carter years in France, when you couldn't give away dollars, I felt like a prince. Thank you, Ronald Reagan.

But while my career was taking off, my personal life was in shambles. The mother of my two children, then aged seven and six, had taken me to court in a nasty custody battle which, as a French woman in French courts, she won even though she was the one who had walked out, leaving the children behind. I drifted from woman to woman like a shipwrecked sailor, grasping at driftwood. My latest was a French air hostess named Martine. One perk from her job was that she only paid 10 percent for personal air travel, so I asked her to come with me to Baghdad, thinking at the very least she would shield me from another Iraqi government honey trap. She agreed.

As we landed in Baghdad and taxied toward the arrivals building, the captain came over the intercom to page me. When I lit my light, two stewardesses rushed down the aisle (we were in Business), quickly drawing the curtains beyond us. "Come with us, please," they said.

Two red Mercedes came streaking across the tarmac and pulled alongside the aircraft, led by a green and white police car with its blue light flashing. I nudged Martine and pointed.

"It looks like a welcoming party," I said.

At the bottom of the jetway, a diminutive gentleman in a Baathist uniform was waiting for us. As we got closer to him, I saw the crossed swords and eagle indicating he was a major general. I was impressed.

"Mister Timmerman, I presume," he said, with a British accent and a decided twinkle in the eyes behind his oversize designer glasses. "I am General Ala'a. On behalf of His Excellency, Minister Khairallah, welcome to Iraq."

He ushered us into the backseat of the first red Mercedes, then climbed into the front passenger's seat. We followed the police car across the tarmac, tailed by the second Mercedes and two bodyguards. A few hundred yards later, we pulled up to an elegant VIP pavilion. General Ala'a handed our passports to a gofer and offered us Arabic coffee.

"The Minister has prepared quite a program for you," he said. "I don't know what you did to merit this, but I've never seen anything quite like it. You must be very important!"

He laughed at his own joke, but not in the guarded, I'm-about-to-kill-you-isn't-that-a-hoot way that the Baathists cultivated. He was relaxed, and he laughed for real.

"I understand you want to meet General Amir," he said.

I grinned, a bit taken aback at how quickly he got to the point.

"Well, he's agreed to meet with you two days from now. But first, I think we want to find out what Madame would like to see while she is in Iraq."

With a gentility I never would have suspected from a Saddam Hussein henchman, General Ala'a proceeded to ask Martine what she would like to do with the second red Mercedes (and its driver and body-guards) while I was off with him for official meetings. When she had no ideas, he played tour guide, proposing a visit to a new shopping mall, and of course, a trip to Babylon, recently restored thanks to the efforts of our modern-day Nebuchadnezzar, His Excellency Saddam Hussein.

"We even have a synagogue here in Baghdad that very few people realize still exists," he said, winking conspiratorially.

Martine tossed her short blonde hair to one side and gave me a frightened look. I wasn't quite sure whether this was some kind of trap or a backhanded way of getting me to realize that the brutal dictatorship that came to power after hanging the Jews of Baghdad had turned a corner and was seeking to put on a more practical face.

"A synagogue, really? I'd like to see that," I said.

"Done," he said, slapping his knee.

+ + +

He accompanied us up to a gigantic suite on the top floor of the Baghdad Sheraton, where a silver champagne cooler and two perfectly iced bottles of Dom Perignon awaited us by a vast bed. Through the picture windows and the balcony beyond, we could see the Tigris as it wound through Baghdad. The *masgouf* joints on our side of the river were lit up with strings of Christmas lights, but the other side was a vast, dark hole. This was where Saddam hunkered in his palace.

"I am sure you would like some time to relax after your journey. Shall I pick you up for dinner at eight o'clock?"

"That would be great," I said.

Once General Ala'a departed, I popped the cork on a bottle of Dom Perignon and poured us each a glass.

"Nineteen seventy-six," I said, savoring it. "Who would think, in the middle of a war."

We drank and enjoyed ourselves and the deep pillows and fluffy comforters until the alarm went off at 7:00 PM, waking us to prepare for dinner.

General Ala'a took us that evening to an Ottoman-era caravanserai, a tavern and boarding house for travelers that had been made over as a nightclub for senior Baath party members. A bottle of Johnnie Walker Red Label was waiting for us at the table, and General Ala'a drank like a trooper. As the evening went on, and the noise level rose to raucous, a belly-dancer bounced and jiggled her flesh from table to table, egging on the men to place money in her bodice.

"Is she Iraqi?" Martine asked.

"She must be Syrian," General Ala'a said. "We breed our women more Spartan," he winked.

The next day, we drove south of Baghdad to visit Babylon, which Saddam had begun rebuilding four years earlier, even as the war with Iran dragged on. The site emerged from the mud of the Euphrates in vague, dreamy shapes seen through mist. Like Flaubert's depiction of ancient Carthage in *Salammbô*, a study in the color ochre, so Babylon was a study in sepia-colored mud, fashioned into archways, hundreds of cool inner chambers, and buried corridors with spiraling ceilings, all of them fake, melding together into a single indistinguishable mass of mud.

"You see these?" General Ala'a said, pointing to the raised lions imprinted into every brick. "They are exact replicas of the original lions fashioned by Nebuchadnezzar that decorated the entire palace."

We emerged from the cold inner rooms into the winter sunshine, with tall date palms hiding the river in the distance. General Ala'a led us to an isolated statue on a slight rise overlooking the river. He asked me if I knew what it was, but it was so eroded that I didn't have a clue. So he cupped a hand to his ear and recited: "'*By the rivers of Babylon we sat and wept, as we remembered Zion.*'"

"This is the famous lion?"

"Yes. This is the precise spot where the Jews came to lament their captivity."

Again he gave me that inquisitive look, eyes twinkling, to see if I grasped his meaning. I knew the story of King Nebuchadnezzar taking the people of Jerusalem captive and bringing them as slaves to Babylon. Saddam claimed to be his natural successor and boasted that he would do the same thing to the Jews of today. But the end of the story was more dicey, at least if you were a Baathist general speaking to a foreign journalist. For the Jewish captives were ultimately set free, not by Nebuchadnezzar or his successors, but by the Persian Emperor Cyrus the Great, after he had smashed the Assyrian empire and captured Babylon.

✦ ✦ ✦

The next morning, I was scheduled to interview defense minister Adnan Khairallah. But when General Ala'a arrived in the red Mercedes to pick me up at 9:00 AM, he announced that there had been a change of plan.

"Not our plans, unfortunately. But the Iranians. Last night, they launched a surprise attack in the south and captured the Fao peninsula, so the minister has flown down to Basra to personally supervise the battle to expel them."

"When do you expect he will return to Baghdad?"

"That, my friend, is not mine to know. But my guess is you will not be meeting with him on this trip. My apologies, but it is beyond our control."

Instead, we went to the Iraqi Staff College in Rustumiya, near al-Rashid Airbase on the outskirts of Baghdad. While that might sound like a snooze to many American readers, remember: this was Saddam Hussein's Iraq, a closed dictatorship suspicious of foreigners, which for decades had been a strategic ally of the Soviet Union and an implacable enemy of Israel and the United States. Add to that the mutual and often murderous suspicion that existed between the Baathists and the regular army since the Baath party first seized power in 1958, and the willingness of my hosts to open up this inner sanctum of the Iraqi professional military was nothing short of extraordinary. I was the first journalist ever to be allowed inside. I learned to my astonishment that there was zero Soviet indoctrination, at least of the military. Instead, all the textbooks on military theory and strategy were British and dated from post-World War I protectorate days.

"Iraq's military doctrine and teaching is all its own," the staff college commander, Brigadier General Abdul Razzak Yacoub, claimed. "Our most important training manuals were written by my esteemed friend, General Ala'din Maki Khamas," he said with a nod to my host.

General Ala'a shrugged, acknowledging the compliment. "I have tried to make my contribution," he said.

As we were leaving, I paused at a glass case with plaques offered by visiting dignitaries, most of them written in Arabic with the flags of neighboring countries. In the middle, one was written in French and signed, "Pierre Gallois."

"So General Gallois came here two years ago?" I said.

"Ah, yes. The father of the French nuclear strike force," General Ala'a said dreamily.

"I interviewed him not long ago. He is quite an admirer of your president."

As we drove back, I pondered whether this was yet another clue General Ala'a was offering me of Iraq's most deeply held secrets. General Gallois was famous for steering France into a "third way" between NATO and the Warsaw Pact, guaranteed by its independent nuclear strike force. American Francophiles liked to point out that having French nuclear ballistic missile submarines, theoretically independent of NATO, complicated the calculations of the Soviet high command, all while no one in NATO ever questioned their ultimate allegiance. Was General Ala'a suggesting that Iraq was a secret US ally? Or was he suggesting, more simply, that Iraq still aspired to acquire nuclear weapons, despite the Israeli air strike that had demolished its French-built nuclear bomb plant in 1981?

+ + +

The next day, General Ala'a had arranged for me to meet the famous (and previously elusive) General Amir, the man the French arms salesmen lusted after and feared all at once, the man whose signature meant the difference between a life of constant hustling and a comfortable retirement on the Côte d'Azur.

"So this is his office after all!" I said when General Ala'a told our driver to turn into the small walled compound I had visited the year before.

"Right address, wrong introduction," General Ala'a said. "Today he is waiting for you and will answer all your questions."

The same lieutenant I had met a year earlier ushered us into the modest office of Major Zuhair, who apparently was the general's aide-de-camp. He had the lieutenant bring us tea, British shortbread, and dates, and after speaking with General Ala'a in Arabic, turned to me.

"I was telling the general about your visit last year, but he seemed already to be informed."

All three of us had a good laugh at that. Then a door behind the major's desk swung open, and a diminutive man in a crisp Baath party uniform emerged from the padded leather of the inner door. He wore giant, steel-rimmed aviator glasses and a Charlie Chaplin moustache. I noted that his shoulder boards had an additional star to those of General Ala'a, making him a *fariq*, or lieutenant general. "So you are the famous Mister Timmerman!" he bellowed when he caught sight of me.

"And you are the famous General Amir," I said. "So famous, that no one seems to know your last name."

"Ha," he said. "Let's keep it that way."[25]

Over the next two hours, General Amir provided detailed answers to my questions about Iraqi arms purchases and the difficulties of integrating Soviet and French weapons systems into the same force. He

---

25   Lieutenant General Amir Rashid al-Ubaidi, who then headed the military's Scientific Research Coun-
      cil, was in charge of Iraq's ballistic missile development in addition to Air Force procurement. He went
      on to become the vice minister of Industry and Military Industrialization, and later, minister of Oil. He
      was the six of spades in the US military's Deck of Cards of top Iraqi leaders during the 2003 liberation
      of Iraq. He surrendered to the US in late April 2003 and was quietly released in July 2012.

confirmed that Iraq had built an electronics plant, known as Saad 13, with the help of the French, and was even willing to discuss future arms purchases, a subject I knew would make my editors and readers salivate. The one thing he wouldn't confirm was the Iraqi purchase and massive use of the South African G-5 gun. He didn't deny it; he just said that he knew nothing about it.

On the way back to the hotel, General Ala'a congratulated me on the conduct of the interview. "Even I learned things I didn't know," he said.

"What's with the G-5?" I asked. "He had no problem confirming all kinds of things, including the French radar deal and Saad Thirteen?"

"You're forgetting one thing: he's Air Force," General Ala'a said. "If you want to see your South African guns, watch the news this evening. I think you call it…B-roll."

When I opened the door to our suite, Martine lay propped up in the gigantic bed watching soap operas. I sat down at the desk and worked for several hours transcribing my interviews, well after the sun went down and the Christmas lights along the Tigris became visible through the trellised outer wall of the balcony. At 8:00 PM, I got up to switch the channel to the Iraqi news. Martine patted the covers next to her.

"Turn that off. Come to bed," she said with a pout.

When the footage from Fao came on, I turned up the volume. The TV anchorwoman was telling about the valorous counter-offensive being led by the minister of defense. The B-roll showed endless columns of Iraqi tanks and tracked vehicles on tank transporters, and then I saw what I was looking for: row after row of G-5 howitzers, identical to the one I had fired in South Africa, their muzzles lighting up the darkness so you could see the gun crews covering their ears, pounding away at the Iranian lines.

"There it is!" I said excitedly. "That's the final confirmation."

"*Chéri*, turn that off and come to bed," Martine repeated.

At that moment, something in me clicked, like a switch being thrown. We had traveled to a country in a life-or-death struggle and were privileged to get a glimpse of history being made, with little (if any) risk to ourselves. I wanted to see more, hear more, learn more. That's why I was here. But to Martine, it made no difference.

We were planning to get married in less than six weeks' time, and suddenly, I realized we had little in common—and little to say to each other. Martine was a practical woman. She could balance her checkbook, cook family meals, remember birthdays, and make sure the children made it to school on time. She even ironed my underwear, which I initially found quaint. But now her love of order and security and her lack of inquisitiveness left me cold.

Our relationship never recovered from that trip to Baghdad; because in the meantime, I had met Christina. And the contrast between the two women left me no doubt where my heart belonged and where I felt at home.

27: Courtship
Paris

When Christina resisted my initial advances, I realized that I would have to court her, a concept I thought had gone out of existence. So I started showing up late in the afternoons at the office she shared with a Swedish businessman on the avenue Victor Hugo, within spitting distance of the Arc de Triomphe. We'd chat for twenty or thirty minutes, then I'd take her out for drinks. It took several weeks of this before she agreed to go out for dinner. She had a Japanese girlfriend in Washington she was planning to visit in the spring, and that made her want to eat sushi.

"We're in Paris," I said. "And you want to eat Japanese?"

"Yes," she said. "A very *good* Japanese."

And she gave a smile that was full of such certainty, if it had been a rock, I could have busted my head on it. She knew what she wanted, and if I didn't get it, that was fine with her. There were plenty of other men.

I spent the next day looking through restaurant guides until I found the best Japanese place in Paris, just off the Champs-Élysées, and made a reservation. We drank three small bottles of warm sake with dinner, and I remember not even caring when I got the bill, which was four times the amount I had ever spent on a restaurant in Paris. We leaned into each other when we got back out on the street to hail a cab.

"I have to work tomorrow," she said as she got in. She gave the driver her address at the back end of the Latin Quarter.

"I'll see you home," I said.

"You don't have to," she said. "You're not coming up."

Once we paid off the cab, we kissed out on the sidewalk, long and searchingly, our bodies pressing together.

"You're still not coming up," she said, coming up for air. "Not tonight."

And with that, she punched in the code to her building and headed inside. She turned just before she let the door fall behind her, blew me a kiss, and laughed.

I walked back across the river to the Bastille, and then up the broad, deserted boulevard Richard Lenoir to the Place Voltaire where I lived. In all the years I had been in Paris, I don't think I had ever taken a woman out for dinner and wound up walking home by myself. But instead of the sting of failure, I was elated. This was different.

A week or so later, she accepted to come for Friday dinner at my place. I had spent the afternoon preparing a *blanquette de veau* and the apartment was ripe with hearty kitchen smells. I had opened two bottles of Vosne-Romanée from a wine grower I had met a few years ago and set them on the sideboard to breathe. I waxed the dining room table and brought out enormous glasses specially designed to reveal the Burgundy's complex bouquet.

"I like to eat," Christina said, giving me a mischievous smile as I arranged pieces of veal in a crater of rice on her plate for a third helping.

"I'm glad you like my cooking."

"I could get used to it."

"I think I'd like that."

"But I like my independence."

For the first time since I could remember, I didn't know what to do with a woman. I desired her fiercely, and yet, she made it clear that she was in charge. So I listened to her with all my senses, trying to shut out her words to better understand what she was feeling.

When we finished the second bottle of Vosne-Romanée, she got up.

"It's getting late," she said.

"You don't have to work tomorrow. It's Friday."

"That's true. And I'm drunk. So you can take me to bed now."

"Okay, then!"

I came around to her side of the table and slid my hands around her waist. She turned around and kissed me, long and eagerly. And then that mischievous smile of hers again. "But I *can* walk."

Later, she climbed off me and turned on the light. "I thought you were getting married. So why are you doing this?"

"Does it matter to you?"

"Not really. It's just sex—and food." She thought about it for a bit, then added, "But if I were her, it would."

"I've cancelled everything."

"*Vaaht*?"

She had a way of pronouncing certain words, especially those with ambiguous consonants, with an exaggerated Swedish accent, accompanied with an equally exaggerated expression of astonishment.

"The wedding is off. The house. Everything."

"You're joking," she said. She was serious now. "Martine folded your underwear. She ironed your T-shirts. She kept the kids in line. She never argued with a word you said. Where are you ever going to find somebody like that?"

"Maybe that's not what I want."

A look of panic crossed her face, and I realized I had said enough.

"What I want right now is another bottle of wine."

"It just so happens, there's another one breathing," I said.

We drank that third bottle slowly through the night as the beginnings of love pushed up between us like pale sprouts at the end of winter.

28: The Damavand Project

On April 22, 1986, the feds struck again. This time, US Attorney Rudy Giuliani indicted seventeen individuals for a fantastic scheme to sell $2.5 billion worth of weapons to Iran. I was in a state of shock when I read the first press reports. I knew some of these men personally and had broken bread with them. And I knew quite a bit about the hardware they were accused of trying to sell to Iran because I had seen telex traffic describing it. Included were the thirty-two—now thirty-nine—F-4 fighter jets I had learned about from Broman and Cutter when they had tried to purchase them from Egypt with me as a cutout. Now the feds were indicting the Frenchman who had initiated the deal, former French Navy pilot Bernard Veillot.

Veillot had smelled a rat when Cyrus Hashemi, an Iranian American who claimed to have opened a new channel to Iran, brought a congeries of money-hungry wannabes through Paris earlier that spring. Until then, the Iran connection had been Bernard's piece, so why did they need me if they now had Hashemi? Bernard wondered. Hashemi tried to convince him to come to New York to finalize the deal and bring along his new American partner, a part-time American oil trader and retired US Marine, John Delaroque. They sat for days in a suite of the Hotel Raphael in Paris, and there were just too many of them, most of them new, hangers-on and profiteers, Israelis and Americans and Germans and Czechs. There were way too many deals and intermediaries and too much money, Bernard told me. When Hashemi sensed his reluctance to come to New York and suggested Bermuda instead, Veillot said no. His instincts were sound: Hashemi turned out to be a confidential informant for US Customs and taped their conversations for prosecutors, while the man posing as the assistant to Khashoggi lawyer Samuel Evans, Joe King, was an undercover US Customs agent who later testified against them. Although Bernard's name was eventually dropped from the indictment, one of the prosecutors in New York told me he could still be arrested at any time.

I spoke to him the day after the indictments were handed down, and he was seething. "I'm not going down easily," he said. "This whole thing goes very high." He insisted that the actions of an over-zealous US Customs commissioner had put the kibosh on a strategic deal that could have brought Iran back into the American fold, his goal all along. "They're throwing the baby out with the bathwater."

Just like Paul Cutter, Bernard wanted me to believe he was not in it for the money but to save the world.

"Don't take my word for it," he grumbled. "Talk to Brenneke."

After Cutter's arrest in July 1985, the French arms dealers were desperate to find a new channel to the US government so they could move US weapons to Iran. So when Delaroque introduced Oregon businessman Richard J. Brenneke as "a personal emissary of Vice President George Bush," Veillot thought his ship had come home. For three straight days that autumn, Veillot huddled with Brenneke and Delaroque in the Hotel Florida in Paris to discuss a new approach toward Iran. Veillot found in Brenneke a willing audience.

"Bernard told me that the Iranian military was spooked," Brenneke said when I spoke to him after the bust. Recent high-altitude bombing runs by Soviet Backfire bombers and an uptick in the long-simmering insurgency in Iranian Baluchestan had convinced them that the Soviet Union was about to join Saddam's war against them. They needed US help and were willing to release the US hostages in Lebanon in exchange for it. Veillot gave him a thick reference binder, code-named Damavand A010186, to back up the Iranian claims and their offer. The dossier contained Iranian intelligence reports on the Backfires, including an aerial photograph of the Soviet bombers taken by an Iranian Air Force pilot near Mount Damavand; reports on Soviet aide to Balouchi insurgents and the location of new Soviet military bases in Afghanistan; a blow by blow account of how the Iranians had captured three Soviet T-80 tanks in the mountains of Kurdistan from Soviet tank crews during field trials; and an Iranian offer to trade the tanks and the hostages for American weapons. (The tanks were so new they had not yet been introduced into service, so they were a top priority item for the US). It also contained a political memo detailing the steps the Iranian government pledged to take to block Soviet influence in Iran and move closer to the United States, to be negotiated during a "high-level meeting" between US and Iranian officials. Brenneke promised to pass the Damavand file to the US government for action. "It was very detailed," Brenneke told me. "A road map."

Brenneke had been around the intelligence world long enough to appreciate the value of the information Veillot had given him; he'd been out of it long enough to know that the only way he could cash in on it would be to convince top-level officials to make the operation their own. So he began shopping the Damavand file around Washington. Starting in November 1985, he showed it to a Marine Corps Counter-intelligence officer, Colonel George Alvarez; to J. William Middendorf II, a former Secretary of the Navy and US representative to the Organization of American States; to the State Department's European bureau director, Ralph Johnson; and to Colonel Douglas Menarchik, military advisor to Vice President George Bush—all of this, course, well *after* the White House-approved arms deals had begun but well *before* the Bible and the cake meeting in Tehran with Ollie North, Bud McFarlane, Michael Ledeen, and Rafsanjani. None of it had yet become public.

As Brenneke told me in taped interviews over several days, the Americans wanted him to "clean house" of the black-market wannabes. They wanted Tehran to know that if they wanted US weapons and spare parts, they had to deal directly. The two busts were part of the plan so the real arms deals could be taken over by General Richard Secord and his network as part of the White House Initiative toward Iran.

Brenneke claimed that Vice President George H. W. Bush personally blessed the Damavand project in a private meeting set up in Oregon by

Republican senator Mark Hatfield. While Brenneke couldn't prove that he had actually spoken to the vice president or his staff, what he told me was familiar. Even the Iraqis were telling me they were starting to feel the impact on the battlefield of US weapons deliveries to Iran.

NSC consultant Michael Ledeen recalled learning from Iranian intermediary Manouchehr Ghorbanifar essentially the same information as contained in the Damavand file at roughly the same time the Iranians were relaying it to Bernard Veillot. "By late 1984," Ledeen wrote, "Khomeini had come to the conclusion that Iran was under severe strain; Iraqi planes bombed major Iranian cities at will... If Iran were to have any chance of winning the war, she would need modern weapons and spare parts. The best weapons, like the spare parts for the crippled Iranian arsenal, were American. Thus, in late autumn or early winter, the Ayatollah informed his foreign diplomats that Iran would seek some form of contact with the West for this purpose, and particularly with the Great American Satan. They were to seek out channels to the Americans, in order to begin the process."[26]

I wrote a column for the *Wall Street Journal*—five months before the Iran-Contra story broke—blaming US Customs for bumbling a strategic initiative that could have ended the covert war between the United States and the Islamic Republic.[27] But I wasn't quite convinced I had enough to make the story stick. After all, I was still peeking through the window at the players inside. Soon all of their actions would become public.

29: 'We Hate Your Country'
Riyadh

My Iraq stories had been a big hit with the defense contractors and uniformed military who subscribed to *Military Technology*, so my editors decided to send me to Saudi Arabia to report on the Saudi Air Force and Navy. If Saddam Hussein was keeping revolutionary Iran in check with the blood of his soldiers, the Saudis were providing the bread and the milk that nurtured them. For the contractors, Saudi Arabia was the mother lode, the cornucopia so full of riches that everyone got their share.

---

26 Michael A. Ledeen, *Perilous Statecraft: An Insider's Account of the Iran-Contra Affair* (New York: Charles Scribner & Sons, 1988), p111.

27 Kenneth R. Timmerman, "U.S. Customs Stumbles into Deep Mideast Waters," Wall Street Journal-Europe, May 5, 1986.

While the Saudis had only encountered the Iranians once on the battlefield—a brief skirmish two years earlier when two Iranian F-4s flew a provocation run into Saudi airspace and were promptly shot down by Saudi F-15s—rumors were afloat that the Iranians now were planning to take their war to the Saudis in hopes of cutting off Saddam Hussein's financial pipeline after cutting off his access to the Gulf at Fao. My job was to get a feel for the morale, training, and equipment of the Saudi forces, while taking the temperature of the contractors and the diplomatic community.

During a three-week tour of the Kingdom, I was provided access to front-line officers and military bases that few Western reporters had ever visited. My guide for much of the time was a thirty-one-year-old Army captain named Saleh, who was nearly as wide as he was tall. He was courteous, if reserved, and his English was perfect.

"I spent five years doing pre-med in Oregon," he said, "then I came back to join the Army."

"You weren't tempted to stay in America?"

"Not once," he said. "Before, many young Saudis left and our country was run by foreigners. I wanted to come back to serve my country."

Darkness fell quickly in the desert, and even though we were on the outskirts of the Saudi capital, I was astonished not to see the lights of a city ahead of us. Huge walled compounds, some of them dark, some of them lit like Baghdad fish restaurants with strings of Christmas lights, rose up out of the endless dark expanse of the desert.

"What do you have that's old in Riyadh?" I asked.

"You Americans," he sneered. "You like to see old. There, look," he said, gesturing almost contemptuously toward a dark palace. "That is very old."

Try as I might, I couldn't see much difference between the concrete, Lego-like structure and what seemed like its twin a bit further down the road, except that one was dark and the "new" one was full of light.

"How old is it?" I asked.

"Maybe ten, maybe fifteen years," he said, completely serious now. "The wealthy people, they get tired of their palaces, so they build new ones. That one is very, very old."

We rode in silence for awhile. Like Mary, after encountering the mysterious words of the archangel, I pondered his words. I sensed an inner hostility in Captain Saleh, not directed at me in any personal way but at me as an American and at those of his countrymen who embraced American ways. I would learn much more about this over the next three weeks.

+ + +

As in Iraq, the contractors were eager to fill me in. Most of them were Americans, working on everything from the Riyadh airport to an endless series of military programs involving the expanding Royal Saudi Air Force F-15 fleet, its AWACS aircraft, and other air defense systems. Those I met on the job with their Saudi bosses were deferential. "They have technology you won't find anywhere else," one expat working for the Riyadh airport authority told me. "Our job is to make ourselves obsolete, to train the Saudis gradually to replace us."

The Americans I met in their walled compound in Riyadh told a very different story, especially the wives.

They carped about being forced to wear black robes and head scarves whenever they left the compound, including the supermarket, where they had a tendency to catch the airy robes in the wheels of their shopping carts. "Just last week a guy cornered me as I was bending down to unwind it," one woman complained. "He pinched my butt and would have done more if I hadn't ripped the damn thing out of the wheels."

When their children turned fifteen, they were no longer allowed to attend school and were sent home. Why? "So they won't pollute the Saudi youth with Western values," another woman said. "Once they turn eighteen, you can't even get them a visa so they can visit."

High-powered binoculars had become very popular among Saudi motorists who drove past the walled American compound. There was a hill beyond the swimming pool where Saudis would get out and ogle the men and women swimming together. "So they complained to the authorities that we were breaking the law," the woman went on. "That put an end to mixed bathing."

The latest incident occurred when a Lebanese woman living in the compound gave a slideshow to the Expat Women's Club of her trips to the interior, showing the backward conditions of Saudi villages. Then she showed slides of Lebanon where women drove cars and appeared in public not only unveiled, but in clothing designed to accent their female attributes. "The Saudi women who attended got mad. They shut us down," the woman said.

Several of their husbands worked on the AWACS program and confirmed that the Saudi AWACS had been stripped of the most sensitive hardware. "If they let you onboard, just look at all the empty panels in the racks—and that's nothing compared to what's been left out behind the panels that *are* there."

They also confirmed that in the confrontation with the Iranian F-4s, it was a US AWACS crew that guided the Saudi pilots to come up behind the Iranians and fire before they had visual. "The real problem is, there just aren't enough Saudis," one program manager said. "The ones we get can be very good. But the pilots don't fly if they don't feel like it, even if they are getting orders from Central Command. If the Iranians ever seriously probed, they'd find the Saudis to be a paper tiger. I hope we're out of here before then."

From the expats, I learned to pay attention to office dynamics, to observe the differences between the Saudi managers and their expat employees. The Saudis were invariably dressed in impeccable white *thobes* and sat around clean, air-conditioned offices without a shred of paperwork drinking tea, whereas the expats had grit beneath their fingernails or scanned multiple computer screens in hot, cramped cubicles with phones ringing off the hook. Whether it was at the airport authority, the military bases I visited, the Taef military hospital, or elsewhere, I saw it repeatedly and resolutely kept it to myself. Clearly, it was extremely sensitive. But I didn't know enough to make it an issue.

+ + +

The King Faisal Naval Base in Jeddah was the main port of the Saudi navy and home to their new French frigates. It was thus a big "get" for me to tour the base and meet with its commanders, since the Saudi contract was the biggest ever for French naval equipment manufacturers. I was escorted on board the *Bouraida,* an eleven-thousand-ton oiler that two years earlier had steamed out of La Ciotat, the naval shipyard just outside of Marseilles, and now served as a support and command ship for the fleet. My escorts apologized for the captain, Lieutenant Commander Ghanim al-Oufi, who was unable to greet me when I was piped on board. "He is at prayers, *yani,*" they told me. No Iraqi, Egyptian, Lebanese, or Palestinian commander I had ever visited had excused himself because of prayers.

Once he joined us, Commander al-Oufi was quick to praise the French, who were delivering the best ships in their arsenal to the Saudi Navy. "We have named this program *Sawari* after a great naval victory of the Muslims," he said. "We hope our Sawari program will be as successful."

I jotted down the reference but paid little attention to it at the time. Nor can I recall any French journalist or defense ministry source ever commenting on the name Sawari or what it meant to Muslim culture. Since I was the first foreign journalist to view the new French ships or to visit this brand new naval base, inaugurated just three years before, I had other fish to fry. To my editors, and indeed, to the rest of the media that was paying attention, *Sawari* meant dollars for France.

Later, I learned more. The *Dhaat al Sawari*, or the Battle of the Masts, was the first major naval victory of the new Muslim empire. Fought in AD 655 against the Byzantine armada off the coast of Egypt, it put an end to a millennium of peace that had joined continental Europe to North Africa and the Levant throughout the Greek and Roman empires. Sawari shattered Christian domination of the Mare Nostrum and sealed the fate of the Holy Roman Empire, which had been limping along for two hundred years under a series of "barbarian" kings and princes after the sack of Rome. From then on, the Mediterranean ceased to be a crossroad of civilizations and became a roiling danger zone dominated by Muslim raiders. The Dhaat al Sawari ended trade between North Africa and Europe, most notably cutting off access to Egyptian papyrus. Without a replacement material on which to copy books, literacy in Europe, which was widespread at the time of the battle, was extinguished within a generation. A generation! Muslim raiding parties became increasingly bold and repeatedly struck the Mediterranean coast of today's France and Italy, looting the coastal cities and driving the inhabitants to fortified hilltop citadels, where insular feudal lords replaced the Roman governors and their cosmopolitan ways. In short, the battle of Sawari ushered in what we now call the "Dark Ages."[28]

Such was the high accomplishment this Saudi naval commander and his royal masters apparently aspired to repeat.

---

28 For generations, British-born historians, Gibbons among them, purveyed a view that Islamic culture benefitted the West. Belgian scholar Henri Pirenne dismantled that myth with factual evidence showing that the Muslim invasions "broke the unity of the Mediterranean world and turned the Middle Sea... into a battleground." See the excellent analysis of Emmet Scott, *Mohammed & Charlemagne Revisited: The History of a Controversy* (Nashville: New English Review Press, 2011).

+ + +

We flew into Taef, the summer capital of the Kingdom, in a Saudi army helicopter. My pilot purposefully circled the rugged moonscape surrounding the city, pointing out the brilliant white fortresses, each seemingly isolated on its own ravine, where royal households spent the hot summer months.

Major General Abdulaziz Henaidy was the commander of King Faisal Air Base. "Our goal is to maintain and operate our F-15 squadrons without foreign assistance," he said. It was a tall order, in a country when many of the pilots learned to fly before they could drive a car.

He gave me sweeping access to the base and to his squadron commanders, as well as to the aircraft hangars and the tarmac. In the ready room, I chatted with Major Muqrin Abdulaziz as he was suiting up. As the most senior F-15 pilot in the Royal Saudi Air Force, he was in charge of qualifying younger pilots who "graduated" from flying F-5s. In just twelve flights, they were considered operational. "Of course, we have not yet been tested in combat," he said.

"What about the Iranians?" I asked.

"The Iranians? Let them come. We'll go get them."

The handful of pilots in the ready room were sitting around, drinking tea. They nodded their heads in agreement, *let's go get the Iranians,* but there was no sense of urgency, no tension, no sense of danger. Prince Muqrin and his F-15 pilots were weekend flyers, playing with their winged Ferraris. On his helmet was emblazed the call-sign, "Rocky." Princes in fantasy-land.[29]

That evening, I strolled through town during the witching hour as the sun began to fade and the coolness of the desert rose up like a cold breath from the stones and dust of the public gardens. A pair of Saudi women carrying shopping bags approached me, talking to each other, laughing. Suddenly, one of them elbowed her friend, pointing to me, and they lowered their voices. As we continued to approach each other, I could see their eyes locked on my body behind the gauze-thin black veils, undressing me layer by layer. A desert breeze pressed their abayas against their bodies, the setting sun from behind me penetrating the thin black cloth so I could see that both women were naked underneath. I felt my blood rising and continued to walk

---

29   Prince Muqrin briefly became Crown Prince after the death of King Abdullah in January 2015.

until a wisp of the thin black cloth brushed against my bare arm, then blew away. And then they were gone.

On the streets of Paris, such an encounter would not be unusual. But here, in Saudi Arabia? Troubled soup beneath the veil, I thought.

+ + +

As my tour came to its end, I went back through my notes, highlighting quotes for articles. I kept returning to the interview with the naval commander in Jeddah who had mentioned the Battle of Sawari. I had jotted down the theme of our last exchange, "New tech, old ways." He was explaining how the Saudi military was assimilating new technology from the West but was determined not to allow it to change them. "Saudi Arabia is a country devoted to God, and this will not change," the commander said. "We also have close family ties, and this will not change. We do not want it to change. Even here, as you see, we stop for prayer. We have six or seven mosques on this base alone! Our religion is part of our strength."

Another commander, from the King Abdul Aziz Military Academy, put it this way: "The strategic importance of this country is not military. It is Islam. One billion Muslims turn to face us five times a day. Think of that!" he said. "Three hundred years ago, no one had heard about oil. But even thirteen centuries ago, they had heard about Islam. We don't want to appear on the world map as a black dot of oil but as the land of the Holy Cities of Islam."

I decided to probe a bit deeper on this theme with my guide, the squat Captain Saleh. On our last evening together, I repeated to him these things that I had heard from other commanders.

"You don't let your women drive, you don't allow Western influences into your society, you ban Western television shows from the airwaves. But you can't keep it out forever. Can you?"

I will never forget the Oregon-educated Captain's sneering response. "We hate your country," he said. "We don't want to be like you. We hate your openness. We hate the way your women show themselves like whores. We will buy what we need from you for now. But in the end, we will destroy you. Islam will destroy you and anybody who tries to be like you."

I thought of what had happened to the Shah of Iran and shuddered. Because we were going down the same path, repeating the same mistakes, without realizing it. This alliance with Saudi Arabia was not going to end well. In our arrogance—or perhaps, it was just the Western liberal mindset that believed in the perfectibility of man—we viewed history as having just one major plotline, from Adam until today, with enlightenment as the common future all men would share regardless of their background, their situation, or their beliefs. What if some cultures thrived in darkness and backwardness? What if they defended with greater vigor that darkness than we defended our freedom? Could they set back the world clock, the common march toward the future? What if the future they aspired to was totally different from ours and no effort on our part could convince them to adopt our goals?

30: Fanning the Flames

It took several more months, but I finally convinced Christina to move in with me that summer at the rue Pache, overlooking the Place Voltaire. She cut ties to the apartment she shared across the river with a friend from the south of France, and with it, her ability to run away from me easily. Life changed overnight for both of us. We became inseparable, each other's best companion. She wanted to know everything about everyone I met and interviewed and never failed to find some motivation behind their behavior I had missed. Luckily, she was there when I learned from the French court that I had lost visiting rights to Julian and Clio after their mother sued to gain full custody over them. You could have swept me off the floor with a broom, but she rebuilt me, piece by piece.

In mid-September, I took her to Greece to meet Kostas Drakos, the owner of the inn and restaurant at Mylopotas on Ios, where I had spent many wonderful summers. Together, we discovered nearby Kimolos, island of ship captains, where tourists seldom disembarked. It was a two-hour walk across the island along donkey trails through rock-strewn vineyards and pounding cicadas and a heavy sun to the only beach, a magnificent horseshoe of white sand guarded by a tiny stone chapel on the hillside above. Snorkeling out beyond the headland, I dove down twenty feet and swam through the streets of a sunken city, stunned to realize it was the same Rose City I had imagined in a novel years earlier. Back in town, we learned there *had* been a city once on that headland, but it slid into the sea in 1500 BC in the earthquake that formed the caldera on Santorini, wiping out Minoan civilization.

I made my veal stew for her birthday, October 26. We joked that this was how I had first seduced her. But by now, just eight months after meeting her, I knew that I wanted to spend the rest of my life with her. She was fifteen women all wrapped into one. We joked about seeing ourselves in ancient Greek statues, in Ptolemaic urns, in tapestries of medieval unicorn hunts, in Brueghel and Botticelli images. We felt we had known each other at different times and different places for ten thousand years.

I found an emerald that caught the radiance of her eyes and took it to a jeweler who turned it into a pendant. I gave this to her over dinner and asked her to marry me.

"Aaa-ah," she said in her Swedish sing-song, her eyes catching specs of light from the small diamonds in the setting. It was one drawn out syllable, all vowel. "I'll have to think about it," she said.

"You could just say yes."

"That would be too easy for you."

We were both Scorpios, as was my six-year-old daughter, Clio, who Christina won over the first time they met. We joked that only Scorpios knew how to deal with Scorpios. She said yes nine days later, on my birthday.

Life has never been the same since.

✦ ✦ ✦

It was Christina who encouraged me to put all the stories I had been saving of arms dealers and intrigue and put them into a book. I called it *Fanning the Flames: Guns, Greed, and Geopolitics in the Gulf War.*

I had started working as a stringer for *Newsweek* earlier that year. Bureau chief Fred Coleman was an old Moscow hand, but he was fascinated by the Middle East and the odor of sulfur that seemed to linger over the arms and intelligence world. He assigned me a tiny closet in the Paris bureau on the rue du Faubourg St. Honoré and an IBM Personal Computer, which in those days was just getting introduced into the news business and cost several thousand dollars. I wrote most of *Fanning the Flames* on that clunky machine, saving it to floppy disks that were still floppy and printing out hard copies on perforated computer paper.

While working for Fred, I got to meet and interview French prime ministers, defense ministers, and former intelligence chiefs. I met Angolan guerilla leader Jonas Savimbi, Iranian dissidents, and many others, including Vice President George Bush, who did not strike me as devious or clever enough to orchestrate the grand bargain with Iran my sources later wanted me to believe he had embraced. My favorite, though, was Marcel Dassault, the aircraft pioneer, who at ninety-three seemed to have physically shrunk to the size of a wizened pre-teen. He spoke with a high-pitched twang that would have been a whine in anyone else, but for Dassault, it was a voice that commanded attention and respect. He was impressive.

Much harder than meeting or interviewing celebrities was not getting intimidated by the *Newsweek* office manager, a wizened Chinaman named John (yes, we all called him a "Chinaman"), who had escaped Communist Party rule shortly after the rise of Mao. You had to wade through his vast library in the center of the office to get anywhere, so there was no escaping his seemingly endless storehouse of anger and resentment. John saw himself as our sergeant major. He spent his days clipping dozens of newspapers in more languages than I recognized and compiling files on every subject imaginable. He kept biographical files on French and European politicians. He kept files on French sex scandals and crime stories, on summit meetings and political party chiefs. He compiled directories of officials at various embassies and companies based in Paris and on organizations as disparate as the International Atomic Energy Agency and UNESCO. He even had files on the annual selection at the Cannes Film Festival, including the runners up and wannabes, going back twenty-five years. When General Vernon Walters came to town on a "secret" mission, John handed me a background dossier with articles on him dating back to the 1950s. From John, I learned to keep files. Some of them, from the pre-computer days, I continue to truck around the world.

A few days after the Lebanese daily *As-Safir* revealed that a group of Americans, including senior officials from the National Security Council, had traveled to Tehran carrying a Bible for Ayatollah Khomeini signed by President Reagan and a chocolate cake in the shape of a key, I paid a visit to Jim Hoagland, who at the time was Paris bureau chief for the *Washington Post*. I had bumped into him a couple of times since he came to Paris that March. He shared our office space at *Newsweek*.

The *As-Safir* story from October 1986 marked the official beginning of the Iran-Contra scandal, although it would be called "Iran-gate" for many more months by the media, ever hopeful of following the money and taking another presidential scalp. As I laid out the strategic underpinning to the black-market arms deals with Iran, Hoagland leaned back in his chair. The more I spoke the further back he leaned, until I thought he would fall over. I tried to hand him the transcribed interviews with Brenneke, but he waved them away. "You want me to believe that the vice president of the United States is dealing arms to Iran? On the basis of what, a statement from some arms dealer out to make a buck? You've got to be kidding me," he said. And he gave me such a look of disdain I wanted to shrink into the cracks between the creaky floorboards.

I knew I was sitting on a huge story, and I was confident it was true. But I didn't see how to get it the attention I knew it deserved.

I didn't yet understand the notion of juice. But that's what I needed.

+ + +

Help came from where I least expected it.

At one of our Anglo-American Press Club lunches, I got talking with an older gentleman, dressed like a stockbroker from the 1950s, who worked for the *New York Times*. He wore matching ties and pocket scarves, slicked back his thinning black hair with Brylcreem, and had the voice of a World War II newsreel. I spoke to him about my book project. He invited me to lunch later that week.

Paul Gendelman didn't work on the news side but headed the New York Times Syndication Sales service. Not only did they syndicate *Times* columnists and news articles, but they also bought books and sold excerpts to publications around the world. As I explained the structure of *Fanning the Flames*, broken into distinct chapters that could be sold as magazine articles, he got excited. We signed a contract a few days later. The Iran-Iraq war had set off the biggest arms bazaar in history, with thirty-nine countries selling weapons to the belligerents, twenty-four of them to both sides. Every arms manufacturer in the world was trying to get a piece of the action, and I had the goods on them all.

Gendelman was very good at what he did. He took the manuscript to the Frankfort book fair, and by the end of 1986, he had sold cover stories based on my as-yet unpublished book to some of the biggest newsweeklies in Europe. I was being translated into Dutch, French, Swedish, and

Portuguese. He had book deals in Arabic, French, and German. Barry Lando, who was a Paris-based producer for Mike Wallace at CBS's *60 Minutes*, talked about doing a story. Instead of living hand to mouth, I was now making three and four times my monthly expenses. To me, that was serious money.

Christina had become my accomplice. Together we traveled to Stockholm to interview Swedish customs officials and pore over thousands of pages of documents on the gunpowder cartel. The Swedes were happy to share, since they didn't recognize the French, British, Spanish, and Italian companies in the purchasing documents they had seized, whereas I had interviewed many of the company officials who had signed them, either in Baghdad or at various international arms shows. Iran and Iraq were engaged in an artillery war the likes of which hadn't been seen since World War II. Each month, they fired off more than five hundred thousand rounds of 105mm or 155mm munitions. No one manufacturer could supply either side, let alone both. So they created an innocuous-sounding trade association to divvy up the contracts and keep both belligerents in ammo. My reporting on the cartel for the French magazine *VSD* occasioned my first award for investigative journalism, and Gendelman made the most of it.

He also set me up with the *New York Times*.

I had gone to the United States that November to visit nuclear weapons labs and other facilities associated with the Strategic Defense Initiative, the only American among a group of European reporters handpicked for a propaganda tour by conservative scholar Bob Pfaltzgraff. If this was propaganda, it sure beat Saddam Hussein and his thuggish flaks. We spent an evening with Hungarian-born physicist Edward Teller, the legendary father of the hydrogen bomb. Teller mesmerized us at a dinner with academics at the Hoover Institution in Palo Alto, CA, leaning on his cane as he walked about, describing a world where the destructive forces he and his colleagues had unleashed had been tamed by exotic new technologies. "I believe…" was how he seemed to start every sentence. It was easy to see how Teller could mesmerize politicians. He was a visionary who communicated a future where nuclear weapons became useless with a power and directness that made you feel it was already upon you.

Just in case we weren't taken with Dr. Teller's futuristic vision, our tour guides made sure we saw its opposite by taking us to America's nuclear war-fighting command, deep inside Cheyenne Mountain. From the observation balcony in the heart of the mountain, we watched the giant screen where Soviet missile launches would light up in flashing trajectories on their way to the continental United States. We watched the pale war-fighters manning consoles and telephones in the pit below. The whole command center had been built on gigantic coil springs, so it could absorb the shock of a thirty-megaton nuclear blast, larger than any weapon ever tested by the United States. (The Soviwwet Tsar Bomba, tested once in 1961 but never built or deployed, was the only weapon big enough to take out the complex). Years after *Dr. Strangelove* fantasies of nuclear war had terrified a generation of Americans, the NORAD complex at Cheyenne Mountain continued to fuel Hollywood imaginations.

After a final round of interviews in Washington, DC, I popped up to New York to visit my bosses at *Newsweek*, Mike Ruby and chief of correspondents Bob Rivard, as well as the offices of the Grey Lady herself. *New York Times* foreign editor Warren Hoge gave me a tour of the newsroom and introduced me to investigative reporters Jeff Gerth and Stuart Diamond, whom he had assigned to work with me on the Damavand project. We were going to make history by cracking open the story of the US-Iran arms connection. I had found the juice.

When I got home from the whirlwind US trip, I found a note from Christina awaiting me in my desktop planner. "Are you still happy to have me here?" she wrote.

She had gone out to the kitchen to get a bottle of bubbly wine, Swedish caviar, and chopped onions—her favorite appetizer—and a warmth flowed over me, starting in my stomach and spreading to the rest of my body. She always seemed so strong, so sure of herself, so un-needy, that to glimpse this other side of her overwhelmed me. I went to join her in the kitchen and opened the wine.

"Of course I am!" I told her, brandishing the note. The words seemed so small and superficial compared to what I was beginning to feel for her.

"You should have taken me with you," she said.

"You know it wasn't my choice."

"If you're going to keep traveling, I want to go with you."

I knew I had to respond but was afraid that anything I said would be insufficient.

"I want you with me everywhere," I said.

"Reall-y?" She turned to me mischievously, wagging the knife. "And not just in your bed?"

"That's always a good place to start, isn't it?"

31: Bernard, the Arms Dealer
Paris

I filed half a dozen lengthy dispatches to Jeff Gerth and Stuart Diamond after returning from New York in early December, laying out in great detail what I had learned from Paul Cutter, Bernard Veillot, and Richard Brenneke about covert US arms sales to Iran.

The final player I wanted to interview, Mark Broman, had disconnected his phone, so one evening, I ventured over to rue Bonaparte, where he had bought a small apartment on the top floor of a six-story walk-up. From seven o'clock onward, the Latin Quarter was packed with revelers, even in cold weather, so it was an unending conga dance from the Saint-Germain-des-Prés metro to the Procope and down to the rue Jacob. Broman had gone to ground closer to the Seine, sheltered by a world of old money and culture he had always aspired to join.

I knocked on the door several times in the dark before I heard movement inside.

"What do you want?" a wheezing voice whispered.

He had seen me through the peephole.

"I need to talk to you," I said.

We had parted more than two years earlier on bad terms and hadn't spoken to each other since.

"Why should I talk to you? You're a reporter," he said.

"Yes. But I'm the only one who knows you didn't do what they are all saying you did."

That got his attention, and he opened door a crack so I could see the chain bolt and the fact that he was in pajamas and a silk nightgown at eight o'clock, and with no female in sight. He clearly was not well. For someone who had been military-fit when I last saw him, it was a shock. His eyes were red, and he was out of breath, even though he obviously hadn't taken more than a few steps to the door.

"I'm waiting for a heart transplant," he said. "Can't you just leave me alone to die in peace?"

That threw me back.

"Let me in," I said. "I won't stay more than a few minutes."

His small apartment smelled like an infirmary, and I felt pity for him. I didn't want to torment him, but I did want the truth. I told him that I was working on an investigative story for the *New York Times* on the Damavand project. I couldn't guarantee how he would come out. But if he talked to us, at least he could tell his side of the story.

"I've got all the documents. Paul is in jail. The Frenchmen want to spill their guts. All I need from you is to confirm to the *Times* that we have talked. I'll run some quotes past you if you give me a new phone number."

"Don't give them this number," he said, writing it out in neat block letters on a scrap of paper. "I'm not supposed to get excited or stressed. The French doctors say it could kill me," he said. "They aren't sure they'll have a heart for me before I die."

He was in full melodramatic mode by this point.

"If I don't answer, I'll be in the American hospital in Neuilly," he said. "If we're both lucky, you'll find me there alive."

+ + +

A few days later, Christina and I drove the three hours southwest from Paris to a suburb of Tours to visit with Bernard Veillot. I had recently bought a used Renault 14, which the French marketed as the first "*voiture en forme de poire*," as if that were a great attraction to car-lovers. Translated, it meant "the first pear-shaped car." It sounded like an overweight American with a large rear end.[30]

"I've known Bernard for years," I told her as we were driving down the A-10. "He's the real deal. He was a French naval aviator, which nowadays means an elite so small they could fit in the back of this car. And he's furious because the Americans indicted him. He thought he was doing them a service."

"So you think he's going to tell you the truth?" she said.

"Actually, I do."

In normal times, Bernard was moody and emotional, prone to dark

---

30 The marketing slogan was a take-off on the absurdist title Eric Satie gave to one of his most famous piano compositions, "Trois Morceaux en forme de poire." I suppose that was supposed to lend an air of sophistication to the car. Welcome to French marketing.

thoughts and depression—not exactly what you would expect from a top gun pilot, but hey, he was French. He had deep rings around his eyes and always seemed bathed in a haze of cigarette smoke, like many a character I had met during all-night drinking bouts in old Paris watering holes around Les Halles. But this time he was worse. Like Broman, he was physically a wreck.

"I had an abscess in a tooth," he said. "I didn't pay it any attention. Neither did my dentist. Until the infection spread to my brain and they took me to the emergency room, where they told me I would be lucky if I survived."

Christina knew someone in Sweden who had had the same problem, she said. It was the dentist who failed to diagnose the seriousness of the abscess and took her friend off antibiotics before the infection had been cured.

"That's exactly what happened with me!" Bernard said. "They stopped the antibiotics too soon."

Later on, our children would call Christina "Madame Catastrophe" because she always had a disaster story she could recite in magnificent detail for every horror story someone we knew or had just met was undergoing. And they were all true. This was the first time I had witnessed this extraordinary talent of hers. At first, I thought she was just making it up.

Bernard, the arms dealer, was living in a cookie-cutter suburban villa in a quiet neighborhood of similar houses. I was a bit surprised at the modesty of his circumstances. I wanted to ask him who had paid the bill for the fancy hotel in Geneva where he claimed he had spent months negotiating with the Iranians. He must have plunked every franc of his military retirement into the deal.

Over a long morning that stretched way past lunch, Veillot told us his story.

He had flown US-built Corsairs for the French navy. That is why he spoke English and had a familiarity and respect for the US military: they had trained him. In 1980, he started flying charters to Iran out of Ostend, a tiny freight airport outside of Bruges, Belgium, bringing in supplies for the gum arabic industry. "But there were other things as well," he said.

Through the charter business, he got to know pilots at Iran Air, and through them, Iranian Air Force officers. It was a tiny, close-knit elite, and as a pilot flying into Iran, especially once the war with Iraq began, he was part of it.

In 1983, his Iranian Air Force friends asked him if "something couldn't be done" about the US arms embargo. They had sent two hundred agents to scour the arms markets in Europe, and many of them were claiming they could deliver US equipment and spare parts. But they all failed.

Some of them, like Colonel Faroukh Azizi, were getting rich off of the scams. "He was friends with Rafsanjani. Smoked opium with him. The Air Force guys hated him," Bernard said. "He wasn't one of them."

But he controlled the money. He was *the guy*.

Azizi telexed Veillot in late 1983 and then phoned him in Tours, asking if he could get American-made missiles. "I told him I wasn't an arms merchant," Bernard said. But the more he talked with his Iranian friends, the more he sensed there was a political opening that shouldn't be missed.

The US arms embargo had virtually grounded the Iranian Air Force. Of the four hundred fifty combat aircraft purchased by the Shah, only seventeen F-4s, five F-5s, and two or three F-14s could be maintained in combat readiness. And they had no weapons to shoot down the Soviet Backfire bombers that had started flying across their airspace way above the range of Iran's Hawk air defense systems. The Iranian officer corps was divided over what to do. One faction favored putting out feelers to the United States, in the hope that healing the political breach would lead to reopening the arms and spare parts pipeline so they could threaten the Soviet bombers. An opposing faction—equally as powerful—favored accepting Soviet and Chinese offers to re-equip the IRIAF with Soviet-designed fighters.

Veillot's friends belonged to the pro-US faction. They argued that if they failed to get the US planes back in the air, the pro-Soviet faction would take over the air force—indeed, the entire regime—and the United States could forget about reconciliation with Iran "for at least the next ten years." Already, they were creating new squadrons equipped with Chinese MiG-21s and Chinese copies of Sidewinder missiles—Bernard gave me the contracts with the specs. These squadrons formed the backbone of an entirely new air force within the Revolutionary Guards Corps. Bernard's friends were getting desperate.

"So I told them I would help, but only if they were willing to make a political deal, not just buy planes and munitions," he said.

Veillot teamed up with the other Frenchman, Claude Lang. Lang phoned Boyle—the codename he used for his NSA friend—to see if the Americans were interested in pursuing the Iran opening. Boyle told him to proceed. Soon they were meeting in Paris with a retired US Air Force major general, L. W. "Swede" Svendsen. Tall and powerfully built, Svendsen wore an Air Force tie clip and cufflinks. "He looked like a second-generation immigrant who desperately needed to show he was American," Bernard said. "He was always grooming his nails." His partner, retired USAF colonel Norman A. Callihan, was the first of many Americans to reassure the Frenchmen that their deal had been blessed "at the highest levels of the US government." They would need an end-user certificate to clear the deal with the US authorities, but it was merely a formality, Callihan said. So Veillot and Lang hopped on a plane to Buenos Aires, where they purchased the Paraguayan document I had shown the Egyptians. To me, it was fascinating. Here was the other side of a story I had experienced firsthand. But I hadn't been able to see the big picture.

I took eight pages of notes during our conversation that day and drew charts of who opened what doors and how the money flowed. For two years, the deal went nowhere because Bernard hadn't found the right Iranians and his partners hadn't found the right Americans. It started to gel during May-June 1985 meetings in Geneva when Iranian Air Force colonel Kiamars Salashour replaced Azizi, the bent political operative who was pocketing the money, and Delaroque brought Brenneke and the White House into the mix. Bernard gave me the serial numbers of the thirty-nine F-4 aircraft they now planned to get from the US Air National Guard, and the numbers checked out. No one outside the US government could have supplied such information. The planes were being retrofitted at the Ogden Air Logistics Complex at Hill Air Force Base in Utah, apparently to Iranian specifications. (Colonel Salashour was insisting that an expensive low-smoke modification be made to the engines.)

"While we were sitting together in Geneva, we got a telex from Boyle's friend at the CIA," Bernard said. He dug through his papers and found a copy. It read, "Re Damavand project. Just completing our arrangements. Can you meet with us in Paris, Monday, June 10? Advise Mr. Lang." It was signed H. R. Jones, a name that was unfamiliar to me.

When Christina and I got back to Paris, I called David Twigg, the

US Army criminal investigator who had contacted me after the New York and Bermuda busts. We had met at the Paris embassy, but now he was back in the States. He, too, was happy to talk. It turned out that "H. R. Jones" was a codename for Paul Cutter. Had Bernard forgotten that I knew Cutter?

"Forget about Cutter," Twigg said. "The key is Boyle. He is a real person, and he really did work for NSA. I briefed NSA on Damavand in February 1986. They denied knowing anything about it. But *they knew*. They asked me to drop our investigation." I took another six pages of notes and filed them to Jeff Gerth and Stuart Diamond at the *Times*.

We were getting close, I thought.

+ + +

I was making so much money by this point from the *New York Times*, *Newsweek,* and other freelance contracts that we were able to rent a small apartment at the Trois Vallées ski resort, Les Menuires, for the Christmas and New Year holiday. Christina's son Niclas flew down from Sweden. He was just one year older than Julian, my oldest, and almost the same size. We packed our ski clothes into flat bags and made a bed in the back of the car by folding down the rear seat, then tucked the three kids in on top and drove all night down to the Alps to avoid traffic. They were so close in age—Niclas was then eight, Julian was seven, and Clio six—they quickly became co-conspirators.

Christina agreed with me that we should treat them exactly the same—no favorites, no special dispensations, no separate authority. If we were going to build a family, it started here with the two of us and the three children we already had. We both had to be parents to each of them.

Chapter 6:
Treachery

32: Game of Missiles
Paris

Investigating Iran-Contra was like digging into an ant hill: the sawdust on the surface led to rotten wood beneath and, as you kept on digging, to a maze of tunnels leading deep underground.

On the surface, of course, were the hostages in Lebanon—Americans, Brits, and Frenchmen—all of them held by Iran or Iranian proxies. Since I knew three of them personally and had shared their fate, however briefly, this was a big hook for me. The currency for successfully winning their release was weapons. And since the weapons couldn't be transferred openly or purchased through state budgets, getting them to the Iranians involved a murky underworld of intelligence operators, arms dealers, and influence peddlers, most of them tied to prominent politicians.

Some, like Paul Cutter, were in it for the money. Others, like Veillot and Brenneke, claimed to be operating out of patriotism and geopolitical interest.

But there were many others involved in the game, people whose paths I had yet to cross. And they played for keeps.

Swedish prime minister Olof Palme was shot in front of his wife while walking home from the movies in Stockholm on February 28, 1986. Palme's murder had all the hallmarks of a professional hit and remains unsolved to this day. But as I dug into it with Christina, we found that Palme had agreed to secret arms shipments to Iran and then, just months before his death, abruptly shut them down. In November 1985, he called back two ships carrying Bofors howitzers en route to Iran, one off St. Helena's Island on the Atlantic side of the Cape, the other off the coast of Mozambique. The Iranians were furious. And then he was dead.

In July 1986, just months after he had visited Paris to meet with Veillot and Delaroque, Cyrus Hashemi died suddenly in London, allegedly from a "rare and virulent form of leukemia" that was diagnosed only two days earlier. In the Paris suburb of Neuilly, an American playboy named Glenn Souham was mysteriously murdered on September 24, 1986, while out for a walk with his cover-girl live-in partner. No one paid attention to his demise at the time. But a friend at the US embassy in Paris told me that Souham had known Ollie North and that a photograph of the two them in Granada would soon make its appearance in the press.

John Barry at *Newsweek* wanted me to look into Manouchehr Ghorbanifar, the Iranian intermediary whose name had now surfaced in the Iran-Contra deals. We knew that his brother had a carpet shop in Paris. I pinged my Iranian sources and former French and Israeli intelligence officers who were well connected to the arms and intelligence underworld. Pulling together my notes from a half-dozen interviews, I realized I had compiled quite a file on the not-so-mysterious Iranian. I was getting ready to file my Ghorbanifar backgrounder when John the Chinaman buzzed me on the internal line.

"There's a gentleman here wanna see you."

"What's his name?"

"He no wanna give no name," John said.

"Is he armed?" I asked facetiously.

"I dunno. He don' look it."

I went out to the front office, intrigued. The person waiting for me was sitting nervously, wearing a tatty suit and heavy overcoat. He had large tortoiseshell glasses, a sharp nose, and a receding hairline. He could have been any French intellectual from any left bank café, reeking of stale dark tobacco. Except that he was clutching a document case on his lap. A thick one.

"Is there someplace where we can talk?" he said in a clipped, almost British accent I couldn't identify. It was almost a lisp but not quite. I didn't know whether it was an affectation or just the way he spoke.

"Sure. I've got a cubicle in the back," I said.

Thus began an extraordinary relationship that continues to this day.

"I have something that I think will interest you," my guest said once he had taken off his coat. He pulled a single sheet of paper from a large stack inside his document portfolio and placed it on my desk. "LE JEU DES MISSILES," it read. "SECRETS DES VENTES D'ARMES DANS LA GUERRE DU GOLFE, PAR KENNETH TIMMERMAN."

I had never seen the French title before, as Gendelman was still in negotiations with several French publishers to sell the rights. But there was no mistaking it: this was the cover page of my own book translated into colloquial French.

"What is this?" I said with unfeigned indignation.

"I work for the Quai d'Orsay," he said. "Do you know the CAP?"

I did not.

"It's like your bureau of intelligence and research, INR. We call it the Centre d'Analyse et de Prévisions. Since I am half-British, they asked me to review the translation."

"Just the title page?"

"No, the entire book. They had some questions. I told them the simplest thing was to speak directly to the author. That's why I'm here. In exchange, there are a few areas where I think I can help you."

He wouldn't be drawn into a discussion of how or why the French foreign ministry came into possession of a copy of my as-yet unpublished book manuscript. I didn't even have a copy of it myself! I kept the text files on floppy disks here at the Newsweek office. The only printout I had made I gave to Gendelman. I realized in a flash that he had Xeroxed it and circulated it to book publishers and major news magazines—discreetly, or so I had thought. Had the French acquired it from a friendly publisher? Or had they broken into his office near the Madeleine and helped themselves to a copy?

"I understand you are interested in Ghorbanifar," my guest went on.

Now I was really spooked. Was he able to read my mind? Or my notes?

"A lot of people are," I said casually.

"We have a mutual friend, a certain Jean-Pierre L——," he said. "He told me about your recent conversation."

The Jean-Pierre in question had worked in Africa and the Middle East for the SDECE, the French CIA. His specialty was setting up offshore proprietaries for clandestine arms deals. I had indeed asked him about Ghorbanifar.

"Okay. So what do you know that Jean-Pierre didn't?"

"Ghorbanifar is still active. He is down in Marbella this week, staying at Khashoggi's villa. Last week, your friend Michael Ledeen came through Paris, flying up from Malaga, the airport that serves Marbella."

Ledeen's name was just beginning to surface in the media as one of the intermediaries involved in the Iran-Contra affair, but no one at *Newsweek* or the *New York Times* knew that he was still actively engaged with Ghorbanifar. And I did not know him, so he was not my "friend." That would come later.

"Ledeen met Ghorbanifar through their mutual friend, [former CIA officer] Ted Shackley. Ghorbanifar has a real Portuguese passport under the name Pereira. He also has a Greek passport," my guest said.

Was I ready to forgive the apparent theft of my manuscript? Absolutely.

Before leaving, my guest gave me a French paperback, *Dossier A... comme armes.* It had a subtitle that reeked of scandal: "*Arms trafficking, kickbacks, and political shenanigans.*"

"I am an author, too," he said.

"So this is you? Eric Gerdan?" I said.

"Yes.... Well, not exactly."

"What do you mean?"

"That is a pen name. The editor thought it was too dangerous for me to put this out under my own name. We went after some of the old Gaullist intelligence networks in Africa and the Middle East. We knew that some of the people we named were not going to be very happy."

"And so did they ever go after you?"

"What do you mean? They didn't know who I was. Look, you can call me Gerard."

"Is that your real name?"

"Yes. Gerard Willing."

We exchanged phone numbers and agreed to stay in touch.

Game of Missiles, I thought. Good title!

33: The Paris Ayatollah

Ali Pahlavi was the black sheep of the former shah's family. For six years as a child, he had been the crown prince of Iran, while the new shah remained childless. Ali's father, the shah's younger brother and heir apparent, died in a helicopter accident when Ali was just seven years old, thrusting him to the fore. Many suspect that a jealous brother was behind the crash.

Ali's mother was a Swiss national and a Christian, so he was brought up between two countries and two faiths. Depending on the season, he either went by his Muslim name or his Christian name, which was Patrick. At eighteen, he joined the Imperial army, where he was trained as a commando and a combat helicopter pilot. Unlike his soon-to-become-famous younger cousin, who became known as "Baby Shah," he was not a weekend pilot but a real fighter. He refused to flee Iran with his family after the revolution, preferring to remain on an ancestral cotton plantation in Mazandaran province near the Caspian Sea, which he turned over to his workers. By that point, he had become a devout Muslim. The new regime tolerated him for a few years but never granted his wish to join the battle against Iraq. He was forced to flee about three years after the revolution, joining the ranks of the political refugees in Europe. The Queen Mother, Farah Diba, and especially the former Shah's twin sister, Ashraf, loathed him because he always spoke his mind and refused to play by their rules. His military toughness and willingness to take risks made him a walking insult to his cousin, thirteen years his junior, who had neither of those qualities. So he wound up penniless in Paris, where I interviewed him for *Newsweek*.

One afternoon, Ali/Patrick suggested we have tea with Ayatollah Mehdi Rouhani, the dean of the Iranian Shiite clergy in Europe.

"Ken, if you want to know what Khomeini and the mullahs think, you need to speak with Ayatollah Rouhani," he said.

And he was right.

Dr. Rouhani lived in a large apartment in the shadow of Trocadéro, across the river from the Eiffel Tower. Patrick and I got off the metro at the Passy station, made famous in the final scene of *Last Tango of Paris*, and walked down the steps to a stately nineteenth-century building along the *quai*. Patrick rang an unmarked buzzer in the hallway, and we headed up a broad spiral staircase that circled the lift. Halfway up, we heard someone crack open a door just above us in the dimness. Small tinted windows with leaded panes let in ancient light.

"*Bonjour, mon ami*," the Ayatollah greeted Patrick, taking both his hands in his own. Except for his luminous, almost mischievous smile, he looked like a younger version of Ayatollah Khomeini, with the same fierce beard and pale forehead, the dark, piercing eyes, and the black turban of the *seyyed*, or descendant of the Prophet. When I remarked on this later, he told me that he and Khomeini were indeed blood relatives, as were most of Iran's top clergy.

Dr. Rouhani ushered us through dark corridors into a vast sitting room flooded with soft light and curtains that obscured a magnificent view of the Seine. In the place of honor on top of a rosewood console was a framed photograph of him as a younger man with Pope Paul VI. Before the revolution, he led the first ecumenical exchanges between the traditional Shiite clergy and the Vatican. After he poured us glasses of tea, he showed us photographs of himself with the Grand Rabbi of France as well.

"Monsieur Timmerman," he said, his eyes sparkling with humor. "It always amuses me to hear that President Reagan is looking for a moderate mullah in the so-called Islamic Republic of Iran. The most moderate of them all is Khomeini. Believe me!"

Mehdi Rouhani came from a family of clerics and was something of a child prodigy at the seminary in Qom, where at the age of twenty-five he earned the title of "ijtihad," one who is qualified to interpret Islamic texts.[31] Two of his older brothers, Sadegh, and Mohammad-Sadegh, were grand ayatollahs, the highest clerical rank in Iran. "None of the traditional clergy accepts Khomeini and his invented concept of *velayat-e faghih*, absolute clerical rule," Rouhani said. "There is no precedent for this in the entire history of Islam! That's why Khomeini has placed under house arrest almost every grand ayatollah in Iran, including my brothers. Their very presence as free men was a challenge to him."

Dr. Rouhani loved to talk about Islam, its founder, and the thousands of stories about him, known as the Hadith. But he always had an original interpretation, a unique spin. He liked to challenge the rigid interpretations of the Wahhabis and of the ruling clerics in Iran, who in his view were using religion as a tool of military conquest and political domination.

"I am guessing that you cannot go back to Iran and say these things," I ventured.

He gave a quick shake of his head, accompanied with a cluck of his tongue. Obviously not.

"The best way to get rid of Khomeini is through the clergy," he said. "I was in Paris in 1978 when Khomeini set up camp in Neauphle-le-Château. I refused to meet him, although he was staying only twenty miles away from me and his people were begging me to come. Khomeini was an extremist, a revolutionary. There was no possible meeting of the minds. But," he said again with that twinkle of his, "he is the most moderate of the lot."

---

31   The very notion of "ijtihad" is one of the many things that distinguishes the Shiite clergy from their Sunni, and especially their Saudi and Wahabbi brethren, for whom the notion of interpreting Islamic scripture is blasphemy.

I spent many afternoons with Ayatollah Rouhani over the years to come, discussing religion and politics. He was an inveterate gossip. He knew every Iranian who had fled Iran and had stories about most of the men who were now ruling the country. For example, Ali Khamenei, then president, started out life as a rural cleric who earned his livelihood by traveling from village to village on a donkey to perform weddings. "He never made it past the fourth grade," Rouhani laughed. "And now he's trying to call himself *hojjat-ol-eslam*." Of course, today he is the Supreme Leader and calls himself a grand ayatollah.

For all his "moderation," Rouhani acknowledged that Islam was not just a religion dealing with personal salvation but that it also sought to codify rules for every conceivable human behavior and interaction, from marriage to economics, science, government, and even the arts.

"How should you raise your children? Islam has the answer. When are you allowed to divorce your wife? Islam has the answer. Should we teach the sciences to women or allow women to vote? Should we teach children to play musical instruments? Again, Islam has answers for this and for every conceivable question you might ask governing man and society," he said.

This is a fundamental characteristic of Islam that distinguishes it from other religions and that Western Middle East "experts" frequently seek to obscure or simply don't understand. Yes, Islam is a religion, but it is also a supremacist ideology. It was just the beginning of the many lessons about the essence of Islam I would learn while drinking tea with Rouhani. I became his student, his one-man *hosseiniyeh*. He reminded me more of a Jesuit than other clerics I got to know later in life: always open, always rational, always tolerant, who in the midst of the national tragedy that had decimated hundreds of thousands of his countrymen, never lost his sense of humor.

34: Stabbed in the Back

Paul Gendelman was having a huge success marketing chapters of *Fanning the Flames* to news magazines around the world. In addition to the agreement with the *New York Times*, he sold chapters to the leading news magazines in Sweden, Holland, Brazil, Kuwait, and beyond. The French newsweekly *L'Express* and their Belgian counterpart, *Le Vif l'Express*, ran an excerpt on the cover of their February 6, 1987, editions. And Gendelman was sending me checks that just seemed to grow bigger by the week. I was getting on average around 10,000 francs per chapter, all the while I was getting bylines in *Newsweek* on a regular basis.

When the *New York Times* published the first long investigative story based on my reporting, I was in for a shock. Rather than focus on Iran and what Veillot and Brenneke were calling the strategic "initiative" to woo the Iranian regime away from the Soviet Union, they focused on Mark Broman and another retired colonel whose name was unfamiliar to me and tried to link them through innuendo to the US Customs sting that had landed Paul Cutter in jail. Even worse, they claimed to have "discovered" a 1984 telex message, signed by me, "that appeared to be part of an effort to purchase military aircraft for Iran." Then they noted that Iran "was not named in the telex." Talk about sleazy!

Stuart Diamond had the decency to call me the day before the piece ran to give me a heads-up. I was flabbergasted.

"You're talking about that telex Cutter sent me in Cairo with the pro forma invoice for the tanks and the aircraft. I showed you that."

"This document wasn't in the bunch you gave us."

"So what was it?" I asked.

"We got it from someone else."

"I didn't send telexes except about advertisements for the magazines. What does it say?"

"My editors won't let me share it with you."

"So you mean you've got an anonymous source claiming I was selling arms to Iran, and your editors don't even have the decency to show me the document they claim I sent?"

"Unfortunately, yes."

When the story ran, it included a section on me—not as a reporter, per my contract with the *Times*, but as a participant in the scheme I had reported on—with the subtitle, "An Insider's Account: The Story Checks Out." After finding the telex, Stuart wrote, "the *Times* reinterviewed sources that Mr. Timmerman had previously contacted and found the information that he had provided to be accurate."

When I showed the story to Gendelman, he said I shouldn't be upset. "You're reading it wrong," he said. "They have just confirmed that all the information you provided them checked out."

"But they are making me out like I was an arms dealer."

"So what?"

Gendelman was right. The *Times* rehired me for another month or so, and Stuart ran a lengthy piece about the Damavand project on February 2 that included a straight mention of me and my book.

But thanks to the *New York Times*, I was now officially an arms dealer.

✦ ✦ ✦

"*Bill Dodge*,"[32] I said.

"Who's that?"

"He's the only guy whose name you didn't mention in either of the stories. He's got to be your source."

Over the transatlantic phone line, I could almost see Stuart squirming behind his desk at the NY Times.

"*Bill* was the foul-mouthed lawyer from San Francisco selling the Australian C-130s who got Broman to buy one of the Hercs for the French so they could use it in Chad."

"Look, I'm sorry, but I am not allowed to discuss this with you. I just can't."

Some of the early news accounts on Cutter's arrest mentioned that the FBI got their initial tip-off in March 1985 when Charles St. Clair approached an undercover FBI agent with an Iranian shopping list that included F-4 engines, M48A5 tank engines, and five thousand TOW missiles. Now I was beginning to wonder if *Dodge* wasn't the undercover agent—or at least serving as a confidential informant to keep himself out of jail. We had never particularly liked each other; like Cutter, he was suspicious of me because I was a journalist. But why would he attempt to get me crossways with the *New York Times*? Just spite?

"If it had been my decision, it wouldn't have turned out this way," Stuart said.

"It's okay, I get it."

---

32 Not his real name.

35: Izzy Stone, KGB Spy
Amsterdam

Mark Shapiro of *The Nation* invited me to a conference he was organizing in Amsterdam that May, with the goal of nudging reporters from
a half-dozen countries to collaborate on big international stories. This was
a heavy lift in a journalistic culture big on personalities that had never
believed Ronald Reagan when he famously remarked how much you could
accomplish if you didn't worry about who took credit. For that matter,
most journalists there had never believed Ronald Reagan on anything.

Mark was my age, in his early thirties, and had cut his teeth investigating the alleged ill effects of pesticides in Latin America, a subject I
found a bit overwrought. But after our first chance meeting, I showed
him around Paris and we became friends. He was a self-avowed leftist,
and I enjoyed challenging him on this. I didn't see how you could call
yourself an investigative reporter if you advocated a point of view before
getting the facts. It seemed to me that the politics ought to flow *from* the
facts, not the other way around.

"Why would Monsanto or some other corporation sell something
they knew to be poison?" I asked.

"Profits," Mark said.

"But how could they continue to make money once people realized
their products were poison?"

"Because they succeeded in covering up the truth. That's not a point
of view. It's just a fact."

Maybe he was right, but maybe he wasn't. He and his girlfriend,
Connie, labored to keep up when we went drinking together. I have
always been suspicious of journalists who thought sobriety was a virtue.

Amsterdam was a hoot. *The Nation* put us up in an oversized hostel
run by a left-wing cooperative along a quiet canal with a collective dining
room and meeting halls. There must have been sixty or seventy reporters
in all. I had long discussions with Scott Armstrong, a former *Washington
Post* reporter who had just started the National Security Archive, to
which I subsequently donated a portion of my Iraq weapons archive for
a collection on the Gulf War. I also became friends with Pascal Krop, a
French reporter I teamed up with to write parts of the French connection
to the gunpowder cartel. We were awarded the Joe Petrosino Prize for

investigative reporting later that year by the Certosa di Padula in Italy. The prize was named after an Italian-born New York cop gunned down for exposing mafia drug cartels.

It never occurred to me at the time that this conference was an iteration of long-standing efforts by the Left to mold the media into a weapon it could use against its political opponents. I still believed that my colleagues were motivated by a desire to expose corruption, abuse of power, and criminal wrongdoing by the powerful, no matter who they might be. I was wrong, of course, as the Covid nightmare would show in spades. My awakening to the politics of journalism was still some years off.

The most memorable part of the weekend was meeting Izzy Stone, longtime publisher of *I. F. Stone's Weekly*. Stone was seventy-nine, wizened but fiery, and led a rousing workshop full of anecdotes from stories he had broken—almost all of them, he claimed, by sitting in the Library of Congress plowing through government reports. Remember, this was the pre-internet age.

"Are they dull? Yes, they are dull!" he said. "But no matter how dull they are, they always contain some nugget of secret information if you know how to look for it. The US government is simply too big for the FBI to keep tabs on every Congressional committee, every Labor Department statistician, and every Congressional Research Service analyst and rap them on the knuckles every time they release or point you where to find classified information."

That sounded right to me, and I would return to his advice many times in the years to come.

His mention of the FBI should have been the tip-off. But only later, once the government began releasing the WWII era Venona intercepts and Herb Romerstein and others scoured them to unmask the identities of Soviet spies in America, did it become apparent that Izzy Stone had led a double life in the 1930s, providing information to KGB spies in Washington that they reported in cables back to Moscow Center. He reportedly broke with the KGB after the Molotov-Ribbentrop pact and played hard-to-get until the KGB successfully re-established contact with him toward the end of WWII. From this period until the Soviet invasion of Czechoslovakia, when Stone broke again with Moscow, "it is clear from the evidence that Stone was indeed a Soviet agent," Romerstein concluded.[33]

---

33   Herbert Romerstein and Eric Breindel, *The Venona Secrets* (Washington, DC: Regnery, 2000), p. 436.

No one breathed a word about that in Amsterdam. Izzy Stone was just a good old-fashioned leftist, an investigative reporter of the old school—or so we believed.

36: Legends
Paris

Both Christina and I felt it was high time we celebrated our marriage in public. I wanted a church wedding; she wanted a reception where we could invite our friends. So after our "official" wedding in Stockholm that April with just her family, we got married a second time in June at the American Church in Paris and invited about eighty guests to the Bagatelle pavilion in the Bois de Boulogne.

We had planned to have a long, leisurely afternoon in the park, strolling through the gardens with champagne and Mozart and parasols and laughter, but as soon as we arrived, it began to pour rain. The caterer crowded us into a small farmhouse on the site. A friend who worked at the US Embassy gave us a pair of Baccarat crystal salt cellars. As Christina opened the package, he leaned close to us and stage-whispered: "If you don't want to use them for salt, they're great for cocaine." Everyone within hearing distance broke out in guffaws.

"Is that what you do at the embassy?" said Jack Belden.

"Not officially," my diplomat friend said. "But it is true that everything coming out of official Washington is a bit dopey these days."

Jack had given up journalism in the 1950s after a legendary career, claiming he was a victim of McCarthyism. He had joined the merchant marine in the 1930s and jumped ship in Shanghai, where he became friends with a young communist named Chou en Lai. He made the long march with Mao and later published the first book on the new Communist regime, *China Shakes the World*. During World War II, he followed General Stilwell's death march across Burma and was wounded at Salerno while covering the Allied landing in Italy for *Time* magazine. He was fired toward the end of the war when General Eisenhower barred him from the traveling press corps for allegedly fraternizing with the enemy. (Jack's version was that he had written a story about a family of German civilians and how they struggled to survive the Allied advance.) By the time I got to know him in the late 1970s, he was writing sonnets and a blowhard epic poem on the ills of the nuclear age. He encouraged me to go into journalism and to always focus on the "little" people. "The politicians will always take care of themselves," he said. "Their victims can't."

At one point, Christina tugged on my arm. "Have you seen the children?"

The room was packed, and the kids were easy to miss. Niclas, the oldest, barely came up to my chest; Julian and Clio were even shorter. We had bought new white khakis and white shirts for the boys and a long pink dress for Clio—summer fare.

"Maybe they went outside," I said. "I'll check."

The rain had tapered off, and it was turning into a delightful June afternoon, with the sun beginning to burn the moisture off the grass. I could hear Julian shouting happily in the distance and went in to get a camera, thinking I would surprise them.

And I did. When I got back outside, there was Julian, sliding into home base at the far end of the farmhouse, with the other two not far behind. Leaping up, he elevated his hand like a Roman emperor surveying a triumph, covered in mud from head to foot. Niclas-who-never-dared-get-in-trouble was also covered in mud. I snapped a picture before I broke out laughing. We were building a family.

+ + +

Gerard Willing, the French bureaucrat who presented me a purloined copy of my book manuscript, continued to feed me a dizzying array of inside stories about intelligence matters, terrorism, the arms trade, and corruption. I couldn't use a fraction of what he shared with me at *Newsweek*, and so we gradually developed the idea of publishing a biweekly confidential newsletter, a new business in those days. I called it *Middle East Defense News*, *Mednews* for short. I began test-marketing it at the Paris Air Show that summer and locked in several dozen firm orders at what I thought was the hefty price of $500/year.

The formula was simple. The Brits wanted to know dirt about the French, the French wanted dirt on the Brits, and everyone wanted dirt on the Americans. The Americans were happy to dish on everyone else, and they all hated the Chinese, the Russians, and the Iranians.

I made a brief trip to Washington in September. In addition to buying my first Macintosh computer, I met with US government officials, who were happy to fill my notebooks with juicy anecdotes about arms deals and Iranian leaders. I began to realize that *Mednews* should include data-driven stories, chronologies of state and private visits, statistics on the arms trade and Order of Battle features. These were, of course, "background" stories that few news organizations ever ran, but I felt they were both important and newsworthy. Such background stories could be dramatic: while compiling an early chronology of Iranian relations with Pakistan using the CIA's Foreign Broadcast Information Service, I stumbled across two visits to Iran by a relatively obscure Pakistani scientist named A. Q. Khan. To those in the know, Khan was the head of Pakistan's uranium enrichment programs, so in *Mednews* I suggested that the only reason Iran's Atomic Energy Agency would sign a consulting agreement with him in January 1987 was to launch their own uranium enrichment program. And I was right. But the International Atomic Energy Agency tasked with monitoring Iran's nuclear ambitions didn't connect the dots until 2003, by which time it was too late.

During this trip, I met Dr. Stephen D. Bryen, a deputy undersecretary of defense and director of the Defense Technology Security Administration, DTSA. Steve regaled me with stories about Soviet high-tech espionage networks and the Reagan administration's efforts to rally the Western allies to stop them. He convinced me to include a high-tech espionage section in *Mednews*. It was the beginning of a lifelong friendship, not just between the two of us but also between our families.

Steve introduced me to the legendary Herb Romerstein, who published the Venona intercepts, and to Michael Ledeen. Michael and I compared notes on Iran, and he happily confirmed Gerard's story about introducing the French government to Manouchehr Ghorbanifar, then considered one of the most secretive and illusive figures of Iran-Contra. "Whenever I come to Paris, I *always* see Ghorbanifar," he said. "But I'm not in the business of freeing hostages. I *am* in the business of overthrowing Khomeini—or at least, that's what I thought it was."

✛ ✛ ✛

Shortly after I returned from Washington, Gerard showed up at my cubicle at *Newsweek* and extracted a thick envelope from his briefcase. It contained an eighty-three-page contract between a company called Les

Accéssoires Scientifiques, based in a tiny village near the German border, and Technipromimport, a KGB front used to purchase dual-use technology in the West.

"Your new friend, Steve Bryen, has been busy," he said.

As happened so often between us, Gerard seemed to read my mind. I had not mentioned meeting Steve in Washington, but he obviously knew about it.

The $7 million contract involved the transfer through the French company of US-made ion implanters for making gallium arsenide bubble-memory chips, a military-grade microprocessor. Very High Speed Integrated Circuits (VHSIC) of this type were among the most sensitive technologies then available in the West and were used in the newest generation supercomputers. The Soviet Military Industrial Commission, VPK (the agency responsible for the purchase, theft, and smuggling of high technology from the West), had issued top-priority orders to its collectors to acquire them, Gerard explained. They were also the only computer chips then available that could survive the massive electromagnetic pulse (EMP) generated by a nuclear blast. Chips made of ordinary silicon would melt.

"Where did you get this?" I asked him.

"I can't tell you. But you can use it."

The first issue of *Mednews* came out at the end of September 1987, and Gerard convinced a friend to do the layout using desktop publishing software. I mailed the eight-page newsletter to fifty paying subscribers and to another two or three hundred prospects and called my new consulting-cum-publishing company Middle East Data Project, Inc. By the time the next issue was ready in mid-October, I had learned how to do the layout myself and brought in several dozen new subscribers.

I included in that first issue a brief item on the bubble-memory contract. Without tipping our hand as to the documents I had acquired, I noted that five crates of equipment bound for Moscow had been seized at Luxembourg's Findel airport and that the French owner of LAS, Dr. Aimé Richardt, was locked in appeals in a Luxembourg court to get them released. I hand-delivered copies to several friends at the French newsweekly, *L'Express*. The editor, Jérôme Dumoulin, called me the next day asking to meet.

"This is huge," he said. "This company, LAS, is owned by a subsidiary of the Société Générale, one of the largest banks in France. If it turns out the French authorities sanctioned this type of export, that's betrayal at the heart of NATO."

The cover story in *L'Express,* with my byline, ran on October 16, 1987 with the title, "Le Scandale Français." The president of the Société Générale subsidiary responsible for the exports told us in an interview that he had "total confidence" in Dr. Richardt. "If somebody told me tomorrow these activities were contrary to the interests of France, I would stop immediately," he said. "The French equipment we are selling is also made by our Western competitors, whose markets are saturated. The Eastern bloc countries are our only market. Our high-tech industries wouldn't survive without these exports."

As I continued to report on high-tech espionage networks in the coming years, I would hear this type of argument repeatedly, both inside governments and in private industry. There was a huge battle taking place behind the scenes between the free-traders, who dismissed the strategic impact of these sales and wanted export controls abolished, and those like Steve Bryen, who put security before profit.

And then, of course, there were the spies.

+ + +

One of my sources was a former DGSE officer named Marc G———, who had been detailed to the Ministry of Foreign Affairs as the French representative to COCOM, the NATO coordinating committee for high technology export controls, the group Steve Bryen had spent years to revive and strengthen.

Marc had access to the intelligence files on Dr. Richardt. And they were devastating, he told me.

"We believe he is a Soviet or East German illegal who was sent to France to assume the identity of a child who died during or right after World War II," he said.

How in the world could I use that information, especially since Dr. Richardt had filed a lawsuit against *L'Express*—not for my article, but for the photographs of him washing his car at his home in Alsace-Lorraine, which he claimed constituted invasion of privacy?

"What you can say, on background, is that we find his contacts and his personal background *highly suspect*," Marc said. "And that we continue to monitor his activities."

Marc believed that a young boy named Aimé Richardt had been born near the German border in 1934. The family had two children: the boy, Aimé, whom Marc believed died toward the end of World War II as the Germans retreated from France, and a younger sister who had been committed to a mental institution.

"His parents are dead. His sister has disappeared. No other family members are still living. According to his legend, he was drafted at a young age to serve in the Algerian war and then reappeared miraculously twenty years later to marry the daughter of a wealthy forge owner, once there was no one left who might remember him. If you ask the Defense Ministry, you will find that they have no record of his alleged military service," Marc said.

True? Not true? I went down to Richardt's hometown, Conflans-sur-Lanterne, and found that while he was well known as a local businessman, no one remembered him as a child. No one remembered what he had looked like as a young man. No one could remember him returning from his military service in the Algerian war. "He showed up here in the late 1960s to marry the daughter of a wealthy businessman," one local official told me. "Ever since, he's been a pillar of the community." And as Marc had suggested, when I petitioned the Defense Ministry for his military service record, I was told in writing that they had no information on him.

Could the Soviets or the East Germans have been so sophisticated as to manufacture a legend so thoroughly backstopped as to have eluded all but the most ardent pursuers?

+ + +

Gerard called me about a week after the cover package in *L'Express* appeared, asking me to meet him at the rue de Rivoli exit of the Place de la Concorde metro station. "I'll be there in about thirty minutes," he said. "If you leave now, you should get there just in time. There's some-body I want to introduce you to."

I was learning to not question Gerard's imperiousness. If he said, "Come here, now," I set everything else aside and got moving.

I window-shopped the arcades of the rue de Rivoli down the street from the US Embassy, waiting for him to emerge from the metro. When I saw him accompanying an American in a trench coat, I approached and saluted him in French.

"Let's have a coffee," Gerard said in his clipped English. His companion nodded, lazily surveying the street.

Once we were installed at a back booth, the American introduced himself. He worked with Richard Armitage at the Pentagon and didn't mind telling me that he and his office were in charge of supervising weapons shipments to the Afghan mujahidin. His name was Vincent Cannistraro.

"We've got a problem," he said. "Some of our Stingers have gone missing, and we think the Iranians have them."

An Afghan warlord named Younes Khalis had been ambushed by Iranian border guards as his supply convoy tried to bypass a flooded wadi. Thinking they had encountered an Afghan Army patrol, Khalis fired back, and both sides took casualties. The Iranians called for reinforcements from a nearby Revolutionary Guards post. "When the Guards arrived, they confiscated his trucks, which contained nine Stingers," Vince said.

L'Express published a photograph of an Iranian Revolutionary Guards soldier shouldering a Stinger in the same issue that contained my cover story on Dr. Aimé Richardt. I was beginning to think there was no coincidence to Gerard showing up with Cannistraro.

"Why are you telling me this?" I asked him.

"We want the Iranians to know that we know they have those missiles. So if they think they can use one of them to down a civilian airliner without attribution, forget it. We will hit them mercilessly."

Later, Gerard told me the rest of the story.

"Vince used to work at the CIA and was involved in the Afghan Stinger supply line. He's been sent here to walk back the cat."

"The cat?"

"Isn't that what you call it? Damage control."

37: Saddam's Nephew
Cairo

Christina and I hit the ground running in Cairo that November, when the Egyptians were holding the second International Defense Equipment Exhibition after a hiatus of three years. As I introduced her to friends and contacts among the French defense contractors, it quickly became evident that the French were running scared: their biggest market, Saddam Hussein's Iraq, had run out of money, and their orders were drying up. Plus, Saddam was furious because a French company, Luchaire, had gotten caught making massive shipments of explosives and underwater mines to Iran, a story I helped break in the French media.

One of my best sources had flown in from Baghdad a few days before the show. "We've sold the Iraqis two billion dollars' worth of equipment. They fire off our howitzers until the barrels melt. But we are down to just three full-time staff at BWW. We just can't compete with the Russians on price."

What was BWW? I asked.

He leaned in close so we couldn't be overheard. "Base West World, two hundred kilometers southwest of Baghdad. It's where they do rear echelon maintenance on all the ground equipment they've bought from Western suppliers."

As he provided more details, I made a mental note to run a separate item in *Mednews* on how the Iraqis had shifted management of Base West World from the military to a new civilian organization run by the Ministry of Industry. I was sure my Pentagon subscribers, who had limited access to Iraq, would find that of interest.

And that was how *Mednews* worked. It helped that I was getting high-level access. The Egyptian defense minister, Field Marshal Abdel-Halim Abu Ghazala, spoke to me about Egyptian arms sales to Iraq and their plans to assemble the M1-A1 Abrams tank. He even arranged to have Christina and me tour Factory 100, the still-secret tank repair facility that General Dynamics had built on the outskirts of Cairo. I took a picture of her in an Italian designer suit, looking all business in front of a Soviet tank. "My next car," she joked.

Ryan Crocker, whom I had met in Beirut when the embassy blew up in 1983, was now posted to Cairo as a political officer and gave me a detailed briefing. "You might want to stake out the lobby of the Meridien Hotel in Heliopolis after around 10:00 PM tonight," he said. "I'm told the Saudi foreign minister will be arriving for 'secret' talks." And so I could describe how Prince Saud bin Faisal swept into the hotel lobby with a huge entourage to discuss new military agreements with the Egyptians. One source fed another. I was loving it.

I also managed to corner the Iraqi defense minister, Abdul-Jabbar Shanshal. My French friends called him "Saddam's Kurdish hostage," or "zero-tonne-5," the half-ton general, a pun that played on his bulk and his lack of political influence. He was dripping with sweat as I accompanied from stand to stand at the show. But everyone wanted to know what was on his shopping list.

I sent Christina to talk to the Chinese, who were notorious for their duplicity. The China Precision Machine Import-Export Company exported Silkworm missiles, which the Iranians were using to sink commercial oil tankers, and a broad array of military electronics gear. She cornered two of their sales reps in front of a glass case with two sleek PL-9 air-to-air missiles, a Chinese knockoff of the US Sidewinder AIM-9.

"So, have the Egyptians shown interest in adapting your missiles to their US aircraft?" she said, pointing to the display.

"Missul? What missul?" they tittered.

"Those missiles," she pointed.

"We sell-uh no missul here," they said and continued giggling.

We were meeting a friend from Dassault for dinner. He picked us up at the Nile Hilton in his BMW and drove expertly through the chaotic Cairo traffic without ever honking or jerking the wheel, the only car on the road to do so.

"You drive much better than my husband," Christina remarked.

"I'm a fighter pilot," he said. "It gives you calm nerves."

He reinforced what I had been hearing from others. The French were not only worried about their market in Iraq drying up, they were worried about the stability of Saddam's regime.

"All our contracts have been frozen. Chirac is taking a hard line: no payments, no deliveries," Jacques said. "Saddam has run out of cash and is in hock up to his eyebrows to the Saudis and the Kuwaitis. Saddam calls it blood money—Iraqi blood, their money. But after shelling out forty billion or more, they've about had it with him. They had expected him to finish off the Iranians by now."

Worse: Saddam's playboy son, his cousin, and his nephew were all nipping at his heels.

"The son drives his Ferraris around Baghdad at 3:00 AM after drinking all night with women. There's a rumor that he shot Saddam's favorite bodyguard in the hand after they had an argument. The cousin, who is the real defense minister, is not long for this world. The one to watch is the nephew, Hussein Kamil."

Hussein Kamil had been put in charge of the newly created Ministry of Industry and Minerals, he went on, and had also married one of Saddam's daughters. They were getting into military production in a big way. "Hussein Kamil's plan is to put us all out of business. Just you wait," Jacques said.

Prescient words.

Chapter 7:
Hostage Negotiations

38: How I Became an Israeli Spy
Paris

For me, 1988 will always be the year of the hostages. This was not just because it was a subject that dominated headlines or because of my personal sympathy for the hostages in Lebanon, several of whom I knew personally. It was because some of my sources turned out to be key players in the secret negotiations and asked for my help.

It began innocently enough. A friend who worked at *Paris Match*, Jacques-Marie Bourget, introduced me in January 1988 to a former Swiss police intelligence officer, Jean-Jacques Griessen, who was involved in helping to negotiate the release of German hostages held by Imad Mughniyeh. The former Swiss cop had more information than Jacques could use in *Paris Match*. If I played my cards right, Jacques suggested, Griessen might become a source.

Griessen agreed to meet me for coffee at the Concorde St. Lazare near the train station of the same name. You would never think by looking at him that he went back and forth to Lebanon, speaking with terrorists and their clerical masters. Indeed, if he hadn't noticed me and waved, I never would have picked him out from the crowd. He had plastered-over grey hair, metal glasses, a trim grey moustache, and wore an inexpensive grey suit beneath an ordinary anorak. He also was Honorary Consul in Geneva for the government of Chad, and it turned out we had a mutual acquaintance in a Frenchman who had been running guns to then-Chadian rebel commander Hissène Habré on behalf of the French government in ancient DC-3 Dakotas. We wound up talking for four hours, comparing notes on Mughniyeh and his terror associates. As I pressed him for information on the missing ransom payments, Griessen began talking about Mohammad Bakr Fadlallah, the brother of Hezbollah's "spiritual" guide, and a Lebanese diamond trader named Ali Hijazi. It was a common name and could have been anyone.

"How do you *know* these people?" I asked.

"I was in Beirut last month—on a purely *humanitarian mission*," he added quickly. He pulled out a green plastic folder and showed me the

Lebanese incorporation documents of a Swiss-Lebanese aide organization he had established. "If you want to have influence, you need to be on the ground. People have to see that you are willing to help them with things that they need."

I used Griessen's information, without hinting that he was a source, in a story about the German hostage negotiations later that month.[34]

Through French counterterrorism judge Gilles Boulouques I had developed good sources at the Renseignements Généraux, an intelligence organization that has no equivalent in America. The RG was a relic of the Gaullist days when the government spied openly on its political enemies; since the events recorded here, it has been disbanded. I met repeatedly with top officers and service chiefs in the RG counterterrorism branch to compare notes. My RG contacts helped confirm much of the information Griessen had given me.[35]

Then on April 5, seven Lebanese men hijacked Kuwait Airways Flight 422 out of Bangkok, flew to Algiers, and held the passengers and crew hostage for sixteen days. My sources unanimously fingered Imad Mughniyeh as the mastermind of the operation and told me he had conducted a dry run at a Revolutionary Guards base in Shiraz, Iran, several months earlier.

Everyone now seemed to be gunning for Mughniyeh. The Americans wanted him because he had tortured to death Beirut CIA station chief William Buckley and brutally killed US Navy diver Robert Stethem during the hijacking of TWA flight 847. The French, Brits, and Germans wanted him because he had kidnapped their citizens. The Kuwaitis had a long-standing blood feud with him that began when his brother-in-law, Mustapha Badr al-Din, tried to assassinate the Emir in 1984. Mughniyeh's repeated attacks on Kuwaiti airliners were aimed at compelling them to release Badr al-Din, whom they had sentenced to death.

For all this, no one was able to locate him. Gerard showed up at my office at Newsweek shortly after the latest hijacking with a detailed rap

---

34 "West Germany pursue hostage negotiations 'at highest level,'" *Middle East Defense News (Mednews)*, Volume 1, 8, Jan. 25, 1988.

35 During one visit, I noticed the business card of a Swedish "diplomat" and mentioned that he was a friend. My RG contact was happy to confirm that the Swede was, in fact, a spy and had come seeking information on PKK members his government believed were involved in the Palme assassination, a trail the RG discounted and the Swedes subsequently discarded. The chance discovery of that business card sparked a brief *Mednews* story on the continuing efforts of Swedish intelligence to muddy the waters in the Palme investigation, which continues to this day. See "Kurdish Group Issues Travel Warning," June 27, 1988.

sheet, apparently from French intelligence, as well as a set of pictures of the never-before-photographed Lebanese terrorist.[36] It was very hush-hush information. I took the photos to the RG, who confirmed their authenticity and added that the passport photos had been supplied by Syrian and Lebanese intelligence. Twenty years later, I had to laugh as those same photos resurfaced when Mughniyeh was assassinated in Damascus. Someone had made a blurry scan from the original *Mednews* profile on Mughniyeh, without attribution. I later posted the originals on the internet along with more recent pictures I had acquired from an Iranian defector, who had worked with Mughniyeh during one of his many sojourns in Iran.[37]

After I published the Mughniyeh profile and photos, I got a call from the Israeli defense attaché, who was a subscriber. Born in Lebanon and a fluent French speaker, Jacques Neriah was easy to like and could pass for a Frenchman. Over lunch, we discussed various Arab and Iranian arms deals, Mughniyeh and the hijacking, and the status of the Iranian and Iraqi air forces. In passing, he mentioned his "former boss," Uri Lubrani, who had become a legend for having been the only foreign diplomat in Tehran to predict the downfall of the Shah of Iran. In the wake of the 1982 war, Lubrani was put in charge of Lebanon policy, and he could be colorful when he wanted. (Asked by a reporter why Israel had connections to Druse, Christian, and Shiite militias, he famously remarked that Lebanon was "like a piano. You have to play all the notes.") Uri was still considered Israel's reigning expert on Iran and sat in on meetings between his political bosses and President Reagan's national security advisor, Robert "Bud" McFarlane, during the Iran-Contra caper. "Uri said McFarlane didn't understand anything about the Iranians," Neriah told me. "The Great Satan taking Khomeini a Bible and a chocolate cake? Are you kidding? He probably spat on the Bible and fed the cake to his goats."

When the coffee arrived after lunch, Neriah got down to the real reason he wanted to see me.

"As I read between the lines of your articles, Ken, it would seem you have a source or maybe sources who are plugged into the hostage negotiations."

"You're an astute reader," I said.

---

36 "Imad Mugniyeh: the Real Story," *Middle East Defense News (Mednews)*, May 2, 1988, Volume 1, 15. For years this profile of Mughniyeh remained the most detailed biography available.
37 http://www.kentimmerman.com/news/zakeri-mughniyeh_photos.pdf

"You didn't really try very hard to hide it."

"I guess you're right," I laughed.

The Israeli defense ministry had reached its wit's end, he said. "Two of our soldiers were captured along the border in Lebanon. They're just boys, nineteen years old. Not only can we not get them back, but we also can't figure out for sure who's got them."

"These days it's probably the Iranians," I said. "Have you tried Ghorbanifar?"

"Of course. But he's done nothing to help. Uri was wondering if perhaps you could sound out your sources to see what they know."

"My guy has never mentioned Israelis," I said.

Oops, I thought.

"But maybe the guys your guy is talking to know something," Jacques said. "Ask him if he knows the names of the two soldiers. We haven't released them. If he or his guys know their names, that's a start."

That sounded innocent enough. Jacques wasn't asking me for the identity of my source, or to meet him, or anything that might compromise my reporting. As someone who had been held hostage in Beirut and nearly perished there, how could I not feel sympathy for others undergoing the same fate?

Griessen or 'his guys' soon came up with the names of the two kidnapped Israeli soldiers. Thus began a remarkable adventure that would challenge my identity as a journalist and lead me across a line that most of my colleagues still considered inviolable.

39: The London Safe House

I became a go-between for Neriah and Griessen over the next few months, relaying questions and answers. Griessen had news from Beirut. The intermediaries who claimed they were holding the Israeli hostages were willing to talk, but they were making counter-demands before they would produce a sign that the Israelis were alive.

"What do they want?" Jacques asked.

"They want to know what happened to the Iranian diplomat and his two bodyguards who were kidnapped in 1982 on their way back to Beirut from Tripoli. They were last seen at the Berbera checkpoint."

"This everybody knows. They were kidnapped by the Phallange outside of Beirut. We had nothing to do with it."

"I spoke to a friend of mine who was head of Phallange intelligence at the time. He thinks Elie Hobeika took them and killed them on the spot."

"That is quite possible," Jacques said. "So what do Griessen's friends in Beirut want us to do about it?"

"You are Israel. You must know everything," I said.

Jacques sighed. "I know that's what they think."

"Griessen thinks they would settle for the bodies."

A few days later, Jacques asked to see me again.

"I conveyed your information to Uri. He wants to meet you. He agrees that the three Iranians are dead."

My work took me back to Washington at the end of August, where I met with a Turkish-born desk officer in the State Department's counter-terrorism bureau (S/CT). I asked him about the three kidnapped Iranians. He thought they were alive.

"Look," Kamal said. "No bodies were ever produced. We don't even know which Christian faction took them. To the Iranians, they are like MIAs in Vietnam are to Americans. It's easy to understand their concern."

Sure, I thought—if the leaders of the Iranian regime actually thought as we thought. But they didn't. They obeyed a completely different emotional, political, and social calculus, as Ayatollah Rouhani had made clear. I suspected that the demand about the three missing Iranians was just a negotiating tactic and had my doubts as to Kamal's judgment.

I got back to Paris a few days before the Farnborough Air Show, which began on September 9. Before heading over to London, I met with Jacques, then got a call from him two days later from London: "Uri wants to see you tomorrow. Can you meet us in Oxford Circus in the evening?" I said yes, and he gave me an address.

It would be my first visit to an Israeli safe house.

+ + +

I arrived from Gatwick late in the afternoon, sweaty and disheveled from schlepping my bags. There was no name on the buzzer at 2 Mansfield Street. Uri Lubrani was waiting on the couch in dark suit trousers, an oxford shirt, and suspenders and welcomed me expansively as soon as Jacques got me inside.

"Hello, Ken!" he said, shaking my hand with both hands, as if he had been waiting for me all his life. "Sit, sit. What can we get you to drink?"

Uri was in his early sixties, and while he looked as though he had put on weight in recent years, it was easy to imagine him much younger, more athletic, and much more dangerous. He was effusively charming, with a slight, incongruous stutter that made him seem almost diffident. But beneath it was an air of weariness of someone who had seen it all many times over.

For what seemed like ages, we talked politics. This country and that, who was in, who was out. Eventually, he shared his insights into the Iran-Contra scandal, openly reviewing Israel's mistakes in using Ghorbanifar. "You ask why we did it? One reason: Ollie North. We felt our privileged contact with the NSC was so valuable, such an asset, that if he had asked us to do something about the opposition in Iceland, we would have dropped everything to do it."

Jacques brought us fresh drinks and sat down, leaning forward with his hands on the coffee table. I had passed whatever test they had devised for me. Now it was time to get down to business.

"Look, Ken," Uri said. "We are under tremendous pressure from the families of the soldiers, so we appreciate your offer to help. But this demand about the 1982 kidnapping! Really, we are quite baffled by this."

I noted the way that he had phrased it and almost wondered if they were taping our conversation. As would happen several times as events unfolded, I felt it was important to get the facts straight.

"Uri, look. I am very happy to help. And I will help in any way that I can. But I just want to be clear that this didn't start with me coming to Jacques and saying that I could help get your hostages released."

Uri jumped back, almost as if I had clapped my hands in front of his face.

"No, no, no, no, no, Ken. That's not at all what I meant. Please forgive me if I gave you that impression."

"I'm sorry for mentioning it."

"No, no, not at all. You must, Ken. You must. We want you to feel comfortable about this. This is something all of us must approach very carefully."

Jacques explained. "There are lots of people like Griessen who claim to have information or contacts. You give them money, and it turns out they have nothing. But you never know when you've stumbled on the one guy who has a real connection. He knew our boys' names. That is something."

We discussed the pictures Griessen had shown me of him in Beirut with Sheikh Fadlallah, the Hezbollah spiritual leader. I described Griessen's humanitarian-aid organization, the cover he was using to ransom hostages.

"All of this would suggest that Griessen is serious," Uri said. He exchanged a look with Jacques. "It's worth a try. We are afraid that Iran is losing control of the hostages and that they have been split up between the Dirani group and the Mughniyeh group. Once that happens, we might not have another opportunity."

Dirani was another Iranian-backed warlord from South Lebanon who was in the hostage business. I found it intriguing that Uri felt Israel would have more leverage in getting their soldiers released if they were in Iranian custody.

Uri planned to fly back to Israel the following day to present the case to his "colleagues," who I later learned included the prime minister, the minister of defense, and the director of Mossad. "If they agree that we should pursue this, then we will write you a personal letter of accreditation from my government you can present to the Iranis, so they can be sure who you are."

We had just advanced the ball by light-years from my polite discussions with Jacques over meals and drinks in fancy Paris hotels. Uri was about to go operational. And he saw me as the tip of his negotiating spear.

+ + +

On September 30, Griessen came to Paris, and we met for hours in a café near the Gare de Lyon. I took detailed notes as he showed me proof of his direct involvement in the German hostage negotiations. He had copies of the passports of German hostages Rudolf Cordes and Alfred Schmidt, original Polaroid photos of them in captivity, and handwritten letters to their families. Griessen first got involved in the hostage business a year earlier but evaded my questions as to how, who, and what exact role he had played. He had met the Hezbollah leadership and had photographs of himself at a Hezbollah funeral in Beirut to prove it. He set up no fewer than three humanitarian-aid organizations to funnel ransom payments to the Mughniyeh and Hamadeh Hezbollah factions from the German companies who employed Cordes and Schmidt. He showed me letters, documents, and photos of their offices in Beirut and suggested that one of his intermediaries, Rashid Kasrounian,[38*] had taken the "aid" money from the Germans and run. "The biggest threat we now face is from Ali Hijazi. He is trying to put his fingers into every pie. If your friends have information that could help me to limit his involvement, that would be a big step forward," Griessen said.

In case I had any illusion that hostage negotiations were simple, Griessen became my willing instructor. The group that initially seized a hostage often sold him to some other group for money. The buyer, usually affiliated with Iran, wanted to satisfy their patron's political goals while turning a profit on their "investment." On the other side of the trade, you had former intelligence officers, influence peddlers, and intermediaries who claimed to represent the Western governments, each seeking to benefit. And then there were the anonymous bankers and transfer agents, who skimmed off the top and sometimes diverted a huge portion of the ransom into their own pockets, as happened with both the German and South Korean hostages.

Griessen called a few days later and put his Lebanese Hezbollah contact on the phone. He spoke halting English with a very different accent from that of the Beirut intelligentsia I was used to meeting, who were all French educated. He was ready to go to Beirut to "begin negotiations" but first wanted to meet me and my "friends" face to face. "I need to have information on the Missing Person, the Big One. If I have that, I can bring back proof that the people your friends are seeking are alive." I took him to mean the Iranian diplomat who was kidnapped in 1982 but later learned he meant Moussa al-Sadr, a top Lebanese cleric who disappeared while on a trip to Libya in 1978 along with two Lebanese colleagues. Everyone had assumed Qaddafi had murdered them.

On October 5, Uri phoned to tell me he was back in London at the Onslow Court Hotel in Knightsbridge and gave me the hotel phone number over the open line. He was ready to come to Paris in two days to pursue "the channel" I had opened.

I have thought about that call many times. Uri was clearly not worried that the Iranians would intercept it. I think his intention was to confirm to the Brits and the French what we were doing, which his government had already told them through official channels.

---

38 * Not his real name.

Did that mean that for the British and French governments, I was now an Israeli spy?[39]

+ + +

We met at 9:00 AM that Saturday, October 9, at the Pavillion Montagne Hotel, just behind the Israeli embassy. When I arrived, Jacques and Uri were finishing their coffee. As in London previously, Uri was wearing suspenders, this time with white duck trousers and a blue blazer. Jacques was wearing a suit. I felt a bit out of place in my jeans, leather jacket, and open shirt and asked them lamely to pardon my Saturday attire.

"No, no, no, Ken," Uri said effusively. "We are so glad you are here."

After a few minutes, Jacques moved us down the street to a small café so we could discuss the upcoming meetings in Geneva with Griessen and the Hezbollahi he had put on the phone.

"I cannot meet these people," Uri said. "It's just too dangerous. So I will go with you to Geneva on Tuesday and stay behind the scenes. But you will be the star. My people will be just behind you every step of the way. Can you handle that?"

"I think so," I said.

"You will need a cover story."

"My best story is the truth."

"And what is that?"

Uri exchanged an anxious glance with Jacques.

"The truth is that I am a journalist who runs a confidential newsletter that does stories on arms deals and hostages and intelligence issues. I've been following these negotiations with parties from Israel, the United States, and Lebanon. That's why I am here—in Geneva. To hear what Griessen's partners in Lebanon have to say. What they agree I can write about, I will. What I can't, I will convey to the other parties they would like to reach."

Uri scowled as I was talking, then gradually relaxed and gave a curt nod.

"Ken, they are going to ask you to provide proof about the Irani diplomats before they give you anything about our people. You must resist all attempts to reverse the situation."

"I understand."

---

39   That turned out not to be a concern. It was someone from my own government, a former CIA officer I had met with Gerard, who later whispered to journalists that I was an Israeli spy.

"Let me be frank: my people don't trust Griessen. He has embezzled funds from Swiss humanitarian organizations, and nobody knows why or who he's paying off. These guys are a band of Mafiosi, Ken. But the point is, does he have contact with the people holding our hostages? That's all that really matters. That's what we need you to find out."

I raised Griessen's question about Ali Hijazi, the Lebanese diamond trader he claimed was getting in the way of hostage release deals.

"Don't worry about Ali Hijazi," Uri said. "He has many family members in Lebanon. That makes him…exposed."

Well, *that's* interesting, I thought.

40: Coffee with Hezbollah
Geneva

I arrived in Geneva in the early evening and headed for the Cornavin Hotel, just around the corner from the train station. By Geneva standards, the Cornavin is a modest establishment. I took a seat in a plush leather lounge chair in one of the alcoves, as far as possible from a group of Arabs at the far end of the room. A Swede and a British businessman occupied a nearby booth.

Uri slumped down into the chair across from me, visibly exhausted from traveling back to London before flying here. He was in "operational" attire: a dark polo shirt, slacks, and a nondescript windbreaker. Looking around quickly, he shook his head and muttered, "I hate this town."

"Why?"

"Too many Arabs."

I had arranged to meet Griessen at 7:30 pm, so we didn't have much time. Uri went over my "cover" story one last time. I was a journalist and was prepared to advance modest expense money for Griessen's contact— fifty dollars a day—so he could travel to Beirut to bring back proof that the Israeli hostages were alive.

"I want you to tell Griessen that we are skeptical of his claims. You may tell him that some of his former colleagues don't have very nice things to say about him," Uri said.

He also suggested that I "throw in" Terry Waite and US Marine Corps colonel Rich Higgins, kidnapped by Hezbollah in South Lebanon.

I guessed that was the reason Uri had flown overnight to London instead of coming directly to Geneva.

"I thought the Brits were pretty hostile toward Israel," I said.

He grunted. "Perhaps among the services, but I have no problem with them. We agree to share certain things."

After I checked in (Uri's people had put him in a different hotel), we walked back to the station to call Griessen from a public phone. Griessen was ready to meet in a half hour at the Richmond. As Uri and I strolled down toward the lake in the drizzle, I asked if he was married.

"Oh, yes. My wife is quite used to my travels," he said.

"Children?"

"Four daughters."

"That must be a nightmare," I laughed.

"Oh, but it's good to have them around, Ken. It's good to have them around."

I was tense for the coming encounter, and we parted company at the Corniche. I walked slowly, hyper-alert to my surroundings. It occurred to me that Geneva was inhabited by foreigners because no one knew when to cross the streets. I stopped alongside a French couple, and twice we started to cross before the light had turned, but a stolid-looking Swiss gentleman who could have been John Calvin incarnate glared at us to stop. When the light finally turned, I noticed an attractive Arab girl in her mid-twenties dressed in the latest London fashion come out of nowhere and cross behind me.

I stepped up my pace. Glancing sideways in a shop window, I saw that the Arab girl was keeping up, maybe ten paces behind, so I took the bridge and wandered briefly on the other side of the lake, then doubled back at the next bridge and entered the Richmond. Griessen was waiting in the noisy lobby.

"It's too crowded here to talk," he said.

We walked down the street to the Beau Rivage, but the lobby there was equally as crowded, so we moved a bit further down the lakefront to the Hilton, where we found a table in an empty bistro above the lobby. Five minutes after we arrived, the Arab woman strolled in and took a table by herself a few meters away. Was she one of Uri's or one of theirs, I wondered? The thought of being tracked by Hezbollah watchers—and a snatch team, perhaps?—heightened my alertness. This was real.

Griessen didn't pay any attention to the woman. As I would learn, one of his principal character traits was an ability to remain even-keeled, unperturbed, no matter what storms were raging outside.

+ + +

"So tell me more about your Lebanese friend," I said once our coffees arrived.

"He's a man of modest origins but with big ambitions."

Rafaat was a Shiite from the South who used to work for the Lebanese security services, Griessen explained. He was tied in with Abdel Hadi Hamadeh, one of the hostage-takers, and with the Hezbollah leadership. During the Cordes negotiations, Griessen used him in Beirut to transmit documents to Hamadeh. But in the end, the Germans made an end-run around Griessen, working instead with Ali Hijazi and a wealthy Lebanese businessman named Victor C——.

"Between them, they pocketed more than ten million of the ransom money," Griessen said. "That's the word on the street."

As we were comfortably sipping coffee in the Geneva Hilton, I felt way out of my league. Cheating a terrorist gang out of $10 million? How were those people still alive?

"My guy is also close to the head of Iranian intelligence in Europe, Mohammad Taleh. Your friends will understand the significance of that. The Swiss tried to expel Rafaat not long ago because of that, but I intervened. This is how I control him. He remains here solely because of me."

"My friends are also interested in Terry Waite and Colonel Higgins," I said.

"Ah," Griessen said. "For them, I've got someone else you should talk to."

Like a whorehouse Madam, I thought, Griessen had just the right person for his customer's needs. He went out to phone both men.

Unwilling to drink coffee all night, I ordered a glass of Swiss white wine. As I was speaking to the waiter, a young Arab man wearing a sports coat joined the girl who had followed me on the street. They ordered food, talking quietly, with a great display of intimacy. Couldn't be Hezbollah, I thought.

When Griessen returned from making his calls, he told me a bit more about his network. He claimed to have several dozen former Swiss

Customs agents, police, riot squad, and intelligence officers who were ready to go into action at a moment's notice. The hostage ransom business was just a sideline. For his day job, he protected oil pipelines from sabotage in a Middle Eastern country and tracked down Lebanese jewel thieves for the Swiss federal police. "Only a fool would have worked for what I asked to free the German hostages," he said. "I still haven't collected my fee."

I took that as an occasion to voice the Israeli skepticism about his character. He responded without missing a beat, as if I had been talking about the weather.

"What kind of stories did they tell you?" he asked with a faint smile. "Who were their sources?"

When I didn't answer, he started to speculate.

"Well, maybe they could be talking about the fact that I deal with Libyan arms dealers. But you know, Monsieur Timmerman, the fact that you are tracking an arms dealer doesn't make you one yourself."

"Very true," I laughed, wondering what he knew about me.

"Here's the interesting thing. You find the same people involved in every shady deal: drugs, terrorism, arms, hostage-taking. It's a mafia. Some of them are members of what you would call the intelligence establishment. Some of them are politicians. Some are actual terrorists. And sooner or later, they all come here to Geneva."

"Maybe some of your former colleagues in the Swiss police have been spreading nasty stories about you?"

Griessen thought about that for a second, then shrugged.

"Let me show you something to help you to understand how the Swiss police feel about me."

He pulled out his billfold and extracted a laminated pink ID about the size of a French driver's license.

"This is a concealed carry permit. The Swiss authorities only issue these to serious people."

Unfolding the permit, I made a mental note of his birthdate and his home address. He made a point of showing me that the permit had just been renewed.

He nodded as a heavily built man in a beige trench coat pushed his way through the door. He looked like one of Sheikh Farid's Beirut bodyguards, not too intelligent, but street smart and dangerous. His week-old beard belied his pale features.

"I told our friend Rafaat I would introduce him to someone who worked for the American intelligence services in Paris."

Rafaat was almost upon us, so I said nothing. But inwardly, I groaned. Not only was that not true—it was dangerous.

+ + +

After we shook hands, Rafaat surveyed the room and proclaimed that we should move downstairs to the piano bar. The young Arab woman and her boyfriend didn't so much as glance at us as we went by their table.

Like many Middle Eastern men, Rafaat bore on his cheeks the scars of a childhood illness. He had the reddish-brown hair common among Shiites from southern Lebanon. This came from Circassian blood, someone once told me, rampaging migrants from the North who left destruction and light-featured descendants in their wake. We ordered drinks and got down to business as the piano player filled the silence with boozy nightclub tunes. Rafaat faced the door, as if daring anyone he didn't know to enter.

"It all comes down to proof of life," I said. "Can you and your friends deliver that?"

He brushed off my direct question with a sweep of his hand.

"You need to set up a program."

"That sounds like somebody's Swiss bank account to me," I said.

He and Griessen laughed good-humoredly, but underneath it, Rafaat was deadly serious.

"The Germans went behind our back," he said bitterly. "If they had only followed the program I proposed to them, they wouldn't have had all the problems they encountered."

"Their people spent another six months as 'guests' of the Movement," Griessen added. I took him to be referring to Hezbollah. "And the German government had to come up with more money in the end."

"We don't need that much," Rafaat said. "Say, twenty thousand to begin with."

"Dollars?" I nearly choked.

"Certainly not Lebanese pounds. I must go to Beirut and sit in the Summerland Hotel for a couple of weeks and let people come to me."

As we haggled back and forth over the money, I realized I was on losing ground. I never should have let the conversation go in this direction to begin with. Griessen sensed my increasing reticence and tried to steer Rafaat away from his extravagant plans to leave a trail of hundred-dollar bills in the bars and nightclubs of Beirut's premier seaside resort. He was the consummate intermediary, launching into an endless story about meeting the Hamadehs and Sheikh Fadlallah and eating in cheap felafel parlors in the southern suburbs of Beirut, hoping to absorb us in the details so we would forget the knot of disagreement between us.

"At least get me an official report on the disappearance of Imam Moussa Sadr. *Your friends* in Mossad can prepare this. And a separate report on the disappearance of the Iranian diplomats. We will leak these to the Lebanese press while we are in Beirut. This will open doors," he said.

He explained that the interim leader of the Shiite community in Lebanon, Ayatollah Mehdi Shamseddine, was eager to assume Moussa Sadr's title as head of the Higher Shiite Council but was being forced to wait another five years—unless they could declare Moussa Sadr officially dead.

"An official report of this kind will strengthen his claim," Rafaat explained.

"And it will make him beholden to us," Griessen added.[40]

Rafaat started telling me about other hostage deals he had been involved in and how they had gone sour because the buyers weren't willing to pay the price.

"Just three weeks ago, the group holding the American, Thomas Sutherland, was ready to deal. They wanted three hundred thousand down and three million on delivery because they wanted to get out of Lebanon fast. When your government refused, they went to ground. Now it is going to be much harder to bring them back to the table," he said.[41]

"Look," he went on. "Ali Hijazi is going to Beirut next Wednesday to negotiate the release of Terry Waite. Anything is possible if you have the means. All we need is a budget, and we can get your friends out."

"I'm not in a position to offer you a budget besides a plane ticket and a modest per diem," I said. "Please relay that to *your* friends, and we can talk again tomorrow morning if you'd like."

I grabbed my briefcase, shook their hands curtly, and headed out. They were stunned. I had actually walked away from the table, when both of them thought the negotiations had just begun.

---

40 I would meet Shamseddine many years later in Beirut and was impressed by his urbanity and keen political instincts. He was a Lebanese version of Ayatollah Rouhani.

41 Dean of Agriculture at the American University in Beirut when he was kidnapped in 1985, Sutherland wasn't released until November 18, 1991. He died at the age of 85 in Fort Collins, Colorado on July 23, 2016.

✦ ✦ ✦

Griessen was out of breath when he joined me down at the coat check. I laughed at the thought of him running down the stairs to save the deal.

"I told our friend that you and I needed to talk privately. We agreed to meet again tomorrow morning."

And so, for the rest of the evening, Griessen worked on me. We walked up to the train station and wandered into a pizza parlor and ordered pizza and a half-bottle of wine. Griessen became anxious to know what the Israelis were saying about him, to set the record straight. At around midnight, I said goodnight. We parted ways on the sidewalk, setting off in opposite directions.

I found a phone booth in front of the station and phoned Uri in Room 718 of the Warwick, as we had arranged. Five minutes later, I joined him in the lobby and we ducked into the bar.

"Sorry about the late hour," I said. "Did you manage to get some sleep?"

"Not a wink. But that's alright, I am used to it. I'm just sorry that you've had such a long night."

He ordered Campari and soda. I asked for a Rémy Martin.

Uri listened attentively as I recounted my evening and brushed away my poor impression of Rafaat and abrupt departure.

"This was just a get-to-know-you session," he said. "He and Griessen are professionals. They knew that."

"I didn't feel very professional," I said.

"No, no, no, no, Ken. You did fine," he said. "You played hard to get, which was just right. These people are thick-skinned. And they're coming back for more tomorrow. We can see that."

For the next half hour or so, he drilled me on specifics I needed to cover with Rafaat in our next meeting.

"Press him for more detail on the navigator and the two boys because they are two separate propositions. If he pretends that the same group controls them, he's not our guy."

Ron Arad, the Israeli navigator, had been shot down over southern Lebanon two years earlier in his A-4 Skyhawk. Uri believed he was still being held in the South, probably by Dirani, the local warlord who had "purchased" him from the group that had captured him when his plane went down. I was also to find out more about the type of report Rafaat wanted about Moussa Sadr and the missing Iranians. "We are not in the

habit of concocting this kind of thing," Uri said. "We cannot release something fictitious. It would be bad for our credibility. So stall for time on this,
say you need to consult with your people in person. He'll understand that."

I took notes that I planned to have open in front of me when we
next met. It was getting close to one in the morning, and we were both
exhausted. But something else was troubling me.

"He told Rafaat that I worked for the CIA," I said.

Uri raised his eyebrows in disgust. "That's Griessen for you. These
people are really the dregs of humanity. You cannot allow him to do this,
Ken. You know how rumors fly. You must be careful about your reputa-
tion. You want to continue working in the Arab world. Getting yourself
identified as CIA would be fatal to you. Fatal. Look at William Buckley!
You must correct this forcefully, the first thing you do."

He rehearsed my story again with me (my true story!), and my
confidence began to return. Uri's presence was reassuring and powerful.
I didn't start to read good spy fiction until many years later, but once I
did, I recognized Uri in a dozen different characters across continents and
cultures. He was the agent runner whose sole job was to pump me up,
support me, steer me away from danger, and point me toward success.
He was mentor and comrade-in-arms rolled in one.

His last piece of advice was almost humorous.

"Tell Griessen tomorrow morning that you must meet with him
first. Don't worry, he will make the other one wait."

+ + +

I set my alarm for 7:30 AM and called Griessen at eight, as we had
arranged. Just as Uri had predicted, Griessen didn't complain when I
said I had to see him alone before we met Rafaat again. So a half hour
later, we had breakfast together at the Crystal Hotel, near the station.
I told him forcefully that I had to correct the record about who I was.
Griessen fidgeted.

"If you tell him you're a reporter, it might scare him away," he said.
"I'll tell him you're an independent, like me."

"No," I said. "I will tell him. I want this whole CIA business taken
off the table. I have to work in the Arab world, and I would like to do it
without constantly looking over my shoulder."

Rafaat pulled up in front of the hotel in his beige Volvo 740 and
lingered a few minutes in the car. Was he checking for surveillance?

Or just reading the paper? When no one besides the parking attendant showed up, he joined us inside.

I felt much stronger and more confident after my talk with Uri and a good night's sleep. I spelled out my affiliation as a journalist and gave him a copy of *Mednews* to prove it. Rafaat appeared to accept this shift in the terms of our relationship with equanimity. It also made things easier as far as his financial demands were concerned. Clearly, I couldn't be advancing large sums since I was offering to pay his expenses out of my own budget. From $20,000 up front, he came down to a plane ticket and a $50 per diem.

"You can contribute something as well," he said to Griessen.

Flustered, Griessen offered five hundred Swiss francs.

"One thousand," Rafaat said.

"No more."

"A little more," Rafaat tried again with a smile.

"Okay. Five hundred one francs. That's it."

Sighing, Rafaat agreed.

I took out my notebook and began to press him for specific details on the Israeli hostages and who held them. He backed off slightly, saying now that he only had access to the navigator (whom he called the "pilot"). Dirani still had him and was willing to exchange him for a pledge of personal safety from the Israelis.

"The two soldiers are being held by the Hezbollah Shura Council in Beirut. We have no opening there yet," he said.

He pulled out a typewritten report he believed had been written by the Lebanese Forces on the killing of the Iranian diplomat and his bodyguards. It was extremely detailed and claimed that Kataeb faction leader Elie Hobeika had held the three Iranians for two months then assassinated them. The only problem was, the report claimed the abduction occurred in the summer of 1985, whereas it actually happened in 1982.

"Maybe it is a typo or a transcription error from Arabic," Rafaat said. "This is the type of thing we need—but from an official source."

At ten o'clock, I excused myself to make a phone call to my "friend." Uri was scheduled to take a plane back to Tel Aviv at 11:45 AM. We agreed that I needed to wrap up and meet him back at his hotel.

Back with Griessen and Rafaat, I summarized the points we had agreed to: First, my "friends" would provide the reports Rafaat was demanding. Rafaat would then travel to Beirut, and my "friends" would leak the reports to the media while he was there. He expected this would open the doors and allow him to get proof of life, at least for Skyhawk navigator Ron Arad.

As I took my leave of them, I memorized the license plate of Rafaat's car, which was still parked outside. GE 228 171.

+ + +

I got to the Warwick just as Uri was coming out the front door with his overnight bag. He nodded, and I jumped into the cab the concierge waved forward for him. We rode together to the airport, making small talk, two friends sharing a cab to the airport.

The person at the Swiss Air counter was having problems finding Uri's reservation in their computer. "It's under Uri, L," he said. "Uri is the last name."

Once they had sorted it out, we stopped for a final debriefing in an airport coffee shop.

"If we have to speak by phone you must use code words," Uri said.

We agreed that I would refer to the reports Rafaat was seeking as the "*cartes de visite*" (business cards). Rafaat was "the Bishop," Griessen "the Archbishop." Mustapha Dirani, the warlord who was holding Ron Arad, was simply "Mr. D." No mention of Israel, Iran, or Lebanon.

While transparent to anyone who understood the real subject, I supposed that the simple code was designed so our calls would not trigger the word-search algorithms of the NSA's computers.

I took a cab to the Cornavin train station and arrived back in Paris at 4:38 PM. Jacques Neriah beamed at me when I stopped off at the Israeli embassy. He was excited, conspiratorial.

"So, you've just been through your first operation, and you survived."

"I don't think there was any particular danger," I said.

He clucked his tongue. "We had eyes on you the whole time. If nothing else, you will get a good book out of it!" he said.

"Uri said the same thing last night. I told him that seemed to be the only perk I would get out of it."

"Perk?" Jacques said, not understanding.

I laughed. "Uri didn't understand the word either. The only benefit, if you will."

"We don't take these risks for benefit, Ken. We do them to save the lives of our people."

"And I am happy to help. We've always been clear on that."

Jacques had one more item of business. How he handled it betrayed his impish sense of humor.

"You need to use another name when you call me here."

"What do you suggest?"

"How about, Mister Webster?" he said.

Judge William Webster had taken over as CIA director the year before to sort out the Agency in the wake of the Iran-Contra scandal.

"That'll put the French knickers in a twist," I said.

"Let them earn their keep."

Christina and I were now living in a fixer-up house we had bought in Maisons-Laffitte, a twenty-minute ride on the RER train from Paris. I said goodbye to Jacques so I could get home in time for dinner. How is that for congenial "spy" work?

Now the waiting began.

41: Back Door Man

Weeks went by with no news from Griessen or Rafaat. It wasn't until the end of November that Rafaat finally called me from Geneva. He had just spoken with his source in Beirut, "the one who holds the pilot." Over the previous few days, his gunmen in South Lebanon had been under assault from a rival group. "He is ready to negotiate, to collaborate with us on the pilot," Rafaat said. "But he needs something to strengthen his hand. Otherwise, he could be killed tomorrow. They are shelling him bad."

He scaled back his demand regarding the Israeli government report on Moussa Sadr. "It can come from you or from someone in the Arab media. But we need new information." He also stopped making financial demands.

When I connected with Uri by phone in early December, he was glum. Everything was blocked on his end because hung elections in Israel had created a political impasse.

"We'll wind up with a national unity government with rotating prime ministers. But for now, it's all horse trading," he said. "Such is Jewish politics. If you have two Jews in the room, there will be three political parties and five opinions. And nothing will get done."

And that was when Israel lost eyes on Ron Arad, just when a deal seemed within reach. To this day, he has never surfaced. His family can thank the politicians.[42]

+ + +

In mid-January 1989, I received a cryptic call from Griessen in Geneva. By that point, I was deep into an investigation of the Pan Am 103 bombing over Lockerbie, Scotland, which had taken place just before Christmas. Griessen was concerned because "someone" had been taken in South Lebanon in connection with Ron Arad. I took him to mean that the Israelis had kidnapped someone close to Dirani. He also said that his nemesis, the Lebanese jeweler from Geneva, Ali Hijazi, had now entered the scene as a key player in negotiations for Arad's release.

For several months, I had little contact with Jacques Neriah or Uri Lubrani as Israeli politicians sorted out their power-sharing arrangements. Then, in early April, I met a former French case officer, Daniel Burdan, who had written a "tell-all" book about his nine years in the counter-terrorism division of French counterintelligence, the DST. Daniel's big story involved how wrangling among politicians and corrupt intelligence officials had caused the DST to dismiss actionable intelligence on a terror network that exploded on Paris streets in a series of bloody bombings. If they had acted in time, he claimed they could have prevented the bombings.[43]

Daniel seemed to know something about everybody, which is how he stayed alive. So I asked him about Ali Hijazi.

"The Ali Hijazi I know has been under Israeli control for at least three years, when Mossad lured him into a honey trap in Paris," he said. "The girl had a Polish mother, a Jewess, and a Danish father. Blonde, well-built. A real looker, named Elisabeth. She became Hijazi's mistress and often visited him at his apartment on the avenue Foch. She came to me later for protection. That's when she told me about working for Mossad."

---

42 The November 1, 1988, Israeli elections led to two months of political horse-trading and did indeed give birth to a national unity government, just as Uri had predicted, that took office on December 22, 1988.

43 A good friend, Bill Dowell, who was then working as a stringer for *Time* magazine in Paris, introduced me to Daniel. Bill was one of the most generous reporters I had met and enjoyed sharing sources with me who had stories he knew he would never be able to report. He had introduced me to Pierre Salinger several years earlier and induced him to share files on the Iranian revolution and early Iranian arms deals I incorporated in my first book, *Fanning the Flames*. Daniel's book, written under a pseudonym, appeared under the title *DST: Neuf ans à la division antiterroriste* (Paris: Editions Robert Laffont, 1990).

If Daniel's story was accurate—and I had no reason to suspect it was not—then it did much to explain Uri Lubrani's mysterious remark that the Israelis were "not worried" about Hijazi's involvement in the hostage negotiations. He was their back-door man.

Not long after this, Jacques Neriah told me that they had decided to cut off all contact with Griessen because he was "unreliable." According to Uri, he had been fired by Swiss intelligence after being caught with his finger in the till. "The Swiss warned us off Griessen. They said he was 'dynamite,'" Jacques said. "They were tracking every move he made and told us that at any moment, they were going to arrest him. If we continued to work with him, we would have put in jeopardy our relationship with the Swiss services. We cannot operate in Switzerland without their approval, just as in France."

As it turned out, my days as an Israeli "spy" were barely enough to fill a chapter, let alone an entire book, as Uri and Jacques had said. But Griessen's story was another matter. He continued to play in dangerous fields, although he was never arrested by the Swiss. I continued to visit him and compare notes about the hostages in Lebanon, his investigation into the murder of West German politician Uwe Barschel, and his complex relationship with a murky intelligence broker and hostage negotiator named Werner Mauss—right up until his suspicious death.

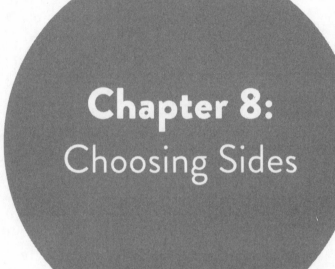

Chapter 8:
Choosing Sides

42: The Baghdad Arms Fair
Baghdad

Saddam's minions billed it as a birthday celebration. But for the French, British, German, and other arms merchants he "invited" to take part in the festivities, it had all appearances of a summons, and a very expensive one at that. Many of them were subscribers to my confidential newsletter and complained to me in private of the huge sums the Iraqi government was forcing them to pay for display space at the First Baghdad International Exhibition for Military Production, the arms fair that officially opened on April 28, Saddam's fifty-second birthday.

Many of these same subscribers had been telling me that my newsletter would be going out of business now that the eight-year Iran-Iraq war had come to a close. But here they were, lining up to kiss the ring of Hussein Kamil al-Majid, Saddam's son-in-law, the man they believed held the keys to fabulous new contracts—and retirement in St. Tropez.

As I visited the exhibits of French defense contractors I had known for years, they pointed out their competitors from Italy, Spain, and Britain. "The gang's all here," one of them joked. So much for the end of war as we knew it.

Among the exhibitors was Gerald Bull, the soon-to-become deceased inventor of the supergun, a monstrous fixed artillery piece that Saddam built into the side of a mountain, which he hoped to use to annihilate Israel. Outside of a handful of intelligence officers and artillery experts, nobody knew who Bull was at that point. Those who noticed the 1/35 scale model of the supergun he displayed thought it was a joke.

British machine-tool company Matrix Churchill had an entire pavilion, slapping stickers for an Iraqi company, "Nassr," on top of their brochures. "Nassr" boasted of manufacturing all sorts of bombs and rockets in Iraq, as well as producing five-axis machine tools capable of manufacturing just about anything, but it was just a front. The Brits were supplying all the know-how and doing all the work.

Atlanta-based bankers Paul Von Wedel and Christopher Drogoul arrived at the show after touring one of their projects in northern Iraq.

They ran the Banco Nazionale del Lavoro's money-laundering machine that funneled US taxpayer dollars into Iraq's weapons industry in the guise of commodity credits and export guarantees from the Bush administration. And these were just a few of Saddam's guests.

I did a double-take when I walked into a pavilion of Iraq's military industrialization ministry. In the middle of the room, I found a five-axis machine tool bearing the serial-plate "AVQBQ-SHW" in an area devoted to Iraq's ballistic missiles.

Here's why it was a big deal.

During my investigation of Soviet high-tech espionage for my new book, *La Grande Fauche*, I identified a number of West German machine-tool manufacturers selling to the Soviets and went to visit them. Christina and I had toured the Waldrich-Siegen plant in Burbach, West Germany, just four months earlier. Waldrich-Siegen was under investigation for selling a giant composite tape-laying machine, made with technology from its US parent company, Ingersoll Rand, to a Soviet military aircraft factory. While we were on the factory floor, Christina noticed a shipping crate with "Iraq" written on it and distracted our hosts for a few minutes so I could examine it. I noted down the serial number, just in case. Waldrich-Siegen officials later told me it was a common-place "civilian" export to Iraq. But here was that very machine, with the same serial plate, identified by the Iraqis as part of their ballistic missile program.

Over the previous three years—thanks in good measure to my deepening relationship to Reagan appointee Steve Bryen—I had come to understand that in the event things went bad in a country such as Iraq, exports of dual-use technology were far more dangerous to US interests than actual weapons sales. For example, the United States had exported billions of dollars of state-of-the-art weaponry to the Shah of Iran in the 1970s: F-14s, Phoenix missiles, Huey Cobra attack helicopters, and much more. When the United States slapped an arms embargo on Iran after the 1979 revolution and war broke out a year later, the sudden lack of spare parts grounded Iran's air force. In multiple interviews several years later, Abolhassan Bani Sadr—who had been president at the time—provided me with chapter and verse on the disaster of the broken supply line and how he scoured sprawling warehouses without inventory lists, unable to locate vital spare parts he and Iranian officers knew were there. Iran's revolutionary government felt it had been painted into a box and sent arms buyers scouring the world to buy spares. Their enterprise became the subject of my first book.

Saddam also felt the sting of an arms embargo, and it motivated him to develop his own weapons industry, just as Israel and South Africa before him, by importing generic or dual-use manufacturing equipment his experts adapted to produce weapons. I was beginning to understand the relationship between dual-use exports, which many American companies were actively lobbying to expand, and dangerous weapons programs in countries such as Iraq, Syria, Libya, and North Korea, thanks to Steve Bryen and Bill Triplett, a staff lawyer who worked for Senator Jesse Helms. At the time, the fact that my best sources were Republicans, whereas I had always believed that "big business" was a Republican interest, went beyond me. I just assumed that the restrictions on high technology exports these Republicans were trying to get Congress to impose had broad bipartisan support.

As I later found out, I was wrong.

+ + +

While the Baghdad arms fair was a big deal for the arms merchants, it went almost totally unnoticed in the press. The only Western reporters present were me and Christopher Foss of *Jane's Defence Weekly*, an industry publication. Later, once the Iraq arms scandals became front-page news, I am sure that the more honest reporters then covering the Middle East must have kicked themselves for missing such a huge opportunity.

I spent two hours on opening day in a beige suit and tie in the hundred-degree heat, taking pictures of every dignitary who ascended the steps of the VIP pavilion. I was using a Canon EOS 650 with a 100–300mm telephoto lens and had to turn off the autofocus because the guests were moving in a nearly constant line. They bowed and scraped as if they were about to meet the God of Mammon himself. Many of them I didn't recognize at the time, but I shot them anyway; a Lebanese friend in Paris, who went over the contact sheets with me later, spotted Saddam's younger son, Qusay, as well as a number of arms dealers whose names were familiar but who had never been photographed.

My favorite was a photo I snapped of French aircraft magnate Serge Dassault and his top arms salesman, the ever-elegant Hugues de l'Estoile, shuffling before Hussein Kamil and his two sidekicks, Lt. Gen. Amir

Rashid al-Ubaidi and Lt. Gen. Amir Hamoudi al-Saadi. Unbeknownst to the outside world, those three Iraqis controlled Iraq's entire defense establishment, from conventional weapons production to uranium enrichment, nuclear-bomb design, chemical weapons, and ballistic missiles factories. And I had them in a single photo.

One poignant scene took place beneath the wing of a French-built Mirage F1 EQ5 fighter-bomber. General Maurice Schmidt, the French Army Chief of Staff, had come to Baghdad as the personal representative of French Defense Minister, Jean-Pierre Chevènement, an ardent admirer of Saddam Hussein. I had met General Schmidt a few times in Paris and thought it would be interesting to follow him around. When he saw what the Iraqis had done with the Mirage, I didn't need to eavesdrop because he was shouting so anyone could hear.

"What [expletive deleted] is that?" he shouted at Dassault's De l'Estoile, pointing to an unfamiliar missile hanging beneath the wing of the French fighter.

"Well, *mon générale*, if you ask me, it looks like an AS-14," the arms salesman replied.

The AS-14 Kedge was a Soviet laser-guided missile that the Iraqis had bought in large quantities. The French believed it was a knock-off of their own AS-30L, although it had three distinct advantages: it had a slightly longer range, packed twice the explosive punch, and it was much less expensive than the French missile.

Schmidt looked De l'Estoile in the eye: "What have you people been up to over here?"

"Don't look at me. We had nothing to do with this. The Iraqis have been working all by themselves."

De l'Estoile then steered the General in his white képi and summer dress uniform over to a MiG-23 sitting on the tarmac of Al-Muthana Airport. "See that refueling probe?" De l'Estoile pointed to the nose of the Soviet fighter. "*That's* one of ours."

Schmidt was not amused, even though De l'Estoile hastened to explain that the Iraqis had adapted the French refueling probe to the Soviet fighter without asking advice from Dassault.

After publishing those photos in *Mednews*, I sold a package of pictures from the arms fair to the Sygma photo agency. They included a famous picture of Iraq's al-Hossein missile that still gets reproduced today and the only pictures then available of General Amir and his associates. They became a big hit once Saddam invaded Kuwait the following year. [44]

But the pictures I took of the French chief of staff and the Dassault arms salesman arguing beneath the wing of the Iraqi Mirage F1 that day would cause a diplomatic incident of major proportions. Three years later, they nearly got me expelled from France.

43: Search Warrant, French-Style
Paris

My new book, *La Grande Fauche: La Fuite des Technologies vers l'Est,* hit the stands in September 1989, just months before the Berlin Wall fell. It included several chapters on the alleged Soviet or East German illegal, Dr. Aimé Richardt, the biggest techno-bandit in French history.[45]

The French media was not accustomed to the type of fact-driven reporting I was doing, and they lapped it up. Sections from the book appeared in the big circulation weekly, *Paris-Match*. Major French TV networks invited me onto prime time shows.

The book also attracted the attention of Richardt's lawyers, who filed a criminal complaint for document theft and violation of professional secrecy laws. This was aimed at a French bureaucrat the lawyers alleged had provided me with the eighty-three-page contract to sell bubble memory production gear to the Soviet Union.

Jacques Dournel, sixty-two, was France's top export licensing official. For over two years, he had avoided my calls, making the attempt by Richardt's lawyers to prosecute him all the more absurd. Not long before the book went to press, he finally agreed to sit down to an interview. He believed Richardt was not just seeking to get his own exports approved but was "attacking the system" in an effort to undermine the authority of the government to control high technology exports. "If he were selling barley and hops, nobody would care," Dournel said. He also confirmed

---

44 *Mednews* published a double issue devoted to the Iraqi Arms Industry on May 8, 1989 (Volume 2, 15/16) that included the first-ever list of Iraqi weapons plants, data that US military planners used for targeting later on. I also published extensive interviews with the Generals Amir (Amir Rashid al-Ubaidi and Amir Hamoudi al-Saadi). I describe the arms fair in more detail in Kenneth R. Timmerman, *The Death Lobby: How the West Armed Iraq* (Boston: Houghton Mifflin, 2002), pp. 333–334.

45 Paris: Les Editions Plon, 1989. The official English title was *Gorbachev's Technology Wars*. The colloquial phrase used in the French title roughly translates as "the grand heist."

the name of the politician who was putting pressure on him to approve Richardt's Soviet exports, a well-known Gaullist member of parliament. "Every man has his price, even me," Dournel said. "But my price is too high for Mister Richardt."

It was a great interview.

Richardt's lawyers were accusing Dournel of having provided me with the contract because the excerpt we published in *l'Express* "included marginal notations written by Mr. Dournel." That was a surprise, since I had assumed the comments had been written by Richardt himself.

+ + +

Early that December, I got a call from an inspector at the Police Judiciaire (PJ) asking me to meet him in Paris that morning. I agreed immediately, thinking he had information for me.

When I arrived at his office, he presented me with a search warrant on my house and office. The pretext was to determine if I was in possession of stolen documents.

I was floored and asked the inspector to go over the file with me while I took notes. That's how I learned that an earlier demand by Richardt's lawyers to search my house had been denied.

"You realize who this guy is, don't you?" I said to the inspector.

"*Cher monsieur*, if you only knew," he sighed.

"Your own people believe he's a Soviet agent."

The inspector gave one of those magnificent Gallic shrugs, hands spread wide, which implied he knew much more than he could possibly tell me and was powerless to do anything about it.

"My instructions are to accompany you to your home office to look for these documents," he said. "Now, I have some business to attend to with another colleague for the next twenty minutes or so," he added. "Perhaps you would be kind enough to wait here for me? Feel free to use the telephone if you need to. Just dial nine for an outside line."

He actually winked at me as he said this and got up.

"Twenty minutes, that's it."

As soon as he had shut the door behind him, I picked up the phone and called Christina.

The good news was that I had put all the sensitive files on Richardt, including the contract, in a locked metal case two years earlier. The bad news was that the case was in our bedroom.

"I can take it next door to Armelle's," she said. We had very good neighbors who always sympathized when I told them about the French government's shenanigans in Iraq or elsewhere.

"Make sure you keep the clipping files in the file cabinet where they can find them," I said. "It wouldn't be credible for them to find nothing at all."

Just to play it safe, Christina gathered up sensitive documents on several terrorism cases, including classified French government reports, and hid them amidst school papers in our children's rooms.

Twenty minutes later, as promised, the police inspector returned, and we put on our coats. A colleague of his joined us, so we said little for the forty-minute drive to Maisons-Laffitte. I escorted them to the garage we had converted into a comfortable office and introduced them to Christina, who was nine months pregnant. She directed them to the file cabinet containing our alphabetical persons files. She let them find the Richardt news clippings themselves.

Visibly embarrassed by her advanced pregnancy, the other inspector asked her if we kept any files in the house.

"I don't allow my husband to bring work home at night," she said. "Everything stays out here."

The two Frenchmen looked at each other, then at her.

"But, of course, I can show you around upstairs if you like," she added, holding up her baby with both hands.

"No, no," the inspector who had given me the warning said. "That is quite enough of this farce."

He made me sign a receipt for the files they had "discovered" in their search and bade us good day.

It was nice to think some Frenchmen in positions of power knew which side of the Cold War they were on.

+ + +

They never succeeded in prosecuting me for document theft (which I did not commit), nor did they ever discover who my source had been for the contract. Eventually, Aimé Richardt and his lawyers dropped the case.

But that wasn't the end of my legal troubles over the book.

Not long after Christina gave birth to our daughter, Diana, I got a call from my publisher's lawyer. British media magnate Robert Maxwell had just filed a one-million-franc defamation suit against us.

I was much more worried about Maxwell than I was about Richardt. For starters, he had a lot more money. I had written about a $34 million contract for computer equipment, data base systems, and high-speed modems that Maxwell Communications had signed with the Federal Institute for Scientific and Technological Information of the Soviet Academy of Sciences, VINITI. As I explained in the book, VINITI was a well-known collector of open-source information for the KGB's high-tech espionage effort. Maxwell didn't contest the accuracy of my information, since it was based on his own press release, but he was furious about the way I described it. I had titled this section, "Maxwell puts the KGB online." He had never expected anyone to identify the true functions of an obscure Soviet institute.

The French court vindicated me completely in record time—just three months!—and ordered Maxwell to pay damages. I joked with the lawyers that the only thing worse than being an American in a French courtroom was being British. I think the French judge actually enjoyed condemning Robert Maxwell, who never showed up in court, as an absent representative of perfidious Albion. As everyone in France has learned from childhood, "*les absents ont toujours tort.*"[46]

44: Pierre Salinger's Yogurt

Pierre Salinger became an avid *Mednews* client. For several years, we had been comparing notes on Iran and on terrorism cases. As European bureau chief for ABC News and their roving investigator into all things murky, he had a healthy respect for the intelligence underworld, which I shared. He was eating yogurt at lunchtime when I arrived at his London office. I made a joke about English food, but he made a sour face. "Diet," he grunted.

The biggest case for all of us at this point was the downing of Pan Am 103 over Lockerbie, Scotland, in December 1988, which took the lives of 270 people. Pierre had spent most of the previous year investigating different leads. I had worked around the edges. Both of us knew much more than we could write or put on TV.

---

46 Loosely translated: If you don't show up, you lose.

Like me, Pierre paid almost obsessive attention to details. We talked about bomb-makers and the signatures they incorporated in their bombs. We talked about witnesses who had been jailed in Germany but never charged. We talked about several CIA teams linked to the bombing: one shadowing the bombers, another caught on board and killed when the plane went down. We were happy campers.

I had just run a story about a report commissioned by Pan Am from a shadowy investigative group, Interfor. The report alleged that Pan Am 103 was a CIA-protected drug route, operated by Syrian businessman and wanted arms dealer Monzer al-Kassar, which had been doubled by real terrorists who used the CIA protection to smuggle a bomb on board. The Americans believed that al-Kassar could get the US hostages in Lebanon released, so they allowed him to use the drug route as payoff, the report alleged. The head of Interfor, Juval Aviv, claimed to be a former Mossad operator.

Pierre wasn't buying it. "There is no proof that Monzer was involved," he said. "When I met with him in Damascus, he said he was willing to do an on-camera interview and would deny any involvement. ABC New York said no."

The big elephant in the room was Iran, I argued. I showed Pierre recent photos a Lebanese source had given me of Ahmed Jibril, the Palestinian terrorist widely believed to have carried out the bombing, meeting with Iranian clerics in Beirut. The Iranians had motive, given that Rafsanjani himself had pledged to retaliate against the United States for the shooting down of Iran Air 655 over the Persian Gulf in July 1988 by the *USS Vincennes*. Iran was engaged in a covert war with the United States, taking US hostages in Lebanon, blowing up the US Embassy and the US Marines in Beirut, and now—I believed—downing Pan Am 103.[47]

In the end, it wasn't Pan Am 103 that Pierre had brought me over from Paris to discuss, but Panamanian strongman Manuel Noriega, who had just surrendered to invading US forces in Panama after a standoff at his presidential palace. Wanted on drug charges in the United States, Noriega was believed to have stashed assets around the world, including in France. Pierre wanted me to find them and hired me on the spot for three months at $5,000 per month on the strength of my contacts with French officialdom. Thus began many years of cooperation between us.

---

47   The Jibril photos: "Alliance in Terror," *Middle East Defense News (Mednews)*, April 17, 1989, Volume 2, 14. The early Pan Am 103 stories: "Pan Am 103: The search for the illusive 'Godfather,'" November 13, 1989, Volume 3, 2; and "Pan Am 103: New Revelations," January 19, 1990, Volume 3,7/8.

45: The Intelligence Underworld
Geneva

In another life, Swiss private detective Jean-Jacques Griessen could have been a character in a soap opera, driven to gossip by a life of boredom in the suburbs. But Griessen gossiped about the rich and powerful. Despite his low-key demeanor and his casual Swiss drawl, I sensed he was always on edge, knowing he was pushing the limits.

We were walking toward Lac Léman to have lunch when he nodded toward a car parked up on the sidewalk. "We have company," he said in his sing-song French. "Some of my former colleagues appear to have taken an interest in you."

I had to agree—no Swiss citizen would ever think of violating the public order in such a way, so it had to be the police.

"No matter. We are in Switzerland," he said. Meaning, we were safe.

Griessen had a steamy story for me this day. Once we sat down, he pulled an eight-by-ten-inch photograph from his briefcase and slid it across the table.

"Do you recognize any of these individuals?" he asked.

The photo was taken at the Richmond Hotel. People were coming down the cotillion staircase, dressed in tuxedos. The photographer had focused on three men huddling at the bottom of the stairs. I thought one of them looked familiar.

"That's got to be Robert Mitterrand," I said. He was a thinner version of his famous brother, the French president.

Was Griessen reading my mind? Just the day before, I had spent hours at the Tribunal de Commerce in Nanterre, pulling the corporate documents for Danubex SA, a company run by Robert Mitterrand. (This was pre-internet, so you had to actually go to the courthouse to find corporate records). The registry listed Bulgarian directors and East European clients. Among them was the notorious Bulgarian state-owned arms export corporation, Kintex, which the KGB used for smuggling weapons to terrorist groups. Gerard had suggested I start digging into the business interests of the elder Mitterrand. What was he doing at the Geneva gala?

"Next to him," Griessen pointed, "is my good friend Ali Hijazi. And this other gentleman is a senior official in the French DST, Jean-François Clair."

I was dumbfounded and grabbed the photo to scrutinize it carefully. It wasn't crystal clear, but the likenesses were good enough to be recognizable. Jean-François Clair had been the head of the Middle East branch of the French FBI at the time the photo was taken. Since then, he had been promoted head of their counter-terrorism division. I knew many of his close subordinates.

"What could these three have to yap about?" I wondered.

"That's a good question, isn't it?"

Griessen's thin grey moustache twitched ever so slightly, his Calvinist version of a smile. "One can only wonder why the brother of the French president, for whom the French hostages in Lebanon have become a political albatross, would come to Geneva accompanied by the Middle East director of the DST to meet with a Lebanese intermediary who boasts of his ability to contact the hostage-takers."

"Ransom payments?"

"Certainly not!" Griessen said, looking around him furtively. "We're talking about foreign aide, *mon cher monsieur*. It's just that the aide money doesn't always come from government accounts."

A political slush fund to ransom the French hostages? It was a huge story—if it was true.

+ + +

The next day, Griessen showed me an internal French intelligence "note" on dark finance networks in France. It was headlined "Financial network of Ali Hijazi, banker, in Cannes and Geneva, linked to General Mitterrand and to Swiss jeweler, Victor C———." General Mitterrand was the eldest brother of the French president and ran the GIFAS, the government-affiliated aerospace association that hosted the bi-annual Paris Air Show.

"Remember when the American, Eugene Hasenfus, crash-landed in Nicaragua?" Griessen said. That was the event that had triggered the Iran-Contra revelations. Hasenfus, an American contractor working for a CIA proprietary, confessed on Nicaraguan state television to delivering arms to the Contras for the CIA. "The Sandinistas found two business cards in his plane: one for Jean-Paul Cuché, a banker with the Union des Banques Suisses in Geneva. The other was Ali Hijazi's," Griessen said.

I could feel him building a case. While I suspected that Hijazi had been co-opted by the Israelis, Griessen painted him as a powerful figure in the intelligence/arms/terror underworld, whose access and contacts went deep. "You find the same people involved in every shady deal. And they are all here in Geneva," Griessen said.

He went on to tell me about Werner Mauss, a former associate from West Germany. Mauss had hired Griessen to help get West German hostages Rudolph Cordes and Alfred Schmidt released. "Both hostages were held by the Hamadeh clan," Griessen said. "Mauss was authorized to offer up to fifteen million each. But when time came to pay, the Hamadeh brothers never received the money. At least, that's what their Beirut lawyer told me."

Griessen believed that the companies actually paid Mauss $50 million to get their employees released and that a courier pocketed the money during trips to Beirut instead of delivering it to the kidnappers.

"In the end, Hamadeh freed Schmidt anyway in exchange for a German pledge not to extradite his brother to the United States, where he was wanted for murder.... We could have done so much more with those aid organizations if Mauss hadn't sabotaged them, as I tried to tell your Israeli friends."

The café where we had been having breakfast had emptied out, and our voices seemed to bounce off the walls, so we decided it was time to move. As we reached the lakefront, Griessen nodded toward a late-model sedan parked up on the sidewalk. This time, I could see a man inside. Across the street, two men were gawking at clothes in shop windows, clearly uninterested in what they were seeing. We crossed the boulevard and headed into a small street behind the lake. A man wearing a black trench coat, buttoned up to the neck, rushed toward us, head down, without saying a word. Griessen tipped his fedora to him without eliciting a response.

"That's strange," he said once the man had passed. "They usually say hello to me."

"Who's they?" I asked.

"That one was a former colleague. The others came on board after my time."

We ducked into a Mexican restaurant off the rue Mont Blanc to weather out the remainder of the pre-lunch hour. Less than five minutes later, four of the watchers came in. Three of them took a table at the far end of the room. The fourth, who appeared to be Lebanese, came right up to us and took a seat two tables away. After ordering a coffee, he got out a book.

I was starting to get spooked by all the attention we were getting. Were they watching Griessen? Or watching me?

"Lubrani is now offering a global prisoner exchange: Lebanese detainees in Israel—including the Hamadeh's friend, Sheikh Obeid—in exchange for the Israeli soldiers, the navigator, and all the Western hostages," I said quietly.

"Be careful," Griessen said. "Two people in France have already been killed over this business. You don't want to become the third."

+ + +

When I got back to Paris, I met with Daniel Burdan, the former DST agent and now author. He knew all about Jean-François Clair and had no doubt why he had been meeting in Geneva with Hijazi and with President Mitterrand's brothers.

"That's his style," Daniel said. "I worked with him for eight years. I saw it."

He also knew one of the couriers Griessen had mentioned who had been murdered in Paris.

"His name was Antoine Makdessi," Daniel said. "He was my agent."

Bingo! I thought. Daniel had recruited Makdessi because of his access to a Libyan intelligence officer who was running a mole on President Mitterrand's staff. "He may well have had holes in his pockets," Daniel acknowledged. "But he also had several holes in his chest." Makdessi was gunned down on July 22, 1989, in front of the Hotel Queen Elizabeth in Paris.

"He was lured by a woman to the hotel entrance when a guy pulled up in a Renault Twenty-Five and pumped seven shots into his chest with a Colt forty-five. Makdessi managed to roll under a car. The killer got out, changed magazines, and pumped another four or five rounds into him while he was under the car—twelve or thirteen rounds in all."

"Who did it?" I asked.

"Not Arabs," Daniel said. "Their weapon of choice is a nine-millimeter pistol. Not Israelis—they use a twenty-two magnum or a twenty-two Walther PKK/S. That's a very small handgun. This guy was using an eleven/forty-three," the European term for a standard .45 ACP round. "If I had to guess, I'd say it was a contract hit. A professional killer. Mafia, most likely."

I briefly mentioned Makdessi's murder in a *Mednews* story I wrote about the West German hostages, along with another tantalizing clue that Griessen had mentioned and Daniel confirmed: Makdessi had set up a fake investment company in Switzerland along with top French officials—including "J. L.," the suspected mole on Mitterrand's staff—as a front for a lucrative scheme to ship toxic waste from Europe and North America to sites in Lebanon's Bekaa Valley.[48]

How deep did the rot go? Griessen and Burdan took me to the edge of the pit, where we peered down through the haze into the underworld of the rich and powerful. As I had been doing since I started *Mednews*, when I didn't know the answers, I dangled the information in a manner that invited people who had answers to reach out to me.

I just hoped we were all on the same side.

46: A Communist, a Capitalist, and a Socialist...
Prague

Just five months after the fall of the Berlin wall, the new Czechoslovak president, playwright Václav Havel, stunned the world by announcing that the former communist regime in his country had exported one thousand tons of Semtex-H plastic explosive in the 1970s and 1980s, most of it to Colonel Qaddafi in Libya. It was enough, Havel noted, to keep terrorists in business "for the next 150 years." He made the revelation after investigators in Britain had determined that a small amount of Semtex, packed into a Toshiba boom-box cassette player, had brought down Pan Am 103 over Lockerbie, Scotland.

It was one of those stories. Everyone knew that Czechoslovakia was the only manufacturer of Semtex, but no one was impolite enough to point it out. Havel pledged that his government would shine light on the misdeeds of the previous communist regime. I was eager to see if he really meant it and hopped on a plane to Prague to investigate.

My first stop was the huge unfinished glass and concrete office complex that housed *Rudé právo*, the former Czechoslovak Communist party daily. The building was a monument to Socialist realism, with thick steel gates on rolling tracks and a giant bas-relief with the slogan,

---

48   "West Germany's hostage saga; or the Case of the Missing Ransom," *Middle East Defense News (Mednews)*, March 5, 1990, Volume 3, 10.

"Workers of the world, unite." A calendar in the reception area bore the portrait of V. I. Lenin. Václav Bervida, my former reporting mate from Beirut, was now the foreign editor.

"After Beirut, the news agency offered me the Rome bureau, but for a number of reasons, I didn't want it," he told me in his office upstairs. "So just before the revolution, I left CTK to join *Rudé právo*. All my former colleagues said, 'How sad, what happened to Bervida.' But then, this place got privatized. And CTK basically ceased to exist. So now I have a job, and they don't."

He gave me a quick rundown of the players involved in the Semtex investigation and agreed to meet again in a few days to compare notes.

My next stop was the main office of Civic Forum (Občanské Forum), the movement founded by Václav Havel and his colleagues during the Velvet Revolution. I spent several hours with Professor Tomáš Pstross, head of their international affairs department, discussing ghosts.

"There are so many rumors, so many stories, about the previous regime," he said. "When the whole world was admiring our soft revolution, we were too soft on the security forces, the STB. We let them destroy the evidence of their despicable acts, including official records of the Semtex exports," he said.

I visited the police criminal lab, a half-dozen government ministries, and the offices of Omnipol, the official Czech government exporter of Semtex. Given the stupor with which I was received, I guessed that I must have been the first journalist who ever darkened their doorway. You could tell the communists by their evasiveness, their inability to remember facts or figures, and the new officials by their enthusiasm.

One evening, I went to a nightclub and found myself dancing in a group with a pretty Czech woman around my age. She introduced me to her husband, Rečak. Before long, he was telling me about his brother, who had been shot dead by Soviet soldiers during the 1968 Prague spring uprising. "You cannot imagine what freedom means to someone who has spent forty-two years in prison," he said. "We will never forget. And we will never forgive."

He worried about a communist comeback in the upcoming parliamentary elections, the first since freedom from the Soviet occupation. "Even if the communists get just twenty percent, they win," he said. "Our democratic parties are too splintered to unite." The communists still had huge assets and controlled government buildings, meeting halls, offices, and thousands of private villas they claimed had been registered in the names of individual party apparatchiks. "You must teach us democracy," Rečak said.

Havel was en route to Israel for a much-heralded state visit where he was going to announce the end of Czech military training to Palestinian guerillas and arms exports to terrorist regimes. But a top foreign policy aide, Alexandr "Sasha" Vondra, agreed to meet with me at the Castle. This was the same imposing castle of Franz Kafka fame, a huge, ornate complex that dominated the orange tile roofs of the city that seemed to flow from its tall windows down to the river in orderly concentric circles. It had been the seat of the communist dictatorship. And now it was the seat of the first post-communist government. As I walked through long corridors and empty, ornate reception halls, everything was freshly painted, and all of it was white: white walls, white ceilings, gorgeous white enamel moldings and window trim. In the public rooms, old Czech masters were the only decoration on the walls.

Vondra's office was just as white and fresh—and completely empty. Papers were scattered all over the floor. They had no filing cabinets, no books, and one computer he told me had been donated by Czech exiles in the US, which in fact remained off the entire time I was there. His secretary was a former actress, and many of the staff were former theater people, rock singers, or composers. Vondra wore jeans and a bohemian shirt with large sleeves and no tie. Havel said that the main reason he had chosen Vondra as his foreign policy advisor was that he had never been out of the country. That way, he could look at the world "with fresh eyes."

The kids have inherited the Castle, I was thinking. The amateurism was a surrealistic reversal of the dreary, starkly organized communist regime. As the US military attaché, USAF colonel Ed Motyka, told me later, the new regime was only superficially in power. "They've replaced the people at the top, the ministers, the department heads. But beneath them, the whole bureaucracy remains staffed by Communist Party members, the burrowers."

And yet, even Colonel Motkya was amazed by the extent of change in just a few short months. "Figures, names, places, dates: this is the type of stuff we simply can't get from them. If I went to Omnipol, I'd be wasting my time. But the Czech top brass is interested in closer ties to the US military. Their generals want to meet our generals. Their educators want to meet our educators. Sometimes I wonder what my job is, especially when everyone back at the Pentagon is still a Cold Warrior!"[49]

At one of the best restaurants later that week, Václav and I were comparing notes when a waiter excitedly approached.

"He has new apéritif to propose to us," Václav explained.

The waiter was carrying four bottles between his fingers like so many cigars and started pouring from them into giant brandy glasses. Gin, vodka, Campari, vermouth…. Like so many others in this town, he seemed drunk on freedom.

"A communist, a capitalist, and a socialist get together for a drink one week after the revolution," Václav said as we tasted the waiter's concoction. "The socialist arrives late. 'Sorry, I was waiting in line to buy meat,' he says. The capitalist says, 'Lines? What's that?' The communist just shakes his head: 'What's meat?'"

Such was Prague, finally free after forty-two years of Soviet occupation.

47: Affairs of State
Geneva

With the assassination of ballistics genius Gerald Bull on March 22, 1990, Pierre Salinger now wanted me to work at full throttle on Iraq. All of a sudden, the idea that Saddam Hussein had commissioned Bull to build a giant artillery piece capable of hurling nuclear or chemical warheads at Israel was no longer the joke people had thought it was at the Baghdad arms fair just ten months earlier.

Pierre had me team up with a US-based producer, Richard Greenberg, who fed me leads from US sources on middlemen and front companies helping Saddam. My job was to track them down in Europe.

I scoured corporate registries in France, Belgium, and Switzerland. I found the offices of Gerald Bull's Space Research Corporation on the rue de Vermont in Geneva. The name plate on the ground floor office had recently been removed, and the double doors showed signs of a recent break-in. The real estate agent in charge of the building told me Bull's company had vacated the premises a month earlier—several weeks after his murder. No surprise.

---

49 I devoted an entire issue of *Mednews* to developments in Prague, with stories on the Semtex scandal, Czech arms exports, and Václav Havel's vow to cut off aid to Palestinian terror groups. See "Havel to Israel," *Middle East Defense News (Mednews)*, April 30, 1990, Volume 3, 14.

I visited with Georges Starckmann, a French arms dealer who was fighting a French bank that had seized $5 million from his account, claiming it was owed to one of their clients. His name had appeared on a $100 million Iraqi letter of credit that an Egyptian intermediary in Minneapolis was shopping around.

Starckmann was something of a celebrity in the arms underworld for his exploits in selling useless "Startron" night vision systems to Qaddafi and living to boast about it. More recently, he had purchased a left-bank nightclub in Paris, the Alcazar. A former DGSE operative I knew who had worked with Starckmann during the Algerian war helped set up my meeting. Starckmann, now sixty-three, was full of bluster, colorful, and profane. Like so many arms dealers, he loved to talk.

I started off as I always did, by letting him tell his story. His primary concern was to convince me that he was no longer in the business. "What they want to buy today, you can't deliver. Even worse, the clients need financing." When I showed him the $100 million letter of credit for Iraq, he dismissed it as *bidon*—nonsense.

"Somebody did the trash," he said, rapping the document with his fingers. "Yes, I was in contact with VUF AG," the Swiss company to which the letter of credit was addressed. "No, I never finalized that deal with Iraq—which, by the way, was for civilian equipment. German trucks, if I remember correctly. Oh, and if anybody's counting, I never paid back one cent to the Libyans, out of all the millions Paribas-Suisse claimed I owed. And the Libyans are still my friends."

But if he wasn't doing deals with Iraq, of course he knew lots about other people who were. He dished on the pair of Germans involved in the VUF AG operation, one of whom he claimed to have gotten arrested three times. He also confirmed what I had been hearing about Iraq's growing insolvency. "The Iraqis dangle these letters of credit for a year or more and nobody will take them. Banks are now demanding thirty-five percent to confirm them, and that's before expenses. Everybody knows the Iraqis will never pay. If you are doing business with Iraq in the morning, expect to go bankrupt by sundown."

I travelled onward to Berne to speak with several Swiss parliamentarians who claimed to be investigating VUF AG, but they admitted they had come up dry. "We don't have judicial powers, so all we can look at are their tax returns. And on that score, there is nothing out of the ordinary," Deputy Olivier Vodoz told me.

My favorite was meeting with a former VUF AG board member named Pierre Weisser. "I know nothing about the company," he told me with a straight face. "I only approved the books."

Another parliamentarian I met in Berne, Jean Ziegler, published a book about this syndrome, *La Suisse Lave Plus Blanc.*[50]

As I always did when in Geneva, I took time to meet with Griessen. He wanted to talk about a case he had been investigating since October 1987: the still-unsolved murder in a Geneva hotel room of West German politician Uwe Barschel.

I am convinced it was this investigation that ultimately got him killed.

+ + +

I began to receive anonymous packages with intelligence documents and internal files apparently pilfered from arms dealers I was researching. Some of them bore Swiss postmarks and stamps from an anti-arms trafficking group calling itself *Le Ramoneur* (The Chimney Sweep). Others were sent from France. The documents were authentic and always seemed to arrive when I had reached a brick wall. I decided to ask Gerard about these mysterious packages the next time we met to see if perhaps he was behind them.

"This one is very interesting," he said, picking up the transcript of a phone conversation between an unidentified party and a Geneva-based arms dealer, discussing a clandestine arms sale to Iraq. "The group claiming responsibility for tapping the arms dealer's phone are a bunch of lefties in La Ferney," the French suburb bordering Geneva. "But actually, I have never seen this document before. Interesting!"

In his deadpan way, Gerard was telling me that he had seen lots of documents from *Le Ramoneur*, perhaps in French government files, but was not responsible for sending them to me. Then out of the blue, he asked me if I had known about the South African deal to buy surface-to-air missiles from Matra.

That was ancient history as far as I was concerned. It took me a few seconds to shift gears.

"The whole thing was brokered by Jean-Christophe Mitterrand. You know, '*Papa m'a dit*,'" Gerard said with a grin.

---

50   Loosely translated, "Switzerland Launders Best."

Jean-Christophe Mitterrand was his father's principal advisor on African affairs and worked out of the presidential palace. If they mentioned him at all, the French media used the sobriquet "Papa told me" to identify him. They claimed it was the way he began his conversations with African leaders. He was Daddy's emissary—and was notorious for banging the tin cup. At this point, the French still had no legal way to finance their political campaigns, and so they raised dark money through the intelligence/arms political underworld.

"That's why you were followed when you went to South Africa," Gerard said. "I read all about your trip, including the weekend excursion to the Kruger Game Park. Fascinating," he said. He gave what I was beginning to think of as his evil laugh—the laugh he used whenever he was instructing me in the black arts of French intelligence.

How did he know that? I wondered. Could it be true that the French had followed me during my three-week trip to South Africa? I had never written or even spoken to anyone about the weekend in the game park. Now that he mentioned it, I vaguely remembered overhearing talk at several Armscor plants about ongoing deals with France. But followed? Really? Why would the French government expend such an effort? After all, I was just a journalist.

✦ ✦ ✦

A few weeks after that, Christina was nursing our newborn, Diana, upstairs and called me by intercom in the office behind the house.

"You've got to come up here and look at this."

"Look at what?"

"Just come," she said. "Now."

I joined her in the baby's bedroom overlooking the street. A utility truck was parked outside, its ladder extended to the telephone pole just across from us. A man was fiddling with the wires.

"Those are our lines," I said.

"Get your camera," Christina said.

So I went back to the office to fetch my Canon EOS with the 100-300mm telephoto lens and opened the window so I could get a clear shot of the linemen. I made no pretense of hiding and was pretty sure they could see me taking pictures.

"I'm going to talk to them," I said. "With this."

I showed her the micro-cassette recorder I had brought from the office.

Outside, the lineman up on the ladder continued to fiddle with the box on the pole. I asked his colleague by the truck what they were doing.

"Just routine maintenance," he said.

"When do you expect to finish?"

"Oh, that could take some time."

"We haven't noticed any problem with our lines," I said.

"Don't worry," he grinned. "You will."

I couldn't believe what I was hearing.

"Who do you work for?" I asked.

"Private contractors," the man said.

"That's the first I've heard of the PTT using private contractors to repair the phone lines," I said.

"Oh, no. It happens all the time," he said. "Just ask your friends."

My friends. I suspected I knew exactly what he meant by that, and I didn't like it one bit.

American readers may find it difficult to believe that a foreign reporter in France would actually be assigned a "minder" by the French counter-espionage service, the DST, as if France were some Third World dictatorship. But for over five years, from 1987 up until my departure from France in 1993, a DST counter-intelligence officer regularly called to check up on my activities. He wanted to find out what stories I was working on, who I was meeting. When one minder was assigned elsewhere, he introduced me to his replacement. It was all very civilized, even agreeable.

I realized there were two ways I could react to the French approach. I could get huffy and indignant and refuse to talk to them—and suffer the consequences. Or I could go along and more likely learn something useful in the exchange. I chose the second approach, much to the relief of my minders, who never missed an occasion to hold our meetings at a good restaurant over lunch. When we spoke over the phone, they made sure I suggested the restaurants, since they picked up the tab—in cash. They were always happy for an occasion to tap into their expense account. From time to time, when they wanted to impress me with their knowledge of my activities, like Gerard, they quoted transcripts verbatim from my telephone conversations or some detail that could only have been obtained by spying on me. As I knew from other sources, the government had a huge listening post in an underground warren beneath the École Militaire, where more than one thousand technicians and translators labored daily. With the end of the Cold War, they faced massive layoffs and were looking for something to do.

So I decided to take the photos of the phony telephone repairmen to "my friends." My current DST minder used the name Jean-Marc.

I chose a one-star Michelin restaurant on a side street near Palais Royale.

"We would really like to nail Vivien," Jean-Marc said over fresh oysters from Brittany and a good Sancerre. Robert-André Vivien was a conservative member of parliament who had gone to bat for Aimé Richardt, the suspected Soviet illegal I had exposed in *L'Express*.

"We interviewed his aide. We believe he lied to us," Jean-Marc added.

Interesting but totally unusable, I was thinking. *And besides, what does that have to do with the price of onions?*

I steered him back to the photographs I had fanned out on the table.

"Even if my service had ordered a wiretap, which is something I could never confirm, of course, I could not discuss what motivated that decision," he said.

And then he proceeded to do just that.

"There are many, many people at the rue Nélaton"—the headquarters of the DST—"who are very unhappy with the information you have been putting out about this disgruntled former colleague, Daniel 'Burdan.' I believe you know his real name."

Jean-Marc had been more than fair with me over the three years or so we had been meeting. He had also tipped me off to several French counterterrorism investigations before they had become public. So I sensed this was a friendly way of saying I had strayed onto sensitive territory.

"I do," I said, "but I've never used it. What in particular has made them unhappy?"

"*Ouf,*" he raised his hands in a Gallic shrug. "These are affairs of state. But you should know there are very powerful people this Mister Burdan claims to have information on who would be very unhappy if his allegations became public."

I went back and scoured my notebooks after that lunch and thought I had pinpointed the most sensitive allegations Daniel had made. They involved President Mitterrand's brothers, his son, and "J. L.," the alleged Libyan mole on Mitterrand's staff. Affairs of state, indeed![51]

---

51 See "Former DST agent talks," *Middle East Defense News (Mednews)*, May 28, 1990, Volume 3, 16; and "DST: Changes at the top," June 11, 1990, Volume 3, 17.

Although by now I had many friends in the French media and regularly appeared on French television and lunched privately with members
of parliament and former intelligence chiefs, the overt telephone tap and
the friendly warning from my DST minder made me wonder if I had
crossed some invisible boundary. Beyond it, if I continued, lay a danger
zone where I wouldn't necessarily see the booby traps until they exploded
in my face. There was an intelligence war raging deep within the French
establishment between Mitterrand and his political enemies, and I had
just wandered onto the battlefield. It wasn't my role as a journalist to
carry their flags—or get shot at, for that matter. I decided to set aside the
Mitterrand "dossier"—unless, of course, I could prove it.

48: The Best Article I Never Wrote

I had been writing for the editorial page of the *Wall Street Journal* for the
past five years with increasing frequency. So when Saddam Hussein began
accusing Kuwait of stealing Iraqi oil through new horizontal drilling tech-
niques at the end of July 1990, I got a call from my editor in Brussels.
How seriously should we take the Iraqi allegations? Saddam appeared to
be deploying troops—some reports said as many as one hundred thousand troops—along the Kuwaiti border. Was war about to break out?

Iraq had not turned out as the business lobbyists had hoped after the
end of the eight-year war with Iran. Saddam was becoming increasingly
belligerent. He'd launched massive poison gas attacks against the Iranians,
then taken advantage of the war's end to massacre more than a hundred
thousand of his own Kurds, systematically destroying Kurdish villages and
deporting their inhabitants to remote areas of the country.[52] He'd also
clashed with his foreign supporters, particularly Saudi Arabia and Kuwait,
despite what appeared to be a full-throated effort by the administration of
George H. W. Bush to open Iraqi markets to US industrial exports.

Even the French, his staunch supporters throughout the war with
Iran, were sounding alarm bells over Saddam's rapidly expanding domestic
arms industry, in particular his ballistic missile programs. In one story I
had published just weeks earlier in *Mednews*, I related a surprising turn-
around in French policy at COCOM. US Customs had just blocked

---

52   This would later be known as the "Anfal" campaign.

the export of four high-temperature furnaces from a company named Consarc in New Jersey that had been headed for a military research center in Iraq. Now US officials were requesting that allied governments scour their own export approvals of missile-technology items to Iraq and do the same. To their surprise, the French complied. "If you had asked me three years ago if Iraq would be capable of developing their own missiles, I would have laughed," a top French defense official explained to me. "I was wrong. All of us were wrong. This is clearly a cause for concern."[53]

All of this came on the heels of the very public trial and execution in Iraq of British journalist Farzad Bazoft on charges of espionage and an increasing number of well-sourced stories in the German, British, and American press about a secret nuclear weapons program in Iraq. When I sent out sample copies of *Mednews* to potential subscribers, I included a flyer with a picture of Saddam holding a pair of krytrons, used for nuclear weapons detonation, which his black-market agents had managed to buy in the West. At first glance, they looked like a pair of titanium balls. "Lose something in Iraq?" was my provocative headline. All kinds of non-defense technology companies were starting to wake up to the potential public relations disaster of discovering their products being used by Saddam to murder the innocent.

But invade Kuwait? Really?

"We're leaving tomorrow," Christina reminded me. We had four children and suitcases to pack, the house to close, and our final mailer to get out. Then we were headed for three weeks' vacation at her summer cottage in Sweden.

One side of me was ready to dismiss Saddam's reported buildup as a bluff. But another side was worried that Saddam was capable of anything. He was just bold and brash and ballsy enough to do it.

So I did what many wise men in such a situation have done before me. I punted.

"We're heading up to Sweden tomorrow," I told the editor. "Let me take a more thorough look at this and get back to you in a couple of days."

Once in Sweden, we set to doing what we normally did in August: hauling the rowboat down to the lake so we could set crayfish traps at dusk and getting up at dawn to row through the mist across the magically still waters to bring them in. The enormous silence of the lake was broken by the spectral calls of a distant crane, like a brass band after a snowstorm.

---

53 "Missile tech blocked to Iraq," *Middle East Defense News (Mednews)*, July 23, 1990, Volume 3, 20.

The next time we came up for air, it was August 2 and Saddam's troops had just invaded Kuwait. I felt like Hans Castorp in Thomas Mann's *The Magic Mountain*, wandering down from his mountaintop sanitarium to find himself in the muddy trenches of World War I.

I could have told you that I foresaw Saddam's invasion and had been writing frequently on his dangerous arms buildup in the months beforehand. And while the second part of that sentence is true, the first is not. I was completely blindsided, just as our government was. It taught me never to underestimate the capacity of Saddam—or any other dictator, for that matter—to do evil on this earth in ways that defied the imaginations of ordinary, sane men.

It was the best article I never wrote.

49: My Contribution to the War Effort

Back in Paris by August 20, I began preparing the next issue of *Mednews*, looking at five scenarios for how the United States would drive Saddam out of Kuwait. I ran a piece about strategic targets in Iraq—chemical weapons, missile, and suspected nuclear weapons facilities—I claimed the United States would take out. I also ran a story about the buried air bases foreign defense contractors in Baghdad had been telling me about for some time.

After that issue mailed, I got a call from a subscriber at the US embassy in Paris, asking me if I would come to meet some "friends."

My country was about to go to war. The longer I lived overseas, the more I found patriotic stirrings in my heart. I said yes immediately.

The "friends" my subscriber, who was a political officer, wanted me to meet at the embassy annex on the rue de la Boétie turned out to be the air attaché and his deputy—or at least, that's how they introduced themselves. I will call them "Roger" and "Steve."

After my subscriber made the introductions, he said he would leave us to our own devices and left.

"That's a very interesting article you published about the buried air bases," Roger said. "It was very helpful that you included the name of the contractor, Sixco. What else do you know about them?"

"Actually, quite a bit," I said. "I developed a source inside the company earlier this year, and he's been feeding me good information. The company's full name is Six Construct."

Steve gave Roger an encouraging glance, but Roger shook his head—not yet.

"We were also very interested in your article on Saddam's French arsenal. Clearly, you've been to Iraq."

"Many times. That's where I got most of the photographs. They don't come out of weapons catalogues."

"Do the French still talk to you?"

"The last time I checked, they did."

"And when was that?" Steve said, leaning toward me.

I took my notebook from the pocket of my suit jacket and flipped to the last page.

"Yesterday," I said.

Now Steve was really egging on his colleague, making hand gestures as if to say, "What are you waiting for?"

"You probably won't be surprised to hear this," Roger said. "But our friends the French have not be very talkative with us. They've sold Saddam every kind of air defense system they make, including a few they've never deployed themselves. And they've sold him versions of the Mirage F1 that are more advanced than those flying with the French Air Force. We would really like to know more of the specifics of what he has purchased."

"Anything in particular?" I wondered.

Steve handed Roger a cable, which he skimmed before reading excerpts to me.

"For example, did Dassault ever deliver a mission planning system to the Iraqi Air Force? How do the Iraqis digitize maps and process them for mission planning? How do they transport their mobile 3-D radars? Can your sources tell us what kind of vehicle they use?"

I pondered for a moment what he was asking. If these weren't state secrets, they were pretty close to it.

"Can't you put those questions to the French directly?"

"We have," Roger said. "That's why we're asking for your help."

"You mean, they aren't being forthcoming with their allies as they prepare for war?"

Roger realized he had perhaps gone too far—I was a journalist, after all—then made a decision.

"Look, I'm going to be frank with you. We deal government to government. I go through the French Air Force liaison office, for example. Steve goes through the liaison office for his service. They tell us they are 'working on it.' We just want to make sure they aren't still 'working on it' by the time our planes are in the air. Would you be willing to help us—as an American, a patriot, not a journalist?"

These were extraordinary times. On the one hand, my heart was stirring with an eagerness to help, mixed with outrage at the French. On the other, I knew what the French would call anything that strayed from my journalistic endeavors.

"In my travels, I have collected a huge number of weapons brochures. Some of them are very specific—not the kind of thing you see at the Paris Air Show, for example. I can pull them together for you by category so your tech guys can go through them. Call it a consulting project."

"We can't pay you," Roger said.

"I'm not asking you to. It's my contribution to the war effort."

Beyond that, I said that if I were to call my French industry contacts with specific questions such as the ones Roger had mentioned, I could only do so by being totally open about my purpose, even publishing most—but not all—of the results.

"I know these guys. The ones I would call are all very pro-American. I can sit down with them and tell them that their government is not making this information available to their allies and ask them to help unofficially. I'm sure they will."

Over the next few months, I published a series of detailed articles about electronic countermeasures systems the French had sold the Iraqi Air Force. I wrote about Soviet signals-intelligence gear, Iraqi air bases and strategic sites, German helicopters, and the sale by the French of a laser designation pod built originally sold to France by US aerospace manufacturer, Martin Marietta. I published a cover package for *L'Express* with a broad overview of French arms sales to Iraq that appeared as a giant poster on every news kiosk in Paris. It was a hoot walking around Paris that week. Everywhere I went, there was my cover![54]

When the United States launched the first wave of air strikes on Iraq on the night of January 17, 1991, they knew exactly where to find the command-and-control nodes of the French-designed CORAD air defense network and which radar frequencies they used,

---

54 "La Verité sur l'Arsenal Irakien," *L'Express*, September 7–13, 1990.

and they succeeded in taking them out in nap-of-the-earth strikes conducted by eight US Army Apache helicopters. In follow-on strikes just minutes later, wave after wave of US Air Force fighter-bombers pummeled Iraq's airfields, including the buried ones built by the Belgian construction company, Six Construct.

I was pleased and honored to have played some small role in that success and in keeping our pilots safe.

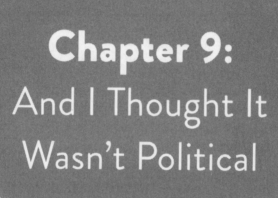

Chapter 9:
And I Thought It
Wasn't Political

50: The Uranium Plant That Couldn't Exist

As the world geared up for war, concerns mounted that Saddam might use chemical or biological weapons against US troops. I intensified my investigation of Western suppliers of dual-use equipment and published a series of stories about suspected WMD facilities in Iraq. "Just how close is Iraq to acquiring nuclear weapons?" I wrote in one of these articles. "The depressing truth is this: nobody knows for sure." I believed in truth-telling, not pretending.[55]

One of the more astonishing stories I broke involved a giant fertilizer plant at al Qaim along the border with Syria that I claimed was being used to process uranium from phosphates ore.[56]

I had a secret source for the story I have never divulged until now: an employee of the Belgian general contractor, Sybetra, who actually built the plant. Philippe Déjardin was the on-site construction manager for al Qaim from 1980 to 1982. He also happened to be Julian and Clio's French grandfather. They knew him as *Gros Papa*.

Philippe frequently stayed on the couch in our small living room in Paris when the children were small, on his way to Iraq or Abu Dhabi or to Orléans for home leave. (His brother Gabriel did the same thing during the Iranian revolution, to and from Tehran where he owned a bicycle factory.) His biggest "secret" mission was to load up on forbidden foods while in France—saucisson, pork sausages, and pâtés—to distribute to his colleagues at the Sybetra base camp in Iraq. Although his daughter and I were barely on speaking terms by now, Philippe and I had remained friends. He seemed to have been expecting my call.

"Can we get together to talk about Iraq?" I asked.

"I thought you would never ask," he said with a gruff laugh.

---

55 "Iraq's Nuclear Shopping List," *Middle East Defense News (Mednews)*, September 17, 1990; Volume 3, 23.

56 I published several stories in *Mednews* in the fall of 1990 that mentioned al Qaim as a uranium processing plant that would figure high in strategic targets for an eventual US bombing campaign. A more detailed description of the plant appeared in "Al Qaim Processing Uranium Since 1982," January 7, 1991, Volume 4, 7.

We met several times over the next few months. According to Philippe, everyone who worked on the construction site in al Qaim was aware there was a smaller, top-secret installation, off limits to all but a handful of workers, at the center of the vast chemicals complex. "We knew it involved uranium," he said. Later, he learned it involved processing uranium from phosphates ore.

As Philippe started naming the various subcontractors installing equipment at the plant, my jaw dropped: many of them lined up with suppliers of dual-use equipment I had been tracking. Coppée Rust, a division of the Groupe Lafarge, was building a phosphoric acid unit. The Danish company, F.L. Smidth, supplied large ovens to enrich fertilizer and corrosive chemicals. Davie Power Gas, a British company, provided gear for processing ammonia and potassium. A US company, whose name he couldn't remember, installed a special production line to make ammonium perchlorate—a key ingredient of solid rocket fuel.

But the key supplier was the Swiss chemical company Alesa AluSuisse Engineering Ltd., which controlled the top-secret unit enclosed behind barbed wire, protected by Iraqi security police. "We were told it was a processing unit to extract fluoride salts from liquid phosphoric acid," Philippe told me. "This included a capability to extract uranium salts from raw phosphates."

It was widely known that most phosphate ore contained tiny amounts of uranium. But the quantities were so small that vast quantities of phosphates had to be crushed, liquefied, and transformed in order to extract minute quantities of uranium. The whole process consumed enormous amounts of electricity as well—one reason why some analysts would later discount my information. "The United States abandoned this technology after World War II because it was just too expensive," one particularly obtuse reviewer of my post-war book proclaimed.[57]

I asked Philippe if the French government was aware of what he had just told me.

"Oh yes," he said. "They've known it for years. Ever since the first time I came back from Iraq, in fact."

---

57   *The Death Lobby: How the West Armed Iraq* was published by Houghton Mifflin in 1992. The reviewer was Gerald Seib at the *Wall Street Journal*—who to this day has never apologized for dissing the book over the al Qaim revelations. "Timmerman could have benefitted from a science editor," he declared. Seib could have benefitted from a bit of humility, especially once the United Nations Special Commission commended me for uncovering the secret nuclear facility.

He then explained a procedure occasionally mentioned in journalistic accounts of French espionage but never formally documented. Philippe had been an "honorable correspondent" for the French foreign espionage service, then known as the SDECE. "Whenever I would come through Paris on home leave, they would send someone to debrief me. Similarly, when I was about to leave for Iraq or Saudi Arabia or wherever else I was on mission, they would run through a list of topics of interest 'just in case' I happened to hear anything." There was never any pay, formal reporting requirements, or orders. But French intelligence expected Philippe and thousands more French executives working abroad to carry out "patriotic missions" while overseas. And as a patriot, he agreed without batting an eye. Philippe never asked anything in return, not even a favor.

Philippe introduced me to his boss at Sybetra, who provided a wealth of additional details on the plant and the subcontractors and specifics on the dual-use technologies they had installed. I began organizing information from these "data dump" interviews in HyperCard, an early form of html database created by Apple and later in FileMaker. It was a natural extension of the data-driven reporting I was becoming known for with *Mednews* and it would help shape the coverage of Saddam Hussein and his complex relationship to the West. I eventually tracked more than 450 companies that had sold dual-use technologies later found in Iraqi WMD facilities.

51: BNL and the Death Lobby
Atlanta

Shimon Samuels was the European director for the Simon Wiesenthal Center and an avid *Mednews* supporter. Christina and I became good friends with Shimon and Graciela, his Argentinean-born wife. The Simon Wiesenthal Center in Los Angeles had just published a report I had written called "The Poison Gas Connection," which explained in layman's terms how Saddam Hussein and Libya's Qaddafi were using seemingly ordinary pesticide plants to produce chemical weapons. Most importantly, I named the suppliers and the individuals involved in the transactions: the bankers, the intermediaries, and the corporate officials who—I argued—knowingly helped these tyrants acquire the means to exterminate large numbers of their citizens.

Thus began a media frenzy focusing on "proliferation." Later, it would be reduced down to a three-letter acronym intended to evoke a mixture of horror and stupidity, depending on your political lens: WMD, weapons of mass destruction. I named 207 companies that had been cited in press accounts for selling dual-use chemicals or production gear to Iraq or Libya at the end of the report, the first time anyone had published such a list.

Shimon thought I should zoom in my investigative lens to focus on the federal prosecutor pursuing fraud allegations against the Atlanta, Georgia, branch of Italy's Banca Nazionale del Lavoro (BNL). After consulting with Rabbis Abraham Cooper and Marvin Hier, who ran the Simon Wiesenthal Center in Los Angeles, we agreed on a budget and an outline for a monograph they would jointly publish with *Mednews*.

And so I traveled to Atlanta in October 1990 to meet with BNL officials and their lawyers and with the federal prosecutor, Gale McKenzie. She was accusing the head of BNL Atlanta, Christopher Drogoul, of defrauding the Italian bank by keeping the $4 billion of allegedly illegal loans he had made to Iraq in a set of "grey books" not declared to the bank. To put pressure on Drogoul, she gave immunity to his partner, Paul Von Wedel, in exchange for his testimony. When I met Ms. McKenzie fourteen months after federal agents had raided the plush BNL office suite on the twentieth floor of Atlanta's Gas & Light tower, she was still having difficulty understanding the documents they had seized, even though most of them were written in English.

"Here's something that looks like a contract," she said, pulling out a multi-page document. "The cover letter shows it was sent to Drogoul by somebody named Hussein Kamil at MIMI. Do you know what MIMI stands for?"

I was floored. I had been writing about Iraq's weapons industry for several years, not just in *Mednews*. Hussein Kamil was the minister I had photographed greeting arms dealers at the Baghdad arms fair in April 1989.

"That's the latest name for the Ministry of Industry, which he heads. It stands for Ministry of Industry…*and Military Industrialization*," I said with emphasis.

"So why would they be buying a steel rolling mill?"

"Who was the end user?"

"The what?"

You've got to be kidding me, I thought.

"When the Iraqis issue these letters of credit, MIMI will appear as the overall government authority for the loan, but it will be pegged to a specific factory or establishment," I explained. "That's the end user."

She gave a kind of snort, as if this was the first time anyone had told her this, then started scouring the contract.

"Okay, so here it says it went to something called taj-eye."

"Do you mind if I have a look?"

She turned the document so I could see it but still kept hold of it. The end user was the Nassr State Enterprise for Mechanical Industries in Taji, about thirty kilometers north of Baghdad.

"That's actually pretty interesting," I said. "Taji is an enormous military industrial complex. I've tracked exports to several state establishments located there for use in manufacturing ballistic missiles, conventional weapons, and uranium enrichment centrifuges. Have you shared this with our friends in DoD? I would think they would want to know everything they can about the site before they bomb it into dust."

"I'm a prosecutor, not an intelligence officer," she said in a huff.

That pretty much ended our interview.

When I spoke to Paul Von Wedel later, he didn't even try to hide his disdain for Ms. McKenzie.

"When the feds raided our offices, they opened the file cabinets and dumped all the papers onto the floor and then stuffed them into giant black plastic garbage bags," he said. "No wonder they haven't handed down an indictment in fourteen months. I'm surprised they can find anything at all!"

I also learned that Ms. McKenzie had shut out the professionals from US Customs. These were the guys who had made dozens of cases against techno-bandits of all flavors, who knew how to read bills of lading and letters of credit, which McKenzie clearly did not, and who understood the weapons applications of dual-use technologies. "She insisted on doing the entire investigation by herself," one of them told me.

In Washington, the BNL case had become a political football, with multiple Congressional committees, all led by Democrats, pursuing the Bush administration for having approved US government credits and export licenses to Iraq's WMD programs. I spent hours with Dennis Kane, the lead investigator for Congressman Henry González of Texas, the chair of the House Banking Committee. He thought McKenzie was stonewalling Congress. "Gail McKenzie has refused to supply documents, she has refused to appear before our Committee, she has refused to cooperate in any manner whatsoever," Dennis told me. "The Attorney General has tried to shut us down and even threatened the chairman—I'll get you the letter before you leave. He claimed we were interfering in a sensitive case with national security concerns. Those are code words for exposing political embarrassment."

I was liking every minute of this. The deeper I plunged into it, the better I liked the provisional title of my monograph, "The BNL Blunder." Dennis and a handful of his Democrat colleagues were extremely helpful, opening their files, sharing documents, and indicating which officials I might want to question for having authorized exports that had increased the lethality of Iraq's military arsenal just as American soldiers and airmen were heading into harm's way.

They were working on parallel tracks with Republican Senator Jesse Helms, whose chief counsel, William C. Triplett, regularly compared notes with me about foreign and US companies providing weapons production equipment to Saddam Hussein or to Libya's Qaddafi. Triplett had a particular gift for making headlines. He published his own list of companies that helped build weapons plants for our enemies. He called it, "Saddam's Foreign Legion."

Also on the team in helping to expose what was fast becoming a policy fiasco were top staffers at the Defense Technology Security Administration, the Pentagon outfit created by Steve Bryen under President Reagan. They had stayed on after Steve resigned and provided me with thick binders of Iraqi industrial projects that included details on suppliers and letters of credit, all of it unclassified. These names went into my databases and fed my stories at *Mednews*.

Republicans and Democrats seemed united in exposing the folly of the Bush administration "tilt" toward Saddam. There was nothing political about it—or so I thought.

+ + +

Not long after returning to Paris in late October 1990, I received a call from Suzanne Gluck, a literary agent working for International Creative Management. She had seen me on ABC News talking about Saddam's weapons plants and thought it might make a good subject for a book. All of a sudden, with Saddam's invasion of Kuwait, everybody wanted books about the Iraqi dictator. "I've got an editor who is very interested in the work you have been doing," she said.

She faxed me an agency agreement, then revealed she was working with Henry Ferris at Houghton Mifflin in Boston.

"He thinks there's a great story in how the West armed Saddam," Suzanne said.

"He's right."

"He also thinks you're the best person to tell it."

My proposal became *The Death Lobby: How the West Armed Iraq.* Houghton Mifflin offered an advance of $150,000, an even larger sum than I had gotten for my book on Soviet high-tech espionage. One month later, I was on a plane to Washington, DC, to conduct additional interviews with Richard Perle, Steve Bryen, Paul Freedenberg, and other former Reagan and Bush officials to nail down the timeline of US exports to Saddam Hussein. As before, my friends on the Hill were generous with their time and now provided me with thousands of pages of export licensing records, which Christina helped me enter into our database.

I had become convinced that providing Saddam Hussein with the industrial know-how and equipment to break his dependence on foreign arms suppliers was a policy error of monumental proportions, driven by corporate and Wall Street lobbyists for material gain. The entire book had four mentions of the word "Republican" and three of "Democratic," each time to identify members of Congress who were opposing the export-driven policy. I remained convinced there was nothing political about my reporting—even though it all appeared to fault two successive Republican administrations.

Follow the facts wherever they lead, was how I saw it. The truth had no party affiliation.

52: 'Our Bible'
Paris

The more I appeared on ABC News, *Nightline*, and on French TV, the more journalists started paying attention to my work. Because of my trips to Iraq and my interviews with the defense contractors, Iraqi government officials, and black-market arms dealers responsible for the rise of Saddam Hussein, the media now considered me a go-to person on Iraq. Reporters from France, Italy, the UK, Germany, Sweden, Switzerland, and Canada called to interview me about arms deliveries to Saddam Hussein. The editor of a US publication called the *American Spectator* commissioned a profile of Saddam Hussein. Even National Public Radio invited me on air.

Tom Hamburger from the Minneapolis *Star Tribune* called me that December. Someone had faxed him the *Mednews* issues with photos from the April 1989 Baghdad arms fair, and he wanted to know about the Soviet AS-14 laser-guided missile hanging from a Mirage F1. "Do you know who supplied the targeting pod?" he asked.

I told him it was the French defense electronics giant, Thomson-CSF.

"And where did they get the technology?" he asked.

"I'm not sure, really," I said. It was a white lie, but I didn't know how much he knew at this point.

He went on to tell me about several exchanges he had had with Martin Marietta. "They claim they sold the laser-designation pod to the French for thirty-seven million dollars in 1975."

"Were any restrictions on the license?"

He hadn't asked but said he would.

A few days later, he called me excitedly with new information.

"The Martin Marietta guys told me that the US arms export license contained a provision that the laser designation pod could not be transferred to third parties without written US consent. The French took over the program in 1979, and that's the last they heard of it until now, when I showed them your photos from Baghdad."

"So it's their pod?"

"Sure looks like it," he said.

I ran a brief piece in *Mednews* on the apparently illegal sale, along with photos of the Soviet missile and the US laser designation pod on an

Iraqi aircraft, and thought no more about it.[58] I figured Thomson-CSF was probably too embarrassed to complain.

+ + +

The six-hundred-square-foot office in our garage was humming in the weeks before the shooting war began in Iraq. I had taken on an intern to help me with research. David was in his mid-twenties and had just gotten out of the US Army, where he had been an artilleryman stationed in Germany. He wanted to get into journalism, and each day arrived on the métro from Paris more excited than the last. I had him buy a half-dozen newspapers before coming out to us, and he spent much of the day clipping articles and entering significant events into a chron file we called "Gulf War news." We had just begun to use a new electronic news service from CompuServe. Even before the internet, the information flow was like sipping from a firehose.

Bill Triplett stopped to have lunch with us en route to Bonn, where Senator Helms was sending him to get additional information from the German government on their exports to Iraq. Friends from ABC News were now reporting from Saudi Arabia, as was CBS *60 Minutes* correspondent Bob Simon, with whom I had worked years earlier on the Damavand project story that never aired. I was chomping at the bit to head into action. But I realized that I had something nobody else had: real information on Saddam Hussein's weapons plants and military capabilities, accumulated over years of investigative reporting when no one was paying attention. So I sat out the war, worked on my book, and did television and radio. As my public profile increased, my agent in New York became increasingly friendly. I was working sixteen- and eighteen-hour days, just as our thirteen-month-old daughter was learning to walk.

During the school vacation in February 1991, we rented a chalet on the ski slopes at Courchevel. I was on a tight writing schedule, but the snow was terrific, and it was such a treat to watch our three older children, who were now twelve, eleven, and ten, chase each other down the slopes. I skied with them in the morning after their ski school lessons, then we all came home for lunch. Christina skied with them in the afternoon while I stayed and watched the baby. When she napped, I wrote. If

---

58   "Martin Marrietta laser technology illegally sold to Iraq," *Middle East Defense News (Mednews)*, December 17, 1990; Volume 4, 5/6.

I was lucky and one of them came home before the lifts closed, I snuck out for another couple of runs at the end of the day.

By now, I was making so much money from my writing that we felt financially secure for the first time. What we lacked now was time. So we tried to make the best of every moment we could steal away from work to just be together. And through all of it, we always ate dinner as a family. Once the shooting war started, I added a prayer for the men and women who were defending our freedom when I said the grace before dinner.

+ + +

Washington, DC

As soon as the shooting war was over, I was invited to DC to address a special conference hosted by my rabbis from the Simon Wiesenthal Center on the arming of Saddam Hussein. It was a dry run of the thesis I would develop fully in my book, *The Death Lobby*, namely that the massive transfer of dual-use industrial technologies to a known psychopath verged on a criminal enterprise. This judgment, based on years of investigation and firsthand evidence I had gathered in Iraq, put me at odds with the Bush administration, which I blamed for lifting export controls and encouraging US corporations to help Saddam build dozens of weapons factories. While the companies and the banks and complacent Commerce Department officials claimed they had "no way of knowing" Saddam's true intentions, I argued to the contrary. "With the gassing of the Kurds in Halabja in March 1988, and the massive use of chemical weapons in the final battles with Iran that summer, you would have to have been deaf, dumb, and blind not to understand what Saddam was up to by that point," I said. Like dictators before him (and many after), Saddam went out of his way to let us know his intentions with exquisite precision. Gerry Bull's supergun had but one target: Israel. Saddam threatened darkly he would annihilate the Jewish state.

Rabbi Cooper had gone to Israel when the air war began in mid-January and stayed for the duration, meeting with current and former prime ministers, including Yitzhak Rabin. He could now report on what he had seen. Iraq's thirty-seven missile strikes were far more damaging than the Israeli censor had allowed the press to report, but key targets in the heart of Tel Aviv somehow remained untouched, he told the conference.

"When asked to explain why those key targets escaped damage, Rabin told me, 'If I were an Orthodox Jew, I'd have said it was a miracle.'" Also miraculous was the astonishingly low casualties Saddam's missiles had inflicted, despite the devastation wrought on homes and apartments of innocent civilians.

"On January twenty-first, sixteen hundred apartments in Ramat Gan were totally destroyed," Rabbi Cooper said. "On January twenty-fifth, four hundred fifty apartments and two public buildings were hit. In a single day, twenty-six buildings suffered so much damage they needed to be totally rebuilt, while more than one hundred seventy people were wounded. The Iraqi missiles just barely missed hitting several strategic facilities, including the Damona nuclear plant," he added.

In public, Israel minimized the damage to keep Saddam guessing about the accuracy of his missiles. In private, Israeli leaders were seething at President Bush, and especially Secretary of State James Baker, for pressuring Israel not to respond to the Iraqi missile strikes. "The language Baker used was pretty ugly," Abe told me. "His anti-Semitism was showing."

The Israelis were also seething over Baker pressuring them to start peace talks with the PLO. "That is a total non-starter," Rabbi Hier said. "Even the Israeli peaceniks have changed their position with the war."

Ambassador Jeane Kirkpatrick gave a stinging speech, ripping into the Arabists at the State Department—including Baker—for what she called their "Lawrence of Arabia complex: the tendency to excuse away the excesses of Arab strongmen."

She warned of the lies being spread in the media by the likes of former president Jimmy Carter, who blasted Israel for violating UN Security Council resolutions since the Six-Day War. "This is simply not true," she said. "There are no UN resolutions that call for an immediate withdrawal of Israel from the West Bank, Gaza, and the Golan. Those resolutions call for an Israeli withdrawal in the context of peace in the region, direct negotiations, and the right of all nations in the region to secure and recognized borders, something the Arabs are nowhere near ready to concede."

Her brilliant defense of Israel and her blunt criticism of the United Nations were my introduction to a new flavor of Washington politics, a notion that continues to resonate today: national sovereignty. "We can't base our actions on shifting UN majorities, nor can Israel," she said. "Israel is not required to commit suicide on the basis of a temporary UN majority."

· She also reminded her audience of the obvious: "It was not arms reduction agreements that brought an end to Iraq's occupation of Kuwait. It was the force of arms. That is a hard fact. One of the lessons of this war is that military superiority counts. Israel must maintain its military superiority over its neighbors because it is the only state in the region whose existence is always at stake."

The rabbis introduced me to her afterwards, and I recognized a kindred spirit. Like Richard Perle, she had been a Democrat up through the mid-1970s, then joined the Reagan administration because of Reagan's willingness to confront the Soviet Union and stand up for Israel. I was beginning to think of myself as a Reagan Democrat as well. Ambassador Kirkpatrick later led a team of former Reagan administration national security officials who endorsed me when I made my first unsuccessful run for public office in 2000 in the Republican US Senate primary in Maryland.

Over dinner, the rabbis asked me how my trip to Rome had gone the week before. They knew I was supposed to be meeting with Cecilia Danieli, a female tycoon whose company had built several steel plants in Iraq and who was also working in Iran. She had written the rabbis a letter of complaint after we had published *The BNL Blunder* in January.

"She couldn't deny the facts," I said. "She just denied what the facts meant."

"I'll bet we're going to find out a lot more about her steel plant once the UN inspections begin," Abe said. "You should pay her another visit once it comes out that the US targeted the complex because it was a WMD facility. Maybe we can get her to cooperate."

And that was precisely what we did. Ms. Danieli flew to Paris at the end of March 1991 in her private jet to meet with me and Shimon Samuels, the Wiesenthal Center's European representative. By now, the media was all over the Western companies that had built Saddam's war machine, in great part thanks to the work Shimon and I had been doing.

"I will admit," she said as we sat together in Shimon's tiny office, "I never thought about the political implications of this business with Saddam. It was business, period."

We discussed a billion-dollar contract she had signed recently to build a similar steel plant in Iran. "Really," she said. "This plant has no military content whatsoever."

"But it's being built right next door to a facility in Isfahan known to make ballistic missiles," I said.

"I wasn't aware of that," she said.

"Well, now you are," said Shimon.

It was a tactic Shimon and I would refine over the next eighteen months or so: naming and shaming the Western companies who were enabling the murderers of tomorrow. We were particularly tough on the Germans, who despite their history of gassing the Jews during World War II, virtually single-handedly built poison gas industries in Iraq and Libya. When you looked over the type of equipment and direct chemical weapons precursors the German government allowed German companies to sell to Middle Eastern tyrants, you could only conclude that anti-Semitism—now cloaked as a left-wing, anti-Israel movement—was alive and well in Germany and other European nations.[59]

+ + +

Even as I was racing to finish the manuscript of *The Death Lobby* by my June 1 deadline, the next chapter of the Iraq drama was beginning to play itself out in New York, Vienna, and across Iraq. It involved the international inspections just getting underway with the International Atomic Energy Agency (IAEA) under the leadership of a new international body headquartered at the UN in New York, the UN Special Commission for the Disarmament of Iraq (UNSCOM). I worked to develop sources at both the IAEA and UNSCOM, and senior officials at both agencies became *Mednews* subscribers. Since the international inspectors responsible for mapping out Saddam's WMD capabilities and dismantling them expected (and received) no cooperation from the Iraqis, they turned to Western governments and even to Russia for intelligence. But Iraq's biggest pre-war suppliers—France, Germany, the UK, and the United States— were often coy in the information they made available. That's why the inspectors turned to me. My databases on the companies that had provided dual-use equipment to Iraq provided a map. Once *The Death Lobby* came out, UNSCOM chief ambassador Rolf Ekéus started giving copies to inspectors. "I told them it was our Bible," he later told me and Christina. I became convinced we were doing God's work to expose the proliferators.

---

59 See, for example, Kenneth R. Timmerman, "Germany Built Saddam's War Machine," *Wall Street Journal Europe*, March 28, 1991.

"We always say 'never again,'" Simon Wiesenthal told me when I met him at a private dinner hosted by an Iranian friend in Paris in May. "But what does that mean? How can we be serious about preventing another Holocaust if our governments continue to allow these companies to sell the equipment and the know-how to kill off Jews in the future?"

That evening, hosted by Colonel Hassan Aghilipour and his French wife, Nelly Chadirat, was the beginning of a relationship I came to cherish. Simon was sharp-tongued and witty, tough on his enemies but charming and attentive to those he loved; fiercely convinced of the justness of his cause in public, while in private secretly fearing failure.

"How much can one person do? Can you really make a difference?" he asked. "I've always believed that you can. You are the future, Ken. Never give up!"

53: 'Oh My, That's the Defense Minister!'
Le Bourget

Expectations ran high at the Paris Air Show that June. US defense contractors were basking in the afterglow of a successful war, where their products had performed with stunning accuracy and lethality. The French were morose, since their client lost the war on prime-time television using their weapons. Talk about bad publicity! Even so, the French aerospace manufacturers association, GIFAS, which hosted the show, convened reporters to tell us not to believe our lying eyes. Military aerospace orders had actually *increased* as a share of overall French aerospace exports for 1990, they claimed. What they left out, of course, was that 1989 had been an abysmal year because Saddam Hussein wasn't buying.

As was his custom, GIFAS president Jacques Mitterrand escorted his brother, the French president, Defense Minister Pierre Joxe, and visiting foreign dignitaries on a tour of the main exhibits before the show officially opened its doors. Defense correspondents, such as myself, were allowed to tag along. Usually the pre-show tour was drop-dead boring. Not this year.

Tensions between the US and France over the Gulf War were still simmering, especially among the military and the intelligence community. Indeed, Mitterrand had been forced to replace the previous defense minister, a well-known Saddam crony, because he had refused to coop-erate with the US-led war effort. (His most famous stunt was to dispatch the only operating French aircraft carrier to join the war with trucks and helicopters on the flight deck, after announcing to the press that no French combat jets would take place in the fighting.)

But Joxe had his own baggage. The son of a known pro-Soviet politician, the Americans suspected him of being a closet communist. Making matters worse, the French had been caught just one month before the show spying on US high-tech companies in France and in Houston, Texas. Pierre Marion, a former chief of French military intel-ligence, the DGSE, boasted to a reporter that France spied on its allies and acknowledged that his service had planted electronic bugs in the hotel rooms of visiting US executives. Tensions between the two coun-tries were high.

The Pentagon had authorized Lockheed Martin to bring a F-117A stealth fighter to Le Bourget, the first time it had ever been put on public display. The Nighthawk had been one of the stars of the "shock and awe" campaign, credited with dropping bombs down the chimneys of Iraqi government buildings in the dead of night. Very little was known about the radar-deflecting coatings on the fuselage. They were highly classified and sought after by intelligence agencies the world over.

The US Marines had roped off the Nighthawk from the public, and they were tense as the official delegation approached. The French presi-dent exchanged niceties through an interpreter with the USAF colonel standing at attention in his flight uniform in front of the aircraft. And then the officials moved on to the next exhibit.

But Joxe lingered at the back of the small crowd and began to move toward the stealth fighter. The Marines saw him but remained immobile until he stepped over the rope and made a dash toward the aircraft, his hands extended in front of him as if he had lost his balance. One of the Marines sprang to life, intercepting him before he could touch the plane. Without a word, he pinioned Joxe's arms to his sides and lifted him back over the rope line like a sack of flour. *Oh my,* I remember thinking, *that's the defense minister!*

When I asked the air attaché at the US embassy about the incident later that day, he laughed. "It's an old KGB trick," he said. "They put a special glue on their hands or a cloth that can pick up minute particles of the radar-deflecting coating. Obviously, since this was the first public appearance of the F-117A, our guys were on the lookout. But the defense minister himself? That was a surprise."

Not a single French reporter mentioned the incident in their accounts of the air show. The French defense ministry kept silent, as well.

+ + +

The American defense contractors were ebullient. All of them seemed to have fresh war stories about how their equipment had performed. Many had petitioned the Pentagon to allow them to bring in aircraft and Patriot Missile batteries from the Gulf War theater. A Mr. Campbell at the Martin Marietta chalet regaled me with stories about the opening salvo of the war, when Apache helicopters used Martin Marietta Hellfire missiles to take out Iraq's French-built radar.

"Did our guys ever see the Iraqi Mirages in the air?" I asked.

"Not that I know of," he said.

"So the Iraqis had all that technology, the Exocet and the AS30L, and they never once tried to launch against our ships?"

"They didn't dare. We owned the skies."

I don't recall whether he invited me to the bar at this point, but our conversation took a more confidential tone.

"Were you the reporter who broke the story about the laser designation pod?" he asked.

"I was."

"We got a call from a Minneapolis reporter who said he'd read about it in some confidential newsletter published in Paris."

I grinned and handed him my favorite promotional flyer with the picture of Saddam Hussein showing off his titanium balls.

"Well, for the record, Thomson-CSF never asked us for an export license. That was our pod, and we never knew they sold it to Iraq. We've gone back and done a full review. The Pentagon is truly pissed, I can tell you that."

Bob Trice, the Middle East rep for McDonnell Douglas, told me a similar story later that day.

"Everyone wanted to know what happened to that damn targeting pod," he said. "It's the latest NATO technology, one of those things that gives us our qualitative edge over the Soviets. If it went to Iraq and it went to India, you know it went to Mother Russia. But what do you expect of the French? They make these beautiful aircrafts but have never been able to make radar worth a damn. Great for impressing your mistress, I guess. They look great at air shows but are worthless in war."

Game on. And I would be caught in the thick of it.

54: 'Saddam's Secrets'
Vienna, Austria

The United Nations inspections of Iraqi WMD sites that began after the war quickly became front-page news. I developed relationships with top inspectors in Vienna and New York and shared with them sections from my book to help them identify secret weapons plants and WMD production gear they should be destroying. In exchange, they fed me lists of dual-use equipment they found during the inspections that I published in *Mednews* and the *Wall Street Journal*. My database of European and US suppliers who had helped build Saddam's weapons machine was growing by the day.

As Triplett put it, "before the war we thought Saddam had one nuclear weapons program and was five years from the bomb. Now we know he had five nuclear weapons programs and was just one year from the bomb."

My work caught the attention of Barry Lando, a CBS *60 Minutes* producer in Paris I had gotten to know. Barry was working with Mike Wallace and plied me with questions on what I was calling an export control scandal. I sent him a series of memos on the weapons inspections and what they had found. Initially, Barry asked me to focus on Lieutenant General Amir Hamoudi al-Saadi—who had just been identified as a key planner of Iraq's secret bomb project—since I was the only Western reporter who had ever met him. But as news of fresh discoveries in Iraq surfaced, they decided to zero in on chief nuclear inspector David Kay, who also happened to be an American. Kay became a media star during his four-day parking-lot standoff with the Iraqis, which was broadcast live on international television. I arranged for *60 Minutes* to interview Kay and other nuclear inspectors at IAEA headquarters in Vienna, Austria.

Although I had worked with *60 Minutes* before, I hadn't been prepared for the Hotel Imperial and the lifestyle to which Mike Wallace was accustomed. A few minutes' walk from the Vienna Opera House, the Imperial was a former palace, with a majestic central staircase, paneled in marble, leading up to a ring of chunky balconies arrayed with Greek statues and enormous crystal chandeliers. My room came equipped with an inlaid writing desk and cameo-style portraits of Habsburg royals and looked out onto the Kartnerring. I took the metro out to the IAEA and spent the day doing pre-interviews with David Kay and his deputy, Maurizio Zifferero, and going through their files. I came away with pages and pages of notes on companies and equipment found at facilities I had identified as part of Saddam Hussein's clandestine nuclear weapons archipelago.

"You have been right about these things," Zifferero told me. "Many of us never wanted to believe that Saddam's people were technically capable of this. He fooled us. He really fooled us."

Mike Wallace flew in late that afternoon and closeted himself off in his suite to recover from jet lag. Barry called me that evening to go over our game plan. "Be at the suite by 10:00 AM," he said.

The next morning was hectic. Wallace's palatial suite was flooded in sunlight as Barry worked with the production crew to position the light umbrellas for the set. Mike Wallace was seated at an Empire breakfast table in his nightgown, drinking coffee, as a make-up artist fussed over his hair. "So you are Mister Timmerman," he boomed in greeting. He was reading one of my memos and looked at me over his reading glasses with milky eyes. "Do you think this goes up to the White House?" he asked.

I shrugged. "It's hard to see how it doesn't. The tilt toward Saddam was pretty open once Bush took office."

"So I gather from your reporting."

"But I can't prove that the president himself knew anything about Saddam's nuclear weapons program."

"Hmp!" Wallace said. He turned to Barry to shout out something about needing to close the heavy floor-to-ceiling drapes once they started shooting.

While Mike Wallace was famous for the "gotcha" interview, that wasn't what he was planning for this show. When David Kay arrived, I greeted him and introduced him to the production team and to Mike Wallace, who was now dressed and extremely gracious.

"You've become something of a hero to ordinary Americans," Mike said.

"I don't know," Kay said. "But to my State Department friends, I'm the skunk at the garden party. They all wish we'd just go away."

Barry had me stand in the background with him during the shooting. It was a treat watching Mike Wallace go to work, leading his witness through his story until he reached the moment he wanted to immortalize. That was when his eyebrows went up and he recomposed all the crevices of his face into a mask of astonishment.

"And yet, for years Saddam escaped detection. How was that possible?" Wallace asked.

"No one thought the Iraqis were as capable as we now know they were," Kay replied.

He used a similar trick when he interviewed me later.

We were talking about the companies that had provided dual-use equipment to Iraqi weapons plants, my specialty.

"Is it possible they just didn't know what they were doing?" Wallace asked with feigned innocence.

I paused as if giving his question a lot of thought. "It's very hard to believe they didn't understand what was going on," I said finally.

The show, titled "Saddam's Secrets," aired on November 17, 1991, just as I was finishing a week-long book tour in Boston, New York, Chicago, and Washington, DC, thanks to my publisher, Houghton Mifflin. *The Death Lobby* got a tremendous amount of press. It was reviewed in three separate articles in the *Boston Globe*, twice in the *New York Times*, and in hundreds of other publications across the country. The *New York Times* also invited me to write an op-ed about Saddam Hussein's relentless pursuit of nuclear weapons, right beneath the eyes of international inspectors and the export control authorities of Western governments, including the United States. They titled that piece "Surprise! We Gave Hussein the Bomb." In it, I singled out the efforts of former Pentagon official Steve Bryen, by now a personal friend, in getting US Customs to block the shipment to Iraq of high-temperature furnaces for the nuclear program. It's obvious to me now that the headline they chose was aimed at slamming President Bush.

The growing Iraq export control scandals, which I helped fuel, came at a time when Bush's approval ratings were way over 60 percent. His ratings were so high, in fact, that the Democrat National Committee was having trouble recruiting candidates to oppose him in the 1992 elections.

As this and related stories began to take their toll on the president's approval ratings, that would change.

Chapter 10:
Visitors

55: 'No Arms Shipments, No Scandal'
London

So far in my career, with few exceptions, I had sought out my sources. Now, as my work on Saddam's weapons plants became more prominent, people were coming to Paris or to Maisons-Laffitte to meet me.

Norb Garrett was a twenty-nine-year veteran of the CIA. He had been chief of station in Cairo and ended his career as chief of East Asia operations before he joined the corporate intelligence network of former US prosecutor Julius Kroll. Norb asked to meet me in Paris in December 1991 to talk about their star client, the government of Kuwait.

"We are looking into Saddam Hussein's secret financial holdings around the world on our client's behalf and believe you can be useful," he said. "We know he has significant assets here in France."

He offered me $500 a day to help in their investigation.

"Most of this work is being done out of our London office," he added. "We don't really trust the French."

So in January 1992, I made the first of many day trips to London, where I met with Norb and a former senior MI6 officer, Michael Oatley, at their offices in Leconfield House, the former MI5 headquarters on Curzon Street in central London. If Norb looked like a former linebacker in a suit, Michael was right out of central casting—tall and lanky, with big bushy eyebrows and a patrician accent. They had an entire office suite segregated from the rest of their operations that was dedicated to the Iraq project, where we poured through the corporate records of Saddam Hussein's bagmen in Luxembourg, France, Switzerland, Germany, and Italy. At lunchtime, Michael took me down to a fish restaurant called Wheeler's just around the corner.

"The Chablis is rather ghastly," he said. "But I could recommend the Mâcon-Lugny."

On days when we had less time, it was off to the Red Lion pub for lighter fare.

Michael was a former Director of Operations for MI6 and was liaison with Israeli intelligence in the early 1980s when they were targeting the Iraqi-Argentinean Condor missile program through sources inside German supplier companies. He called CIA Director Bill Casey a devout Cold Warrior, who came up with "crazy schemes," like an attempt to overthrow the pro-Soviet regime in the People's Democratic Republic of Yemen. "All of us toyed with the idea of overthrowing the PDRY," he told me. "But we concluded that the regime would disappear anyway because of tribal conflicts."

He liked to poke fun at his French colleagues and their conspiracy theories. "Soldiers make bad intelligence people. They are too hot, too impulsive, too nervous," he said, referring to the French military intelligence service, the DGSE. He preferred the DST, the French counter-espionage service, which MI6 worked with extensively on terrorism. "They are level-headed, cool—very un-French," he said.

In the rare phone conversations or faxes we exchanged after our first meeting, we referred to this work as Project Gander, or just "Gander," for short.

It was through Kroll that I first sat down with an Iraqi businessman who was assisting their investigation. I had met him briefly at a conference of Iraqi exiles in Paris a few months earlier. Now, Michael Oatley insisted that I pay him a visit at his tiny office at 199 Knightsbridge, just across Hyde Park from Kroll. I was to look for a plaque that said "CardTech."

It was hard not to like Ahmad Chalabi. Bald at an early age, bubbling with energy and an almost cherubic smile, he ushered me into the tiny cubicle he used for his political activities in what he explained was a thriving commercial enterprise to bring Visa card services to the Arab Middle East. For hours, we talked about Saddam Hussein and his bagmen. Ahmad appeared to know many of them personally. He knew their families, he knew their companies, and he knew where they hid their secret bank accounts. I took pages and pages of notes.

Michael Oatley and his team relied extensively on Chalabi for leads. They relied on people like me to track them down and confirm them. Chalabi never once deliberately steered me wrong, as the CIA would later claim he did them.

+ + +

Another person who swung by Maisons-Laffitte was Arch Roberts, a Democrat staffer on the House Foreign Affairs Committee. Having spent much of the previous two years investigating the Iraq export licensing fiasco for the Democrats, I didn't find this visit strange or unusual. Arch wanted to discuss what I knew about US weapons diverted from Jordan or other legitimate buyers to Saddam Hussein's Iraq.

"That's a red herring," I said. "Saddam's main arms suppliers were France, the Soviet Union, Brazil, China, South Africa. Lots of others got into the game, but those were the big ones. The US never sold weapons to Saddam."

"We think King Hussein diverted US Mark Eighty-Two bombs to Iraq. And howitzers," Arch said.

"Never happened. Believe me. I would have seen them on the ground. Besides, Saddam was churning out dumb bombs like the Mark Eighty-Two by the thousands in his own factories. Which we helped build. Or at least, finance."

Arch wasn't happy. I later learned he had heard these stories from a left-wing reporter named Murray Waas who had called me several times over the previous year peddling dark tales of secret dealings between George H. W. Bush and Saddam Hussein.[60]

"But I did see the helicopters. You know about them, right?"

Arch's bearded face lit up. "You mean, the ones sold by Sarkis Soghanalian through the CIA?"

"Yeah—well, no, actually. The CIA had nothing to do with it. He sold them during Reagan as civilian helicopters and got a Commerce Department license. Customs later went after him for falsifying documents and put him in jail. Wanna see a picture? Dressed in Iraqi livery?"

"You have a picture of American helicopters converted to military use in Iraq?"

"Yes. Well, sort of," I said.

I rummaged in a bookcase and pulled out a file with my photos from the 1989 Baghdad arms fair and starting leafing through them.

---

60 I later stumbled on one of Murray's screeds, "In the Loop: Bush's Secret Mission," which the *New Yorker* ran on November 2, 1992, the day before the presidential election. He co-wrote the piece with Craig Unger, an early victim of Bush derangement syndrome, whom I later encountered at the fortieth reunion of the Paris Metro in Paris in 2016. See, "Celebrating 40 Years of the Paris Metro: Where have all the Journalists Gone?" Frontpage, September 30, 2016. https://archives.frontpagemag.com/fpm/celebrating-40-years-paris-metro-kenneth-r-timmerman/.

"Here you go."

I handed him a crystal-clear shot I had taken with my 100-300mm telephoto lens, blades still turning, less than a minute after the Bell 212 had landed at Al-Muthana Airport. It was painted in desert camouflage, with the Iraqi flag prominently featured near the tail.

Arch screwed up his eyes, examining the helicopter. "No rocket pods. No weapons...."

"Right. These helicopters were sold to the president's personal security detail. He uses them to fly around to his palaces."

He handed the photo back, disappointed.

"What about the biowarfare agents? They were licensed by the Commerce Department and shipped from the Centers for Disease Control in Atlanta."

"That's true," I said. "I wrote about that in *The Death Lobby*. When Steve Bryen at DTSA learned what had happened, he came down on them like a ton of bricks. Those were the first and only bioagent samples sent to Iraq."

"And the chemicals?" Arch asked.

"Same thing. The first shipments, in 1984, came from a US company in Baltimore called Alcolac. When Steve learned about them, he got Customs involved and nothing more left the US. He got Commerce to ban the export of chemical weapons precursors after that."

"So no arms shipments. No chemical weapons. No anthrax. No scandal."

"Oh, there's a scandal, all right," I said. "It just isn't quite as sexy. Steve Bryen and Richard Perle later got overruled—not on direct arms shipments, that never happened—but on the sale of dual-use equipment to Iraq. That's what BNL was all about. The United States government helped finance the sale of computers and machine tools that went into Iraqi weapons factories. Instead of shipping weapons, we helped Saddam make them."

Arch got up. "It's an important story. But not my jurisdiction," he said.

We agreed to meet again during my next trip to Washington.

56: Return to Lebanon
Naqoura, Lebanon

I flew into Ben Gurion airport at the end of February and spent the night in Jerusalem with an old friend from Paris. David Winn was now the US consul general in East Jerusalem. Normally caustic and deeply cynical, he was in shock from his wife's sudden illness and death. Renée had been diagnosed with multiple sclerosis early in their marriage, which made them decide never to have children. An accomplished biologist, she traveled frequently to Madagascar as a newlywed to study lemurs in their natural habitat. Later, as the illness progressed, she kept lemurs as pets. She made light of her MS, even when she started using a walker. Through it all, she made David laugh.

They moved to Jerusalem and then, out of the blue, she got liver cancer and died within months.

David was happy for the distraction my arrival provided, and we spent hours talking people and politics and drinking Palestinian wine from Ashkelon.

"I just can't believe she is dead," he said. "But let's not talk about that."

"Let's have another glass of wine. That's what Renée would have wanted."

"Hear, hear," he said. "Another glass of wine."

The next morning, I rented a car and drove up north. My goal was to drive the road along the Lebanese border past Bint Jbeil, the home village of Imad Mughniyeh, and spend the night in a kibbutz near Sasa about halfway across the Galilee. I planned to visit the United Nations border post at Naqoura the next day.

By the time I reached the turn-off just south of Kiryat Shemona, it had started to snow. And then night came down like a curtain crash.

The narrow road wound through the hills of Galilee in the darkness, with the snow swirling in ever-thicker clouds that sucked all the light from my headlights. I could barely see the road and could feel my summer tires spin as we climbed. If I couldn't keep up speed and stay in third gear, I would never make it to the top, so I gunned the engine, weaving sloppily up the hill. Luckily, I was the only car on the road.

Once I reached the plateau, there was a long straight stretch before Sasa. Out of the blackness beyond the swirling snow, I saw lights flashing. As I approached, the flashing became rhythmic, and the lights became yellow and more distinct, and as I got closer, I saw smaller lights wandering off along the side of the road. All of a sudden, a soldier in a parka was standing in front of me, his bearded face chunky with ice, waving me to continue forward. Off to the side, I saw a dark metallic dinosaur, chained to a transporter, all lights extinguished, stuck in a ditch at an impossible angle. I had to laugh as I realized it was a Merkava tank weighing close to sixty tons and that it had slid off the road. A half-dozen soldiers stood around, trying to figure out what to do. Good luck pulling it out of the ditch!

As I started to descend the other side of the plateau, the snow tapered off, and I could see the electric border fence and the dark hills of Lebanon where Hezbollah lurked, and then on the Israeli side the yellow lights of a settlement, grouped together like wagons circled together in the wilderness in the valley below. Between them was nothing—not a house, not a light, not even a car. Just death, lurking in the utter blackness.

+ + +

I was anxious crossing the border by foot, but there was no other way to do it. I walked through the shantytown of Naqoura, with its gigantic potholes full of melted snow and its tin-roofed shops, each with a Mercedes or beaten-up BMW parked in front, all of them potential car bombs. It was the first time I had been back in Lebanon in nearly ten years. The Palestinians were gone, but Hezbollah had taken their place, and they were avid hostage-takers.

I found the Turkish-born spokesman for the United National Interim Force in Lebanon (UNIFIL) behind the dirty, whitewashed wall, crowned with barbed wire, that housed the UN complex by the sea. Timur Goksel had agreed to come down from Tyre to brief me, then hand me off to the commander of the French contingent, who would escort me through his sector of the hot border between Israel and Lebanon.

UNIFIL was established in the wake of Israel's limited incursion into Lebanon in 1978, ostensibly to prevent cross-border attacks by Israel or the PLO, which then occupied South Lebanon. Pakistan, France, Norway, Nepal, and Fiji contributed troops, and each commanded their own sector of the border, but they were powerless to prevent the Palestinians from shelling Israel or the Israelis from retaliating. When I was held hostage in Beirut during the 1982 war, Jean-Yves Pellay recounted to me the famous moment when the commander of the French contingent, facing an Israeli armored column several miles long, decided to drop his trousers and moon his Israeli counterpart, rather than attempt a suicidal resistance.

Timur Goksel had seen it all. "Volunteered" by his government in 1979, he became the go-to source for journalists, intelligence officers, and government officials in South Lebanon. Over the past year, he told me, Hezbollah had moved in, replacing the Amal Shiite militia that had been disarmed under the Taef accords. "We are now in an exceptional situation," he told me over tea. "We have never had so many weapons and so many gunmen in our area at one time. I try to appeal to their sanity, but it doesn't always work."

The border had become a free-for-all. "Two Fijian soldiers got wounded trying to stop gunmen from moving in with their weapons. We tried to delay the Israelis from attacking them; didn't work. We tried to stop Hezbollah; no dice."

The Israelis weren't targeting UN troops—at least, not obviously, he said. Another bunch of Fijians were wounded by an Israeli helicopter, but that was because they were standing right next to a Hezbollah gun position. The closest to actual fighting came when the Israelis crossed the border with seventeen tanks through the Nepali sector. This was precisely the type of incursion UNIFIL was supposed to prevent—but so were the Hezbollah rocket attacks into Israel that had prompted the Israeli response.

"The Nepalis called for reinforcements, and when they didn't arrive, they tried to block the road with their cars. Luckily, everybody put down their weapons and fought it out with their fists. The Israelis won. So they smashed our vehicles and went on through. An Israeli captain was killed up the road later on—I'm told, by Hezbollah gunmen."

Goksel admitted that after thirteen years, he had become "part of the local scene." Everybody knew him, and he knew everybody. He had become the chronicler of the region's ill, the memory man.

"When your Colonel Higgins was kidnapped four years ago, three thousand Amal militiamen went looking for him. The Hezbollah guys who took him had planned multiple escape routes, decoys, and safe houses along the way. They had four separate kidnap cars roaming the area. It was a very professional operation. We don't really know how he died. We think he was taken out of the region quickly or maybe killed by accident by a guard or in anger. It was stupid, really. He was valuable as a hostage."

It was fascinating—and appalling—to listen to his stories. He seemed to know so much and yet remain so impotent. I got the same impression from the French commander, Jean-Paul Chessel, when I toured his sector with him. The UN were hapless chroniclers of evil, not knights of the good.

When I returned to Naqoura later that day to walk back across the border into Israel, a T-shirt in a shop window caught my eye because of the Swedish flag. "I'm a silent UN soldier and would like to be with you," the slogan read. "If the answer is yes, then SMILE."

A mortar went off from somewhere in the dense brush along the road just as I crossed the border: a single round, heading north into Lebanon. It was an undeclared war, what the experts called a "low-intensity conflict." I saw no reason to get caught in the middle. I found my car and headed south to Haifa before Hezbollah could respond.

57: Saddam and the Jews
Haifa

Amatzia Baram, an Iraqi-born Jew who was becoming a popular scholar on all things Saddam, had invited me for dinner that evening in Haifa, about an hour's drive from the Lebanese border. The roads were awash with record flooding. He and his wife lived in a modest flat in a dingy concrete and glass building that seemed to have no heat. We drank pots of tea, a bottle of wine that I brought, and every drop of wretched alcohol he could find to keep the damp winter chill from penetrating our bones. I took pages and pages of notes—about the Iraqi opposition, about the failures of Israeli intelligence to remain focused on Iraq after taking out Saddam's nuclear reactor in 1981, and about regime insiders, including Hussein Kamil, the son-in-law who became chief of Saddam's weapons programs.

But especially we talked about Amatzia's own efforts to get the United States to make Israel part of its "tilt" toward Saddam, in an effort to get the Iraqi dictator to covertly recognize Israel's right to exist and drop his support for the worst of the Arab terrorist groups murdering Jews.

Amatzia had studied the complex clan structure of Saddam's Iraq and believed it was the glue that held Saddam's regime together. "Why is Izzat Ibrahim so important?" he said at one point, referring to a low-key deputy remarkable for his red hair and green eyes, a sign of Circassian (some said Assyrian) blood. "Because he is from ad Dour, the second most important center of power after Tikrit. Many of Saddam's top generals come from ad Dour."

"That's where the Iraqis had Thomson-CSF build Saad Thirteen, the military electronics plant."

"Exactly," Amatzia said.

"And that's why Saddam had him marry his eldest daughter."[61]

But Amatzia had another reason for suspecting that Saddam might not be a die-hard anti-Semite, as most of his fellow Arab leaders were.

"Saddam's mother was a fortune-teller," he said. "She went around carrying seashells, or holding beads in her hands, and would approach passersby and offer to tell their fortunes. When she was pregnant with Saddam, she told her friends she had the Devil in her womb and sought to abort him. She was convinced that if he lived, he would do evil things.

"But there was a Jewish family who lived nearby—one of just two Jewish families in Tikrit in 1937. And they sympathized with Oum Saddam. They convinced her not to abort her baby. Later, when Saddam was a child and he misbehaved, his mother used to scold him by saying, 'You'd be dead if it weren't for the Jews.' That's why he's not truly anti-Semitic the way Arafat is. He just pretends to be," Amatzia said.

I went to bed on a sofa on his glass-enclosed balcony, shivering throughout the night, thinking what a great novel this could be: the evil Iraqi dictator, feared of his subjects and his neighbors alike, who felt secretly indebted to the Jews. Even when they chastised him, say, by blowing up his nuclear reactor, they were acting justly, as his mother had done whenever she punished him as a child.

---

61   Izzat Ibrahim ad-Douri was hunted by the US-led coalition during the 2003 invasion as the King of Clubs of Iraqi leaders. He went underground, and by 2014, he was believed to be leading the stay-behind Baathist networks that joined forces with the al-Qaeda in Iraq remnant to form ISIS. My sources say he died, possibly of natural causes, in 2015, although he was reported killed in 2018 and in 2020. He was never found by US forces.

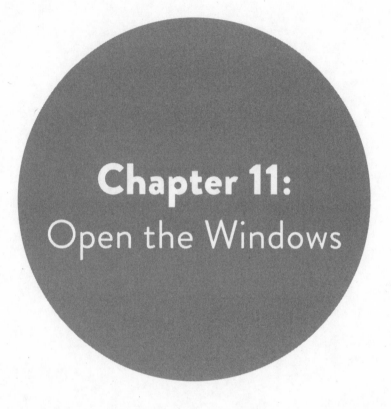

Chapter 11:
Open the Windows

58: Bill Clinton's 'Funny Facts'
Washington, DC

My rabbis at the Simon Wiesenthal Center in Los Angeles agreed that it was time to start looking for the next Iraq, a phrase I used at the end of *The Death Lobby*. The shortsightedness and willful blindness of Western governments that had allowed Saddam Hussein to purchase sophisticated dual-use technologies was being repeated with other countries that hadn't yet emerged as major security threats. They commissioned me to do a larger study that looked at the growing defense industrial base in Iran, Syria, and North Korea, and offered me a generous travel budget.

Non-proliferation was becoming a big business. I went to Washington in March for a conference hosted by Sandy Spector of the Carnegie Endowment, packed with muckety-mucks from previous Democrat administrations. It was also becoming increasingly political. As Governor Bill Clinton of Arkansas started rising in the polls, his advisors began to emerge from the woodwork. While in Washington, I met with a missile expert named Janne Nolan at the Brookings Institution. A former Carter administration official at State, she became a protégé of Senator Gary Hart in the 1980s and was a rising star in the Democrat Party's national security establishment. She knew of my work, and we hit it off.

"President Bush and his people don't want to hear about strengthening the IAEA or about strengthening regional non-proliferation agreements that address the root cause of nuclear proliferation," she said. "Instead, they talk about a nuclear expeditionary force that would stomp on bad countries. It's missing the point."

She worked with a small group of foreign policy advisors to the Clinton campaign, headed by Sandy Berger and a former State Department policy planning director named Tony Lake. If I was interested in helping the campaign, perhaps I could compile a brief paper on the weaknesses of President Bush. "Call it, 'funny facts on proliferation,'" she said. I should put the information into bullet form, with dates when President Bush vetoed proposed sanctions against proliferators, the value of contracts he approved for Iraq, and data on US companies helping Iraq.

It seemed an almost innocent proposal, certainly not anything political, I reasoned. After all, this was just the type of thing I had been publishing in *Mednews* for the past four years.

While in Washington, I traveled to the CIA for a meeting on Syria, Iran, and North Korea with Gordon Oehler, the national intelligence officer for weapons of mass destruction and proliferation issues. While it was a broad-brush briefing, Oehler was able to confirm information I had from my own sources on Chinese missile sales and Syria's success in producing both chemical and biological warheads for their missile fleet. Iran had an "aggressive" program to develop longer-range missiles, he said. Because of this, and the Chinese willingness to sell anything to anybody, the Bush administration had recently established a Non-Proliferation Center at CIA. "Now all our proliferation disciplines are gathered together under one roof, instead of spread across the bureaucracy," he said. That was just the opposite from I had heard from Janne Nolan.

As Gordon escorted me out, I mentioned that this was the first time I had actually visited CIA headquarters. "It's a bit ironic, given that the French are constantly accusing me of working for the Agency," I chuckled.

"Oh, the French," Gordon said, rolling his eyes.

Bill Triplett, chief counsel of the Senate foreign affairs committee, then chaired by Jesse Helms, was fuming. "The Senate is so upset with administration double-talk on China that once again we voted to impose conditions on the renewal of Most-Favored-Nation trading status for China, but the president vetoed it," he said.

I found it reassuring that conservative Republicans and Democrats agreed on the threat from Communist China and their proliferation activities. When I got back, I blasted the Bush administration in *Mednews* for caving into business interests who were demanding an easing of export-licensing restrictions.[62]

But there was a lot more going on behind the scenes that none of us picked up on until later.

---

62   "Bush's China Card," *Middle East Defense News (Mednews)*, March 30, 1992, Volume 5, 13.

+ + +

Amman

Just before going to Washington, I met twice with Michael Oatley of Kroll Associates, first in Paris, then in London. Both meetings focused on a new aspect of their investigation into the black-market and money-laundering activities of Saddam Hussein in Jordan. They wanted to send me to Amman to get ground truth on the Iraqi procurement fronts and oil-export agents they had been hearing about from Ahmad Chalabi and other Iraqi exiles.

"Don't push it," Michael said to me when we met in mid-March in London. "The Iraqis can be very thuggish when they put their mind to it. Just see what you can get them to say."

My target list included a software company, a small aerospace company that worked with a British producer of thermal imaging equipment, a company that made armored dune buggies, several banks and financial institutions, and a handful of trading companies. The crown of them all was the Iraq-Jordan Land Transportation Company.

Jordan had become notorious as Iraq's open door to the world. During the Iran-Iraq war, the port of Aqaba went from a sleepy backwater to one of the world's busiest ports, bringing in 90 percent of Iraq's weaponry, food, and industrial goods that could no longer make it past the Iranian navy in the Persian Gulf. To haul this vast quantity of goods, the Iraqi government purchased hundreds of twenty-ton and forty-ton Mercedes trucks and sent them in endless convoys from Aqaba to Baghdad. They also bought a fleet of tanker trucks to export oil. The Iraq-Jordan Land Transportation Company continued to manage the import-export trade after Desert Storm. Kroll estimated that Saddam recently had transferred $5.2 billion in government funds to the Arab Bank in Amman to facilitate the black-market trade. He also asked me to investigate claims that the Central Bank of Jordan was laundering secret Iraqi government funds in Switzerland through commercial banks such as Jordan's Housing Bank, the Jordan Gulf Bank, and the Arab Financial Corporation.

As I went from office to office in Amman, innocently asking questions about trade with Iraq, I encountered a lot of embarrassment. One Jordanian government official, publicly fired by King Hussein because he was too close to Saddam and re-hired on the sly, explained that nothing had changed since the UN sanctions on Iraqi oil exports had been imposed. "We have always exported Iraqi oil through Aqaba. Today, we just pretend it's not happening," he said.

I had phoned Khaled Marzoumi, Iraq's commercial attaché in Amman, to arrange a meeting. He reminded me that we knew each other from Paris but said that unfortunately he would be traveling to Aqaba that evening until the end of the Aid al Fitr celebrations, several nights hence. When I showed up the next morning at the offices of the Iraq Land Transportation Company, I found him hosting a delegation that had just arrived from Baghdad. He was not happy to see me.

"Mister Khaled," I said when I saw him. "I thought you would be gone."

Marzoumi looked the part of a polished Middle Eastern interme- diary. Tall and elegant in his expensive French suit, he sported a trim moustache tinged with grey, as was his wavy black hair.

"Ah, Mister Kenneth," he said. "As you see, *yani*, I had a change of plans."

I knew from the file that Marzoumi was a key figure in Saddam Hussein's clandestine trade network who had helped establish a front company in Paris, Babil International, believed to be the hub of sanc- tions-busting activity. When he disappeared upstairs into the offices of the State Oil Marketing Organization (SOMO), suddenly it all clicked. He was the trade attaché, oil was Iraq's main export, and trucks were the only way for it to breach the international embargo to reach foreign markets. That is why SOMO and the Iraq-Jordan Land Transportation Company shared offices. Nobody had connected the dots between Marzoumi, Amman, and the sanctions-busting network until that moment, when I saw it with my own eyes. He was *the guy*.

+ + +

It took me three days to set up my interview with Crown Prince Hassan, the younger brother of King Hussein. When the Palace finally approved my request, I was summoned hurriedly at 10:30 AM on the Thursday before Aid al Fitr and asked to wait.

They ushered me into an inner office at the Royal Scientific Society three hours later, where I was greeted by a short stocky gentleman in his mid-fifties, dressed in an open-collared shirt, a windbreaker, and slacks. This was the Crown Prince. With no fuss or bother, we got down to the interview.

Hassan spoke a mile a minute in British-accented English, laden with technical terms and jargon, a real policy wonk. Every now and then he paused to give a repressed laugh, which had the effect of sucking in the entire lower portion of his face. I was impressed by the scope of his knowledge, the detail of his almost donnish presentation. But a politician he was not. His main complaint was the influx of Palestinian refugees from Iraq and Kuwait. These were not your run-of-the-mill refugees of war but the engineers, economists, bankers, and managers who had run the Iraqi and Kuwaiti economies until their luck ran out and they were expelled.

"Wouldn't they be a benefit to Jordan?" I asked him naively.

"They are costing us billions!" he said.

So much for the endearing love between the Arabs and the Palestinians.

When I asked him about the allegations that Jordan was helping the Iraqi regime to skirt the embargo, he got defensive. "You can't expect a country that borders another country that has been subjected to international economic sanctions to commit hari-kari," he said. "We can't put up an iron curtain overnight. Where is Jordan supposed to jump?"

And jump they did not. I reported my findings not only to Kroll but also to the *Wall Street Journal* editorial page, which ran a series of columns with my byline from Amman. Jordan continued to help Saddam's Iraq skirt the international trade embargo for years to come.

59: A Matter of Physics
London

After returning to Maisons-Laffitte for time with my family, I went back to London for a debriefing. Michael Oatley introduced me to a former colleague at MI6 named John Christie, an old Middle East hand. Christie had been posted to Kuwait decades ago when an earlier Iraqi dictator had threatened to invade Kuwait. He recalled flying up to the border in a Kuwaiti army helicopter to determine whether Iraqi tanks had actually invaded the country, as the Kuwaitis were claiming. They hadn't.

After that, he'd been posted to Saudi Arabia, Dubai, Lebanon, Egypt, Somalia, and Sudan, returning to London to become Middle East section chief in the late 1960s. Michael Oatley had been one of his operatives posted in Africa.

Christie himself was more of an analyst than an operative. After retiring, he went to work for investment banking houses and later bought a Middle East newsletter group. He prided himself on his Arabic and his knowledge of Arab customs. Michael had brought him in to critique my reports, playing the role of the Kuwaiti client.

As I watched the interplay between these two old spies, I felt I was witnessing a real-life version of George Smiley and his retired protégé Ned in *The Secret Pilgrim*. Michael was the agent-runner, talented, sensitive, and inquisitive. Christie was full of blusterous old-boy superiority, but he knew his stuff cold. He went over my reports line by line, ostensibly to teach me how to write in the style of intelligence reports, not journalism. The main edits involved removing any indication of how I had learned what I knew, including sources, and presenting my conclusions not as suggestions but as if they were the writ of God. "Because that's what we are. At least, that's how the client wants to think of us," he said.

In truth, I preferred the seductive agent-runner to the pontificating analyst. But I learned much from them both.

✦ ✦ ✦

In between these trips, I had several meetings with my latest French counter-intelligence minder, "Patrick." He came to visit us in Maisons-Laffitte and remarked on our new car—the second in four years. As I escorted him back outside after lunch, he suddenly became very serious.

"Does your wife drive your daughter to day care?" he asked.

"Sometimes," I said. "Especially when I'm not here."

"Hmm."

"Hmm, what?"

I was peeved and let him see it.

"No, no, just thinking," he said. "But it's probably not a good idea."

A few weeks after that, we met for lunch at an excellent fish restaurant near Les Halles. Patrick was by far the best of the DST agents who had been assigned to me. He gave me real information I could use in stories on terrorism or proliferation and asked for little in exchange. He just wanted to know what I was doing. Or so he said.

"You know," he began once we had demolished an excellent *bar poché* and began to attack our *colonels*—lemon sorbet with vodka, "you have made a great mistake, Monsieur."

"What's that?"

"You never should have put your home address on your newsletter."

"It is required by law," I said.

"Well, yes. But you needn't have taken it so literally."

"What do you mean?"

I was starting to get worried.

"Now every intelligence officer in Iran, Syria, Iraq, and who knows where else knows exactly where to find you and your family," he said.

It hit me like a ton of bricks. I may even have slapped my forehead, it was so obvious.

"I guess I should change it."

"It's too late for that," he said.

"What do you mean?"

"You should move."

"But we just finished renovating our house!"

"Actually, it would be best if you just left France," he added. "For your own good, Monsieur. I say this to you as a friend."

Leave France? I was stunned. After four years of *Mednews*, I was making good money and was considered an expert on terrorism and proliferation and Third World weapons programs. I had been invited to lecture in recent months at non-proliferation conferences in Italy and France, was working as a consultant for ABC and CBS News, and had received invitations to consult privately from members of Parliament in several countries—including members of Congress in the United States. The Clinton campaign seemed to share the same goal as I did, which was to rein in an export-driven economy that had armed Saddam Hussein with no heed to national security. I believed these were the same mistakes Western countries had made in the 1930s with Hitler, when they coddled a dictator for profit. Should I now give all of this up? Because of an idle threat?

"We had some inquiries about you recently from our Syrian friends," Patrick said, sensing my consternation. "Also from the Iranians. Both of them are wondering why we would allow a CIA agent to operate so freely in our country."

"Come on," I said.

He threw up his hands in a familiar gesture. *Hey, it's not me, I'm just telling you what they say.*

"But nobody really believes that, right?"

"Right," he said. Convincingly. Or almost.

+ + +

The next time I went to London, I related this exchange to Michael Oatley.

"He asked you about your car? Really?" he said.

"Well, yeah. What's so unusual about that? He thought we should stop parking it on the street and bring it in behind the gate."

"Oh, I'm so sorry," he said.

"What do you mean?"

"Well, not to put too fine a point on it. But you really need to call your wife and tell her not to start the car without opening the windows. Not ever," he said.

"What?"

"It's really just a matter of physics. If you open the windows and a bomb placed under the car or in the engine compartment goes off, there's a fighting chance it will vent enough of the explosion out the window to not kill her. If the windows are wide open, that is."

"You're serious."

"I'm afraid so," he said. "The Syrians and the Iranians can be very nasty. And so can the French, by the way."

I felt a chill come over me. There had been a good many car bombs in Paris in recent years, and the Iranians had bumped off some two hundred dissidents in France, Germany, and elsewhere in Europe. But they had never gone after a non-Iranian, and I pointed that out.

"What about Jean-Paul Kauffman? Terry Anderson? Roger Auque? They were all kidnapped by the Iranians in Lebanon. You knew all of them."

"That's true."

They were among several dozen French and American hostages seized by Iranian-controlled groups in Lebanon in the mid-1980s. I had crossed paths with them—and with Kauffman, crossed swords—during reporting trips to Lebanon.

I called Christina as soon as we got back from lunch and gave her instructions for that afternoon when she planned to pick up Diana. I told her the rest once I got home later that night.

I knew by this point that the French were listening to our phone conversations and possibly following my movements. My previous DST minder had told me as much; so had Gerard and Michael Oatley. It was entirely conceivable that Iranian or Syrian agents who had penetrated the French government—and there were many of them—had gained access to that information. From there, it was scarcely a leap to pass that information to operational teams. Would they actually take the risk of assassinating an American journalist living in France? The whole thing seemed preposterous.

But what did I know, especially compared to the professionals who were warning me?

+ + +

The next piece of the puzzle fell into place shortly afterwards, when I was making a presentation on proliferation at the Centre des Hautes Études Militaires, a French government think-tank that was part of the French War College.

One of my fellow panelists was Michel Ferrier, who headed the strategic export control unit at the SGDN, the intelligence branch of the Prime Minister's officer—something akin to our National Security Council. Once the discussion got going, Ferrier launched into a scathing attack on journalists—and then on me personally—for not knowing "the full picture" of government operations, which was only available to persons in positions of power and knowledge such as himself.

I remember thinking, *Wow. He'd have a hard time getting away with that in the States, where journalists are always second-guessing politicians.* The "full picture" he wanted to present was just the French government spin, whereas I had published information not available in France or anywhere.

When it came my turn to bat, I spoke about the depth of knowledge Western governments had at their disposal about Iraq's WMD programs. "We had identified companies and individuals aiding Iraq years before Desert Storm, but none of us—not the Americans, not the British, not the Germans, not the French—did anything about it. We knew, but we did not act, all the while Saddam became a serious threat to us all."

As I was saying these words, Ferrier got up in a huff and stomped out—to the general astonishment of the colonels, flag officers, and armaments engineers. Ferrier was a technocrat who sat at the pinnacle of political and strategic responsibility. And yet, he was simply incapable of confronting contradiction. He was a bit like a teenage shop major who never grows up and simply can't understand that girls do not function with the regularity of an internal combustion engine.

Or so I thought.

But this was just another warning, another dot I failed to connect.

60: SCUDS on Tel Aviv
Jerusalem

Christina and I flew to Israel in mid-May to continue my research for the new Wiesenthal Center report. The Israeli government had agreed to give me extensive military intelligence briefings on the WMD programs of Iran and Syria, and they kept their word. I spent hours with the top science officer at AMAN in his office in the Kirya, Israel's defense ministry. The Israeli colonel went country by country, program by program; it was a *tour de force* for a wonk like me. He confirmed my conclusion, based on export licensing records, that both Iran and Syria were working on biological weapons programs. He also confirmed my long-held suspicion that the French first gave Syria access to WMD technology. "This is why the Syrians still use the French acronym, CERS, for the Syrian Scientific Research Center," the colonel said. "It was the French who built the first science center in Syria in 1976. CERS remains a publicly declared civilian technology agency, and not everything is military. But nearly everything it does is military-related," he said.[63]

While at the Kirya, I stopped in to visit with Uri Lubrani. His negotiations for the release of downed navigator Ron Arad had stalled, although he thought he had found a fresh channel for communicating with Tehran. Since the Gulf War, both the Syrians and the Iranians were trying to convince the Bush administration they had been "housebroken" when it came to terrorism, he said. "But Damascus is still a terror bazaar."

63　CERS = Centre d'Etudes et de Recherches Scientifiques. The English name, SSRC, was Syrian Scientific Research Center. This was the site the US and the French bombed in April 2018 in retaliation for an alleged Syrian government chemical weapons attack.

As for the Iranians, he was convinced they were behind the downing of Pan Am 103, in retaliation for the US shoot-down of the Iranian Airbus. "We think the Libya story is just nonsense," he said.

Back in Jerusalem, I bumped into Rabbi Abe Cooper of the Wiesenthal Center as I was walking past a five-star hotel. We briefly compared notes on my project. He was sending out "demarches" to the German government over sales of dual-use technologies to Iran and to Britain over the supply of a chemical plant capable of producing chemical weapons.

On Saturday, Christina and I took a service cab to Ramallah and then up to Bir Zeit to visit with Albert Aghazarian, the long-time spokesman for the Palestinian university. Albert is a phenomenon. His grandmother fled during the Armenian genocide of 1915 and wound up in Jerusalem; although Palestinians and Armenians were battling each other in Lebanon, Albert adopted the Palestinian cause and became a Jerusalemite at heart.

We drove back to Jerusalem, where Albert took us on a walking tour of the old city. There wasn't a street where half the shopkeepers didn't greet him by name, scarcely a house whose history he couldn't recount.

"Have you ever been on top of the souk?" he asked us.

"On the roofs?"

"Come on!"

From the esplanade of the Church of the Nativity, we took a series of alleyways toward the main souk, until Albert ducked into a dark passageway and disappeared around the curve of a stone staircase. When we caught up with him, he was holding up his lighter.

"That's better, isn't it?" he said, giving us a belly laugh. "Can't see a damn thing!"

We followed his lighter around another turn in the staircase until we reached a small terrace with a spectacular view over Jerusalem. Just below us were the smooth-arched roofs of the souk and beyond, the domes and crosses of several Orthodox churches, their limestone walls etched with windows like caves cut out of a hillside. Behind us was the shimmering gold of the Dome of the Rock, the mosque built by the Umayyad caliph on the Temple Mount.

"This is what Satan had Jesus look at when he tempted him," Albert said, with a grin. "It's remarkable he didn't give in. Don't you think?"

✦ ✦ ✦

That evening, we had dinner with Jacques Neriah and his wife at a fish restaurant in Herzliya, an upscale suburb north of Tel Aviv. Jacques had been promoted since returning from Paris and was now the director of analysis at AMAN.

"I'm trying to retire," he said, "but I'm a victim of my success. My director, Amnon Shahak, has refused me a pension if I retire now. So they are offering me a job as head of the new Arms Control Directorate at the Ministry of Defense."

We had a lot of catching up to do. In 1990 when Saddam invaded Kuwait, Jacques personally predicted that Saddam would hit Israel with SCUD missiles, bucking the conventional wisdom at the time.

"I handed one of your photos of the French chief of staff in Baghdad to Prime Minister Shamir before the war. That became part of the file and undoubtedly contributed to Shamir refusing to let France join the peace process," he said.

The famous photos from the Baghdad arms fair. I was starting to hear a lot about them, in places I never suspected they had reached.

Jacques's conclusion that Saddam would launch SCUDs on Israel was based on a technical analysis, not any particular item of intelligence. Iraq publicly test-fired its al-Hossein missiles out to ranges of six hundred kilometers—enough to reach Israel—several months before the war began. "I knew that Iraq had developed CW warheads. While I didn't think Saddam would use them for fear we would retaliate, this is what convinced the General Staff to issue gas masks to every citizen, including Palestinians," he said.

He thought General Schwarzkopf, the American war commander, was a fool and a publicity hound. "On the first night of the war, here comes Schwarzkopf making a triumphal announcement that allied air power had virtually wiped out Iraq's offensive capability to wage war. They tried to tell us there was nothing to worry about. So when I briefed Peres and Rabin that night, I told them to stay near the shelters between midnight and 2:00 AM. They said, 'Why? Do you know that Iraq will attack?' I said, 'No. I just suggest you stay near your shelter.' The first al-Hossein missile hit at 2:00 AM," he said quietly, with just a hint of a smile. "I couldn't say anything wrong after that."[64]

---

[64]   Peres and Rabin were then in the opposition but returned to power after the elections held just one month later, with Rabin as prime minister and Peres as foreign minister, until Rabin was assassinated on November 4, 1995.

Jacques and his bosses were still bitter about the final hours of the war and Schwarzkopf's unwillingness to commit resources to take out Saddam's missile launchers. "We asked the Americans to go after the supergun in Jebel Makhour. They said they tried but couldn't find it. The UN found it later, exactly where we said it was."

Saddam launched thirty-seven missiles on Israel, many of them with devastating impact. After dinner, Jacques drove us by Ramat Gan, where one of the missiles had slammed into a heavily built-up area and destroyed everything within a three-hundred-meter radius, and all that with a three-hundred-kilogram warhead.

"A member of the German Bundestag came to visit during the missile attacks and asked us what we would do if the Iraqis used gas. He was an arrogant sonofabitch, so I told him, 'You already gassed us once. We won't sit back and let it happen again.' He knew that we knew German companies had built Saddam's poison gas plants; maybe he had read your reports! I let him know that a gas attack would compel my government to respond massively, probably killing thousands of civilians. And that I personally supported that position."

The sky went dark as a cloud of angels, their wings covered in black gauze, swarmed across the moon.

"I think he got the message," Jacques said finally. "After the war, the Germans gave us a six-hundred-fifty-million-dollar submarine. We didn't talk much publicly about Germany's involvement in Iraq. But it doesn't mean that we won't share information!"

Chapter 12:

Persona Non Grata

61: 'If You're Not a Journalist, You're a Spy!'

In early June, I received a phone call from Mike Maloof, an export control specialist at the Defense Technology Security Agency. He was trying to nail down the details of the Thomson-CSF license from Martin Marietta to build the laser designation pod they subsequently exported to Iraq.

"I've found this photograph from a news agency," he said innocently. "It was taken at the International Arms Exhibition in Baghdad in May 1989 and shows an Iraqi Mirage F1 with a Soviet laser-guided missile and what appears to be a Martin Marietta laser designation pod. Have you heard about that?"

"Sure," I said. "I've written about that in *Mednews*. The pod was called Atlis II and it was produced by Thomson-CSF in France. The Martin Marietta people told me that they sold it to Thomson under license in 1979."

"Well, if you hear anything more, let me know," he said.

"Everything I know I publish in *Mednews*," I said. "I believe your office is still a subscriber."

Maloof and I had become good friends. Like Michael Oatley and Gerard, he was convinced my phone was being tapped by the French; after the incident with the lineman out in front of our house, I was, too. So without either of us having to say a word, I understood that he had crafted this conversation to make it appear to the French that he had just "stumbled" upon the *Mednews* photo taken in Baghdad. Something was up, but he wasn't letting on what it was.

A few days later, I released a *Mednews* special report titled "Rafsanjani's Bomb." Using our database, I published a timeline of Iran's clandestine nuclear weapons program.[65] I included lists of suspected nuclear facilities and of companies that had sold Iran dual-use equipment. It

---

65 "Rafsanjani's Bomb," *Middle East Defense News (Mednews)*, June 8, 1992, Volume 5, 17/18. One of the most significant events was the announcement on Iranian radio in 1987 that the Iranian Atomic Energy Organization had just signed an unspecified consulting contract with Pakistani "metallurgist," A. Q. Khan. Dr. Khan's involvement clearly suggested that Iran was seeking to enrich uranium using gas centrifuges, something the Iranians vehemently denied until the Israelis exposed their secret centrifuge plant in 2002 by giving the information to an Iranian opposition group, the MEK.

was the most comprehensive report ever released to the public on Iran's nuclear program. My sources included senior officials at the French Commissariat pour l'Énergie Atomic (CEA), which ran the French nuclear weapons labs as well as civilian nuclear research. They had been critics of earlier French efforts to export nuclear weapons technology to Saddam Hussein and were working closely with the United States at UNSCOM and the IAEA to prevent history from repeating itself. I included an expanded version of this information in the final report I produced for the Simon Wiesenthal Center, which they were now planning to release at a press conference in Los Angeles on August 3.

On June 14, Christina and I headed for Rome, where I was invited to present at a non-proliferation conference. Our hosts put us up in the Il Senato Hotel, in a sixth-floor room overlooking the Piazza della Rotonda. We sat on the tiny balcony in the evenings drinking chilled *spumate* and watching the crowds as if from a box at the Opera, with the advantage of fresh air and privacy.

For those few days, we had not a care in the world.

+ + +

Ten days later, I went out to Le Bourget in the Paris suburbs for an army weapons exhibition called Eurosatory, sponsored by the French defense ministry. I had become good friends with many of the arms exporters, especially the French. I always found them to be intelligent, well informed, urbane, and patriotic.

When I arrived at the press entry to pick up my pass, I was informed that my French Defense Ministry press accreditation had been pulled by the Minister's cabinet. I did a double take.

"Are you sure?" I asked the uniformed female officer who was consulting her list.

"I am very sure, Monsieur. *Désolé.*"

I located a nearby pay phone (this was before cell phones) and called an old friend from the French Press Agency, Pierre Bayle, who now worked as an aide to Defense Minister Pierre Joxe. He checked the files and confirmed that my accreditation had been pulled but didn't know why. Not being a gatecrasher of defense ministry events, I drove back home to Maisons-Laffitte.

Three days later, Pierre got back to me. "There is a dossier on your activities," he said. "Certain contacts you have and certain things you write have been embarrassing to us, so we are cancelling your journalistic accreditation."

I was stunned. Here was somebody I had gotten to know as a journalist, speaking to me with a bureaucratic coldness that made me shudder. My "dossier," he said, included reports from "several French intelligence services." He made it clear that the decision by the French Defense Minister was beyond appeal. "I am sorry that I cannot tell you more," he said.

I smelled a rat. I had just published a book about Western arms sales to Iraq. It had been translated into French, and sales were doing well, and I had become a hot guest on French TV news and talk shows. I thought of any number of stories I had done recently, all of which had left an odor of sulfur behind. No doubt, I had angered many people in powerful positions. After eight years of scratching away at the arms/terror/intelligence underworld, that was not surprising.

As I discussed the situation with French friends and American reporters, it gradually sank in just how serious this was. One of my friends, a senior government official, took me out to lunch. She said she would continue to stay in touch with me, at least for now. "The general view in the French administration is that your newsletter is financed by the CIA," she said. "Even if that's true, that's okay by me."

I began to realize that if I didn't fight this, my life in France would be over.

My DST minder, Patrick, put it succinctly one day over lunch. "If you are not a journalist, Ken, then what are you? What other profession justifies all these contacts that you have with arms dealers, government officials, intelligence agencies, and the like? You will be deported from France as a spy."

"Hello?" I said.

"You will be declared persona non grata, kicked out of France. Or maybe you will simply be prosecuted as a foreign intelligence agent. It's as you wish," he said.

As I digested that news, he waxed apologetic. "I tried to warn you, my friend. It's time that you leave France."

+ + +

But I did not leave France. Instead, I enlisted the help of my colleagues at the French Defense Correspondents Association and got them to appeal directly to the minister of defense. The president of the Anglo-American Press Association, to which I had belonged for years, also agreed to take up my cause. Harry Dunphy, the Associated Press bureau chief in Paris, wrote letters on Association letterhead protesting the withdrawal of my press credentials to the minister of defense, the minister of foreign affairs, the minister of justice, and the prime minister, all of whom had been guests at Association lunches in recent years. Bit by bit, we began getting favorable replies. But for several months, it was touch and go.

That July, Christina and I hosted a garden party at our house in Maisons-Laffitte. This had become an annual event to which we invited friends, neighbors, and professional acquaintances who had become friends. After four years, those friendships were thriving—and so was our garden. I had planted honeysuckle along the wall that filled the air with perfume. The sun was still lingering at the end of our yard when Julian and Niclas, now teenagers, went to work at the barbecue by the garden shed. There were so many people, and it was so far from the house that all we could see were a few glimmers of flame between the branches of a cherry tree. The boys were careful to stay out of sight. When I finally went to check on their progress, they had nearly finished a bottle of bubbly wine and were laughing like fools. What the heck. The sausages and chicken were grilling nicely. And this *was* France, after all.

The mood became increasingly festive, and we all grabbed chairs and sat around picnic tables as the sun gave up the ghost. One of our final memories of Maisons-Laffitte was that of a Kuwaiti journalist friend named Nawaf, whom Christina liked to describe as "wider than he was tall," holding out his glass and his plate of barbecued meat as he sat down into a folding wooden chair. He sat, and sat, and sat lower still, until finally we heard an explosion and the wooden slats flew out in all directions and Nawaf wound up on the grass, grinning good-naturedly as he held out his glass and his plate, still intact and unharmed.

I hoped our landing would be as soft.

62: 'We Will Keep You a Long Time'

Rabbi Cooper and Rabbi Hier flew me out to Los Angeles in early August to release my latest report for the Wiesenthal Center.[66] They had sent copies to the Bush and the Clinton campaigns and had received a letter of thanks signed by Bill Clinton but nothing from Bush. They already had a thick file of media reaction, especially from newspapers in Germany and Italy, where we had identified exporters selling dual-use equipment to Iran and Syria.

Among the biggest surprises in the report were the revelations about Syria's chemical weapons programs. I quoted then Israeli chief of staff Ehud Barak as saying they were even more extensive than Iraq's before the Gulf War. I also identified several hundred major suppliers. These included big-name companies such as Schott Glaswerke, Carl Schenck, and Ferrostaal in Germany and major French pharmaceutical companies. While I felt that the companies should be held accountable, at least through public shaming, they claimed their actions were sanctioned by their governments.

Marvin Hier, dean of the Center, had a riotous sense of humor. At dinner one night at an Italian kosher restaurant, he recalled a visit to the Elysée Palace, where President Mitterrand was sitting like a wax figure in his chair. He was so feeble his aides had installed an emergency button on the arm of his chair in case he needed to stand up to use the facilities. "He buried poor Simon [Wiesenthal] three times as he was presenting him this award, and it was all I could do not to crack up," Marvin said.

After my return, Shimon Samuels organized a separate press conference in Paris, which Simon Wiesenthal flew up from Vienna to attend. Although he was not involved in the day-to-day activities of the Center that bore his name, Simon had taken a special interest in my work, and he let everybody in the audience understand that.

"I have spent my life tracking the murderers of yesterday," he intoned in his inimitable Viennese accent. "Mister Timmerman is tracking the murderers of tomorrow."

I have never been so proud of any comment about my work from anyone.

---

66 *Weapons of Mass Destruction: the Cases of Iran, Syria, and Libya*, Paris/Los Angeles: Middle East Data Project/ Simon Wiesenthal Center, August 1992.

+ + +

At around this time, I took part in a live segment on ABC *Nightline*, hosted by Chris Wallace, dedicated to my revelations about Iran's nuclear weapons program. I drove to the ABC News studio, now relegated to a high-rise office near Montparnasse, at four in the morning, for the live feed beginning a half hour later. On air with me was my friend Bill Triplett (introduced as senior counsel to the Senate Foreign Relations Committee) and Kamal Kharazi, who was the Iranian regime's representative to the United Nations in New York. Kharazi attacked me viciously and personally, calling me a stooge for the "Zionist regime" and claiming that all my information had come from Mossad.

"And so, Mister Triplett, from your perch on Capitol Hill, how do you see Mister Timmerman's research?" Chris Wallace asked.

"Ah, yes," he said, tenting his fingertips together and giving a Cheshire-cat smile. "I can tell you that Mister Timmerman's research is one hundred percent accurate. What we have seen in the classified realm not only confirms it but goes even further. There is no doubt that Iran is seeking to develop nuclear weapons, and this is a huge threat not just to Israel but also to the United States."

I didn't know Triplett would be on the show, let alone as an "independent" authority to judge my work. Kharazi was visibly fuming at being tag-teamed by the two Americans and sputtered on about a Zionist and a CIA plot.

When the show was over, we still had the satellite feed, and I could hear Kharazi berating Chris Wallace about the segment.

"Mister Ambassador," I cut in. "If Iran's nuclear research is intended for purely peaceful purposes, as you contend, why not allow me to bring a team of non-governmental experts to tour your nuclear facilities and report back to the world what we see?"

Kharazi's voice went to ice. "Mister Timmerman, if you come to Iran we will keep you for a very long time," he said. "A very long time."

Later, Triplett and I had a good laugh over that. But we agreed that Kharazi was probably quite serious.

"I wouldn't be going to Iran any time soon," he said.

63: Simon Wiesenthal's Sources
Vienna, Austria

That autumn, I travelled again to Vienna to examine documents discovered in Iraq by inspectors from the International Atomic Energy Agency. Even though I had clashed with one of the nuclear inspectors, Maurizio Zifferero, whose pre-war ties to Saddam I exposed in the *Wall Street Journal*, I was still welcome at the Agency as one of the few international reporters who had in-depth knowledge of Iraqi weapons programs.

While in Vienna, I had lunch with Simon Wiesenthal at the Hotel Europa. I tried to see him whenever I was in town, and he always indulged me. But he rarely responded directly to questions. Instead, like a Talmudic scholar, he launched into a complex narrative that seemingly had nothing to do with what I had asked.

This day, he told me the story of an investigation he had been doing into a suspected Nazi in Milan. He needed to verify that the suspect was indeed the person he was seeking, so he called an old friend in Milan and asked him which bank he normally used for his business.

Is it a big bank? Simon asked.

One of the biggest, his friend replied.

Do you use them often?

Sure, all the time.

Do they know you are Jewish?

Certainly, his friend said.

"So I said to him, look. Call up your bank and tell them you have been offered a business proposition by this man [the suspected Nazi] and that it's a good proposition. But you have some doubts as to the man's background and would like them to check him out."

A few days went by, then his friend called him back. "And I received an intelligence report on this Nazi like you could not believe! When I presented it to the prosecutor in Milan, he just shook his head. 'Tell me one thing, Mister Wiesenthal, just between you and me. My men could not have put together an intelligence report like this. Who are your sources?'

"So I told him, 'Look, sir, I am not asking for your sources, so don't ask me for mine.'"

We had a good laugh over that.

Another case he was working involved a prominent Austrian whom no one had ever suspected of being a Nazi. This individual used to be a lawyer. "I had his name but none of his particulars, not even his date of birth. So I had my secretary call up the Lawyer's Association here in Vienna and tell them that this gentleman had done her mother a favor and so she wanted to send him a birthday present—but she couldn't remember his birthday. They gave it to her. Then she said, 'So it will be his eightieth birthday.' 'No, no,' they said, 'he will be seventy-four.' So not only did we get his birthday but also the year of his birth. The rest was much easier."

That's how he was, right up until his wife died in 2003. Losing his life's companion broke his heart. He died two years later at the age of ninety-six.[67]

64: 500 Million Reasons

I continued to hammer away at the Bush administration for arming Iraq in the *Wall Street Journal* and elsewhere. In a story titled "How Washington Armed Saddam," I detailed some of the US equipment that had been licensed by the Commerce Department for sale to known Iraqi nuclear weapons plants even though the CIA had identified them as "bad end users." This was no accident, I argued, but a policy codified in National Security Directive 26, a top-secret White House order to expand US relations with Saddam signed by President Bush in June 1989.[68]

Senator Patrick Leahy (D-VT) gave me a shoutout for revealing that the Bush administration had ordered a half-billion-dollar bailout of bad Iraqi government loans from the Gulf International Bank in Amman, Jordan, *after* the 1990–1991 Gulf War. "If the information obtained by Mister Timmerman is true," Senator Leahy said, "then it would appear that American money is helping to break the UN embargo against Iraq." He included a letter I had written in response to an inquiry from his staff director with "a list obtained from a confidential source of Jordan-based

---

67   Simon Wiesenthal graciously endorsed me when I ran in the Republican primary for US Senate in 2000. Only later did I learn that I was the first and only candidate for political office in the US he had ever endorsed in his long career. I've posted his letter to Facebook, here: http://tinyurl.com/jmy5efb

68   "How Washington Armed Saddam," *Wall Street Journal Europe*, September 18, 1992.

front companies currently working on behalf of Iraq." In the letter, I noted that before receiving the list I had been in Amman on a reporting trip tracking Iraqi front companies. "Top on the list of suspects at that time was Computer and Communications Systems, a franchise outlet for Digital Equipment Corp. (DEC)," I wrote.[69]

In early October, I met David Aaron, a national security advisor to the Clinton-Gore campaign, at a Paris cocktail organized by Democrats Abroad. It was the first political event I had attended since leaving the United States eighteen years earlier. Janne Nolan had passed on my name, so David knew who I was. He had also seen my Wiesenthal Center studies. He asked me to write up a short paper about how we could reform the export control system to make sure there were "no more Iraqs."

A few days later, Al Gore gave a foreign policy speech that accused President Bush of being soft on Saddam Hussein. I recognized some of the "funny facts" on proliferation Janne Nolan had asked me to compile a few months earlier, taken almost verbatim. Meanwhile, Bill Clinton castigated Republicans for "coddling dictators from Baghdad to Beijing" and pledged that his administration would make countering proliferators a top foreign policy priority. I felt I was in the zone.

Senator Donald W. Riegle (D-MI) invited me to a hearing on October 27, 1992—just one week before the presidential election—to showcase the Bush administration's failure to prevent the arming of Saddam. His staff made arrangements to fly me over from Paris, along with the IAEA's David Kay. I gave detailed testimony based on export licensing records of US technology the UN arms inspectors had found in Iraq. But the hearing was not about facts—it was about politics. It quickly became obvious that David and I had been called as marionettes in an elaborate kabuki dance aimed at discrediting the president of the United States and his national security advisor, Brent Scowcroft. I found it somewhat embarrassing and tried to stick to the facts.[70]

While in Washington, I met with Steve Bryen and a Beltway consulting company called Jaycor. They wanted to enlist my services to set up a "proliferation archive" for the CIA that would help identify milestones in Third World WMD programs based on the type of open-source

---

69 Floor speech by Senator Patrick Leahy, Congressional Record, September 24, 1992; S14969-S14971.
70 I give a more detailed account of this hearing in the opening chapter of *Selling Out America: The Whole Story of Clinton's Corrupt Relationship with Communist China* (XLibris, 2000).

intelligence I had been using.

What they had in mind was a souped-up version of my FileMaker database on Iraq, Iran, Syria, and Libya, coupled with analytical tools I had developed while doing my studies for the Simon Wiesenthal Center. I realized during these meetings, and in follow-on contacts with the Clinton campaign team, that I was one of a small number of people not just outside government but inside as well who had firsthand knowledge of clandestine procurement networks and understood the intersection of technology exports and WMD programs. It was dizzying, especially after many years of feeling out of the loop in Europe.

+ + +

While in DC, I also met with my friends Bill Triplett and Mike Maloof. They told me the real reason I'd nearly been PNG'd from France. It had all to do with money—lots of it.

"Here's what our friend Tony Capaccio put out in *Defense Week*," Maloof told me. He passed me an article about the Pentagon intervening with the Committee on Foreign Investment in the United States (CFIUS) to block the purchase by Thomson-CSF of the missile division of US aerospace contractor, LTV. "The Pentagon review was instigated because of a black and white photo taken at the 1989 Baghdad Air Show. It depicted an Iraqi Mirage F-1 with an ATLIS pod slung from its belly, according to an industry source. The photo was provided by Kenneth Timmerman, an expert on Middle East Arms sales and author of 'The Death Lobby,' an investigation into how the West, including U.S. companies, helped arm Iraq," the article stated.[71]

"'Provided by,'" I said, disgusted. "That's just great. It makes me sound like a US government informant."

"I didn't think he would use your name," Maloof said.

"Look at this," I said, pointing again to the headline. "This is date-lined June 22. That is the same day the French pulled my journalistic credentials. Thank you, Mister Capaccio."

Triplett had even more.

"Thomson-CSF has hired a lobbying firm that has been circulating a white paper on you. It isn't nice."

---

71   Tony Capaccio, "Customs Reviews Whether Thomson Broke Law," *Defense Week*, June 22, 1992, page 1.

"Do you have a copy?"

"You don't want to see it."

He shook his hands, as if to shake off water. "It's all slime."

"But it's good to know," I said.

"Basically, they are claiming that everything you have ever written about them is a lie. They never sold weapons to Saddam, never built a defense electronics plant in Iraq, never sold licensed Martin Marietta laser designation pods to Iraq, the whole nine yards."

When I finally acquired a copy of the Thomson-CSF white paper, it was even worse than what Triplett had led me to believe. Dated June 11, 1992—less than two weeks before my accreditation was pulled—it was headlined "The allegations raised in Kenneth Timmerons [sic] book *The Death Lobby* are baseless." In a detailed two-page section, the Thomson lawyers specifically denied, among other things, that they had built the Saad 13 defense electronics plant. Who had been my source on that story? The Thomson-CSF vice president in charge of Iraq! I had even visited the facility they had set up in a suburb south of Paris for the sole purpose of training Iraqi assembly-line technicians, a facility the white paper claimed did not exist.

But once again, this wasn't about facts—it was politics.[72]

Back in Paris, Gerard filled me in on the back story. It turned out that the CEO of Thomson, Alain Gomez, was a protégé of socialist president François Mitterrand. Gerard believed that Gomez personally made the request to Defense Minister Pierre Joxe to pull my defense ministry press accreditation, in the hope I would be arrested or otherwise forced to leave France.

It's always nice to know you're loved.

In the end, the US government prevented the Thomson-CSF purchase of the LTV missile division because of Thomson's past diversions of US military technology, which I helped to expose. To my knowledge, it was the first time the CFIUS had ever denied a foreign attempt to purchase a US company. Thomson-CSF believed I had cost them a $500 million deal. No wonder they tried to get me arrested or PNG'd from France. They had five hundred million reasons to do so!

---

72 I wrote a detailed account of the Thomson-CSF white paper in *French Betrayal of America* (New York: Crown Forum, 2004), pp. 156–57.

65: The Fist of God
Geneva

In early December, I received an electrifying call from Jacques-Marie Bourget at *Paris Match*. "Griessen is dead."

"*What?*" I said.

"He died of a heart attack in a Zurich massage parlor. Can you imagine Jean-Jacques in a whorehouse? I don't think he would know what to do if he ever met a lady of pleasure."

We both knew Griessen well and resolved on the spot to head to Geneva together to speak to his widow. He had made many enemies in his efforts to get hostages released in Lebanon. But that wasn't all.

"He was on his way to meet somebody in Zurich," Madame Griessen told us. "The last number he dialed on his car phone was the Police Judiciaire in Zurich. Just before that, he left frantic messages with his assistant. This was the man who sometimes backed him up on dangerous missions. He was trying to get him to join him urgently. In one of those messages, he said he was about to meet with three individuals who had the last piece of the puzzle that would reveal who killed Uwe Barschel."

Jacques and I were stunned. We knew Griessen was convinced that the West German politician had been murdered in his bathtub in the Hotel Richmond, but that was years ago. We thought the trail had gone cold.

A few days after Griessen's death, the Swiss police ordered an autopsy, searched his office, and seized most of his files. "Such measures are not taken just anytime someone dies," Griessen's lawyer told us. "The Barschel case bears strong resemblance to the Kennedy assassination, making anything connected to it extremely sensitive."

Griessen believed Barschel's murder was tied to the Iran-Contra scandal. He had documented the simultaneous presence in Geneva of five individuals involved in the hostage negotiations on Oct. 11, 1987, the night of Barschel's death: Iranian Revolutionary Guards Minister Mohsen Rafiq-Doust; Ahmad Khomeini, the ayatollah's son; Adnan Khashoggi, the Saudi businessman and arms dealer; German intelligence operative and hostage negotiator Werner Mauss, an erstwhile business partner of Griessen's who later became his rival; and a German arms dealer named Joseph Messera. Just a coincidence, of course.

Griessen came to believe that Barschel was murdered because he threatened to reveal what happened to the missing hostage ransom payments. Did Griessen suffer the same fate?[73]

+ + +

Over Christmastime, I received a call from author Frederick Forsyth, who had read *The Death Lobby* and asked me to help him with research for a novel on Iraq. He arrived shortly after the New Year on the train from Brussels, where he had been interviewing Monique Jamine, the widow/mistress of supergun inventor Gerald Bull.

For two hours out in my office and another three hours over lunch, Freddy (as he preferred to be called) spun the threads of his plot. The book was to be called *The Fist of God*, after the Arabic phrase *yad'allah*, used by Saddam Hussein to describe the nuclear weapon he had built.

What Forsyth wanted from me was insight into how Iraq could have tricked Western intelligence agencies into believing his program was even one year from fruition, when in fact his scientists were ready to deliver the first bomb in January 1991. He entranced us for hours.

In Freddy's plot, only two people suspected that Saddam might be hiding a doomsday weapon: a twenty-nine-year-old British intelligence analyst and an Israeli who was running an Iraqi agent codenamed Jericho. Through most of the book, we think Jericho is a beautiful woman named Leila, the mistress of the commander of Iraqi ground forces. But when she gets killed, we see the real Jericho looking down at her grave. (It turns out that the ground forces commander himself was Jericho, while the woman was an Iraqi government agent sent to spy on him).

The Israeli tasks Jericho to find the supergun, whose forty-two-meter-long barrel has been dug into the side of a mountain. The camouflage was so successful that the best US spy satellites couldn't see it, despite Jericho having given them the coordinates. "So in the end, for all the might and the technology and the sophistication of the West, it comes down to one man who has to go in there and do the job," Freddy said.

---

73 "Iran-contra killing in Switzerland?" *Middle East Defense News (Mednews)*, December 7, 1992, Volume 6, 5. Many months later, I received a kind note from Griessen's widow, thanking me for my efforts to discover the truth. But she remained fearful that the same people who had killed her husband would come after her or their son if they turned over to me the documents Griessen had hidden in a secret storage locker about the Barschel case. Enough people have died, she said. As for Werner Mauss, he was profiled as a modern-day 007 in a German-language documentary by Stephan Lamby that aired on ARD television on January 17, 1999. Mauss now has a website, http://www.werner-mauss.com, that details many of the public cases he became associated with; I have found nothing about his association with Griessen or his involvement in the hostage negotiations in Lebanon.

The young British signals corps officer chosen to find the supergun and illuminate it with a hand-held laser designator for American pilots is the younger brother of the intelligence analyst who first got wind of the Iraqi nuclear program. Like his brother, he speaks perfect Arabic and was brought up in Baghdad.

Our son Julian, now thirteen, sat spellbound as Freddy spun the threads of his complex story over lunch. I had never seen him sit for so long without saying a word, his eyes growing wider with each twist in the story. What most intrigued me was Forsyth's technique: he had worked out all of this detail in his head, right down to bits of dialogue, before committing a word to paper. "Once you start writing, things tend to solidify and it's very hard to change," he said. "If you keep it in your head, you can keep it fluid while you work out all the details."

Anyone who has read one of Freddy Forsyth's novels knows he is a master storyteller. And here we had a ringside seat to a new one, before it had even been written.

66: Putting on the Chain
Strasbourg, France

My criticism of President Bush and knowledge of proliferation issues attracted the attention of Representative Tom Lantos, a fiery Democrat representing parts of San Francisco and San Mateo County. With a shock of silver hair, an acid tongue, and an anti-government populist streak, Lantos made waves during the late 1980s for investigating fraud and abuse at the Housing and Urban Development agency, HUD.

Born in Hungary, Lantos was saved from the Nazis by Swedish diplomat Raoul Wallenberg, who handed him a Swedish passport on the platform of the Budapest train station. That pedigree gave him instant credibility when attacking the Bush administration for helping arm Saddam Hussein, a dictator who vowed to exterminate the Jewish homeland. As I found out later, Lantos was also a close friend of Hungarian-born billionaire George Soros and did many favors for him as a Member of Congress, a relationship I found extremely troubling even then.

After the Clinton-Gore election victory, Lantos was given a subcommittee chairmanship that thrust him to the forefront of the sexiest foreign policy issue of the day: weapons of mass destruction. Lantos's ambition was to become the "adult" in the Clinton administration's foreign policy stable, but he had not mastered the details of his new brief. He needed me—or at least, that's what Richard Perle told him.

That's how I got a call from his staff director, Bob King, asking me to join them in Strasbourg for an interview, where Lantos was visiting the European Parliament. He asked me to bring Christina, as Lantos was traveling with his wife, Annette.

Our first meeting over dinner was a bit rocky. Lantos wanted to expose proliferators and make sure the United States didn't continue arming rogue states, as Bush had done. On that score, I agreed with him wholeheartedly. But he insisted that to join a congressional staff, I had to become anonymous. "That means no more op-eds, no more radio interviews, no more television appearances," he said.

If all he wanted was someone to ghost-write speeches and op-eds, he didn't need me, I countered. My whole value added was my public profile as an author and an expert on the arms trade and technology transfer. Back in our hotel room, Christina and I chewed on this. Why should I throw my career away to work as a backroom staffer?

The next morning at breakfast, I was more insistent. This time, Tom gave in. "We can co-author op-eds," he said. "The most important thing for me is to remain visible to my constituents in California. If you want to talk to France, I don't care."

We spent much of the day touring the old city of Colmar. Bit by bit, my reservations disappeared.

"You can't afford me," I said over lunch.

"Try me," he said.

I named a figure: $110,000. Tom was taken aback, but his staff director, Bob King, jumped in.

"The committee has a cap on staff at seventy-five thousand dollars," he said. "We can get you another twenty thousand from the personal office—right, Tom?"

Lantos nodded.

"If that works for you, we'd love to have you on board."

Christina had just learned she was pregnant with our fifth child. But like me, she realized we had reached the end of something in France. They wanted me to start on March 1, in six weeks' time.

"I'll need a few months to sell my house and my business," I said.

Bob proposed that I work three weeks on and three weeks off until July 1. That would mean half salary, but it would allow me to come back to France to settle our affairs.

I agreed.

+ + +

Abu Dhabi

I convinced Bill Triplett to join me that February in Abu Dhabi for the first International Defense Equipment Exhibition (IDEX), the ground forces counterpart to the Dubai Air Show. He used his entrée as a Senate staffer to schmooze with the Americans, while I used my *Mednews* credentials to collect information on the Russians, the Chinese, and the Pakistanis, all of whom were presenting significant new equipment for sale in the Middle East.

But most of all, I hung around the Iranians. For the first time ever, they were putting their defense industries on display and sent defense minister Akbar Torkan to lead their delegation. I spent hours picking up brochures, talking to technicians, and asking my contacts among West European arms salesmen what they thought. Before long, a pattern emerged that was similar to what I had seen in Iraq, with European companies—mainly, German—selling machine tools, ostensibly for civilian purposes, that the Iranians installed in military factories. The reporting I did in *Mednews* on this subject is still being read today through an online subscription service![74]

After the show, Bill and I rented a car and drove across the interior of the Emirates to the oasis of Hatta, which was supposed to be a cultural attraction. The village was small and unimposing: squat houses of cinderblock and cement, cooled with window air conditioners. But the site was spectacular: sheer mountains rose abruptly at the end of the village streets, ringing it completely, while a small wadi, gorged with winter rains, ran through luxuriant oasis greenery to where a group of young girls were bathing and playing on the rocks, totally unconcerned by the presence of two foreigners.

---

74 "Iran Puts Defense Industry on Display," *Middle East Defense News (Mednews)*, March 1, 1993, Volume 6, 10/11.

We drove back via Sash, the northernmost UAE village on the Strait of Hormuz. At sunset, we could make out the Iranian coastline, low, dark shadows against the leaden waters of the Persian Gulf. It was easy to imagine Iranian fast attack craft, manned by Revolutionary Guards, suddenly emerging from behind Qeshm Island to attack the oil tankers, as they did in the final year of the Iran-Iraq war. From a vague abstraction, Iran became a brooding, dangerous presence. It reminded me in a way of Beaufort Castle in south Lebanon, overlooking Marjayoun and the Galilee way below.

I was getting ready to abandon everything: my business, my house, and the way of life Christina and I built together, where we worked from home in the easy presence of our children. All the files we had accumulated, the databases, the books, the travels, the recognition and respect I had won as an "authority" on proliferation and the Middle East—gone or put on hold. No more daily "fix" from writing. No more TV appearances.

Triplett commiserated with my dilemma.

"I wouldn't want to encourage second thoughts," he said. "There's nobody competent doing proliferation on the House side, so I'm selfish. It will be great having an ally."

"I hear a *but*," I said.

"Well, yeah! You might find out that you have more influence and are performing a greater service to the cause by publishing *Mednews* than by coming to the House, where you become just another staffer. Are you really sure you want to put on the chain?"

"The chain?"

He pulled out his laminated Senate staff ID, which he had worn around his neck during IDEX.

"That's what this is. It's the chain by which they control you. They tug on it...and expect you to obey. Are you really sure you're ready for that?"

In truth, I wasn't. And I would replay his warning many times over in the months to come.

Chapter 13:
'Watch Your Back'

67: Welcome to the Swamp
Washington, DC

There was no time for second thoughts once I arrived in Washington. It was a constant flurry of activity from the minute I showed up at Lantos's personal office in the Rayburn building. Tom was enthusiastic, warm, and eager to get to work. That first day, we sketched out a series of hearings he wanted to hold on the proliferators I had been tracking in *Mednews*: Iran, Iraq, Syria, North Korea, China. Each of them had gone rogue in their own way. As we talked it through, we started referring to them as "rogue regimes." That became the title of the hearing series. It would stick.

Bob King sent me down to the Sergeant at Arms office to get my House ID badge. I filled out the paperwork, sat for the photo, and waited while they processed the badge. On the bench in the waiting area, they had copies of *Roll Call*, the inside baseball newspaper everyone read. They also had a bowl full of ID card chains. I put one in my pocket, just in case. But for the first few weeks, I kept my badge in the pocket of my suit and took it out whenever I needed to show ID. I wasn't going to "wear the chain," as Triplett called it.

Christina and I had become close friends with Steve and Shoshana Bryen, and they offered to put me up in their basement until I could find a house. Shoshana had given birth to their fourth child, Mollie, two years earlier and was still working from home. So she drove me to the Silver Spring metro in the mornings after Steve and I walked the dog, and I walked from Union Station to the Rayburn building to work. Shoshana hooked me up with a realtor she knew, so in the evenings I went house-hunting and soon settled on a sprawling Victorian house with magnificent woodwork in nearby Kensington. We could move in on July 1.

Those first three weeks went by in a whirlwind. Tom Lantos had me sit behind him at hearings, and when I thought a witness was saying something outrageous, I'd block print a question on a notepad, tear off the sheet, and hand it to him. More often than not, when his turn came around, he would ask the question, sometimes reading it word for word. It sounds like such a small thing—and of course, it was. But to me, it was my first taste of the type of power that fills the swamps of Washington, DC: the power to influence, while remaining in the shadows.

+ + +

I came to Washington with many illusions, the foremost of which was the notion that politics stops at our nation's shores. I had friends on both sides of the aisle, and while working for Lantos, I coordinated my proliferation investigations with Republican staffers in the belief that men and women of good faith could and must cooperate on issues affecting our national interest, regardless of their political persuasion. We could agree to disagree on domestic policy, but on matters of such import as national security and our nation's interests abroad, I felt confident that liberals and conservatives were united. We shared the same goals of preserving our nation's preeminence in world affairs and of holding up a shining example of freedom and democracy in a world ruled by corruption and greed.

I soon learned, however, that bipartisanship was not on Mr. Lantos's agenda.

+ + +

Just two months into the Clinton administration, as I was shuttling back and forth between Washington and Paris, I discovered how sensitive a subject China was to the Clinton-Gore White House.

With Congressman Lantos's approval, I requested licensing records of US high-tech exports to China from the Department of Commerce. My goal was to analyze the data to determine whether US companies had been providing assistance to Chinese weapons manufacturers, as I suspected. If I could pinpoint a few high-profile cases, I felt we could win broader support from security-conscious members of Congress of both parties to tighten the licensing procedures. It was the type of data-driven investigation I had been doing for several years. *I can do this in my sleep,* I remember thinking.

I soon learned that nothing gets done in Washington without a fight. When the Commerce Department finally delivered the several-thousand-page printout of the licensing records to the Rayburn House Office Building, *Democrats* on the House Foreign Affairs Committee kept me from even looking at it for three weeks, despite the fact that the information was not classified and that a fellow Democrat had requested it.

Once the documents were finally turned over to me, I set to work.

In principle, I had three staff members to help me. Marian Chambers worked full time on the committee. She was just out of college, perky, cute, inquisitive, and snarky. In other words, trouble.

"Mr. Lantos didn't assign this to me," she said. "Sorry."

Jonathan Soros was an intern, at least in name. When I explained that I wanted him to enter licensing records into a database on my laptop computer, which I had centrally located at a common work table, he sniffed and left the room. "F—k this," he muttered. As the son of billionaire donor George Soros, he figured he could do what he wanted. And did.

My other intern, Frank Cilluffo, could have walked off the set of *Saturday Night Fever*. He had a New York accent you could pour like molasses, gassed-back hair, and a New Yorker's irreverence. His father knew Tom and had placed him in the Congressional office in hopes he would "graduate" to better things.

"I'm lookin' at lawr enfawc'mint," he said.

I had already started entering the records, using my own Macintosh because the committee PCs had no database software. Out of pity, I think, Frank relayed me from time to time. After a few days, he just stopped.

"Are you sure this is okay?" he said. "Putting government information on a private computer?"

"It's not classified," I said. "As long as you don't enter the company names, there's nothing confidential, either."

"I don't know."

"If you've got a better idea, I'm all ears," I said.

He *har-rumphed* a bit and continued working.

Urgent tasks intervened (members of Congress find most things urgent if they involve donors or friends in the administration). After an initial hearing on Chinese ballistic missile sales in May, Lantos told me to put the China project on hold and focus on our "rogue regimes" hearings.

"Mark my words," Steve said one evening as we walked the dog. "This is going to be Carter II—only worse."

"You mean the retreads?"

Clinton had appointed a lot of former Carter administration to senior positions, including the cabinet.

"Forget the retreads. He is stacking the national security establishment with people who believe that everything is for sale to the highest bidder—and should be."

Just as when I first went to Lebanon and met Maronites and Drusis on the ferry, who explained why they hated the Palestinians, Steve had planted the seeds of doubt.

+ + +

"Welcome to Washington!" a familiar baritone greeted me over the phone. It was Mike Maloof. We chatted a few minutes, then he lowered his voice. "Can you be over here at noon? Something's come up."

DTSA was located in its own office building near the Pentagon, and the Doubletree—where we agreed to meet for lunch—was just across the street. Maloof was now a career employee. I was guessing that he wasn't very happy with his new political bosses and that's why he wanted to see me.

Marian came up to me as I was leaving. "I'll go with you," she said.

She had overheard me telling the office secretary I would be gone for two hours to meet with someone at the Pentagon and actually had her coat in her hand. I stared at her, dumbfounded.

"I'm going to meet with a source," I said.

"Great!"

"He's not expecting to see someone else."

"I won't say anything. I'll just take notes."

I shook my head. "This is somebody I've cultivated for several years. I'll let you know what I find out."

I chalked up her apparent enthusiasm to a sudden onset of a *Scoop, girl reporter* complex and pushed it out of my mind.

Maloof was waiting for me at the entrance to the buffet. We filled our trays and found a table in a dark corner. Once we had settled in, he leaned toward me.

"You'll never believe what these guys are trying to do!"

He made a visual sweep of the room, then slid a manila folder toward me from the pile of newspapers he had brought. "Open that when you get back in your office."

Inside the folder, he explained, was a letter from Deputy Assistant Secretary of Defense Mitchel Wallerstein, a new Clinton appointee, to his State Department counterpart, explaining that AlliedSignal's Garrett

Engine division was seeking approval to export between a thousand and two thousand Garrett TFE-731-2A-2A engines to China. Ostensibly, they were to power a military jet trainer aircraft the Chinese planned to export to Pakistan, but Maloof and the CIA weapons analysts he worked with believed the engines were intended for a nuclear cruise missile. He included a copy of their unclassified analysis of the new Chinese cruise missile program and how the Garrett engines fit a crucial gap in it. It was astonishing information.

"When did he send the letter?"

"This morning," Maloof said. "We believe they don't have a contract for that many engines. We think it's a gimmick so the Chinese can get the production technology."

It took me several months to pull together all the threads of the story, which ultimately led to a series of angry briefings by DTSA and State Department officials and a second public hearing on Chinese proliferation activities that July.

As we walked downstairs, I told Mike about my officemate, Marian, and her sudden desire to join us for lunch.

"You know what that sounds like to me?" he said. "It sounds like they are keeping tabs on you."

"No way!"

"Just watch your back."

68: The China Plan

Christina's pregnancy was more complicated than her earlier ones, and she was frequently in pain. But she was excited about the Victorian house in Kensington and was gearing up to move. In June, I was back in Maisons-Laffitte for my final stint of home leave before joining the committee full time on July 1. We worked day and night packing up the house, selling the car, and tying up loose ends. I even found a buyer for *Mednews*, the proceeds of which covered our moving costs and then some. A chapter of our life was closing forever, but we were too busy to contemplate its significance or to regret what we were leaving behind. We were headed to the New World together.

On September 7, 1993, Christina gave birth to our fifth child at the Columbia Women's hospital in Washington, DC. We named him Simon after the three Simons of our life: Simon Wiesenthal, Shimon Samuels, and Simon Carr, a friend from college whose paintings we had started buying in recent years. We joked that he was the only one of our five children who could run for president, since he was the only one actually born in the United States. Given the problems she had been having with her pregnancy, we were ecstatic that the birth had gone so well. I brought Julian, Niclas, and Diana to the hospital, along with a bottle of champagne. We christened their new brother as I had all of my children: with several drops of wine on his tongue.

One week later, I was headed to Paris for a quick trip to sign the final sale documents on our house, liquidating the last of our life together in Maisons-Laffitte. Just before leaving, I sent a fax to Bob King with last-minute updates on a number of projects, including glowing articles from the *Chicago Tribune* and the *Wall Street Journal* on the hearing we had conducted the day before. No Congressional committee had ever provided the type of investigative detail into potential export violations by US companies selling equipment to Iran, and both the *Tribune* and the *Journal* quoted Lantos liberally. Lantos could be proud that he was now in the forefront of preventing the next Holocaust from taking place—yes, thanks to my efforts.[75]

As I was wheeling my overnight bag to the front door, the phone rang. It was Bob King.

"You got my fax?" I said.

"Yes. But that's not why I called," he said.

He told me he had just gotten out of Lantos's office and that I was fired. "You've pissed off a lot of people," he said. "Including Tom and the chairman of the committee."

I was too stunned to say much. Lantos had never given the slightest hint that he was "pissed off" by anything I had done. On the contrary, he'd complimented me on my work, asked my advice, and enthusiastically read the statements I prepared for him (including the quote used by both the *Tribune* and the *Journal*, that the Commerce

---

75   Christopher Drew, "High-tech sales to Iran called into question," *Chicago Tribune*, September 15, 1993, and John J. Fialka, "Commerce Agency Accused on Exports Allowed for Iran," *Wall Street Journal*, September 15, 1993. Both referred to *Rogue Regimes (Part II): Weapons Acquisition and Supplier Networks*, a hearing of the House Foreign Affairs Subcommittee on International Security, International Organizations and Human Rights, September 14, 1993.

Department "has apparently decided it would exercise a 'don't ask, don't tell' policy" when it comes to proliferation controls). The only conflict involved the China export licensing records, but that was well behind us, and I was now working on a hearing based on what those records revealed about ongoing US exports to Chinese WMD programs. Bob said Lantos agreed to keep me on payroll for another two months so I could land on my feet. They didn't insist that I come to the office every day.

On the way out to the airport, I was of half a mind to cancel the sale of our house and move us back to Maisons-Laffitte.

"You can't do that," Christina said. "You'll find another job."

She was remarkably serene. I had uprooted her from the comfortable and thoroughly enjoyable life we had in France and brought her to a new country where she knew no one. We had a new child, I was suddenly out of work, and we had mortgage and car payments to make. I had let her down. Only her unflagging confidence kept me going through that dark time.

It wasn't until well after I left the Hill that I realized I had stumbled upon a secret Clinton administration plan to expand US exports to China, a plan that no one—including Lantos—knew about at the time. The China Plan was devised by top Clinton administration appointees to recompense Silicon Valley executives for their financial support during the 1992 election campaign. My work, which would have led to greater restrictions on the sale of dual-use military technology to Communist China, was directly at loggerheads with the administration and could have led to the exposure of their corrupt associations. I was a fly in the ointment and had to be eliminated.

To my knowledge, Mr. Lantos never questioned an administration official about sales to China again.[76]

---

76 I wrote about the substance of the China plan in the opening chapters of *Selling Out America: The American Spectator Investigations* (XLibris, 2000). There I exposed the little-known 1992 National Academy of Sciences study by three future Clinton DoD officials—Bill Perry, Ash Carter, and Mitchel Wallerstein—that called strategic export controls a "wasting asset" to be eliminated. I learned about the role of Commerce Secretary Ron Brown in opening the "Big Emerging Markets," starting with China, and described the astonishing shift of the Clinton Democrats from their previous hard line against Communist China to becoming avid supporters of Most Favored Nation (MFN) trading status in the spring of 1993. Most important, of course, was Bill Clinton's corrupt relationship with Mochtar Riady and the Lippo Group, who provided occult financing to his 1992 election campaign, as my friend Bill Triplett would write about in a best-selling book, *Year of the Rat* (Washington, DC: Regnery, 1998). But all that, by now, is history.

69: *Time* Magazine

In the autumn of 1993, First Lady Hillary Clinton was interviewed by a national television network about her troubled health care initiative, which was being called "Hillary-care." To pay for universal health coverage, it included extensive new taxes on every American citizen— exactly the kind of forced health-care coverage that had always infuriated me in France. I was healthy. Why should I be forced to pay 25 percent of my earnings (which is what it came to in France) to subsidize people who hadn't taken care of themselves or had made bad lifestyle decisions? I was willing to pay for catastrophic care in case of accident or unforeseen illness. But surely that shouldn't be so expensive or so intrusive. I knew an infringement on my freedom when I saw one.

Christina's reaction was much more direct. Mrs. Clinton was explaining to the interviewer that the new taxes were not just necessary; they were virtuous. "We know better how to spend people's money than these taxpayers do," she said.

"*Vaa-aaat!*" Christina shouted. "Does she really think she knows better how to spend our money than we do?"

"Unbelievable," I agreed.

I wasn't yet expressing my disagreement with Mrs. Clinton's agenda in political terms, but I was viscerally opposed to it and so was Christina. Both of us had seen socialism up close and personal—she in Sweden, I in France—and we hated it. Masquerading as benign benevolence, it devoured individual liberty and elevated an unelected elite to positions of power where they could make decisions that touched the most intimate parts of your lives. If I had learned anything in Lebanon, it was that freedom was so precious I was willing to give my life for it. It was like air; without it, you suffocated.

Hillary Clinton wanted to chip away at our freedoms. Regardless of politics, I knew I would fight it. I would resist.

Kitzbühel, Austria

After leaving the Hill, I renewed discussions with *Time* magazine, where I had done some freelance work while in Paris, and by early 1994 began working directly for Chief of Correspondents Joelle Attinger as part of a new investigative news team. The first major story I put together for them was a cover package on the assassination of Iranian dissidents in Europe by Iranian government hit teams. I worked with old friend Tom Sancton, who was now the Paris bureau chief. In addition to Paris, where I introduced Tom over lunch to anti-terror judge Jean-Louis Bruguière, *Time* sent me to Berlin, Geneva, Vienna, and Istanbul to meet with prosecutors and with Iranian exiles. At the time, no one except for *Mednews* had been tracking Iranian state-sponsored hit teams in any coordinated way. Our cover package was the first mainstream media effort to put it all together and to suggest that the Iranian regime was using all the instruments of state power to track down dissidents and murder them. And for the most part, the European governments were too feckless to do anything about it, often allowing the killers to escape.

One Friday, I wound up in Vienna, Austria, where Tom's office manager had booked me into the Imperial Hotel (the same one Mike Wallace had stayed in). After an initial meeting with the widow of one of the men murdered with my friend Abdulrahman Qassemlou in July 1989, I had nothing to do until Monday. It was February and had been snowing for three days, so early on Saturday morning, I rented a car and drove into the mountains to ski powder.

The Tyrol is unlike anyplace I had ever been, with sheer rock cliffs thrusting upward from winding riverbeds, majestic, flagpole-straight pines, magnificent waterfalls, and scenic villages unspoiled by shopping malls or modern hotels. I settled on Kitzbühel, and after dumping my bag at a hostel, I rented skis and boots and headed up the lifts, dressed in a leather jacket, jeans, and leather city gloves. The snow had stopped, and it was sunny and warm—absolutely glorious, in fact.

As the afternoon wore on, I got tired of the slopes, where most of the powder had been skied off, and followed some tracks into an open field. I passed well-equipped chalets with their walls of neatly stacked firewood. Then the field plunged down into the woods, where it seemed the tracks continued. I was having a great time. There was about two feet of fresh, dry power—"champagne snow," as it was called out West—and I couldn't have been happier. Now I had to make a decision: climb back up to the slopes, about a hundred meters or so vertical, or continue downward into the woods. I chose the woods. After all, that's where I had learned to ski as a teen in Vermont.

After a couple of turns into a magnificent glade of fir trees, the ski tracks I was following disappeared, leaving only the hoof prints of a deer. *Oops,* I thought. I headed deeper into the woods carefully, taking a couple of turns each time, then stopping to reassess. But instead of leading to another field, as I had hoped, the woods emptied into a steep ravine formed by a narrow, frozen river. *I can ski this,* I was thinking. The river will eventually cross a road, so this was the straightest way down.

I tried to stay high, but the riverbank became a cliff, forcing me into the rocky stream bed. It was only about six feet wide, but it plunged down the mountain at such a precipitous angle that engineers had built concrete retaining walls every thirty meters or so for as far as I could see. I skied down the first stretch, stopped at the top of the wall, and jumped the waterfall to the riverbank below. It was a four-meter drop but manageable.

The retaining walls were getting higher, and when they reached about six meters, I looked for an alternative. The last thing I wanted was to fall (or jump) off a twenty-foot cliff and break a leg in the middle of nowhere.

It was already four in the afternoon, and the light was starting to decline. I could not see the end of the ravine or the valley below. I began getting very slow and methodical in my movements, planning everything out before I did it. At the last waterfall, I took off my skis and threw them ahead of me, shinnying my way down on the rocks. *This is not good,* I thought.

Finally, I came to a logging road that joined the riverbed on the far side, so I took off my skis and followed it up into the woods. The road climbed a ways, and I hesitated, not wanting to climb all the way back up the mountain; the alternative at this point was continuing to follow the ravine. So I slogged my way through the powder until the logging road began to level out. Finally, it hit a ridge and plunged down the far side, so I put on my skis. After fifteen minutes or so of magnificent powder skiing, the logging road emptied onto a real road—that had been plowed! I saw a house and a car parked alongside. Further on, I happened upon a German man in a Mercedes station wagon, who offered to drive me back to the lift. I reached it just before it closed at 4:30.

As I rode the cable car up to the summit for the descent back to Kitz-bühel, clouds of tiny white angels, stirred by the wind, danced in front of my eyes in the last light of afternoon. Once again, God had been good to me, saving me from myself.

The next day, I stayed on the trails.

+ + +

Istanbul

The *Time* office manager in Paris made arrangements for me to stay at the Topkapi Palace Hotel in Istanbul, a sprawling complex of elegant buildings on the banks of the Bosphorus that had been a palace for the Ottoman sultan. The sitting room of my suite had huge sliding glass doors that looked out onto a reflecting pool and a monumental arch.

Because it was Ramadan, the head of the Istanbul police, Necdet Menzir, asked me to join him at 8:00 PM at the military base that served as his headquarters. He was in charge of terrorism investigations. Judge Bruguière held him in high respect and gave me an introduction.

Mr. Menzir held court from behind an enormous Napoleon III desk, with solid-gold metalwork and rich expanses of inlaid wood. No fewer than six telephones sat on the desk, but there was not a single scrap of paper. He looked a bit like a Russian commissar, with a large, broad face and measured speech, where each phrase seemed to include a command. His teeth looked so perfect I wondered if they were fake. He quietly exuded the power of his office.

I made a strategic decision by bringing my own interpreter to our meeting. I told the hotel concierge, who made the arrangements, that I did not want a young man since I was going to the police and did not want someone who might be intimidated. He found me a Turkish woman who spoke perfect English, Olcay Berman, who was married to a second-generation Swede. She was fifty-five or so, diminutive but not dominated. She succeeded in gaining Menzir's confidence after fifteen minutes or so. Soon he was addressing her directly, expecting her to "interpret" (as opposed to just translate) his meaning to me.

Menzir eventually decided he would trust me, and in a wide-ranging discussion lasting nearly to midnight, he had his men bring in their file books. We went through telephone logs, photographs, notes, depositions, arrest warrants, and other documents from their investigations of the Iranian hit teams in Istanbul. It turned out to be a much larger story than I had anticipated. Menzir explained that the Iranians had thoroughly penetrated Turkish society and were targeting not only Iranian dissidents but were murdering Turkish intellectuals who raised their voices against the interests of the Iranian regime or in favor of secularism. Our conversation gave me an appreciation for Turkish police work. They were every bit as good as Judge Bruguière in Paris in tracking down the assassins. We just never heard about it because there were few Western correspondents in Turkey, and until I showed up, none of them had gotten past his door.[77]

70: An Obituary of the "Mainstream" Media
Washington, DC

Time loved the Iran terror investigation, and I soon became the next best thing at Rockefeller Center, the corporate headquarters. Chief of Correspondents Joelle Attinger paired me up with Jonathan Beaty, a legendary investigative reporter who had come down with cancer and saw the end of his career before him. I was groomed to become his successor. Under Beaty's supervision, I did a number of stories out of New York, including a dark tale about the rearming of Saddam Hussein and a ground-breaking "connect-the-dots" story about North Korea's nuclear weapons program that revealed for the first time the existence of a clandestine uranium-enrichment program.[78] Joelle paid my expenses, including hotels at Rockefeller Center when she had me close stories on Friday night with the chief writers and editors.

"Make sure they pay you so much as a stringer they find it's cheaper to bring you on full time," Beaty advised. I did my best. In some months, I pulled in $10,000 to $12,000 in stringer fees, plus expenses.

In early June, I got a call from my friend Triplett, who was still working for Senator Helms.

"There's a guy you've got to meet," he said. "He's been a secret source of my mine for years."

When he gave me Jeff Fiedler's address and told me who he worked for, I began to realize why he had been a "secret" source. Fiedler was the elected leader of the food workers union, FAST, an affiliate of the AFL-CIO. But his real job was as the AFL-CIO's chief investigator into Communist Chinese violations of US labor and human rights laws. He worked with Harry Wu, the famous Chinese dissident who had docu-

---

77 Thomas Sancton, "The Tehran Connection: An exclusive look at how Iran hunts down its opponents abroad," *Time*, March 21, 1994. I got a reporting byline from Geneva, Istanbul, Paris, and Vienna.

78 Kevin Fedarko, "Pushing it to the Limit: Pyongyang plays games on nuclear inspection," *Time*, May 30, 1994.

mented China's Laogai prison labor network and had testified before Congress on prison labor products being sold by US retailers such as Walmart. He and Fiedler were the scourge of the pro-China lobby, led (so I thought) by the Chamber of Commerce Republicans. Given that I hadn't yet stumbled upon the China plan, I thought that made him a great ally of the Clinton administration.

I would soon find out how wrong I was.

The AFL-CIO was so big and so prosperous that it owned its own headquarters building on Sixteenth Street, just one block away from the White House. When I was ushered up to Fiedler's office suite, I remember feeling that I was entering a government building, so closely aligned were the nation's biggest labor union and the Democrats. Fiedler greeted me effusively in his large corner office suite. He wore his long greying-blonde hair in a ponytail and wore jeans and a denim shirt without a tie.

"Triplett tells me you've got a story for me," I said.

"Ah, Triplett," he said. "An unusual ally, indeed. How much did he tell you about me?"

"Only that you worked with Harry Wu on Chinese prison labor."

"Well, that's true. But it's just the beginning."

He pulled out a large file from a filing cabinet beneath his desk and began sorting through documents.

"So here's a report we received from the head of the Machinists' Union in Columbus, Ohio," he said, passing me a stack of papers an inch thick. "It relates a series of visits, all of them past midnight, conducted by McDonnell Douglas officials at the B-1 bomber plant, which you may have heard is being shut down."

"Yeah, I heard the program had been cancelled."

"So what happens to all that production gear?" he said, as I leafed through the report. "It's pretty specialized stuff, all of it paid for with taxpayer dollars. There's not much else you can make with it except make big military airplanes."

The report contained letters on union stationary to the special agent in charge of US Customs in Columbus, Ohio, informing him of the midnight visits to a facility the union boss referred to as Plant 85. The union guys claimed that the visitors were Chinese military intelligence officials, which is why they weren't allowed in by day.

"So did Customs investigate?" I asked.

"It's still a possibility. But they didn't get much support from the head office, let's put it that way."

Fiedler let that information sink in as I leafed through more of the document.

"So Chinese intelligence officers are touring a highly classified US military production plant after midnight to select production equipment they want to buy, and Customs is not investigating?"

"That's right," Fiedler said, tossing me a brochure from a machine-tool auction company. "And the company is pretending they are just auctioning it off. The only stuff being offered for auction are the left-overs, once the Communist Chinese have cherry-picked the best. I'm told that the Customs guys wouldn't be averse to getting a visit from a member of the national media."

It sounded like a pretty good story, so I wrote a pitch and sent it to Joelle and to the DC bureau chief, Dan Goodgame. I proposed to visit the B-1 bomber plant, talk to the union, US Customs, and McDonnell Douglas, then round it out by interviewing people at DoD and the Commerce Department in Washington. To me, it sounded like a fairly straightforward story about a potentially major security breach. I was sure that once we exposed the glitch in a *Time* magazine story, the sell-off of military technology to Communist China would abruptly end.

But I was wrong.

The more I investigated, the bigger the story seemed to get. It turned out that Plant 85 was one of the largest US military production sites in the country. The equipment it contained had cost the taxpayers more than $1 billion when it was first designed to build strategic weapons systems during the Cold War. Even now, with McDonnell Douglas planning to shut down the plant, the equipment was considered so sensitive that divulging technical details about its performance, let alone selling it, required Pentagon clearance.

My contact at the Machinist Union faxed me page after page of equipment being offered for sale. The list included dozens of giant machining centers and gantry profilers the Chinese wanted for their military aircraft plants. Some of the machines were so large they could shape the leading edge of the entire wing of the giant C-17 military cargo jet, working on the metal from multiple angles at once. They were controlled by special computers and required little worker intervention. Each machine was a self-contained, automated production line in itself.

The Chinese buyer, the Chinese Aerospace Technology Import-Export Company, CATIC, offered what amounted to a billion-dollar bribe to McDonnell Douglas: a follow-on contract to produce forty MD80/90 airliners in China, doubling a contract signed in the mid-1980s. But in that same letter, which I obtained, they also threatened that if McDonnell Douglas failed to deliver the production equipment from Plant 85, CATIC would cancel the MD-80 deal outright. Acquiring that production equipment was a top strategic priority for the Chinese military, worth many multiples of the $5 million McDonnell Douglas eventually charged them for the machines.

Joelle Attinger was enthusiastic when she read the copy I filed after visiting Plant 85 in Columbus and blocked out a four-page exclusive for the magazine. In addition to the purely investigative side of the story, I filed extensive background briefs to explain why multi-axis machine tools were key for military production and how the export licensing process worked. When Goodgame objected that the Columbus plant was a one-off affair, I found two additional US military production plants, in Indianapolis and Philadelphia, the Chinese were buying at auction and visited them as well.

I also spoke with former colleagues at the House Foreign Affairs Committee, who were conducting their own investigation into the effectiveness of Commerce Department licensing to China. It never dawned on me at the time why those particular staffers continued to pursue an area where my own investigation had been blocked the year before. In hindsight, of course, it became perfectly clear: they worked for Republicans. The draft report they shared with me blasted the Commerce Department for failing to investigate the Chinese end users to whom US military goods were being sold and for failing to refer licenses to the Defense Department for technical and intelligence community review. Their report shared political blame across the Bush and Clinton administrations and reinforced my conviction that national security concerns should always trump partisan politics.

On June 9, Goodgame sent me a memo that should have sounded the alarm.

After commending me for my reporting, he mentioned that he had just had lunch with a top CIA specialist on China, Korea, and Asia "whom I questioned, without tipping our hand, about the general subject of

China's campaign to buy arms manufacturing technology from the US. He agreed that it's a hot topic that the agency is watching and emphasized that we should look at China's procurement in other countries as well as in the US."

Goodgame's source, who was attempting to put the administration's spin on a potentially damaging story, suggested that Russia, France, Germany, and Israel were also selling manufacturing equipment to China. "If so, as my source says," Goodgame wrote, "what effect would it have for the US to block sales by McDonnell Douglas, Allison, etc.? Wouldn't China buy the same gear elsewhere, depriving American workers of jobs? Is it a better argument—as our sources have suggested in other proliferation stories—that the US and its allies should get together to limit exports of sensitive technologies?"

The language should have been a tip-off. He wasn't talking about the facts I had uncovered but about the "argument" the story would present, the narrative. He followed these comments with twenty-nine questions, most of them like this: "In the interest of fairness and balance, can we get McDonnell to suggest any government or independent experts who share their point of view that this sale is harmless?"

That was the narrative: the sale was harmless. He sent me out to CIA along with Elaine Shannon, an administration scribe, to get briefed by the National Intelligence Officer for China, John Culver, on why the technology was harmless and all of these sales were a ho-hum affair. Culver brought along two specialists, Kimberling Hollins and Scott Reis, to add weight to the argument. I countered with more interviews, more evidence, more documents showing that the Pentagon and even the Commerce Department's Office of Export Enforcement were concerned that the Chinese were robbing us blind.

I also made a quick trip to Europe to report a separate story and took the opportunity to speak with intelligence sources in Germany and France about Goodgame's point that the Europeans were offering similar co-production and technology deals to Communist China.

"I was able to establish during my trip to Germany and France that contrary to what we have been told in Washington, other US allies are *not* supplying this type of technology to the Chinese and are specifically *not* helping China to build up its aerospace industry," I reported back. "This is a potentially major issue, given the very intense interest by the labor unions and their intention to call for Congressional hearings," I wrote.[79]

When the boom came down, it came down hard.

After a Friday lunchtime staff meeting in the DC bureau in mid-July, where my four-page story was still top of the book and closing that night, Goodgame pulled me into his office and fired me on the spot.

"You've pissed off people in the administration with your questions," he said.

"I thought it was my job to ask questions of the administration."

"Yeah, but it's not your job to be an advocate. That's what they think. They think you're being an advocate for a faction that opposes these sales."

Thus ended my brief career at *Time* magazine. I was beginning to wonder if I could last anywhere in Washington without "pissing people off."

Many months later, after I had taken my reporting to the *American Spectator*, a conservative, anti-Clinton monthly, I learned what had pushed Goodgame over the top. And I learned it from an unusual source: Undersecretary of Commerce William Reinsch, a former Congressional staffer who was now in charge of export licensing. Reinsch and I had been sparring regularly but maintained a cordial relationship. He had "summoned" me to his office to complain about my latest article, which in fact was a revised version of the four-page take-out I initially had reported for *Time*.

"Every time you write something, we have to come after you and sweep up," Reinsch joked. He pulled out a thick folder and began leafing through the pages. "We've got a whole file here on your stories—the *Wall Street Journal*, the *New York Times*, *Time* magazine, and now the *American Spectator*. Every time you publish something about us, we have to go back and correct the record."

Reinsch read from a series of letters he and other top Commerce Department officials had sent to news editors over the previous eighteen months in response to my work. I had only seen one of these adminis-

---

79 Culver and his team went out of their way to volunteer that China "does not appear to be seeking long range missile know how through its commercial satellite launching program," where it offered cut-rate launch fees in order to lure US satellite makers into using Chinese launch services to get them into orbit. This piece of mendacity was disavowed in a Pentagon intelligence report just four years later that triggered a criminal investigation into Loral Space & Communications and Hughes Aerospace, as I documented in the *American Spectator* ("Loral Exams," July 1998).

tration screeds. Later, I learned that the *Wall Street Journal* hadn't even bothered to show me the letter they had received from Reinsch and had never contemplated publishing it. When I read it, I understood why: it was packed with misleading statements, inaccuracies, half-truths, and outright lies.

But what caught my attention was the July 1, 1994, letter sent to the editors of *Time* magazine by Reinsch's predecessor, Sue Eckert. Eckert's letter was one of the more extraordinary pieces of *chutzpah* I had ever seen as a journalist. I had gone to Eckert at the urging of my editors at *Time* to lay out in general terms what I had learned in my investigation of Plant 85 and the other military factories the Chinese were buying. I told Eckert we had determined that highly sophisticated machine tools were being shipped to China, possibly illegally, from a number of US defense plants. I also mentioned we had learned that supercomputer sales, which had previously been put on hold, were about to be approved for China over the objections of the Pentagon.

The next morning, Eckert fired off a fax to *Time*'s editor-in-chief in New York. She wrote that she was contacting *Time* to correct several points of my investigation, which, "if not clarified, will present an inaccurate representation of US Government export policy and procedures." Among them was my "implication that the US Government has recently approved export licenses for sales of dual-use technology to military end-users in China. This is incorrect."

That statement was a bald-faced lie. But it got me fired.

I believe this incident formally marks the end of the "mainstream media" as we once knew it. *Time*'s editors showed in July 1994 that they believed their job was not to uncover the truth but to provide political cover to Democrats in power in Washington. If one of their reporters got out of line and stumbled upon something damaging to the Clintons, they believed it was their duty to eliminate him.

It's only gotten worse since then. But *Time*'s willingness to carry water for the Clintons in July 1994 marked a dramatic turning point.

It also woke me up to the fundamental transformation of the Democrat Party that had taken place with the arrival of the Clintons in Washington. The values I thought I shared with Democrats—putting America's national security before the interests of business and exporters—were now being championed by Republicans and vilified by Democrats, with the exception of trade-union holdouts such as Jeff Fiedler.

+ + +

The final click in my political awakening occurred at 2:00 AM, when I awoke from a dream and channel-surfed the TV hoping to fall back asleep. I happened on a university lecture being given by the House minority leader, Georgia Republican Newt Gingrich, on C-SPAN. As I watched, I realized that I had never seen him appear on national television for anything longer than a soundbite. All I knew of him was the ogre-like figure the national media had painted: a white-supremacist, racist hater who was going to dismantle America as we knew it should his party win the 1994 midterm elections.

As I listened to Gingrich, I could feel my jaw dropping—quite literally. He spoke about the Founding Fathers and their vision of an America that ultimately led to a society where government's role was to level the playing field, so that people from diverse backgrounds were assured equal opportunity, but not equal outcomes. He spoke about the heavy hand of government destroying the black community through a welfare system that encouraged single-parent households, promiscuity, and indolence and described reforms that would help people to break the bondage of welfare and get back to work, self-reliance, and dignity. When he first came on, I half-expected to see tiny horns poking out of his hair, but the more I listened, the more I heard a thoroughly rational, calm, thoughtful historian, who sought lessons from our past to improve the way our government worked. It suddenly dawned on me that the media—including my former colleagues at *Time* magazine—had projected a totally false image of the prospective Speaker, not just misquoting his words and his positions but also twisting them into the exact opposite of what they really were. And then I realized, *ta-da!* That was exactly what they had done with China as well, willfully misconstruing aggressive actions by the Chinese to conduct espionage and steal military technology by asserting that Communist China was "not a threat." Why would they do that, I wondered? The answer was suddenly obvious: because the truth did not fit their partisan objectives.

The next day, I changed my Party registration. I became a Republican and felt immediately at home. Both Steve Bryen and Bill Triplett found my sudden awakening amusing.

"I was wondering what took you so long," Triplett said.

I have never once regretted the switch.

Acknowledgments

Most of the people I would like to thank I have already mentioned in the text you have just read. They include Sheikh Farid and Jamal Hamadé, Jean-Yves Pellay, Abdelatif Zein, Dr. Riachi, and Václav Bervida in Beirut; Ali Patrick Pahlavi, Ayatollah Mehdi Rouhani, Jacques Isnard, Jérôme DuMoulin, Stéphane Ferrard, Pascal Krop, Jacques Buob, Percy Kemp, Gerard Willing, Jack Belden, Henri Conze, Hugues and Olivier de l'Estoile, Shimon Samuels, Hassan Aghilipour, Nelly Chadirat, Jacques-Marie Bourget, Gilles Boulouques, Pierre Salinger, William Dowell, Tom Sancton, Fred Coleman, Joel Bernstein, and Jennifer Siebens in Paris; Therese Raphael, my editor at the *Wall Street Journal Europe* in Brussels; Manfred Sadlowski, CEO of Monch Publishing Group in Bonn; Jacques Neriah, Uri Lubrani, Albert Aghazarian, and Amatzia Baram in Jerusalem; Frederick Forsyth and Michael Oatley in the UK; Jean-Jacques Griessen and his widow in Geneva; Simon Wiesenthal and David Kay in Vienna; Ambassador Rolf Ekéus in New York and Stockholm; Steve and Shoshana Bryen, Michael Ledeen, Michael Maloof, Jonathan Beaty, Dennis Kane, Jeffrey Fiedler, Wlady Pleszczynski, and William C. Triplett in Washington, DC; Rabbi Abraham Cooper and Rabbi Marvin Hier in Los Angeles; and the host of arms dealers I have named—and some that I cannot name.

In addition, dozens of sources, many of whom became friends, in the French defense and intelligence establishment helped me with my investigations, often at some career risk to themselves. You know who you are.

A special thanks to Anthony Ziccardi, Publisher of Post Hill Press, for his support and faith in my work, and for the terrific Post Hill production team led by Madeline Sturgeon.

If you've gotten this far, you know that I would not be where I am today if it were not for the direct intervention of my Lord and Savior, Jesus Messiah, who brought me out of the darkness into the light, and for Christina, who worked the secular side of that equation and became the cement of our family. I have been so blessed and give thanks to them both every day. Stay tuned.

Preface: The author reading from his first novel at Shakespeare & Company in Paris, circa 1978.

Chapter 1: Beirut from the north in the early 1980s. Photo by Manoug, courtesy of the National Tourism Council of Lebanon.

Chapter 2: Jean-Yves Pellay's identity card from the South Lebanon militia of Colonel Saad Haddad.

Ten years after sharing a cell together in Beirut, Jean-Yves returned from war in Croatia to visit us in Maisons Laffitte.

L'immeuble de 7 étages n'est plus qu'un amas de décombres que l'on essaie de déblayer pour retirer les victimes.

The building in Sanayeh where we were held hostage in West Beirut, bombed just hours after we were released. Some claimed the huge crater was caused by a "vacuum" bomb or fuel-air explosive (today called a "thermobaric" weapon), but the whole building was an ammo dump. Photo: *L'Orient-Le Jour*, Aug. 7, 1982.

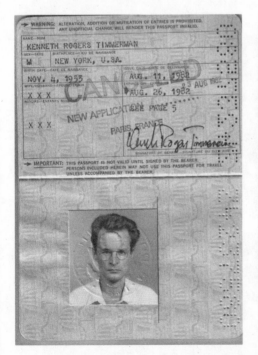

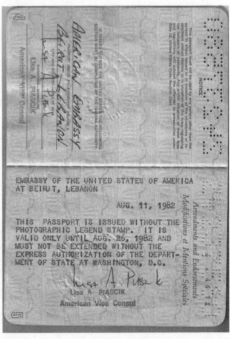

The two week passport issued me without any identity documentation by the US Embassy in Beirut, allowing me to return to France.

Chapter 3: This abandoned refugee camp in Jericho was a rarity, as the PLO was determined to keep Palestinians in the camps, often with physical threats.

A Message from the Mountains: The apartment complex at the Galerie Semaan in Beirut where my friends Farid and Jamal Hamadeh welcomed me in 1983.

Café scene in Ramallah under Israeli "occupation."

Hungry Guns, Exploding Cats: On the flight deck of the *USS Guadalcanal* off the coast of Beirut, just days before Iranian terror operative Imad Fayez Mughniyeh blew up the US Marine barracks at the Beirut airport on October 23, 1983, killing 241 Marines.

Chapter 4: Professor Paul S. Cutter, the elusive executive editor of EDA publications, was at the center of the international arms supply networks that morphed into the Iran-Contra Initiative. This photo was taken during one of his many swings through Paris in 1983.
Courtesy: *Defense Systems Review.*

Chapter 5: Trying out a South African–produced Uzi at an Armscor firing range outside of Johannesburg. It was during this trip that I discovered one of the closest-held secrets of the Iran-Iraq war.

Armscor Chairman Piet Marais, hand resting on a mock-up of the G-6 self-propelled howitzer, as he told me about his massive contracts with Iraq.

Saudi Prince Muqrin bin Abdelaziz and Saudi F-15 pilots in their ready room at King Faisel Air Force base in Taef, boasting about taking on Iran.

"We hate your country": US-educated Saudi Army Captain Saleh.

Fanning the Flames: Vacationing on Ios, with Kostas Drakos (right) and his father, in August 1986.

My home office in Paris.

Chapter 6: Jack Belden (left), Gerard Willing (center), and US diplomat Steve Kashkett at our wedding reception in Paris in June 1987.

Legends: Our wedding day in Paris.

Saddam's Nephew: Catching up with Iraqi Defense Minister Abdul-Jabbar Shanshal in Cairo.

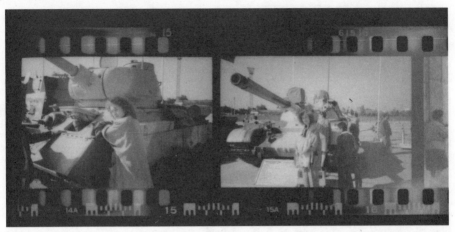

Christina at her first arms show, showing off her next car.

Chapter 7: Imad Mugniyeh's passport photo, which I published in *Mednews* on May 2, 1988, at a time the Iranian-backed terror master was considered a faceless ghost.

The London Safe House: Israeli hostage negotiator Uri Lubrani, who I first met in September 1988 while en route to the Farnborough Air Show. Courtesy: Israel Defense Force.

Colonel Jacques Neriah, the Israeli defense attaché in Paris who introduced me to Uri Lubrani.

Coffee with Hezbollah: Lebanese businessman Ali Hijazi. Screenshot from a 2009 film, "What if I became a hostage," by Marie-Laure Baggiolini and Jean-Daniel Bohnenblust, Radio Television Suisse, *Temps Present.*

Chapter 8: Dassault arms salesman Hugues De l'Estoile with French armed forces chief of staff, General Maurice Schmidt, beneath the wing of an Iraqi Mirage F1 armed with a Soviet-made AS-14 Ketch missile at the Baghdad arms fair in late April 1989. This was the photograph that nearly got me expelled from France.

The Baghdad Arms Fair: Thomson-CSF CEO Alain Gomez (right), who maneuvered behind the scenes to get me declared *persona non grata* by the French government, standing with the heads of Iraq's strategic weapons programs, Lt. Gen. Amir Rashid al-Ubaidi (left) and Lt. Gen. Amir Hamoody al-Saadi.

The author with Hugues de l'Estoile at the Dassault chalet at the Paris Air Show, June 1989. Courtesy: Olivier de l'Estoile.

Search Warrant, French-Style: Christina in our new office in the Paris suburb of Maisons-Laffitte, working before the walls were even painted.

The author standing before the Soviet embassy, Paris, in a publicity photo for the publication of *La Grande Fauche* (Gorbachev's Technology Wars). Courtesy: Philippe Caron/Sygma. Used with permission.

Chapter 9: The author with Brent Scowcroft in the Indian Room, Old Executive Office Building, March 3, 1991.

BNL and the Death Lobby: Holding up a photo I had taken of Iraq's al-Hossein missile in Baghdad while presenting my first report for the Simon Wiesenthal Center at a press conference in Washington, DC.

'Our Bible': Dinner with Simon Wiesenthal in Paris in 1992.

UNSCOM chairman Ambassador Rolf Ekeus became a lifelong friend. Here he is visiting us at Christina's summer house in Sweden in 2008.

'Oh My, That's the Defense Minister!': The presidential tour of the Paris Air Show, June 1991, before the official opening. From left to right: Snecma president Louis Gallois, Defense Minister Pierre Joxe, French President Francois Mitterrand, Aérospatiale CEO Henri Martre.

The Russians were also eager to show off their wares after the first Gulf War, bringing the Sukhoi 27 to the first Dubai Air Show later that year.

'Saddam's Secrets': On the *60 Minutes* set with Mike Wallace at Vienna's Hotel Imperial.

Chapter 10: Leconfield House, the former MI5 headquarters on London's Curzon Street, where I met with Michael Oatley and other former spies now working for Kroll Associates. Together we tracked Saddam's secret billions.

Return to Lebanon: UN soldier in Naqoura, Lebanon, February 1992.

Chapter 11: Albert Aghazarian describing the temptation of Jesus to me and Christina on the roof of the souk in the Old City of Jerusalem.

Chapter 12: The author in the *60 Minutes* mixing studio in Paris. Courtesy: Philippe Lenglin, *Le Parisien.*

500 Million Reasons: Alain Gomez, photographed here at the Dubai Air Show in 1991, had "500 million reasons" to shut me down as a reporter.

The Fist of God: Island hopping with Christina and our four children in Milos, Greece, my last summer before putting on the chain. Diana was just two and a half.

Putting on the Chain: Senate aide William C. Triplett always had the Chinese in his sights. Here he joined me in February 1993 at the IDEX arms fair in Abu Dhabi.

Meeting Marshall Kalashnikov, inventor of the AK-47, at the Paris Air Show in June 1993, the first time I attended an arms show as a U.S. government employee.

Meeting exiled Lebanese General Michel Aoun with Jamal and Farid Hamadeh in Marseilles as a House Foreign Affairs Committee staff representative shortly after the Paris Air Show.

Chapter 13: Christina six months pregnant with our fifth child, Simon, at the Place de la Concorde in Paris shortly before we moved to the United States, where I joined the Congressional staff.